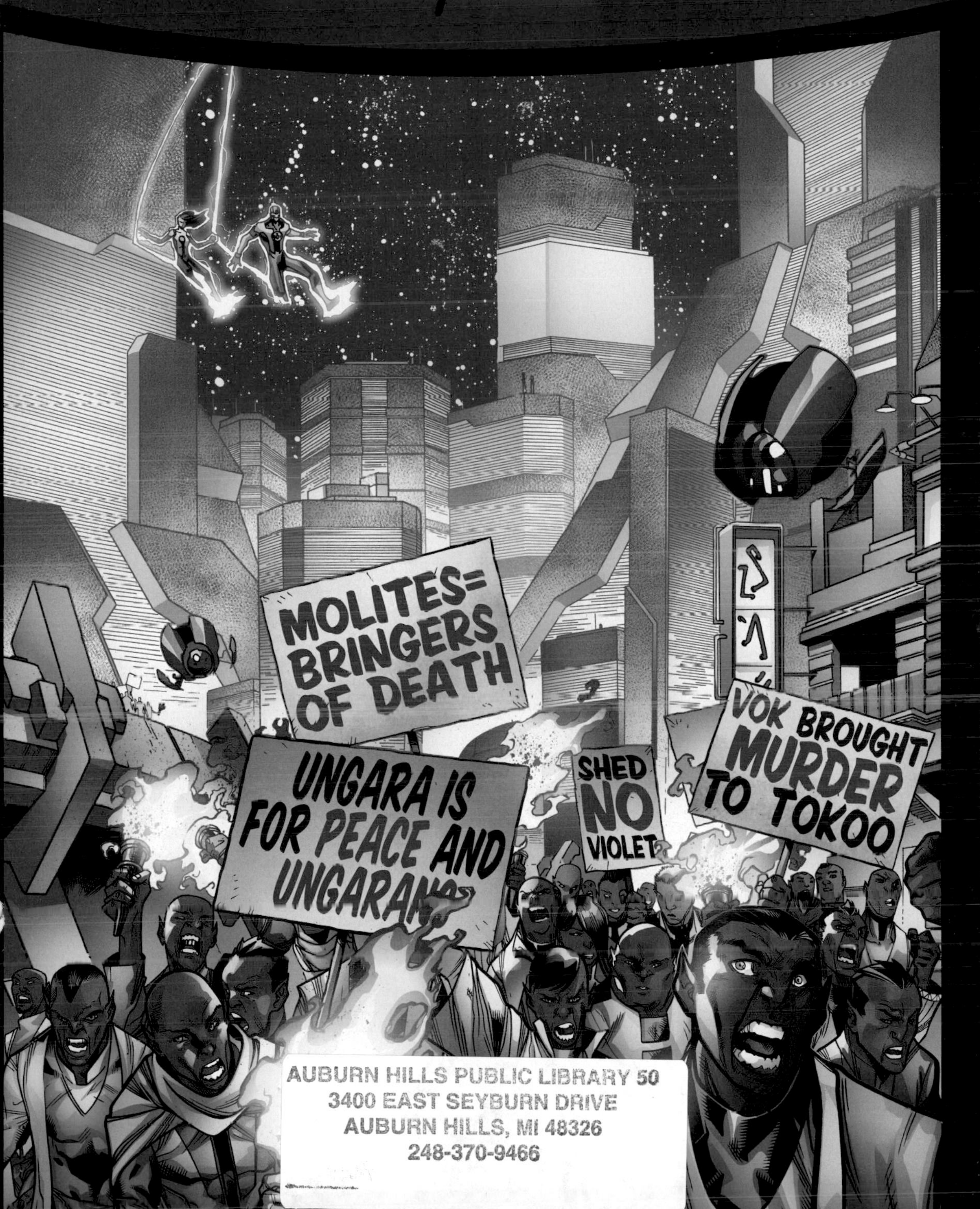
MOLITES=
BRINGERS
OF DEATH
UNGARA IS
FOR PEACE AND
SHED
NO
VIOLET
VOK BROUGHT
MURDER
TO TOKOO

GREEN LANTERNS

VOL.6 A WORLD OF OUR OWN

GREEN LANTERNS
VOL.6 A WORLD OF OUR OWN

TIM SEELEY
writer

RONAN CLIQUET * CARLO BARBERI
EDUARDO PANSICA * GERMAN PERALTA
pencillers

RONAN CLIQUET * MATT SANTORELLI
JULIO FERREIRA * GERMAN PERALTA
inkers

HI-FI
ULISES ARREOLA
ALEX SOLLAZZO
colorists

DAVE SHARPE
letterer

BRANDON PETERSON
collection cover artist

MIKE COTTON Editor - Original Series ✳ **ANDREW MARINO** Assistant Editor - Original Series
JEB WOODARD Group Editor - Collected Editions ✳ **ERIKA ROTHBERG** Editor - Collected Edition
STEVE COOK Design Director - Books ✳ **MEGEN BELLERSEN** Publication Design

BOB HARRAS Senior VP - Editor-in-Chief, DC Comics
PAT McCALLUM Executive Editor, DC Comics

DIANE NELSON President ✳ **DAN DiDIO** Publisher ✳ **JIM LEE** Publisher ✳ **GEOFF JOHNS** President & Chief Creative Officer
AMIT DESAI Executive VP - Business & Marketing Strategy, Direct to Consumer & Global Franchise Management
SAM ADES Senior VP & General Manager, Digital Services ✳ **BOBBIE CHASE** VP & Executive Editor, Young Reader & Talent Development
MARK CHIARELLO Senior VP - Art, Design & Collected Editions ✳ **JOHN CUNNINGHAM** Senior VP - Sales & Trade Marketing
ANNE DePIES Senior VP - Business Strategy, Finance & Administration ✳ **DON FALLETTI** VP - Manufacturing Operations
LAWRENCE GANEM VP - Editorial Administration & Talent Relations ✳ **ALISON GILL** Senior VP - Manufacturing & Operations
HANK KANALZ Senior VP - Editorial Strategy & Administration ✳ **JAY KOGAN** VP - Legal Affairs ✳ **JACK MAHAN** VP - Business Affairs
NICK J. NAPOLITANO VP - Manufacturing Administration ✳ **EDDIE SCANNELL** VP - Consumer Marketing
COURTNEY SIMMONS Senior VP - Publicity & Communications ✳ **JIM (SKI) SOKOLOWSKI** VP - Comic Book Specialty Sales & Trade Marketing
NANCY SPEARS VP - Mass, Book, Digital Sales & Trade Marketing ✳ **MICHELE R. WELLS** VP - Content Strategy

GREEN LANTERNS VOL. 6: A WORLD OF OUR OWN

DC Comics, 2900 West Alameda Ave., Burbank, CA 91505
Printed by LSC Communications, Kendallville, IN, USA. 5/25/18. First Printing.
ISBN: 978-1-4012-8066-6

Library of Congress Cataloging-in-Publication Data is available.

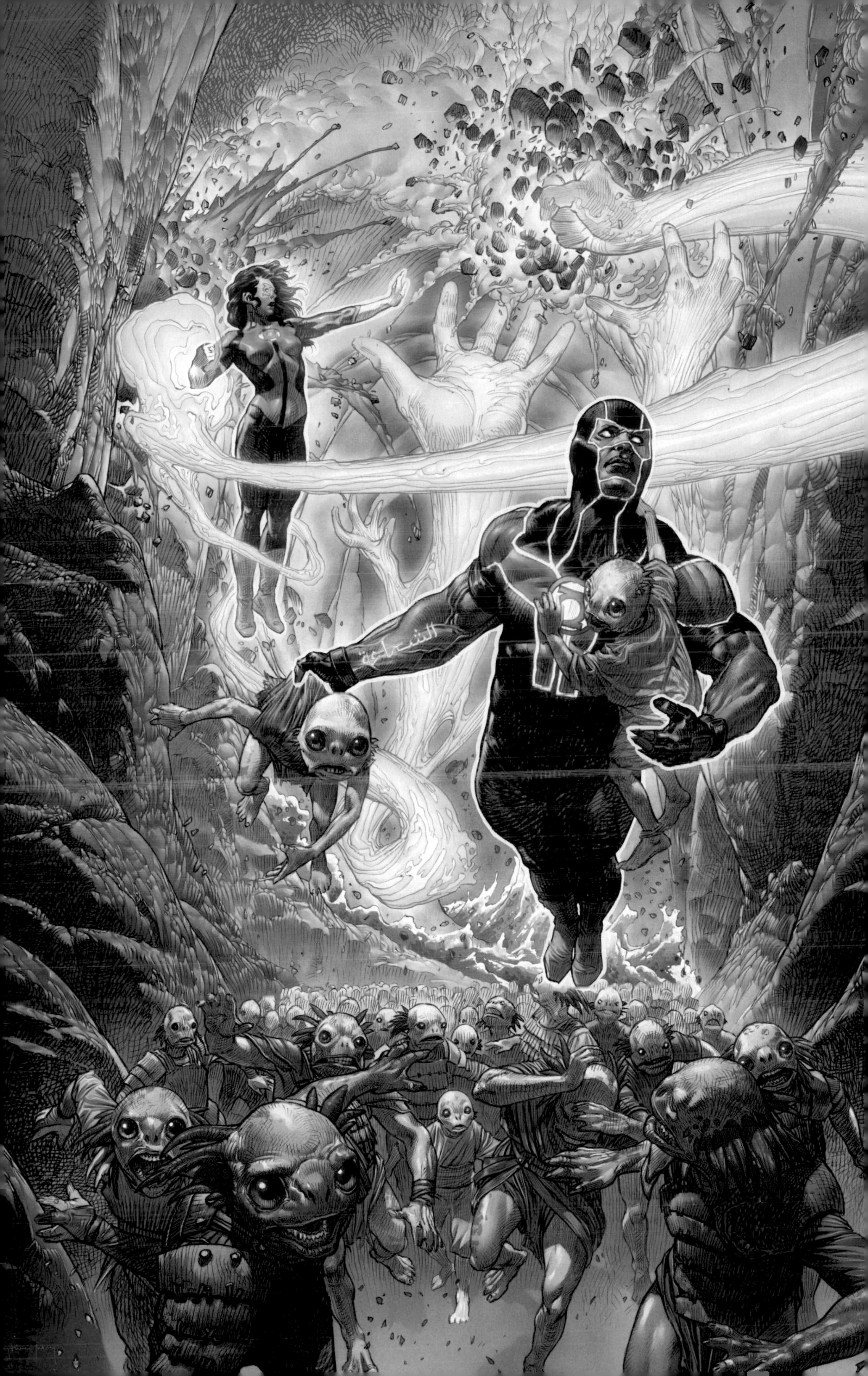

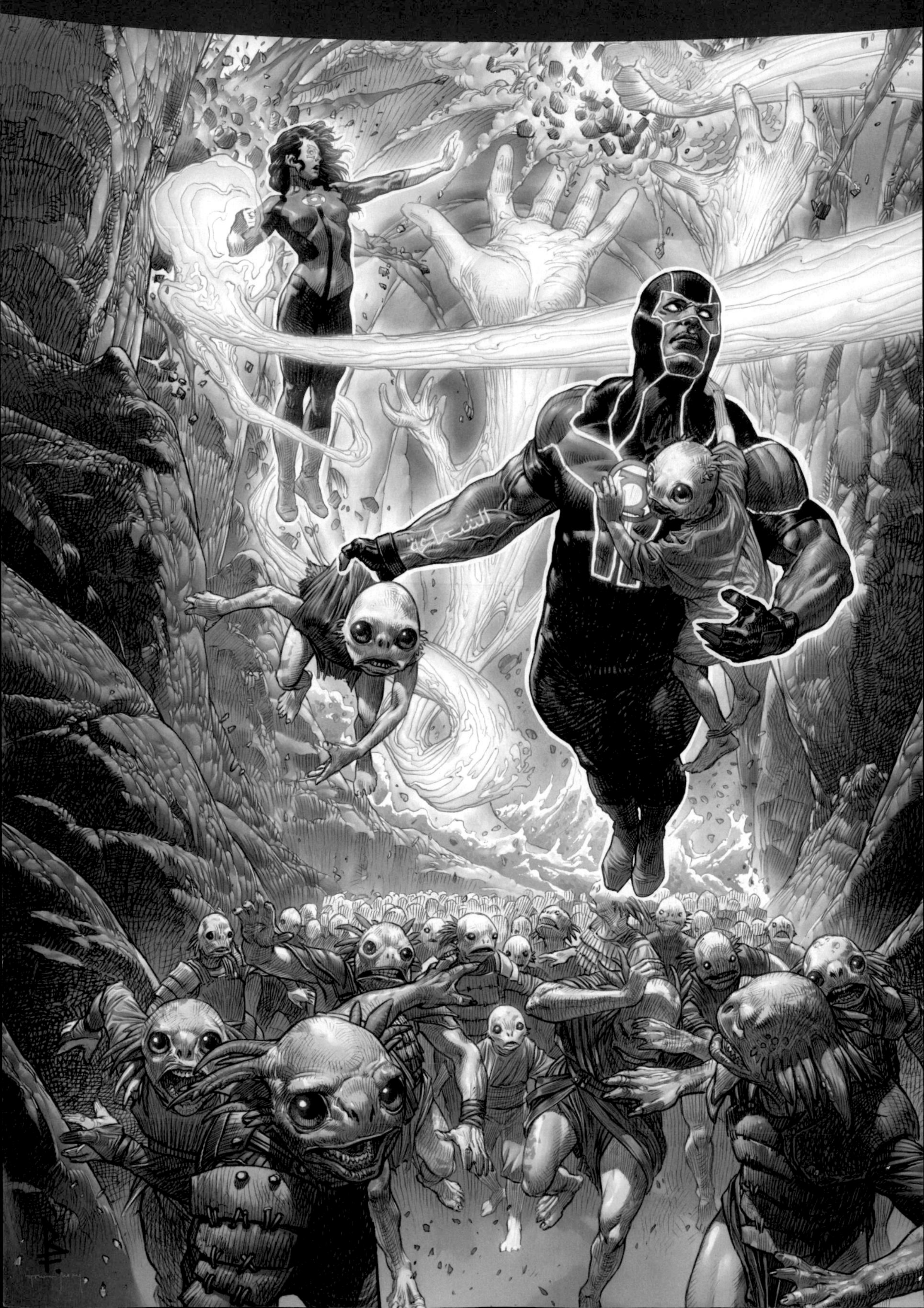

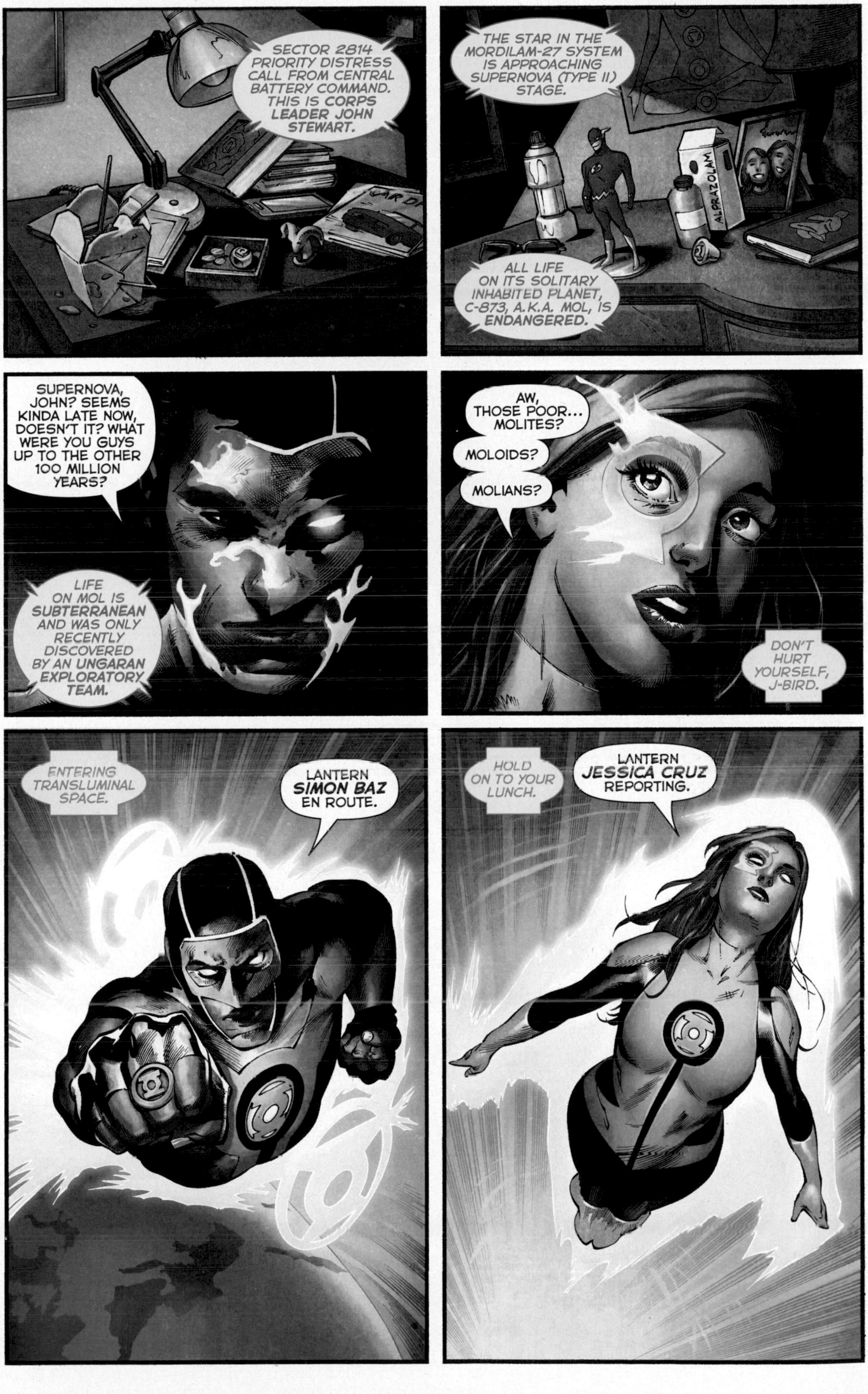
SECTOR 2814 PRIORITY DISTRESS CALL FROM CENTRAL BATTERY COMMAND. THIS IS CORPS LEADER JOHN STEWART.
ALPRAZOLAM
THE STAR IN THE MORDILAM-27 SYSTEM IS APPROACHING SUPERNOVA (TYPE II) STAGE.
ALL LIFE ON ITS SOLITARY INHABITED PLANET, C-873, A.K.A. MOL, IS ENDANGERED.
SUPERNOVA, JOHN? SEEMS KINDA LATE NOW, DOESN'T IT? WHAT WERE YOU GUYS UP TO THE OTHER 100 MILLION YEARS?
LIFE ON MOL IS SUBTERRANEAN AND WAS ONLY RECENTLY DISCOVERED BY AN UNGARAN EXPLORATORY TEAM.
AW, THOSE POOR... MOLITES?
MOLOIDS?
MOLIANS?
DON'T HURT YOURSELF, J-BIRD.
ENTERING TRANSLUMINAL SPACE.
LANTERN SIMON BAZ EN ROUTE.
HOLD ON TO YOUR LUNCH.
LANTERN JESSICA CRUZ REPORTING.

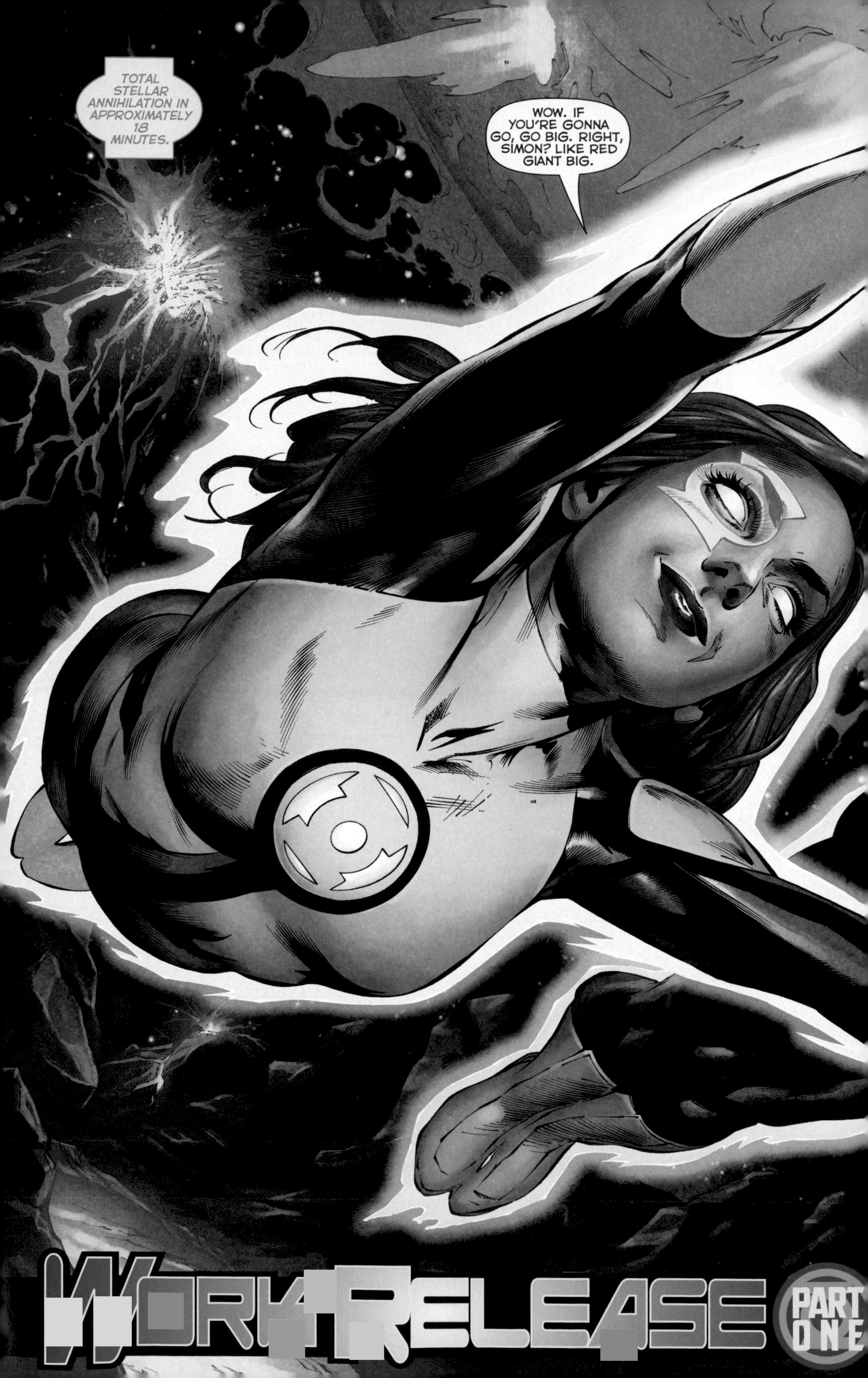
TOTAL STELLAR ANNIHILATION IN APPROXIMATELY 18 MINUTES.
WOW. IF YOU'RE GONNA GO, GO BIG. RIGHT, SIMON? LIKE RED GIANT BIG.
WORK RELEASE
PART ONE

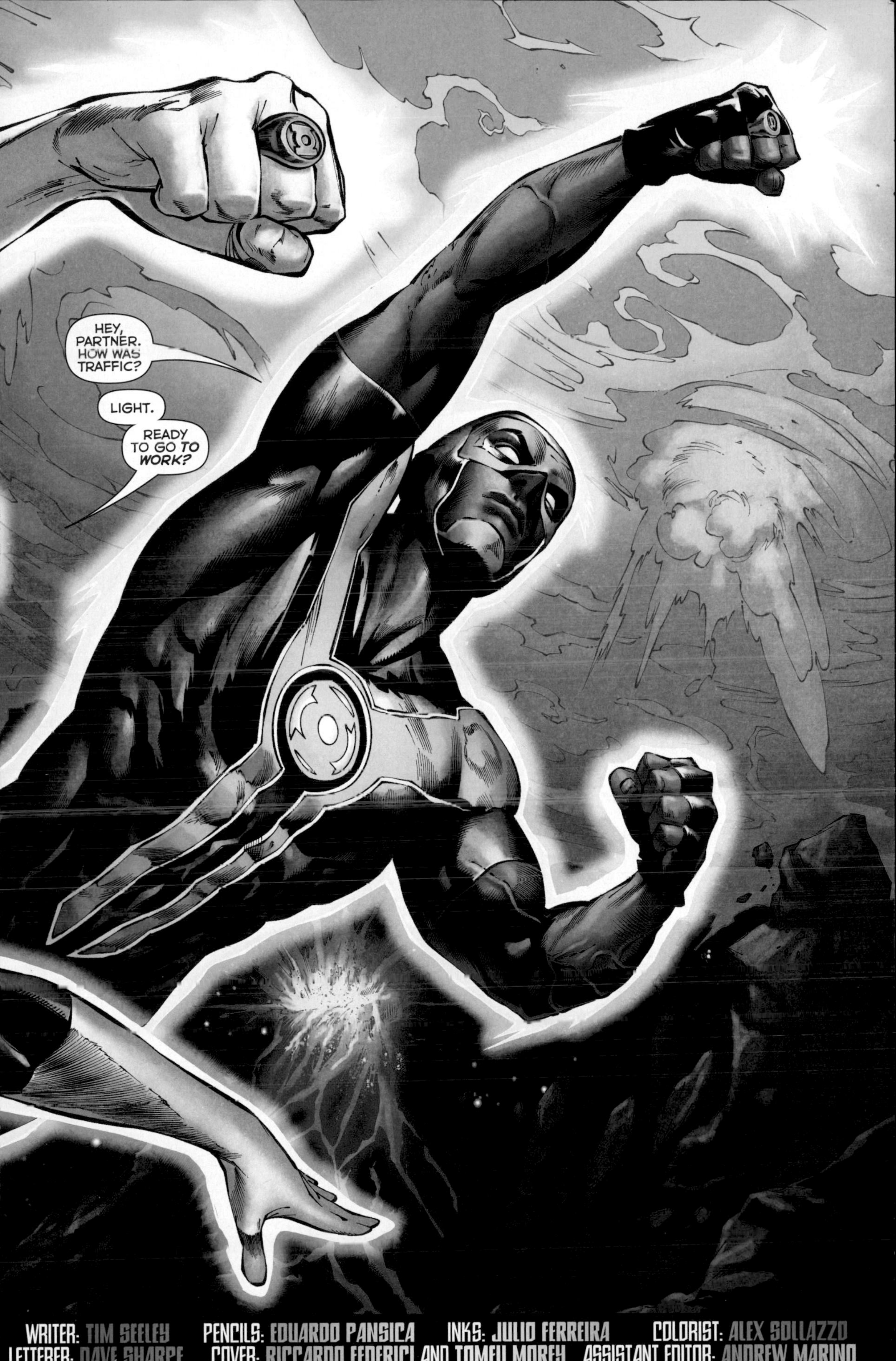
HEY, PARTNER. HOW WAS TRAFFIC?
LIGHT.
READY TO GO *TO WORK?*

WRITER: TIM SEELEY PENCILS: EDUARDO PANSICA INKS: JULIO FERREIRA COLORIST: ALEX SOLLAZZO
LETTERER: DAVE SHARPE COVER: RICCARDO FEDERICI AND TOMEU MOREY ASSISTANT EDITOR: ANDREW MARINO
EDITOR: MIKE COTTON GROUP EDITOR: EDDIE BERGANZA

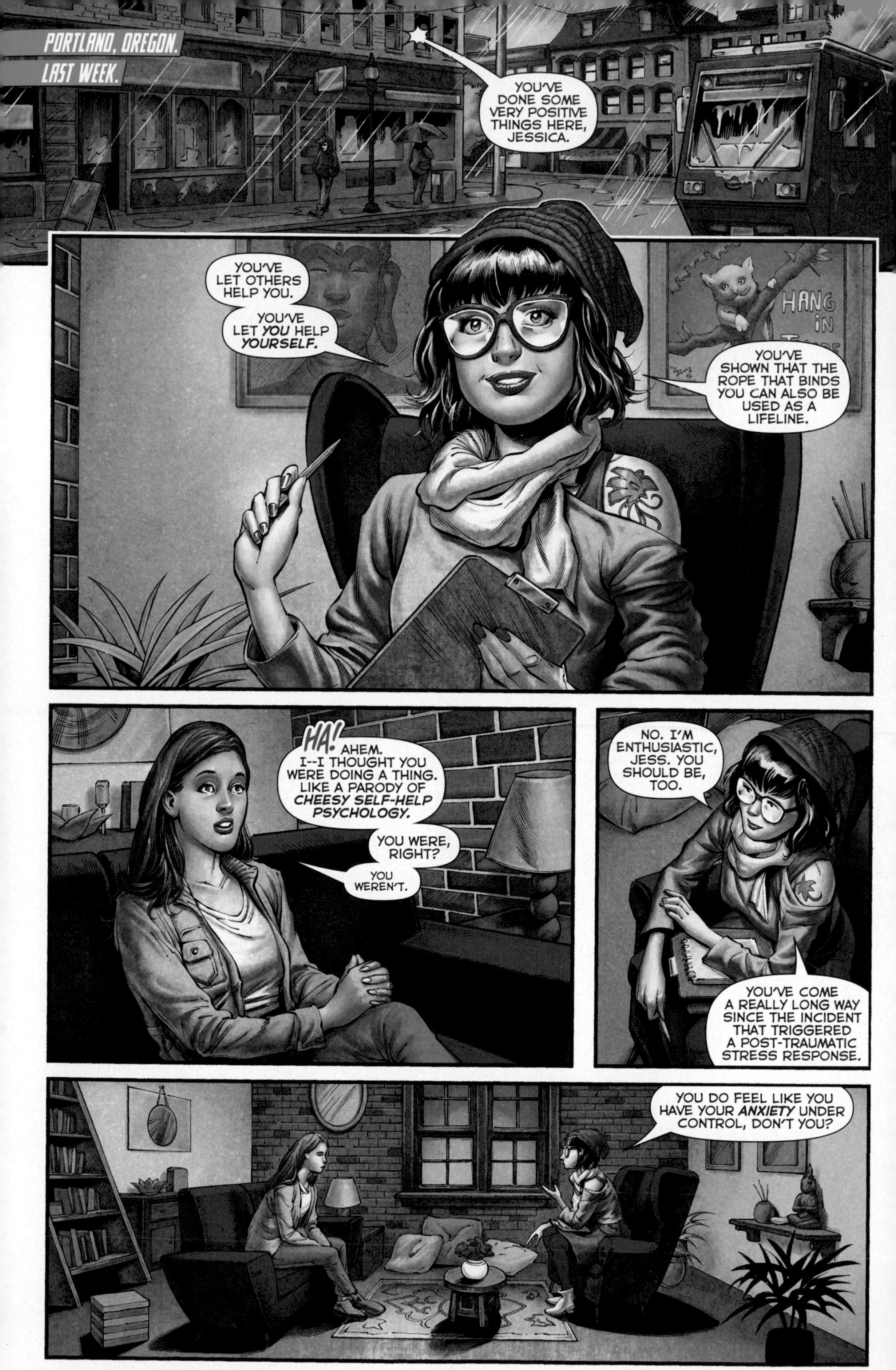

PORTLAND, OREGON.
LAST WEEK.
YOU'VE DONE SOME VERY POSITIVE THINGS HERE, JESSICA.
YOU'VE LET OTHERS HELP YOU.
YOU'VE LET *YOU* HELP *YOURSELF.*
YOU'VE SHOWN THAT THE ROPE THAT BINDS YOU CAN ALSO BE USED AS A LIFELINE.
HANG IN
HA! AHEM. I--I THOUGHT YOU WERE DOING A THING. LIKE A PARODY OF *CHEESY SELF-HELP PSYCHOLOGY.*
YOU WERE, RIGHT?
YOU WEREN'T.
NO. I'M ENTHUSIASTIC, JESS. YOU SHOULD BE, TOO.
YOU'VE COME A REALLY LONG WAY SINCE THE INCIDENT THAT TRIGGERED A POST-TRAUMATIC STRESS RESPONSE.
YOU DO FEEL LIKE YOU HAVE YOUR *ANXIETY* UNDER CONTROL, DON'T YOU?

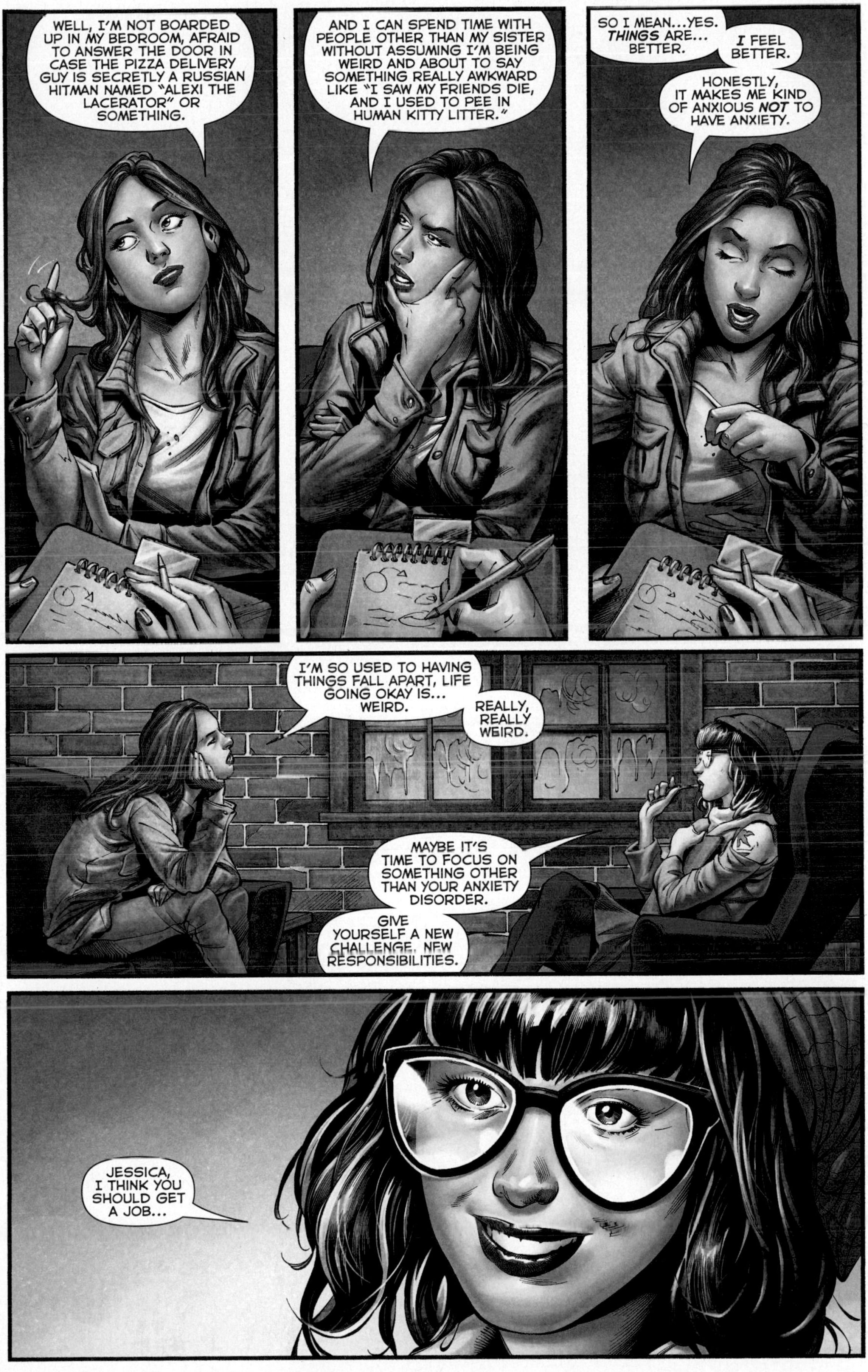
WELL, I'M NOT BOARDED UP IN MY BEDROOM, AFRAID TO ANSWER THE DOOR IN CASE THE PIZZA DELIVERY GUY IS SECRETLY A RUSSIAN HITMAN NAMED "ALEXI THE LACERATOR" OR SOMETHING.
AND I CAN SPEND TIME WITH PEOPLE OTHER THAN MY SISTER WITHOUT ASSUMING I'M BEING WEIRD AND ABOUT TO SAY SOMETHING REALLY AWKWARD LIKE "I SAW MY FRIENDS DIE, AND I USED TO PEE IN HUMAN KITTY LITTER."
SO I MEAN...YES. THINGS ARE... BETTER.
I FEEL BETTER.
HONESTLY, IT MAKES ME KIND OF ANXIOUS NOT TO HAVE ANXIETY.
I'M SO USED TO HAVING THINGS FALL APART, LIFE GOING OKAY IS... WEIRD.
REALLY, REALLY WEIRD.
MAYBE IT'S TIME TO FOCUS ON SOMETHING OTHER THAN YOUR ANXIETY DISORDER.
GIVE YOURSELF A NEW CHALLENGE. NEW RESPONSIBILITIES.
JESSICA, I THINK YOU SHOULD GET A JOB...

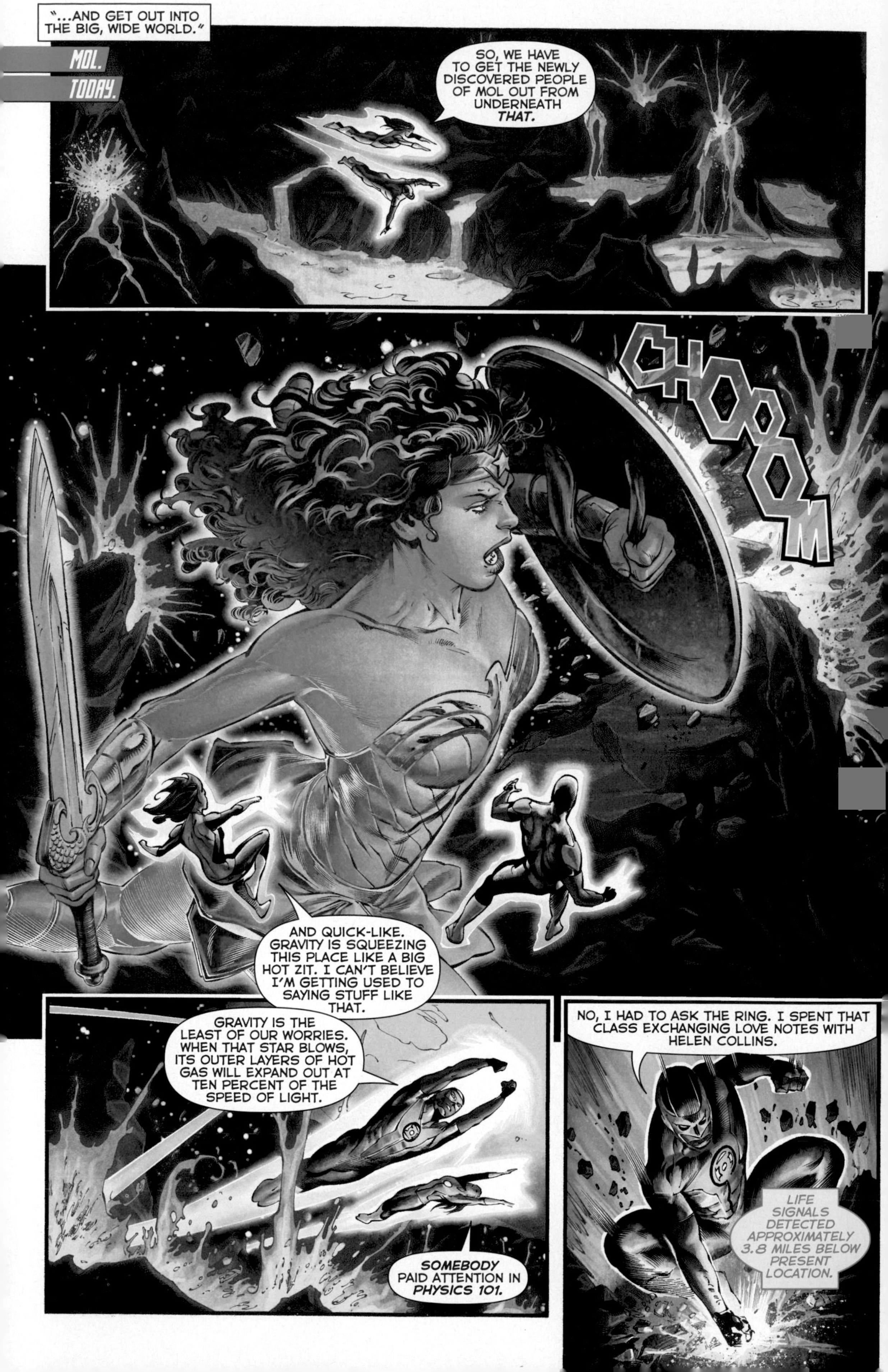
"...AND GET OUT INTO THE BIG, WIDE WORLD."
MOL.
TODAY.
SO, WE HAVE TO GET THE NEWLY DISCOVERED PEOPLE OF MOL OUT FROM UNDERNEATH *THAT.*
CHOOOOM
AND QUICK-LIKE. GRAVITY IS SQUEEZING THIS PLACE LIKE A BIG HOT ZIT. I CAN'T BELIEVE I'M GETTING USED TO SAYING STUFF LIKE THAT.
GRAVITY IS THE LEAST OF OUR WORRIES. WHEN THAT STAR BLOWS, ITS OUTER LAYERS OF HOT GAS WILL EXPAND OUT AT TEN PERCENT OF THE SPEED OF LIGHT.
SOMEBODY PAID ATTENTION IN *PHYSICS 101.*
NO, I HAD TO ASK THE RING. I SPENT THAT CLASS EXCHANGING LOVE NOTES WITH HELEN COLLINS.
LIFE SIGNALS DETECTED APPROXIMATELY 3.8 MILES BELOW PRESENT LOCATION.

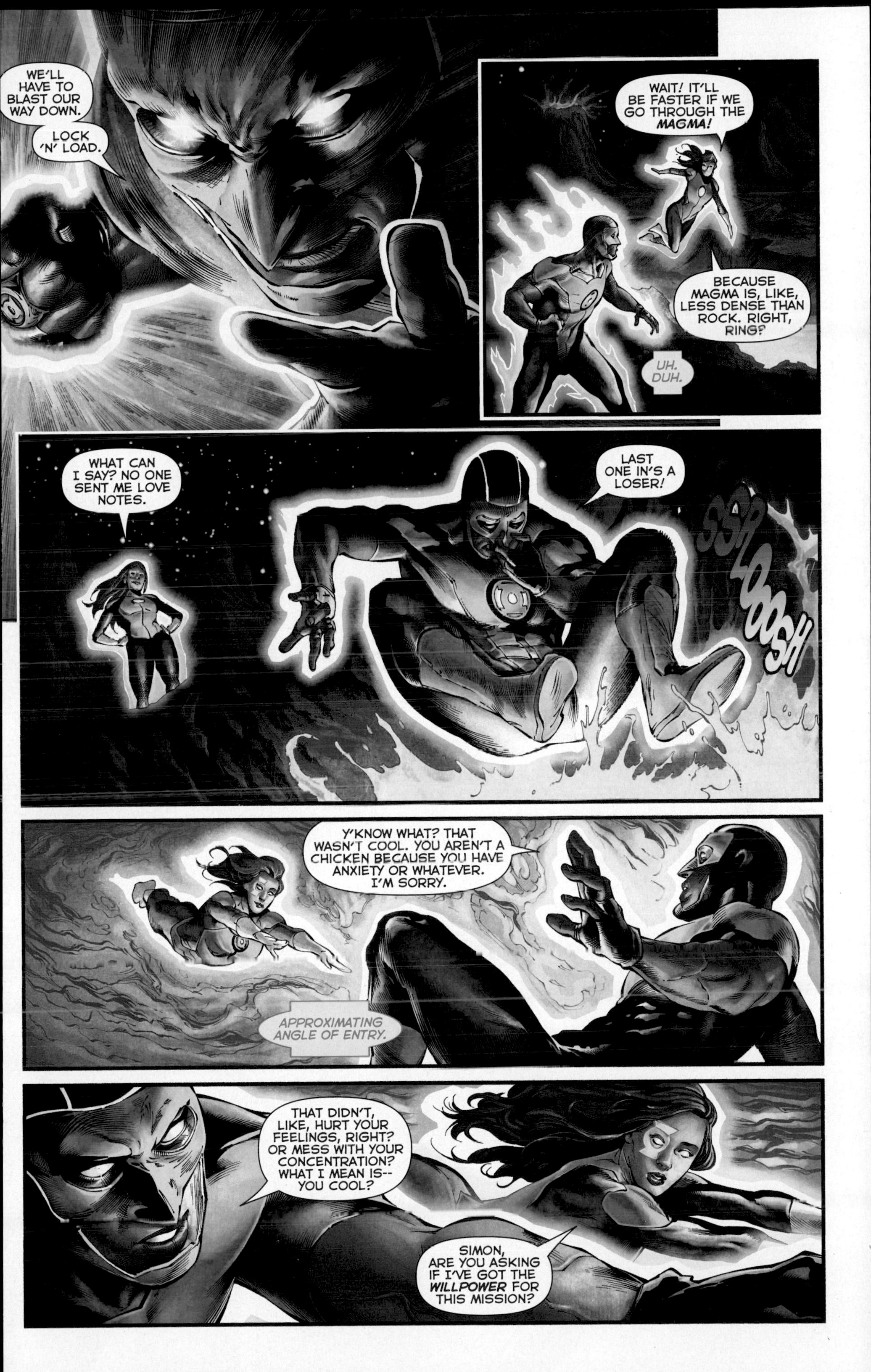
WE'LL HAVE TO BLAST OUR WAY DOWN.
LOCK 'N' LOAD.
WAIT! IT'LL BE FASTER IF WE GO THROUGH THE MAGMA!
BECAUSE MAGMA IS, LIKE, LESS DENSE THAN ROCK. RIGHT, RING?
UH. DUH.
WHAT CAN I SAY? NO ONE SENT ME LOVE NOTES.
LAST ONE IN'S A LOSER!
SSPLOOOSH
Y'KNOW WHAT? THAT WASN'T COOL. YOU AREN'T A CHICKEN BECAUSE YOU HAVE ANXIETY OR WHATEVER. I'M SORRY.
APPROXIMATING ANGLE OF ENTRY.
THAT DIDN'T, LIKE, HURT YOUR FEELINGS, RIGHT? OR MESS WITH YOUR CONCENTRATION? WHAT I MEAN IS-- YOU COOL?
SIMON, ARE YOU ASKING IF I'VE GOT THE WILLPOWER FOR THIS MISSION?

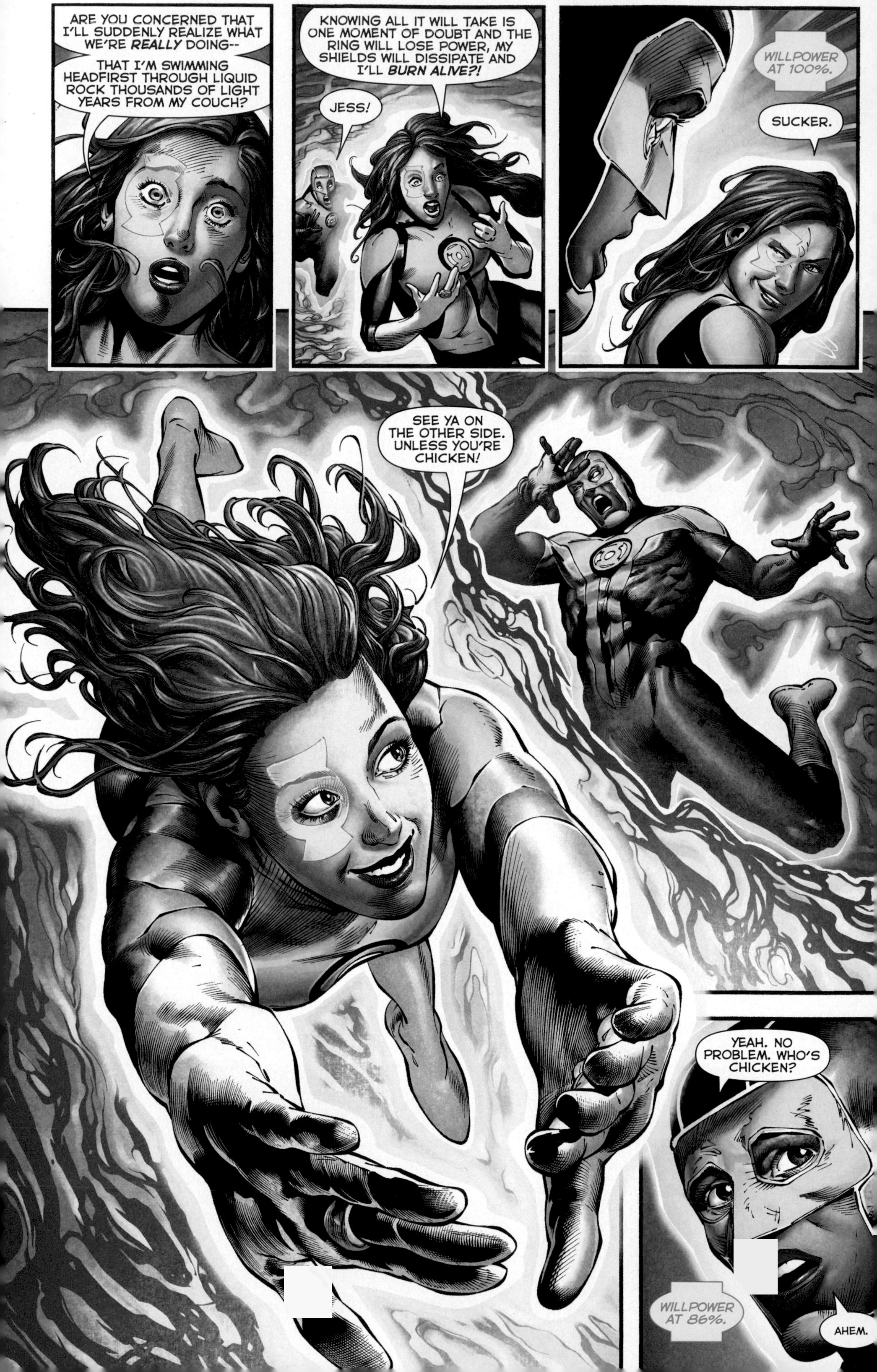
ARE YOU CONCERNED THAT I'LL SUDDENLY REALIZE WHAT WE'RE *REALLY* DOING--
THAT I'M SWIMMING HEADFIRST THROUGH LIQUID ROCK THOUSANDS OF LIGHT YEARS FROM MY COUCH?
KNOWING ALL IT WILL TAKE IS ONE MOMENT OF DOUBT AND THE RING WILL LOSE POWER, MY SHIELDS WILL DISSIPATE AND I'LL *BURN ALIVE?!*
JESS!
WILLPOWER AT 100%.
SUCKER.
SEE YA ON THE OTHER SIDE. UNLESS YOU'RE CHICKEN!
YEAH. NO PROBLEM. WHO'S CHICKEN?
WILLPOWER AT 86%.
AHEM.

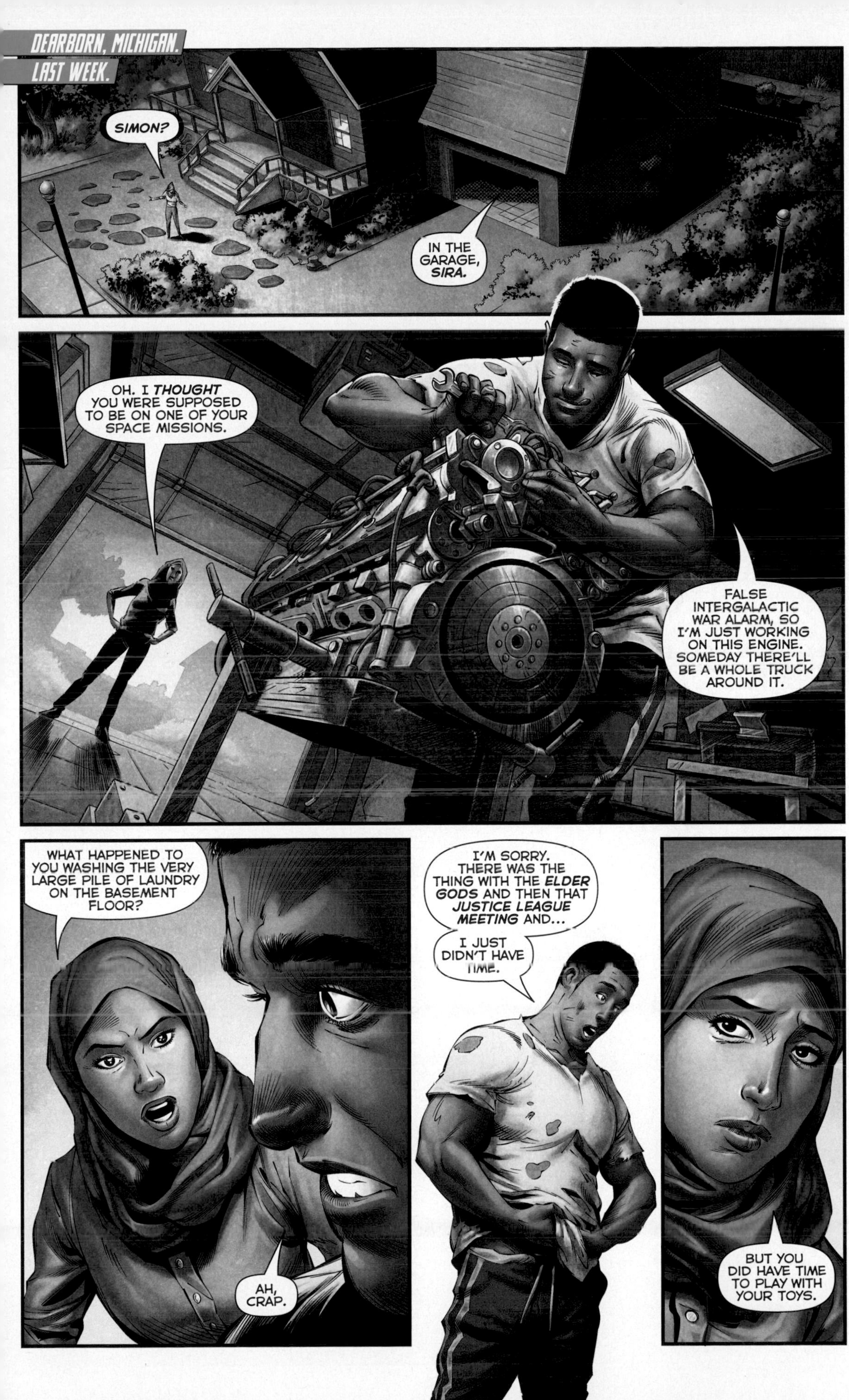
DEARBORN, MICHIGAN.
LAST WEEK.
SIMON?
IN THE GARAGE, SIRA.
OH. I THOUGHT YOU WERE SUPPOSED TO BE ON ONE OF YOUR SPACE MISSIONS.
FALSE INTERGALACTIC WAR ALARM, SO I'M JUST WORKING ON THIS ENGINE. SOMEDAY THERE'LL BE A WHOLE TRUCK AROUND IT.
WHAT HAPPENED TO YOU WASHING THE VERY LARGE PILE OF LAUNDRY ON THE BASEMENT FLOOR?
AH, CRAP.
I'M SORRY. THERE WAS THE THING WITH THE ELDER GODS AND THEN THAT JUSTICE LEAGUE MEETING AND...
I JUST DIDN'T HAVE TIME.
BUT YOU DID HAVE TIME TO PLAY WITH YOUR TOYS.

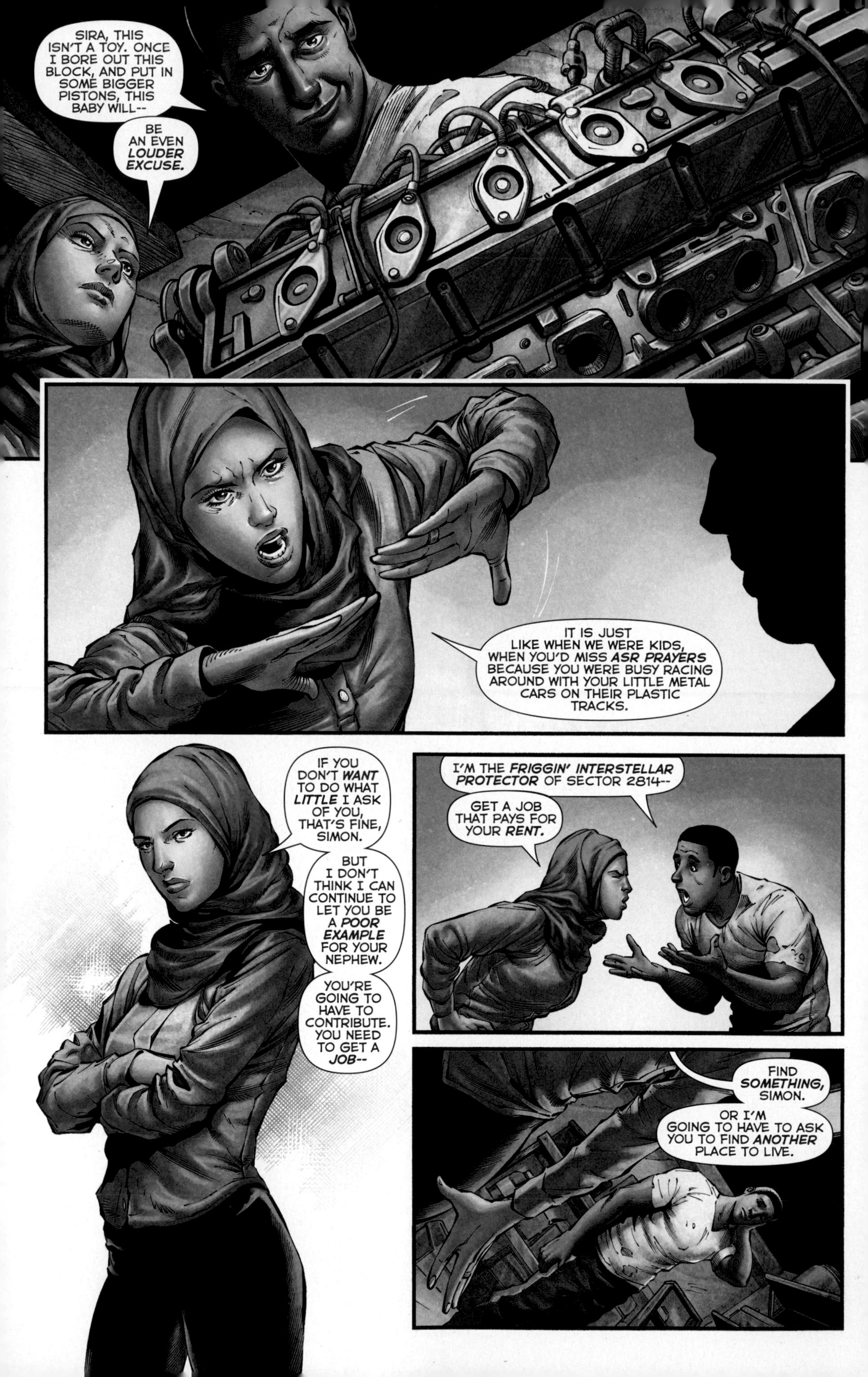
SIRA, THIS ISN'T A TOY. ONCE I BORE OUT THIS BLOCK, AND PUT IN SOME BIGGER PISTONS, THIS BABY WILL--
BE AN EVEN *LOUDER EXCUSE.*
IT IS JUST LIKE WHEN WE WERE KIDS, WHEN YOU'D MISS *ASR PRAYERS* BECAUSE YOU WERE BUSY RACING AROUND WITH YOUR LITTLE METAL CARS ON THEIR PLASTIC TRACKS.
IF YOU DON'T *WANT* TO DO WHAT *LITTLE* I ASK OF YOU, THAT'S FINE, SIMON.
BUT I DON'T THINK I CAN CONTINUE TO LET YOU BE A *POOR EXAMPLE* FOR YOUR NEPHEW.
YOU'RE GOING TO HAVE TO CONTRIBUTE. YOU NEED TO GET A *JOB--*
I'M THE *FRIGGIN' INTERSTELLAR PROTECTOR* OF SECTOR 2814--
GET A JOB THAT PAYS FOR YOUR *RENT.*
FIND *SOMETHING,* SIMON.
OR I'M GOING TO HAVE TO ASK YOU TO FIND *ANOTHER* PLACE TO LIVE.

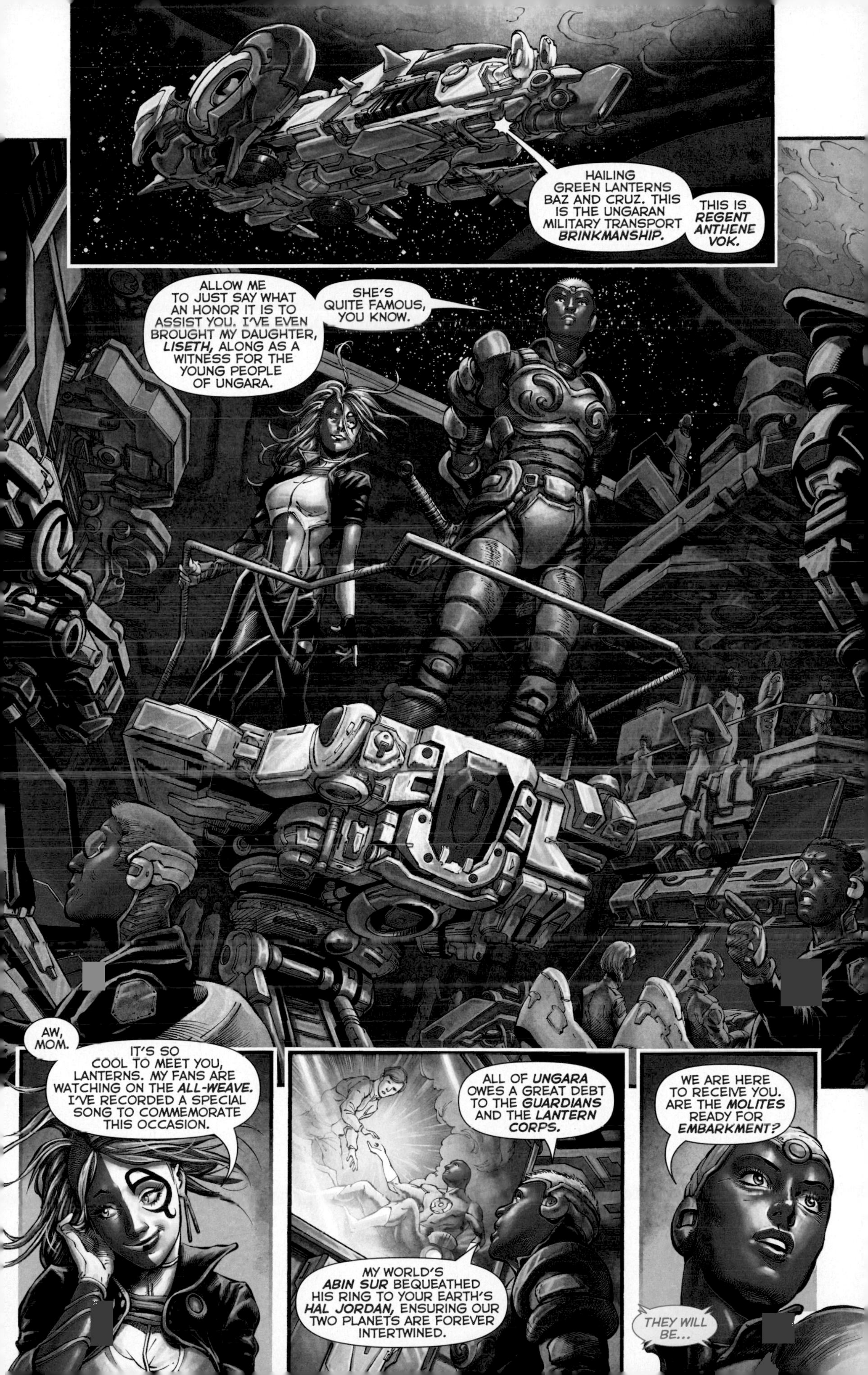
HAILING GREEN LANTERNS BAZ AND CRUZ. THIS IS THE UNGARAN MILITARY TRANSPORT BRINKMANSHIP.
THIS IS REGENT ANTHENE VOK.
ALLOW ME TO JUST SAY WHAT AN HONOR IT IS TO ASSIST YOU. I'VE EVEN BROUGHT MY DAUGHTER, LISETH, ALONG AS A WITNESS FOR THE YOUNG PEOPLE OF UNGARA.
SHE'S QUITE FAMOUS, YOU KNOW.
AW, MOM.
IT'S SO COOL TO MEET YOU, LANTERNS. MY FANS ARE WATCHING ON THE ALL-WEAVE. I'VE RECORDED A SPECIAL SONG TO COMMEMORATE THIS OCCASION.
ALL OF UNGARA OWES A GREAT DEBT TO THE GUARDIANS AND THE LANTERN CORPS.
MY WORLD'S ABIN SUR BEQUEATHED HIS RING TO YOUR EARTH'S HAL JORDAN, ENSURING OUR TWO PLANETS ARE FOREVER INTERTWINED.
WE ARE HERE TO RECEIVE YOU. ARE THE MOLITES READY FOR EMBARKMENT?
THEY WILL BE...

...AS SOON AS WE CONVINCE THEM *NOT* TO DIE.

PODFATHER VOB, I NEED YOU TO GET YOUR PEOPLE READY TO BAIL! THIS IS GONNA BE A *HELLA TOUGH* EXTRACTION, AND WE DON'T HAVE MUCH TIME!

TIME IS NO LONGER WITH US, MY STRANGE SON.

MY PEOPLE ARE DEEPLY IN DEBT TO THE WORLD WE INHABIT. IT IS OUR GOD. IT IS OUR FATHER.

ITS STONE HAS SHELTERED US. ITS WATER AND ALGAE HAVE SUSTAINED US. ITS METALS PROTECTED OUR SOFT FLESH.

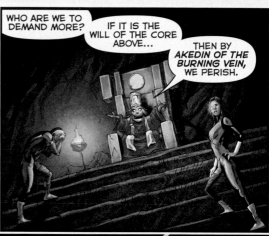

WHO ARE WE TO DEMAND MORE?

IF IT IS THE WILL OF THE CORE ABOVE...

THEN BY *AKEDIN OF THE BURNING VEIN,* WE PERISH.

WE PERISH!

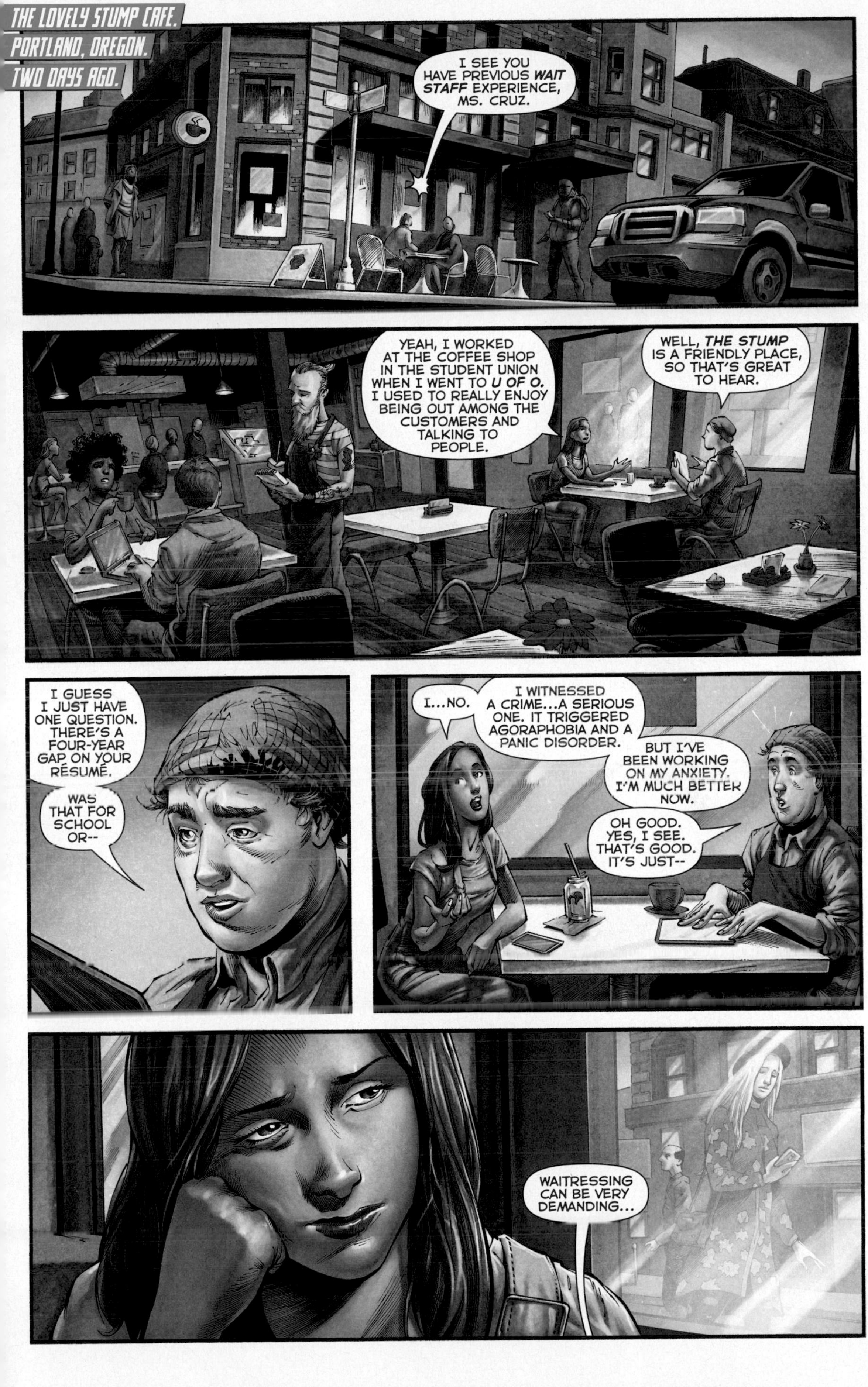
THE LOVELY STUMP CAFE.
PORTLAND, OREGON.
TWO DAYS AGO.
I SEE YOU HAVE PREVIOUS WAIT STAFF EXPERIENCE, MS. CRUZ.
YEAH, I WORKED AT THE COFFEE SHOP IN THE STUDENT UNION WHEN I WENT TO U OF O. I USED TO REALLY ENJOY BEING OUT AMONG THE CUSTOMERS AND TALKING TO PEOPLE.
WELL, THE STUMP IS A FRIENDLY PLACE, SO THAT'S GREAT TO HEAR.
I GUESS I JUST HAVE ONE QUESTION. THERE'S A FOUR-YEAR GAP ON YOUR RÉSUMÉ.
WAS THAT FOR SCHOOL OR--
I...NO.
I WITNESSED A CRIME...A SERIOUS ONE. IT TRIGGERED AGORAPHOBIA AND A PANIC DISORDER.
BUT I'VE BEEN WORKING ON MY ANXIETY. I'M MUCH BETTER NOW.
OH GOOD. YES, I SEE. THAT'S GOOD. IT'S JUST--
WAITRESSING CAN BE VERY DEMANDING...

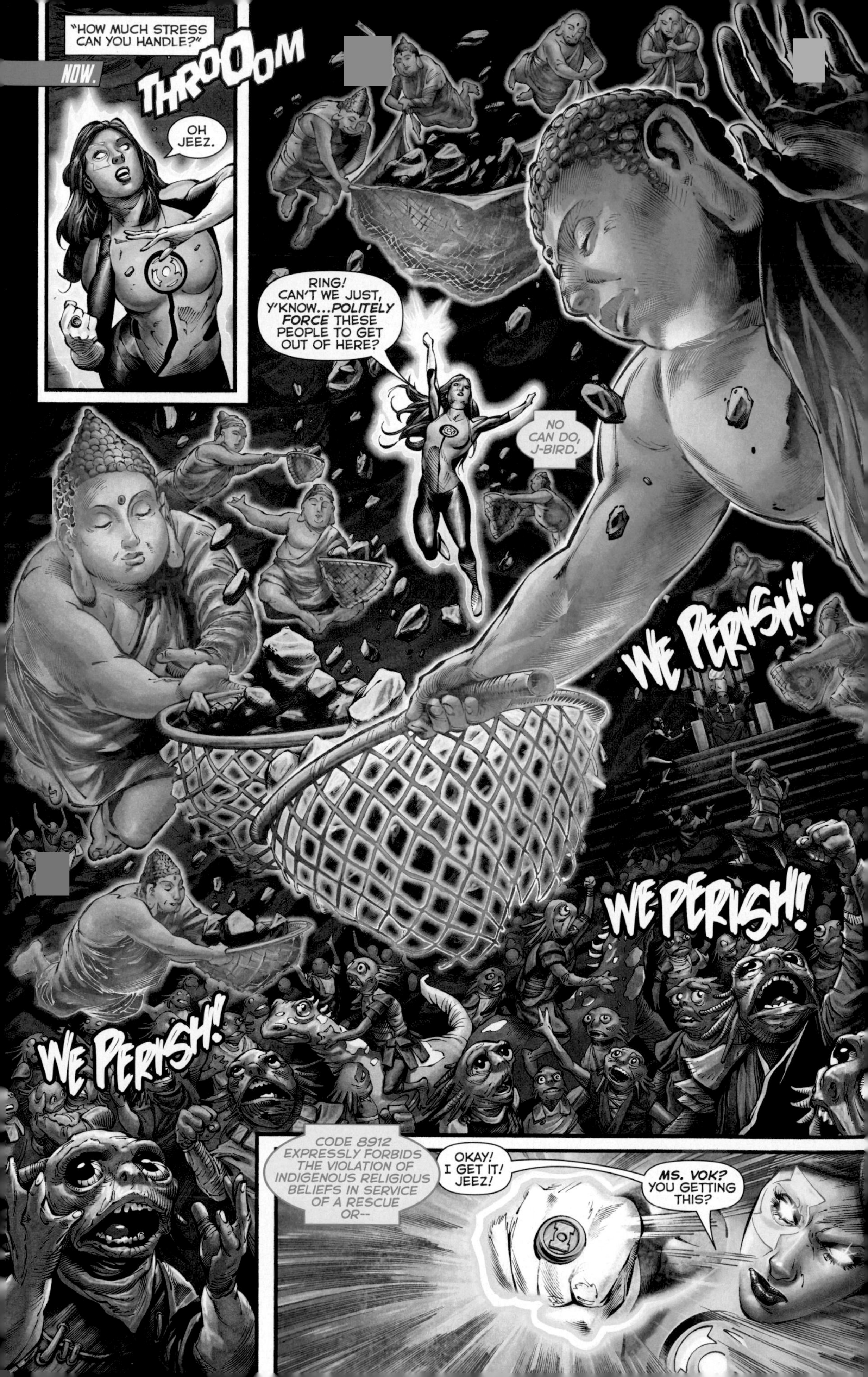
"HOW MUCH STRESS CAN YOU HANDLE?"
NOW.
THROOOOM
OH JEEZ.
RING! CAN'T WE JUST, Y'KNOW...POLITELY FORCE THESE PEOPLE TO GET OUT OF HERE?
NO CAN DO, J-BIRD.
WE PERISH!
WE PERISH!
WE PERISH!
CODE 8912 EXPRESSLY FORBIDS THE VIOLATION OF INDIGENOUS RELIGIOUS BELIEFS IN SERVICE OF A RESCUE OR--
OKAY! I GET IT! JEEZ!
MS. VOK? YOU GETTING THIS?

YES. THE *BRINKMANSHIP* IS MOVING CLOSER TO THE PLANET TO COMPENSATE FOR THE LOST TIME.

OUR *GESTALT COMPLEX* WILL PROVIDE THE NECESSARY SHIELDING.

MOM, I... I REALLY DON'T THINK THIS IS SUCH A GOOD IDEA. ISN'T IT KIND OF RISKY?

LISETH, THIS SHIP IS THE PINNACLE OF UNGARAN MILITARY TECHNOLOGY.

IT'S JUST...

I'VE BEEN FIGHTING WAR SINCE LONG BEFORE YOU WERE BORN. AND I ASSURE YOU, A STAR IS FAR MORE PREDICTABLE THAN AN *OMEGA MEN* KAMIKAZE RAIDER--

WARNING. INCOMING GAMMA RAYS AND HIGH-ENERGY PARTICLES--

SSHRROOM

AGH!

LISETH!

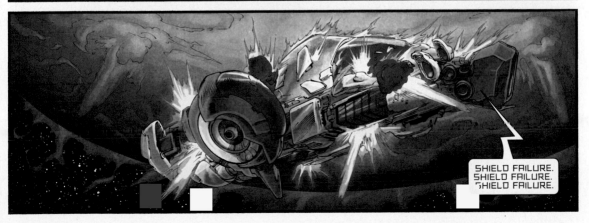

SHIELD FAILURE. SHIELD FAILURE. SHIELD FAILURE.

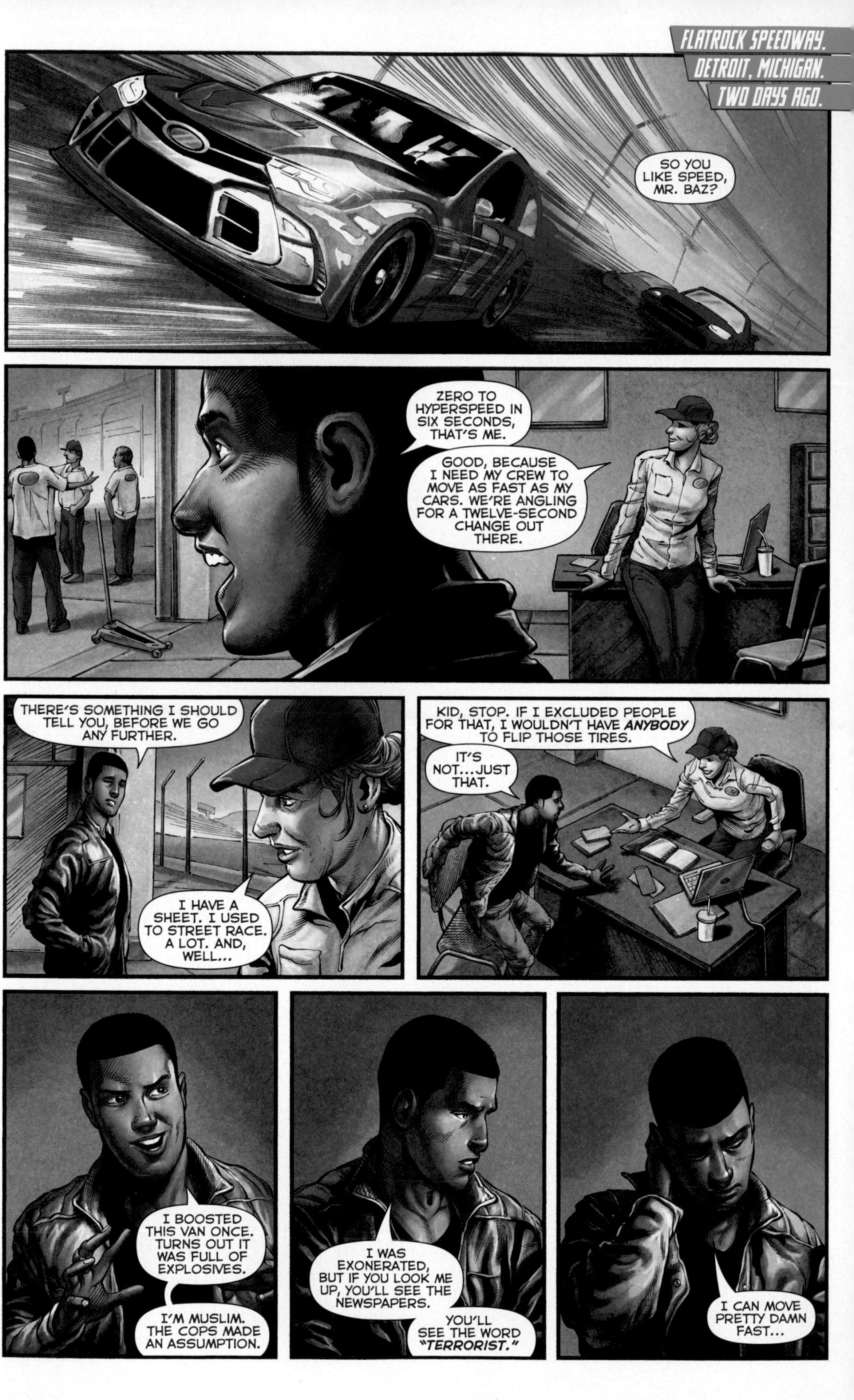
FLATROCK SPEEDWAY.
DETROIT, MICHIGAN.
TWO DAYS AGO.
SO YOU LIKE SPEED, MR. BAZ?
ZERO TO HYPERSPEED IN SIX SECONDS, THAT'S ME.
GOOD, BECAUSE I NEED MY CREW TO MOVE AS FAST AS MY CARS. WE'RE ANGLING FOR A TWELVE-SECOND CHANGE OUT THERE.
THERE'S SOMETHING I SHOULD TELL YOU, BEFORE WE GO ANY FURTHER.
I HAVE A SHEET. I USED TO STREET RACE. A LOT. AND, WELL...
KID, STOP. IF I EXCLUDED PEOPLE FOR THAT, I WOULDN'T HAVE *ANYBODY* TO FLIP THOSE TIRES.
IT'S NOT...JUST THAT.
I BOOSTED THIS VAN ONCE. TURNS OUT IT WAS FULL OF EXPLOSIVES.
I'M MUSLIM. THE COPS MADE AN ASSUMPTION.
I WAS EXONERATED, BUT IF YOU LOOK ME UP, YOU'LL SEE THE NEWSPAPERS.
YOU'LL SEE THE WORD *"TERRORIST."*
I CAN MOVE PRETTY DAMN FAST...

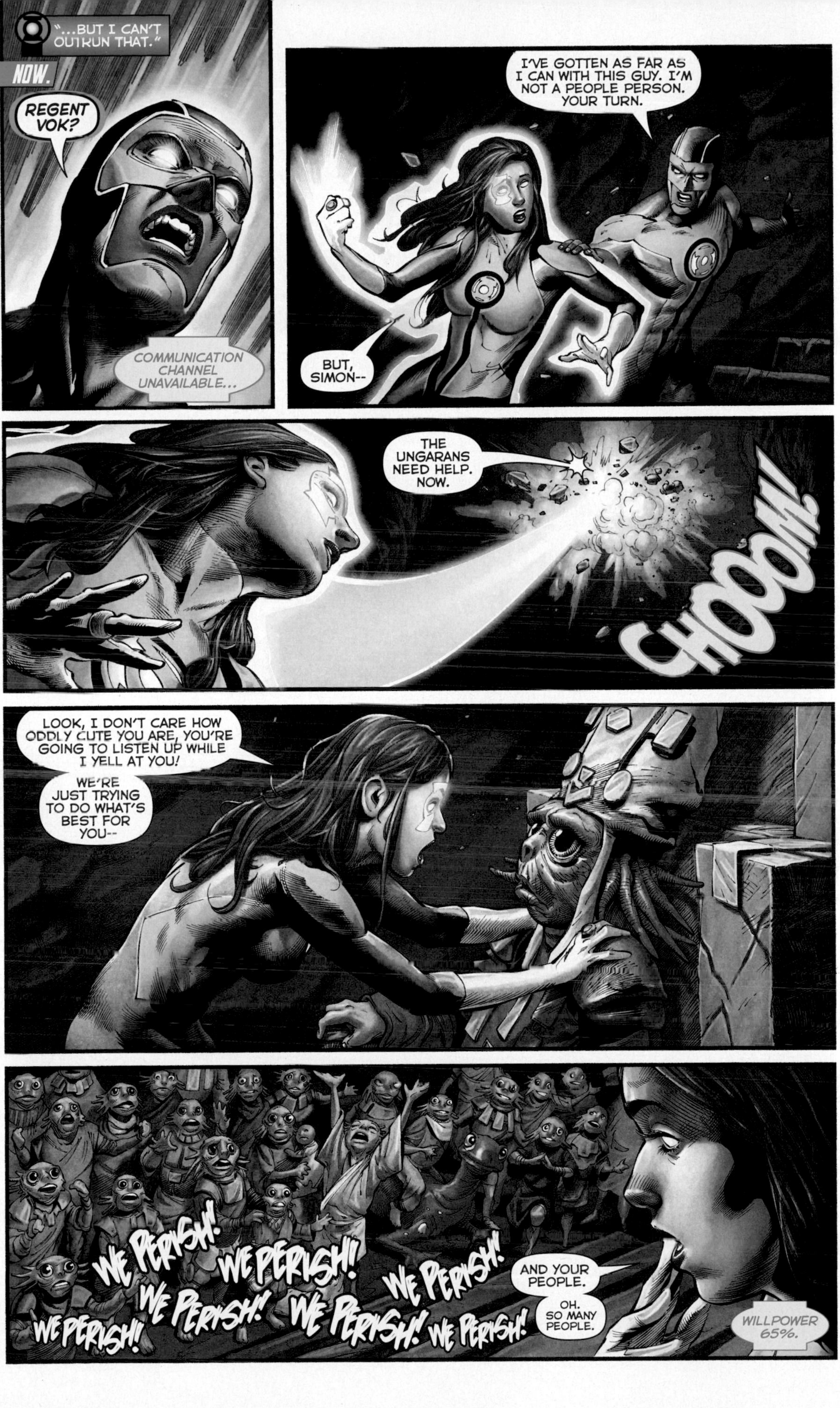
"...BUT I CAN'T OUTRUN THAT."
NOW.
REGENT VOK?
COMMUNICATION CHANNEL UNAVAILABLE...
I'VE GOTTEN AS FAR AS I CAN WITH THIS GUY. I'M NOT A PEOPLE PERSON. YOUR TURN.
BUT, SIMON--
THE UNGARANS NEED HELP. NOW.
CHOOOM!
LOOK, I DON'T CARE HOW ODDLY CUTE YOU ARE, YOU'RE GOING TO LISTEN UP WHILE I YELL AT YOU!
WE'RE JUST TRYING TO DO WHAT'S BEST FOR YOU--
WE PERISH! WE PERISH! WE PERISH! WE PERISH! WE PERISH! WE PERISH! WE PERISH!
AND YOUR PEOPLE.
OH. SO MANY PEOPLE.
WILLPOWER 65%.

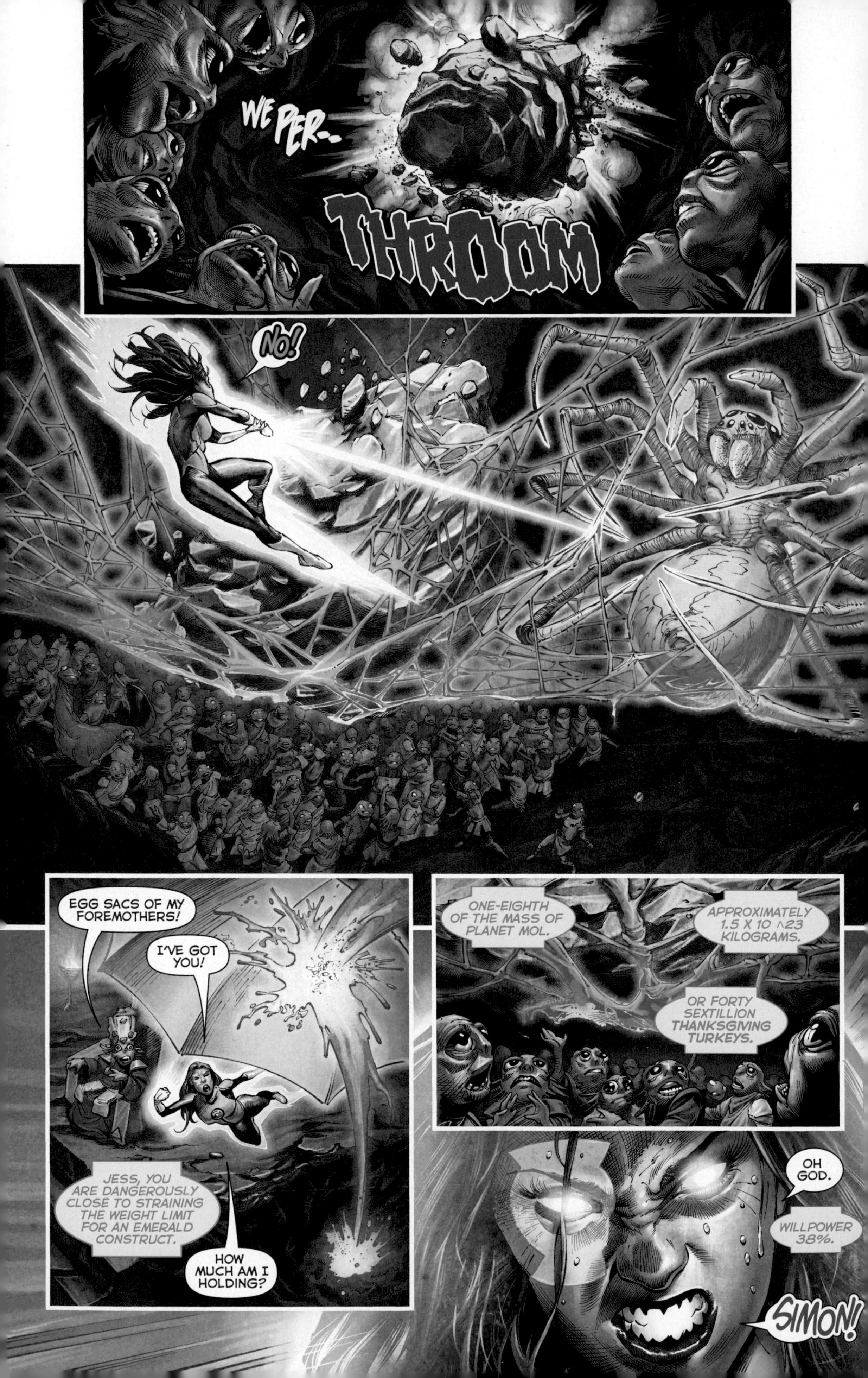
WE PER--
THROOM
NO!
EGG SACS OF MY FOREMOTHERS!
I'VE GOT YOU!
JESS, YOU ARE DANGEROUSLY CLOSE TO STRAINING THE WEIGHT LIMIT FOR AN EMERALD CONSTRUCT.
HOW MUCH AM I HOLDING?
ONE-EIGHTH OF THE MASS OF PLANET MOL.
APPROXIMATELY 1.5 X 10 ^23 KILOGRAMS.
OR FORTY SEXTILLION THANKSGIVING TURKEYS.
OH GOD.
WILLPOWER 38%.
SIMON!

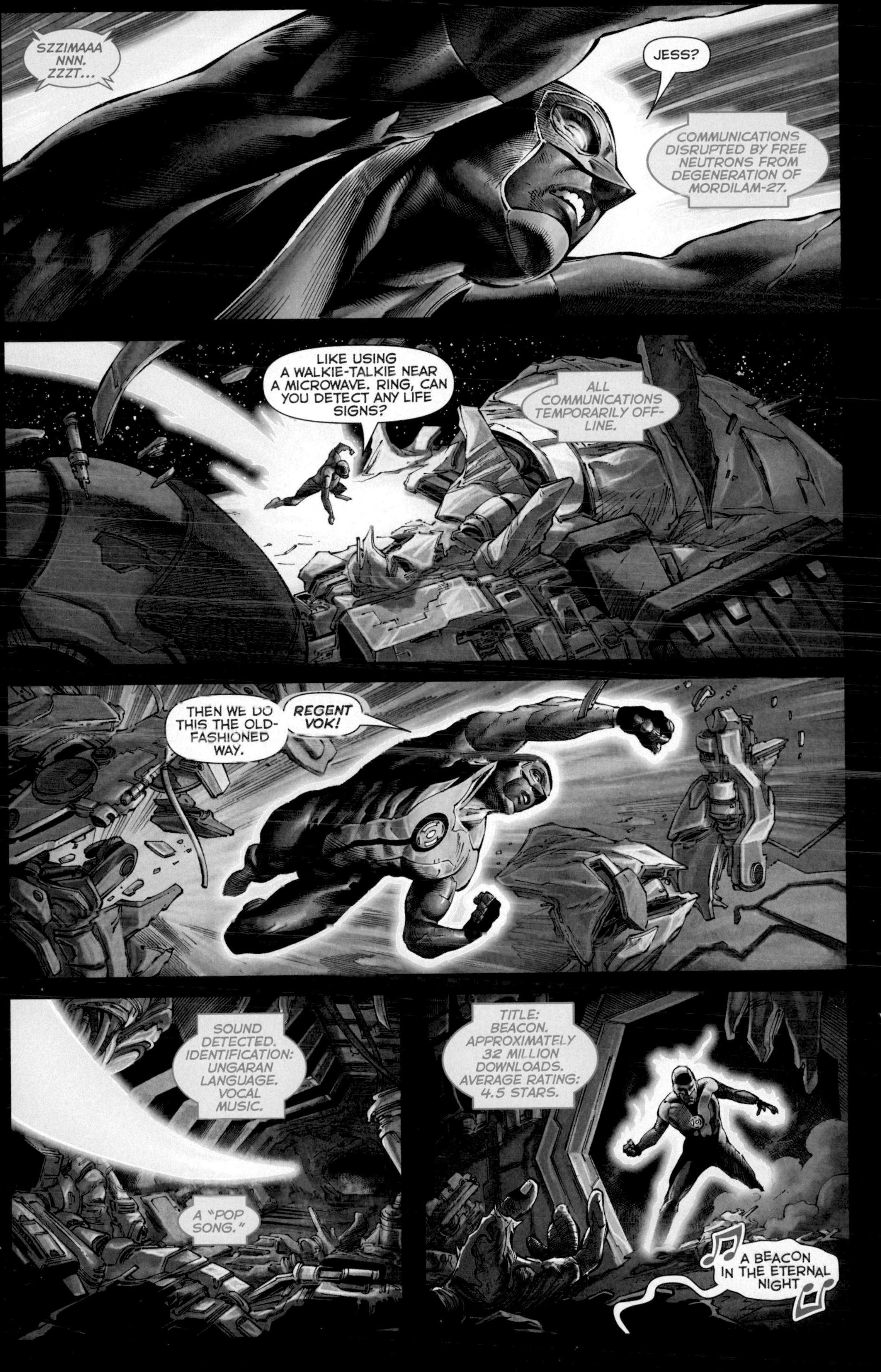
SZZIMAAA NNN. ZZZT...
JESS?
COMMUNICATIONS DISRUPTED BY FREE NEUTRONS FROM DEGENERATION OF MORDILAM-27.
LIKE USING A WALKIE-TALKIE NEAR A MICROWAVE. RING, CAN YOU DETECT ANY LIFE SIGNS?
ALL COMMUNICATIONS TEMPORARILY OFF-LINE.
THEN WE DO THIS THE OLD-FASHIONED WAY.
REGENT VOK!
SOUND DETECTED. IDENTIFICATION: UNGARAN LANGUAGE. VOCAL MUSIC.
A "POP SONG."
TITLE: BEACON. APPROXIMATELY 32 MILLION DOWNLOADS. AVERAGE RATING: 4.5 STARS.
A BEACON IN THE ETERNAL NIGHT

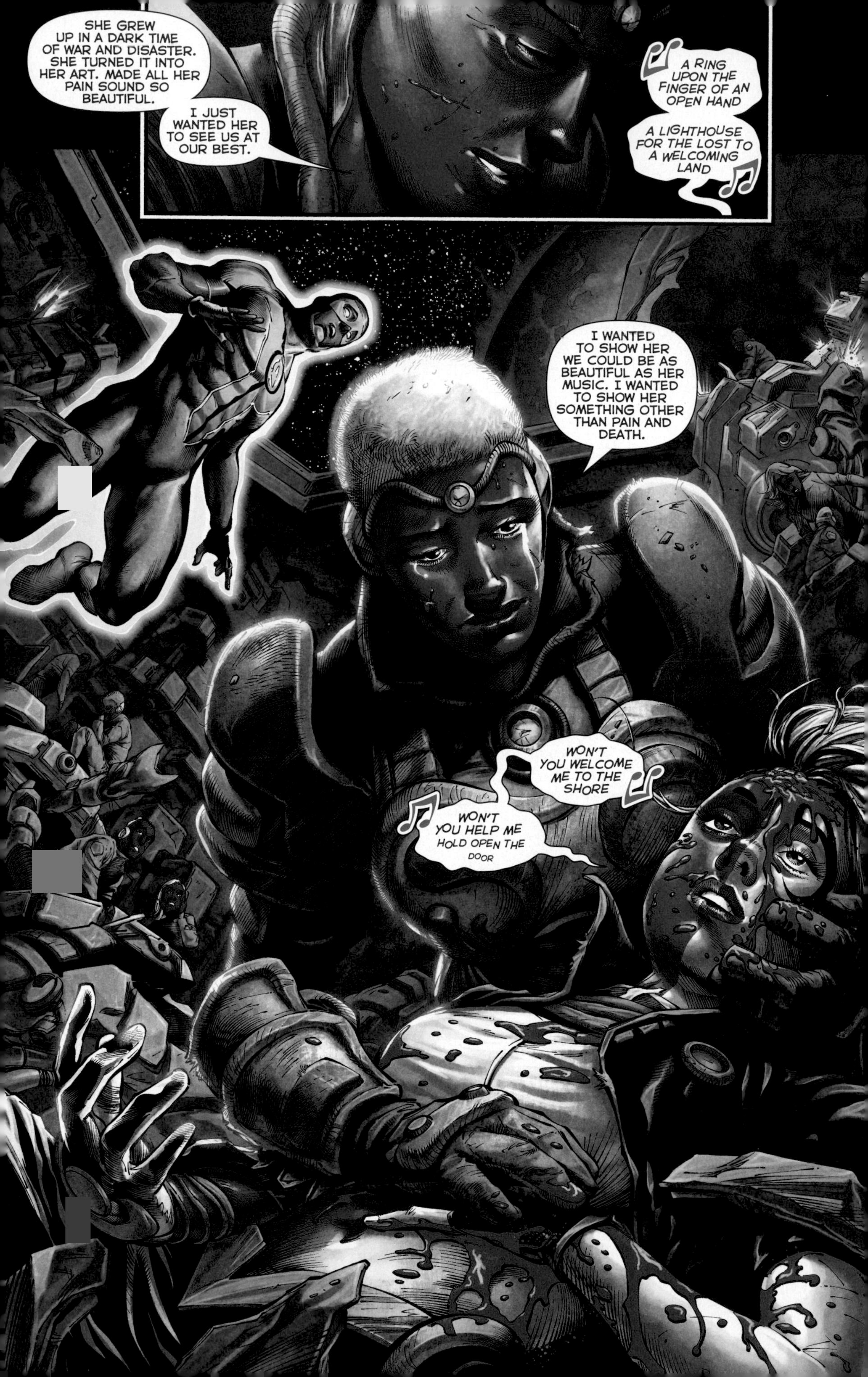
SHE GREW UP IN A DARK TIME OF WAR AND DISASTER. SHE TURNED IT INTO HER ART. MADE ALL HER PAIN SOUND SO BEAUTIFUL.
I JUST WANTED HER TO SEE US AT OUR BEST.
A RING UPON THE FINGER OF AN OPEN HAND
A LIGHTHOUSE FOR THE LOST TO A WELCOMING LAND
I WANTED TO SHOW HER WE COULD BE AS BEAUTIFUL AS HER MUSIC. I WANTED TO SHOW HER SOMETHING OTHER THAN PAIN AND DEATH.
WON'T YOU WELCOME ME TO THE SHORE
WON'T YOU HELP ME HOLD OPEN THE DOOR

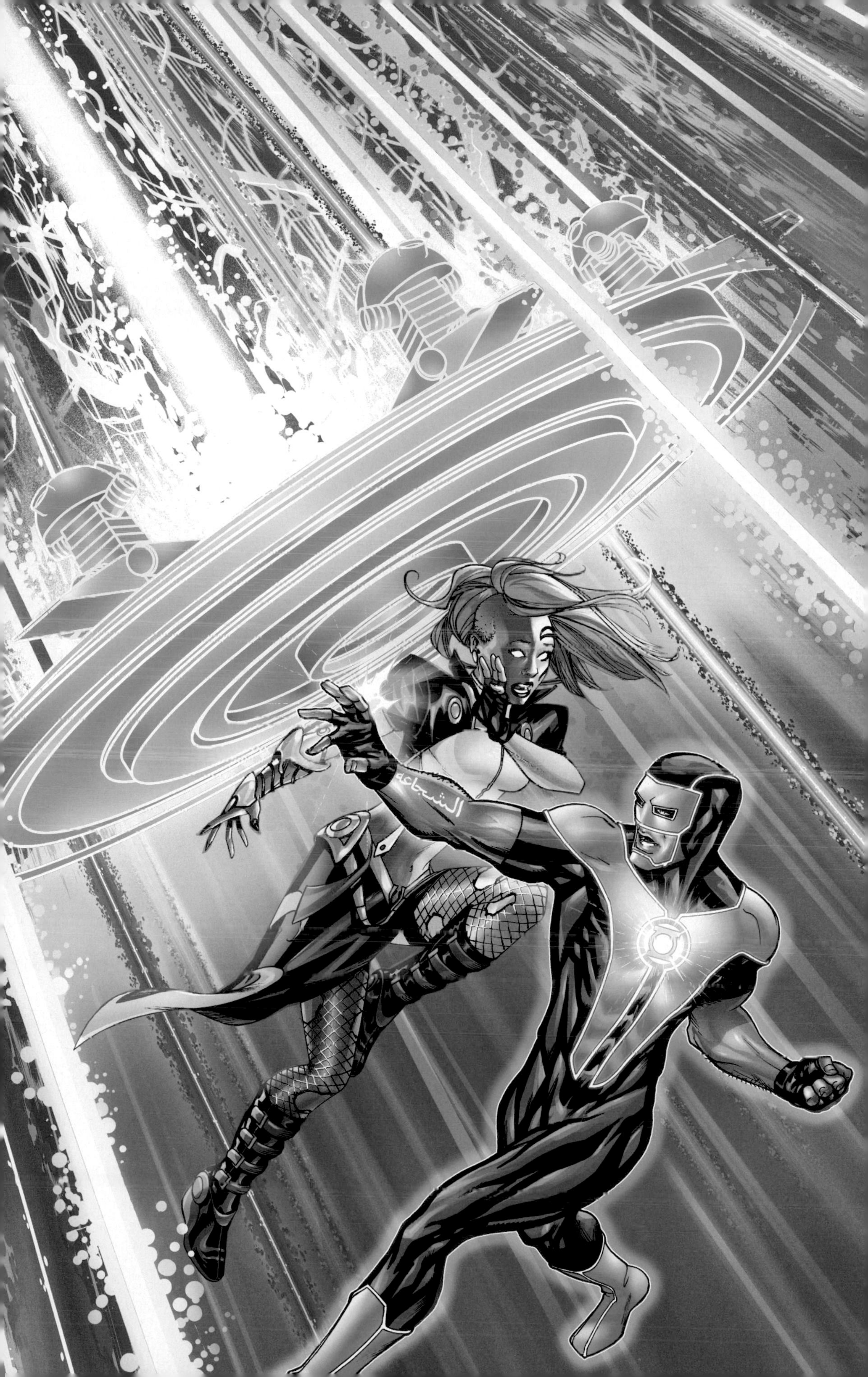
الشجاعة

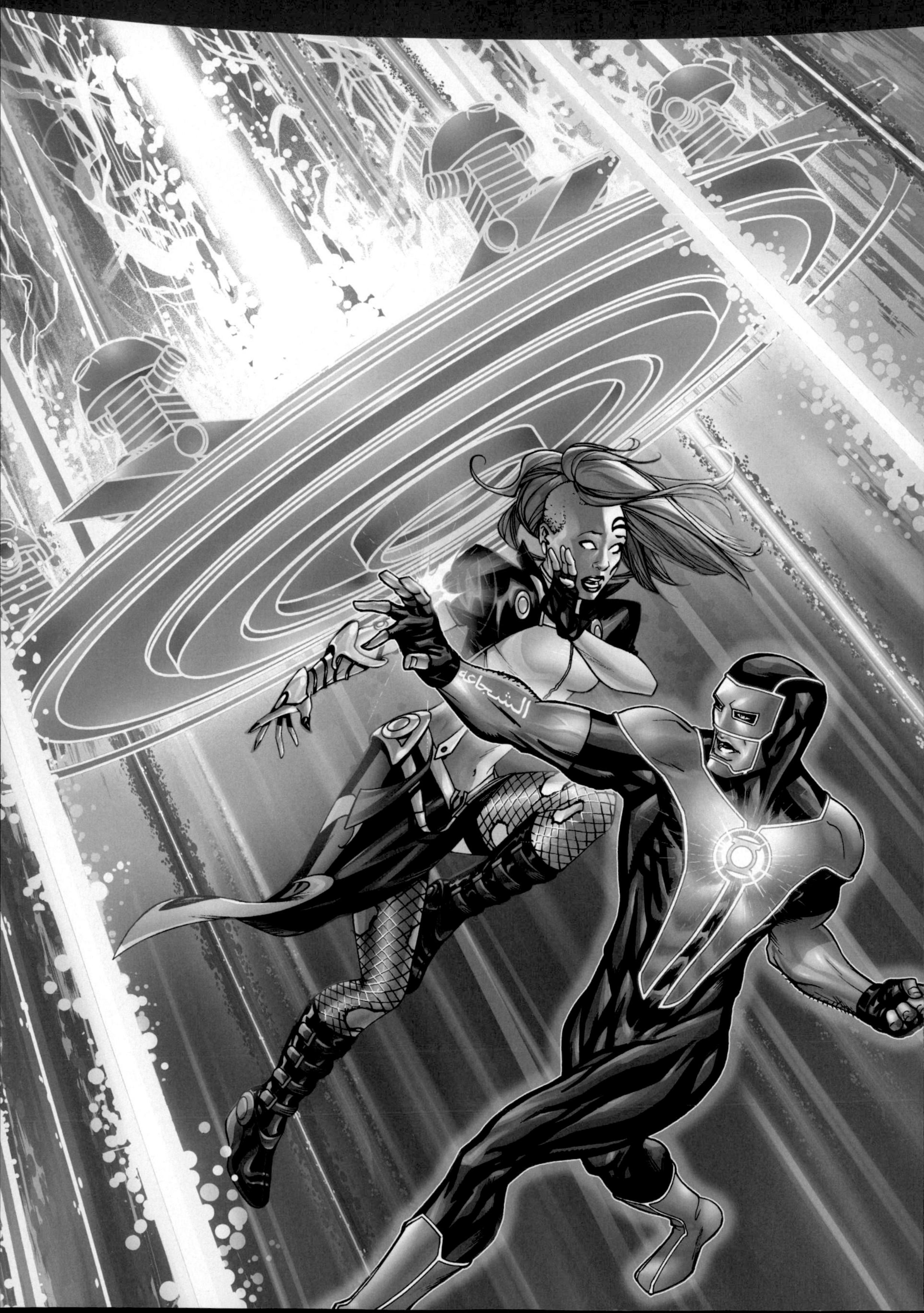
الشجاعة

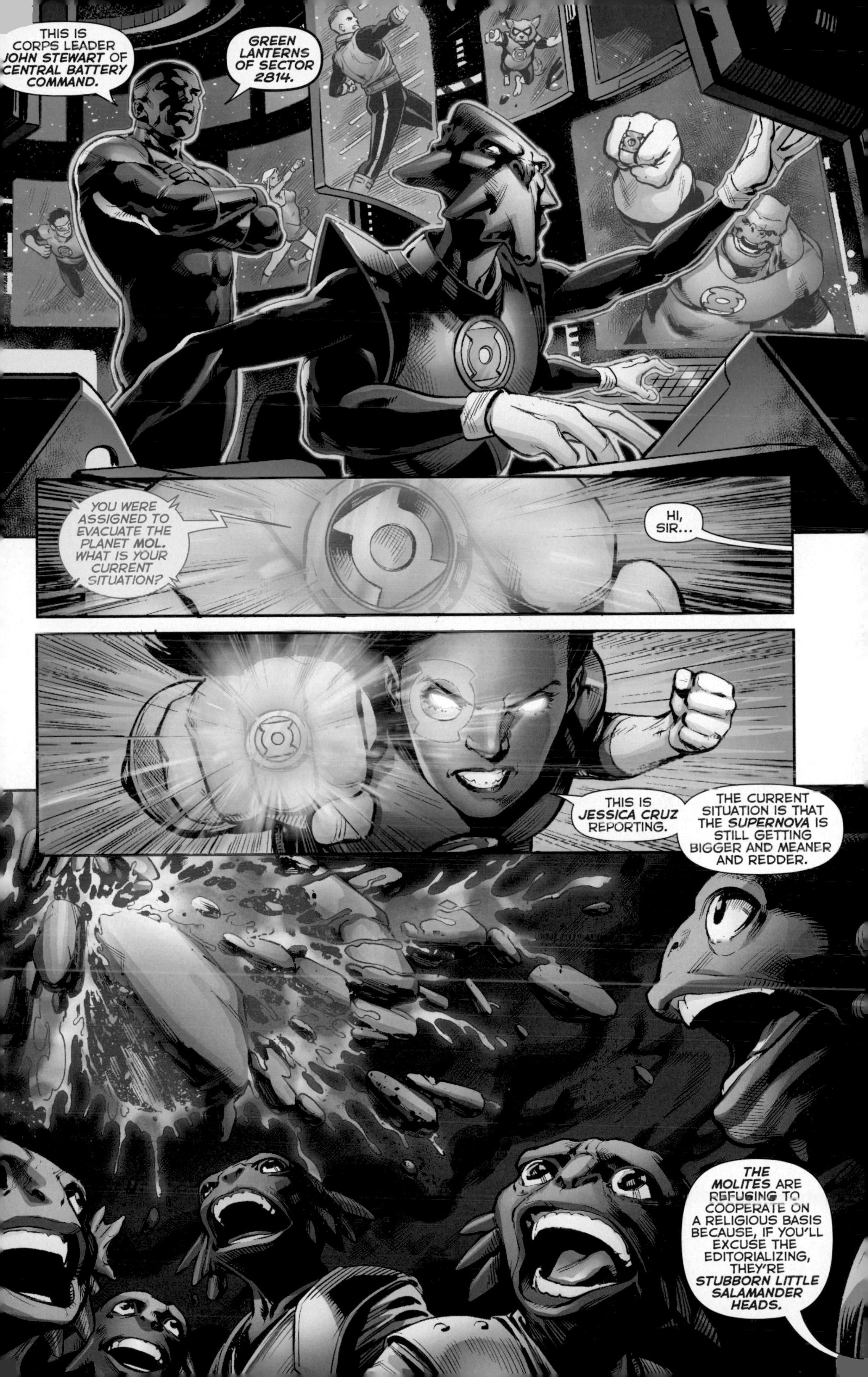
THIS IS CORPS LEADER JOHN STEWART OF CENTRAL BATTERY COMMAND.
GREEN LANTERNS OF SECTOR 2814.
YOU WERE ASSIGNED TO EVACUATE THE PLANET MOL. WHAT IS YOUR CURRENT SITUATION?
HI, SIR...
THIS IS JESSICA CRUZ REPORTING.
THE CURRENT SITUATION IS THAT THE SUPERNOVA IS STILL GETTING BIGGER AND MEANER AND REDDER.
THE MOLITES ARE REFUSING TO COOPERATE ON A RELIGIOUS BASIS BECAUSE, IF YOU'LL EXCUSE THE EDITORIALIZING, THEY'RE STUBBORN LITTLE SALAMANDER HEADS.

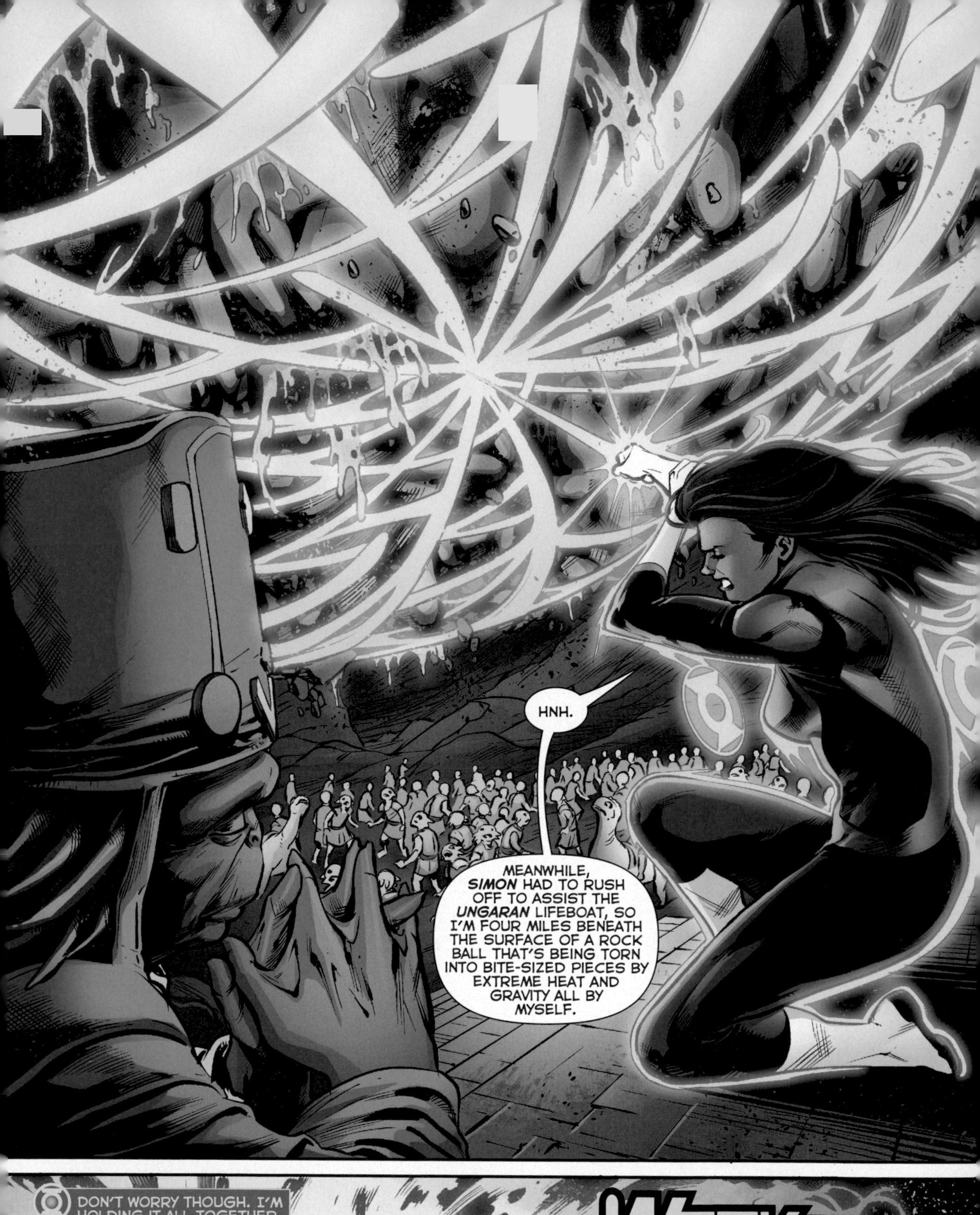
HNH.
MEANWHILE, SIMON HAD TO RUSH OFF TO ASSIST THE UNGARAN LIFEBOAT, SO I'M FOUR MILES BENEATH THE SURFACE OF A ROCK BALL THAT'S BEING TORN INTO BITE-SIZED PIECES BY EXTREME HEAT AND GRAVITY ALL BY MYSELF.

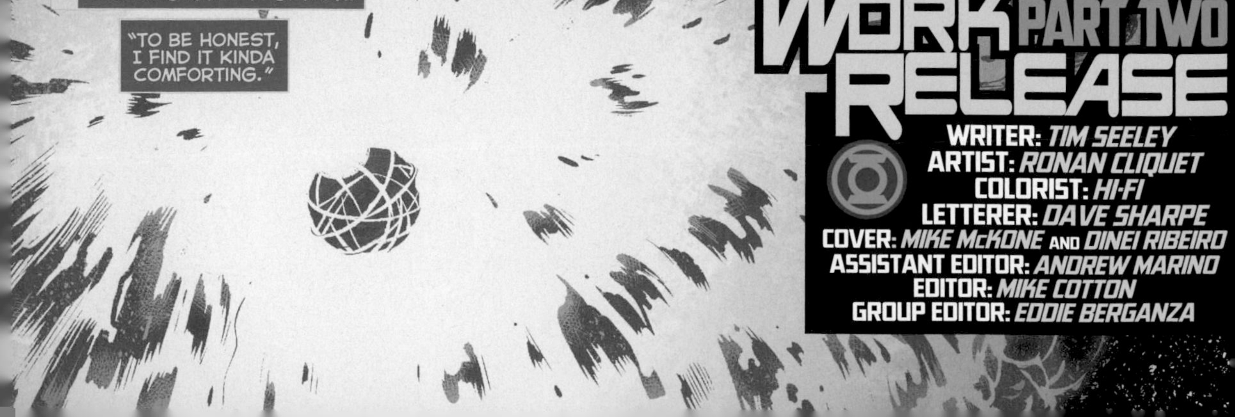
DON'T WORRY THOUGH. I'M HOLDING IT ALL TOGETHER.
"TO BE HONEST, I FIND IT KINDA COMFORTING."
WORK RELEASE PART TWO
WRITER: TIM SEELEY
ARTIST: RONAN CLIQUET
COLORIST: HI-FI
LETTERER: DAVE SHARPE
COVER: MIKE McKONE AND DINEI RIBEIRO
ASSISTANT EDITOR: ANDREW MARINO
EDITOR: MIKE COTTON
GROUP EDITOR: EDDIE BERGANZA

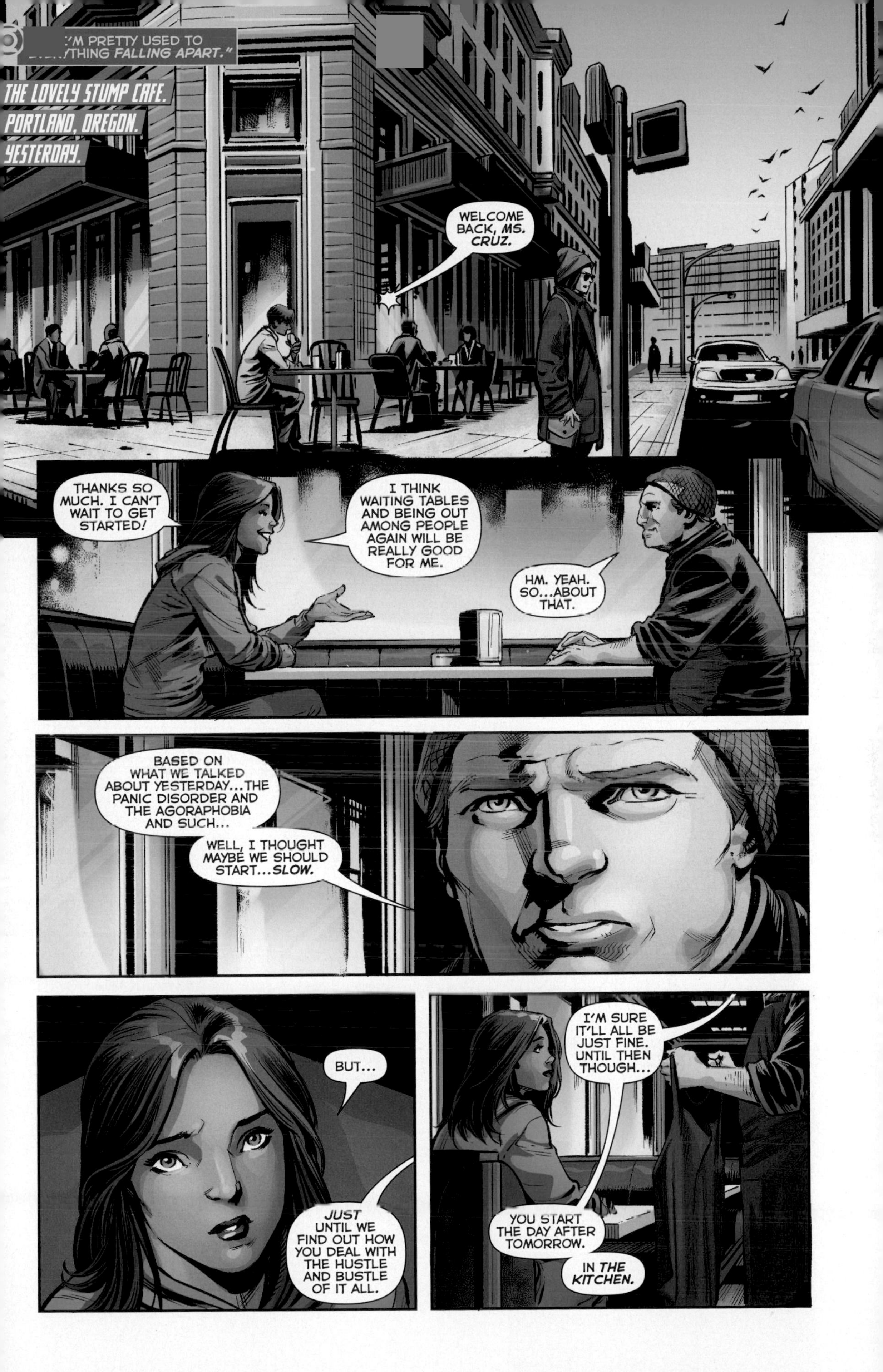
I'M PRETTY USED TO
YTHING FALLING APART."
THE LOVELY STUMP CAFE.
PORTLAND, OREGON.
YESTERDAY.
WELCOME BACK, MS. CRUZ.
THANKS SO MUCH. I CAN'T WAIT TO GET STARTED!
I THINK WAITING TABLES AND BEING OUT AMONG PEOPLE AGAIN WILL BE REALLY GOOD FOR ME.
HM. YEAH. SO...ABOUT THAT.
BASED ON WHAT WE TALKED ABOUT YESTERDAY...THE PANIC DISORDER AND THE AGORAPHOBIA AND SUCH...
WELL, I THOUGHT MAYBE WE SHOULD START...SLOW.
BUT...
JUST UNTIL WE FIND OUT HOW YOU DEAL WITH THE HUSTLE AND BUSTLE OF IT ALL.
I'M SURE IT'LL ALL BE JUST FINE. UNTIL THEN THOUGH...
YOU START THE DAY AFTER TOMORROW.
IN THE KITCHEN.

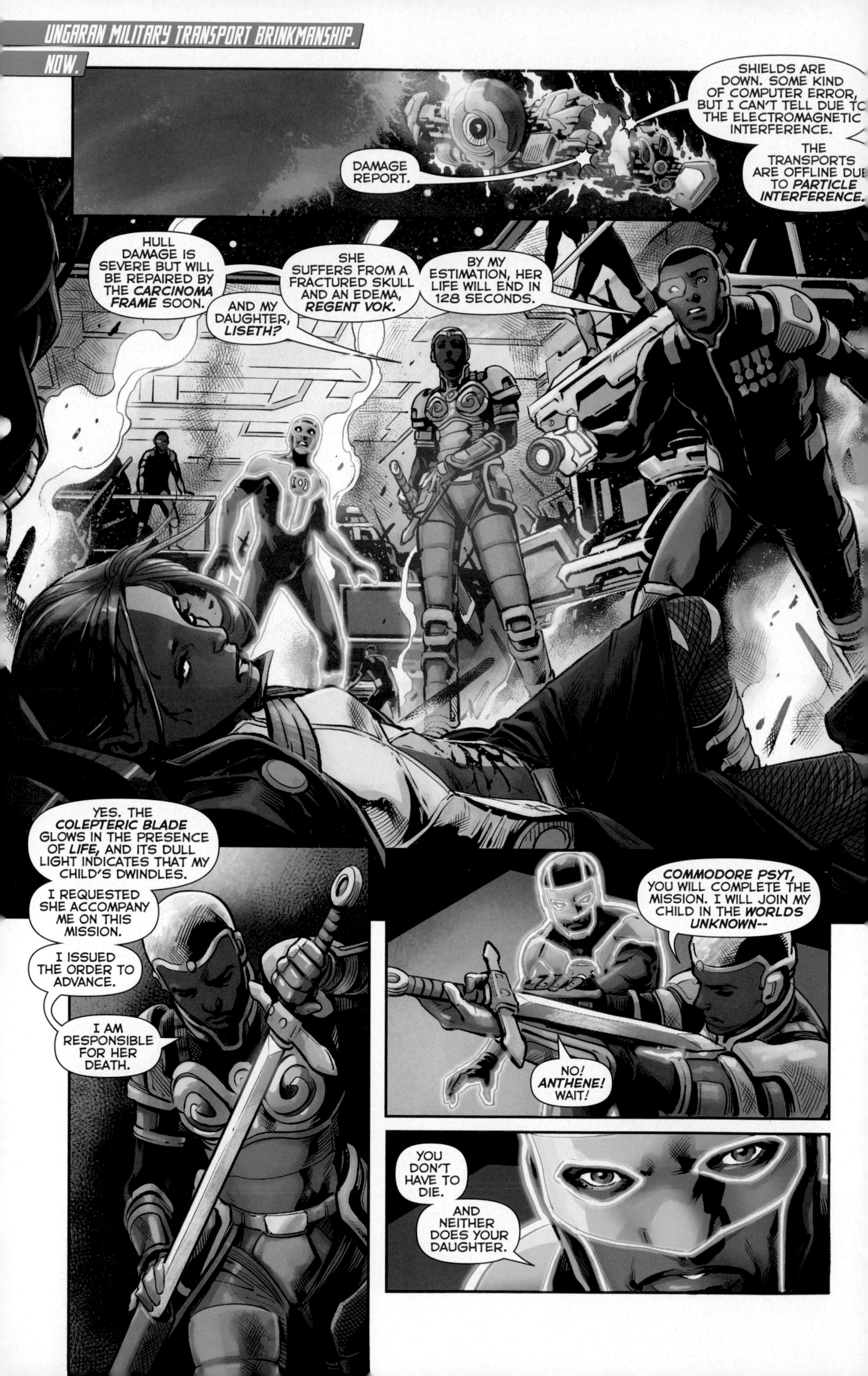
UNGARAN MILITARY TRANSPORT BRINKMANSHIP.
NOW.
DAMAGE REPORT.
SHIELDS ARE DOWN. SOME KIND OF COMPUTER ERROR, BUT I CAN'T TELL DUE TO THE ELECTROMAGNETIC INTERFERENCE.
THE TRANSPORTS ARE OFFLINE DUE TO PARTICLE INTERFERENCE.
HULL DAMAGE IS SEVERE BUT WILL BE REPAIRED BY THE CARCINOMA FRAME SOON.
AND MY DAUGHTER, LISETH?
SHE SUFFERS FROM A FRACTURED SKULL AND AN EDEMA, REGENT VOK.
BY MY ESTIMATION, HER LIFE WILL END IN 128 SECONDS.
YES. THE COLEPTERIC BLADE GLOWS IN THE PRESENCE OF LIFE, AND ITS DULL LIGHT INDICATES THAT MY CHILD'S DWINDLES.
I REQUESTED SHE ACCOMPANY ME ON THIS MISSION.
I ISSUED THE ORDER TO ADVANCE.
I AM RESPONSIBLE FOR HER DEATH.
COMMODORE PSYT, YOU WILL COMPLETE THE MISSION. I WILL JOIN MY CHILD IN THE WORLDS UNKNOWN--
NO! ANTHENE! WAIT!
YOU DON'T HAVE TO DIE.
AND NEITHER DOES YOUR DAUGHTER.

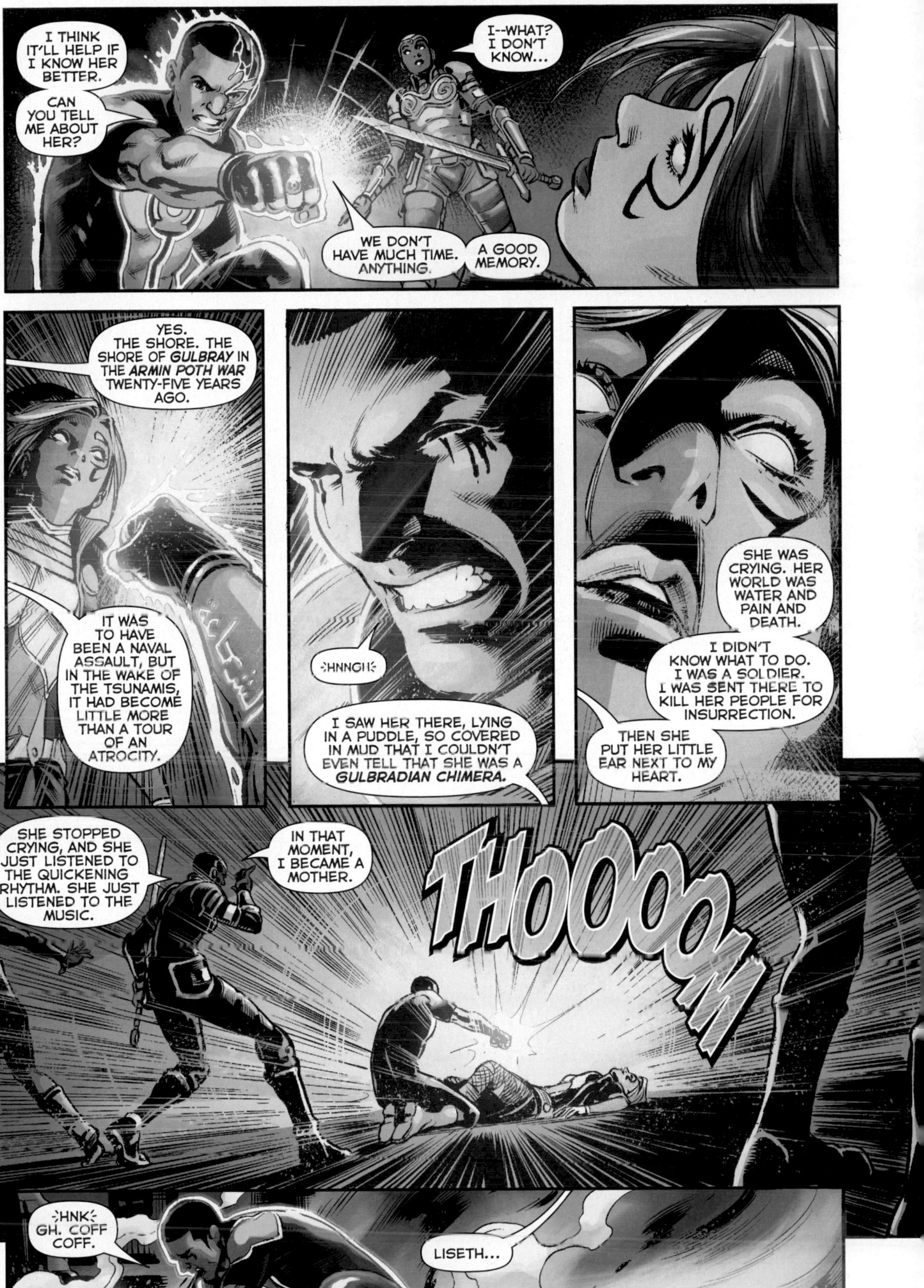
I THINK IT'LL HELP IF I KNOW HER BETTER.
CAN YOU TELL ME ABOUT HER?
I--WHAT? I DON'T KNOW...
WE DON'T HAVE MUCH TIME. ANYTHING.
A GOOD MEMORY.
YES. THE SHORE. THE SHORE OF *GULBRAY* IN THE *ARMIN POTH WAR* TWENTY-FIVE YEARS AGO.
IT WAS TO HAVE BEEN A NAVAL ASSAULT, BUT IN THE WAKE OF THE TSUNAMIS, IT HAD BECOME LITTLE MORE THAN A TOUR OF AN ATROCITY.
HNNGH
I SAW HER THERE, LYING IN A PUDDLE, SO COVERED IN MUD THAT I COULDN'T EVEN TELL THAT SHE WAS A *GULBRADIAN CHIMERA.*
SHE WAS CRYING. HER WORLD WAS WATER AND PAIN AND DEATH.
I DIDN'T KNOW WHAT TO DO. I WAS A SOLDIER. I WAS SENT THERE TO KILL HER PEOPLE FOR INSURRECTION.
THEN SHE PUT HER LITTLE EAR NEXT TO MY HEART.
SHE STOPPED CRYING, AND SHE JUST LISTENED TO THE QUICKENING RHYTHM. SHE JUST LISTENED TO THE MUSIC.
IN THAT MOMENT, I BECAME A MOTHER.
THOOOOOM
HNK GH. COFF COFF.
LISETH...

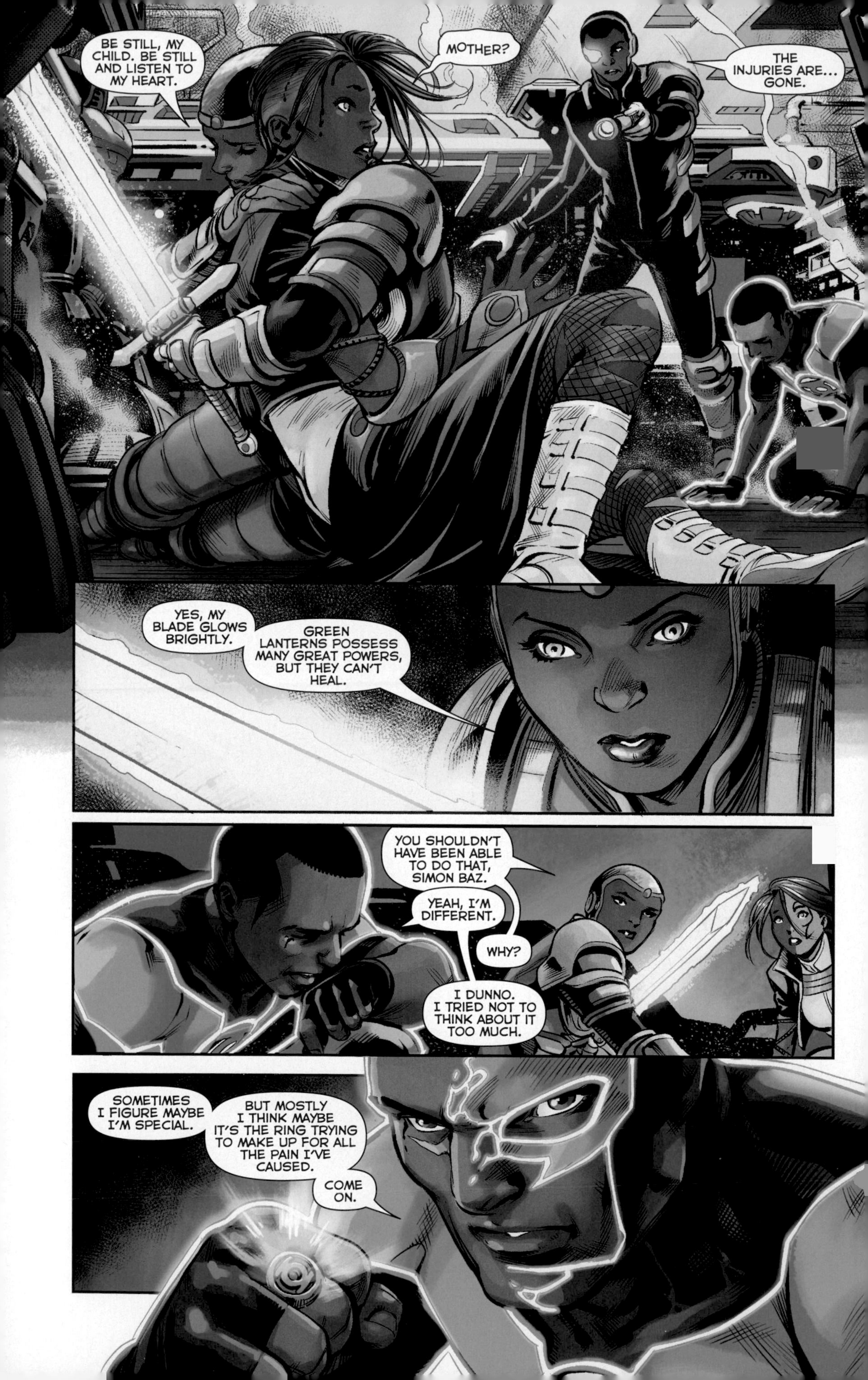
BE STILL, MY CHILD. BE STILL AND LISTEN TO MY HEART.
MOTHER?
THE INJURIES ARE... GONE.
YES, MY BLADE GLOWS BRIGHTLY.
GREEN LANTERNS POSSESS MANY GREAT POWERS, BUT THEY CAN'T HEAL.
YOU SHOULDN'T HAVE BEEN ABLE TO DO THAT, SIMON BAZ.
YEAH, I'M DIFFERENT.
WHY?
I DUNNO. I TRIED NOT TO THINK ABOUT IT TOO MUCH.
SOMETIMES I FIGURE MAYBE I'M SPECIAL.
BUT MOSTLY I THINK MAYBE IT'S THE RING TRYING TO MAKE UP FOR ALL THE PAIN I'VE CAUSED.
COME ON.

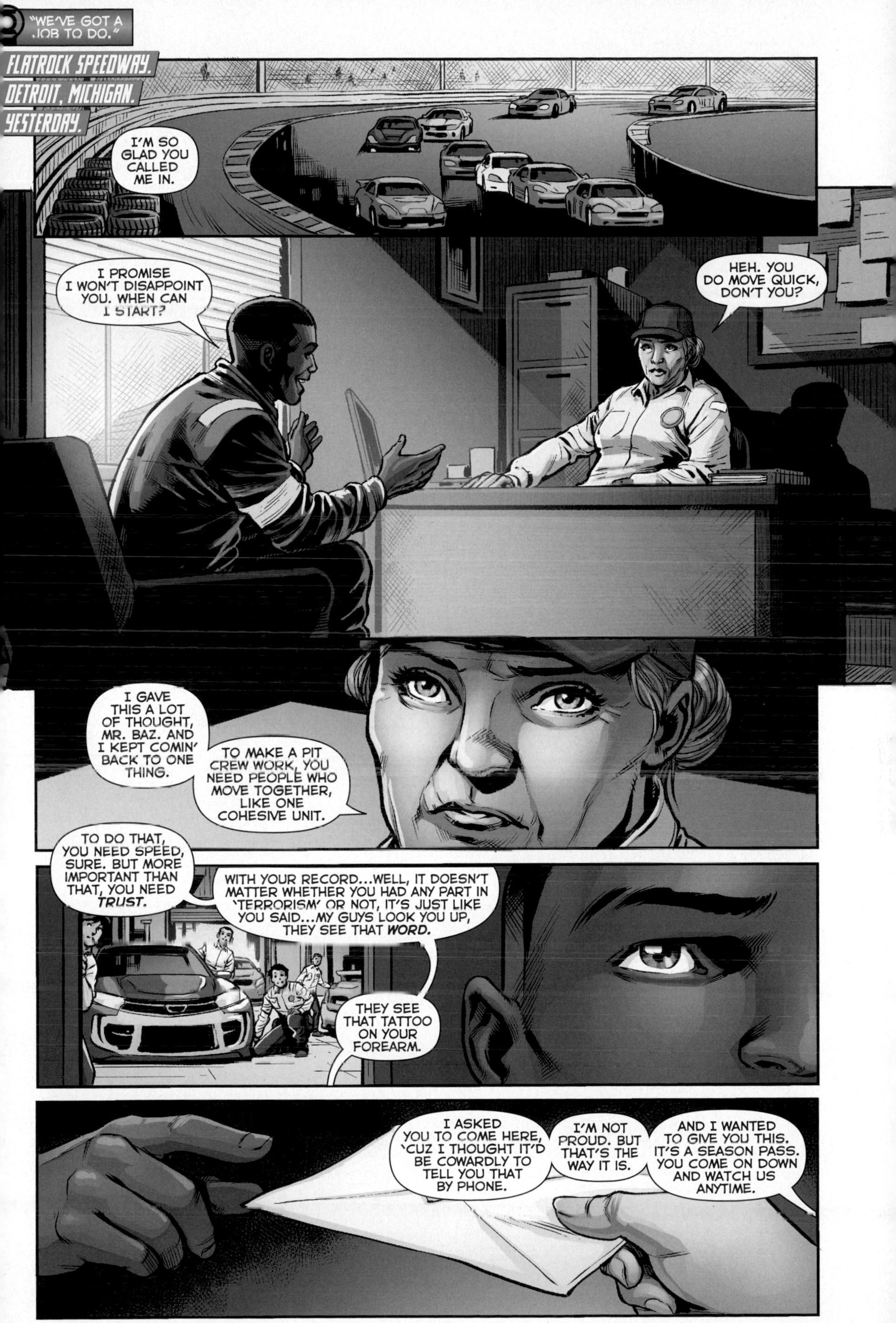
"WE'VE GOT A JOB TO DO."
FLATROCK SPEEDWAY. DETROIT, MICHIGAN. YESTERDAY.
I'M SO GLAD YOU CALLED ME IN.
I PROMISE I WON'T DISAPPOINT YOU. WHEN CAN I START?
HEH. YOU DO MOVE QUICK, DON'T YOU?
I GAVE THIS A LOT OF THOUGHT, MR. BAZ. AND I KEPT COMIN' BACK TO ONE THING.
TO MAKE A PIT CREW WORK, YOU NEED PEOPLE WHO MOVE TOGETHER, LIKE ONE COHESIVE UNIT.
TO DO THAT, YOU NEED SPEED, SURE. BUT MORE IMPORTANT THAN THAT, YOU NEED TRUST.
WITH YOUR RECORD...WELL, IT DOESN'T MATTER WHETHER YOU HAD ANY PART IN 'TERRORISM' OR NOT, IT'S JUST LIKE YOU SAID...MY GUYS LOOK YOU UP, THEY SEE THAT WORD.
THEY SEE THAT TATTOO ON YOUR FOREARM.
I ASKED YOU TO COME HERE, 'CUZ I THOUGHT IT'D BE COWARDLY TO TELL YOU THAT BY PHONE.
I'M NOT PROUD. BUT THAT'S THE WAY IT IS.
AND I WANTED TO GIVE YOU THIS. IT'S A SEASON PASS. YOU COME ON DOWN AND WATCH US ANYTIME.

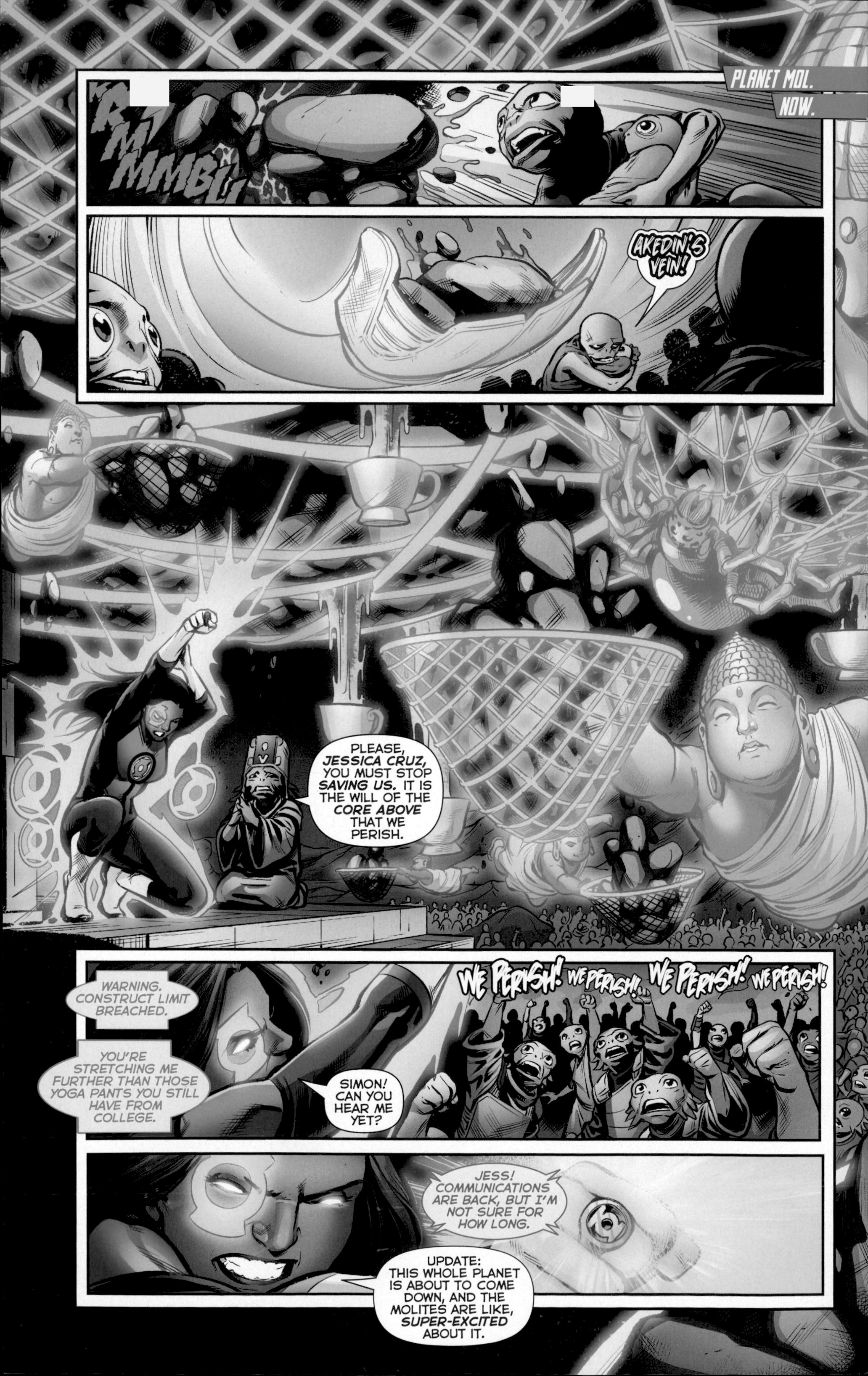
PLANET MOL.
NOW.
RMMMBL
AKEDIN'S VEIN!
PLEASE, JESSICA CRUZ, YOU MUST STOP SAVING US. IT IS THE WILL OF THE CORE ABOVE THAT WE PERISH.
WARNING. CONSTRUCT LIMIT BREACHED.
YOU'RE STRETCHING ME FURTHER THAN THOSE YOGA PANTS YOU STILL HAVE FROM COLLEGE.
SIMON! CAN YOU HEAR ME YET?
WE PERISH! WE PERISH! WE PERISH! WE PERISH!
JESS! COMMUNICATIONS ARE BACK, BUT I'M NOT SURE FOR HOW LONG.
UPDATE: THIS WHOLE PLANET IS ABOUT TO COME DOWN, AND THE MOLITES ARE LIKE, SUPER-EXCITED ABOUT IT.

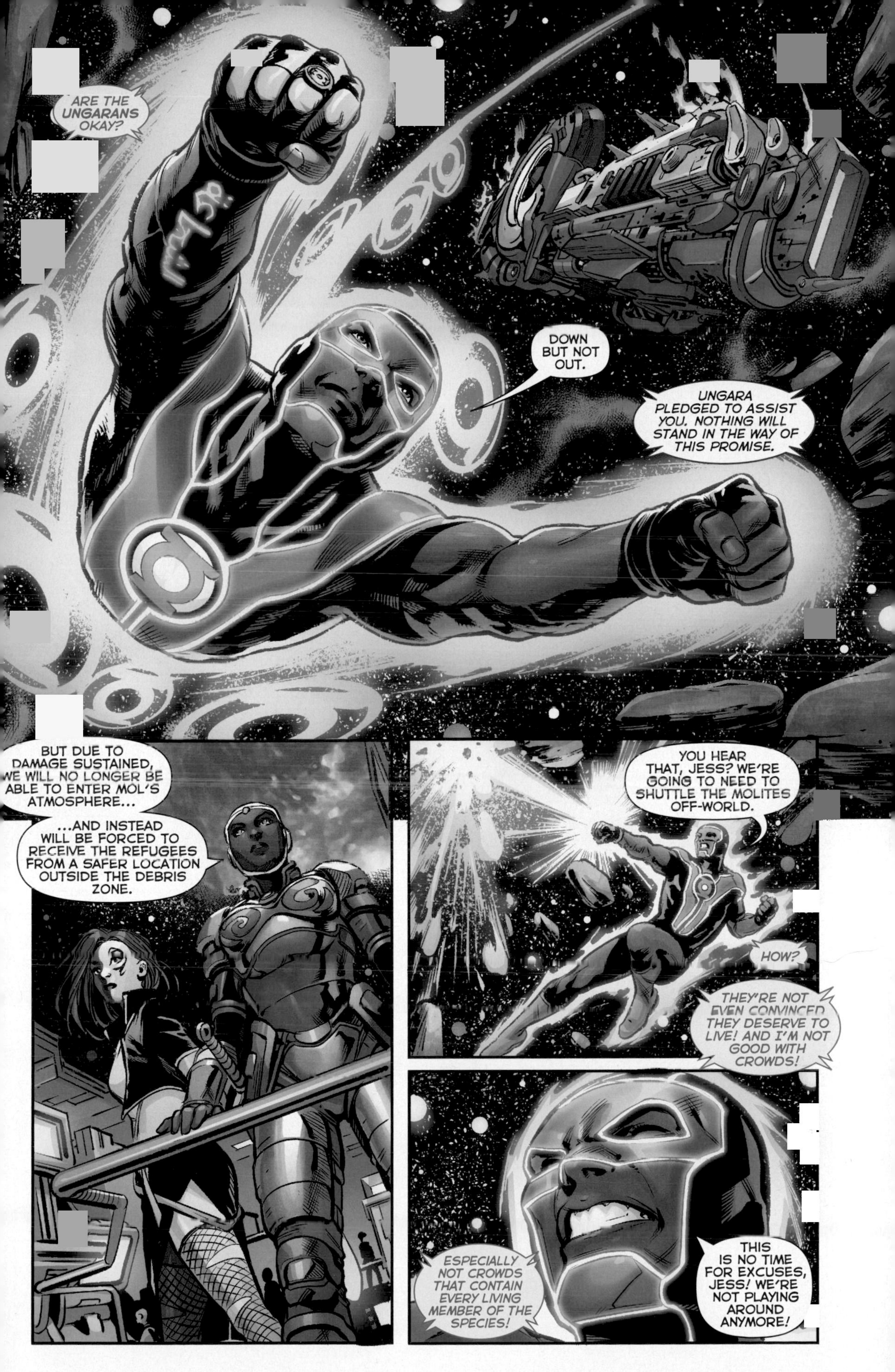
ARE THE UNGARANS OKAY?
DOWN BUT NOT OUT.
UNGARA PLEDGED TO ASSIST YOU. NOTHING WILL STAND IN THE WAY OF THIS PROMISE.
BUT DUE TO DAMAGE SUSTAINED, WE WILL NO LONGER BE ABLE TO ENTER MOL'S ATMOSPHERE...
...AND INSTEAD WILL BE FORCED TO RECEIVE THE REFUGEES FROM A SAFER LOCATION OUTSIDE THE DEBRIS ZONE.
YOU HEAR THAT, JESS? WE'RE GOING TO NEED TO SHUTTLE THE MOLITES OFF-WORLD.
HOW?
THEY'RE NOT EVEN CONVINCED THEY DESERVE TO LIVE! AND I'M NOT GOOD WITH CROWDS!
ESPECIALLY NOT CROWDS THAT CONTAIN EVERY LIVING MEMBER OF THE SPECIES!
THIS IS NO TIME FOR EXCUSES, JESS! WE'RE NOT PLAYING AROUND ANYMORE!

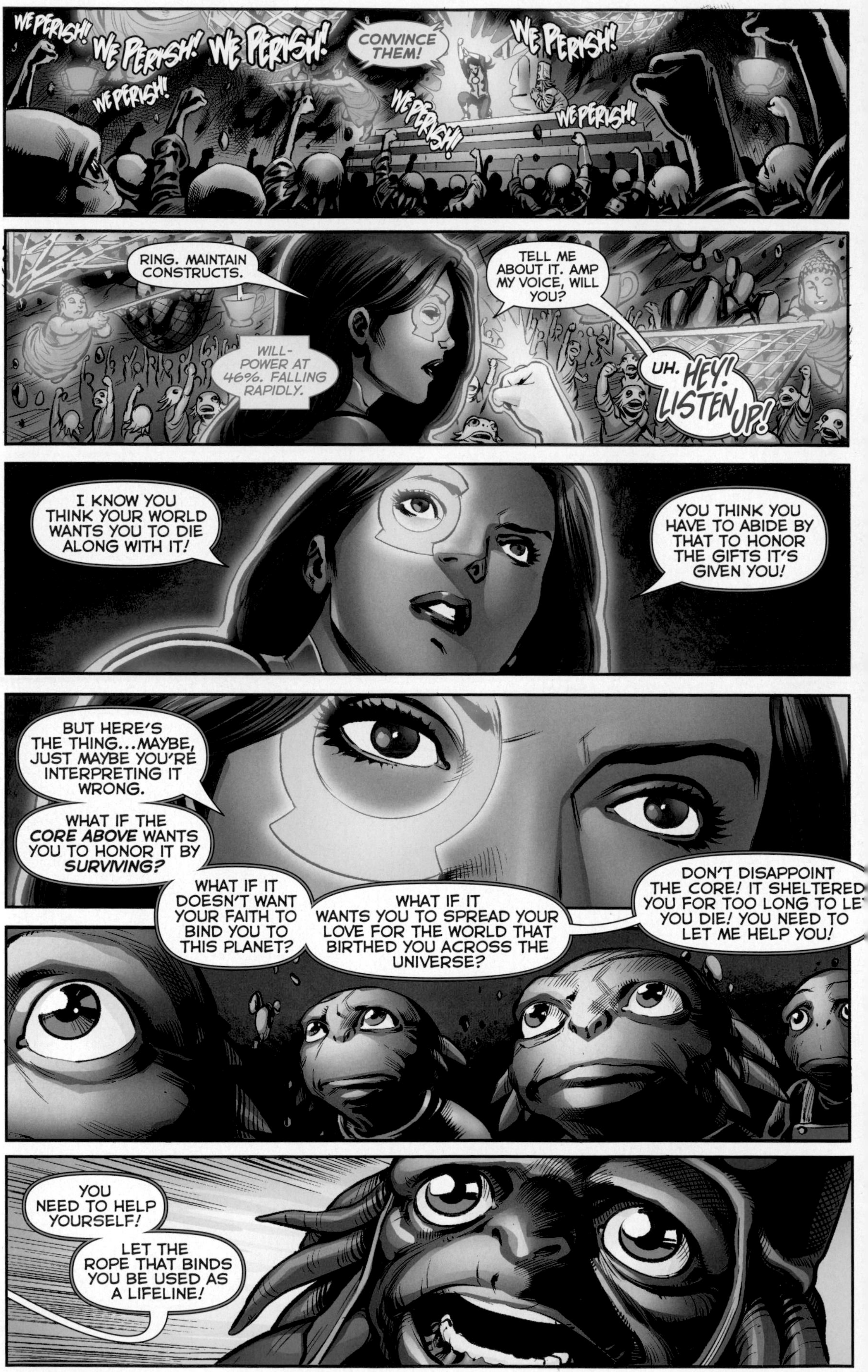
WE PERISH!
WE PERISH!
WE PERISH!
CONVINCE THEM!
WE PERISH!
WE PERISH!
WE PERISH!
WE PERISH!
RING. MAINTAIN CONSTRUCTS.
WILL-POWER AT 46%. FALLING RAPIDLY.
TELL ME ABOUT IT. AMP MY VOICE, WILL YOU?
UH. HEY! LISTEN UP!
I KNOW YOU THINK YOUR WORLD WANTS YOU TO DIE ALONG WITH IT!
YOU THINK YOU HAVE TO ABIDE BY THAT TO HONOR THE GIFTS IT'S GIVEN YOU!
BUT HERE'S THE THING...MAYBE, JUST MAYBE YOU'RE INTERPRETING IT WRONG.
WHAT IF THE CORE ABOVE WANTS YOU TO HONOR IT BY SURVIVING?
WHAT IF IT DOESN'T WANT YOUR FAITH TO BIND YOU TO THIS PLANET?
WHAT IF IT WANTS YOU TO SPREAD YOUR LOVE FOR THE WORLD THAT BIRTHED YOU ACROSS THE UNIVERSE?
DON'T DISAPPOINT THE CORE! IT SHELTERED YOU FOR TOO LONG TO LET YOU DIE! YOU NEED TO LET ME HELP YOU!
YOU NEED TO HELP YOURSELF!
LET THE ROPE THAT BINDS YOU BE USED AS A LIFELINE!

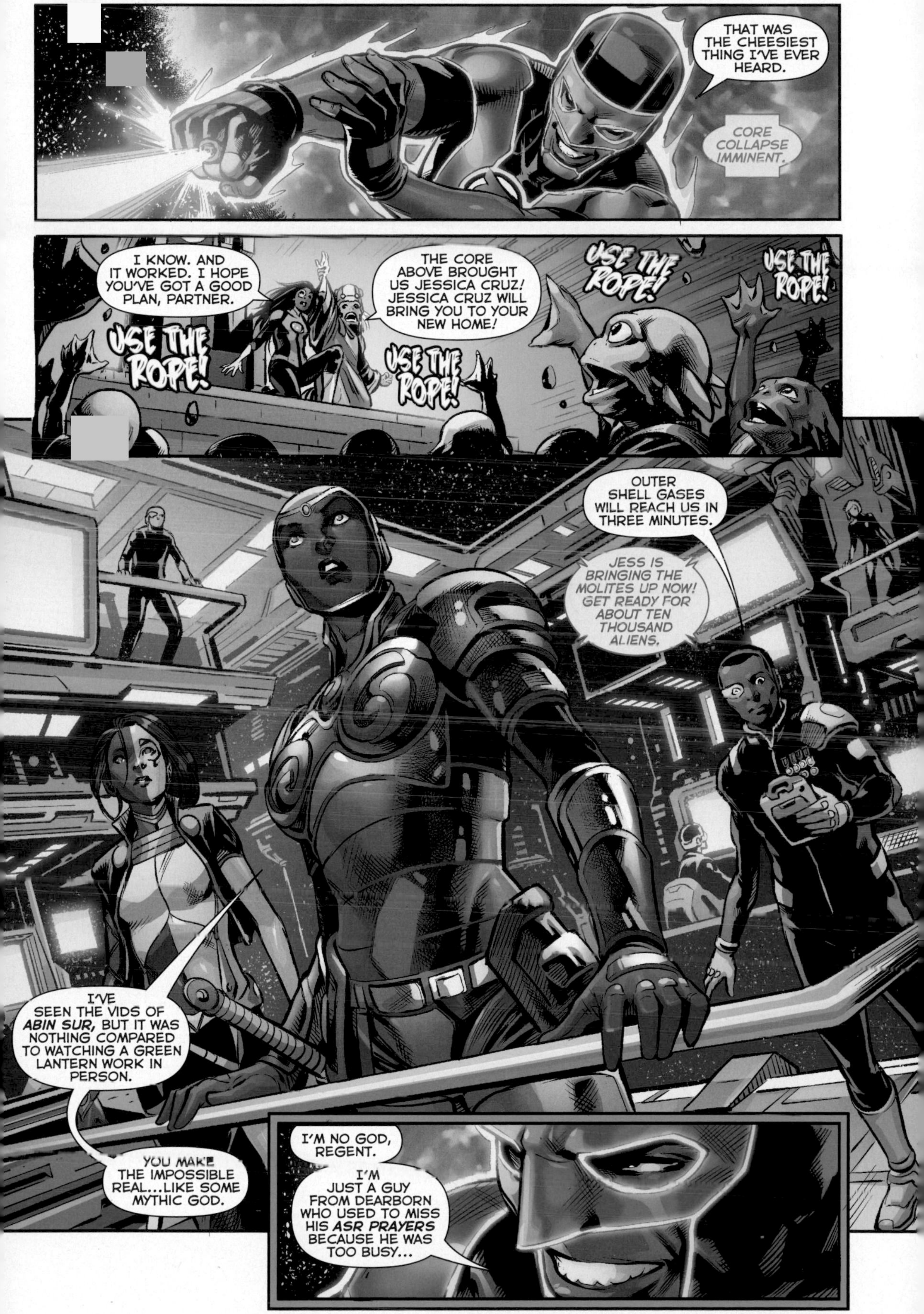
THAT WAS THE CHEESIEST THING I'VE EVER HEARD.
CORE COLLAPSE IMMINENT.
I KNOW. AND IT WORKED. I HOPE YOU'VE GOT A GOOD PLAN, PARTNER.
THE CORE ABOVE BROUGHT US JESSICA CRUZ! JESSICA CRUZ WILL BRING YOU TO YOUR NEW HOME!
USE THE ROPE!
USE THE ROPE!
USE THE ROPE!
USE THE ROPE!
OUTER SHELL GASES WILL REACH US IN THREE MINUTES.
JESS IS BRINGING THE MOLITES UP NOW! GET READY FOR ABOUT TEN THOUSAND ALIENS.
I'VE SEEN THE VIDS OF ABIN SUR, BUT IT WAS NOTHING COMPARED TO WATCHING A GREEN LANTERN WORK IN PERSON.
YOU MAKE THE IMPOSSIBLE REAL...LIKE SOME MYTHIC GOD.
I'M NO GOD, REGENT.
I'M JUST A GUY FROM DEARBORN WHO USED TO MISS HIS ASR PRAYERS BECAUSE HE WAS TOO BUSY...

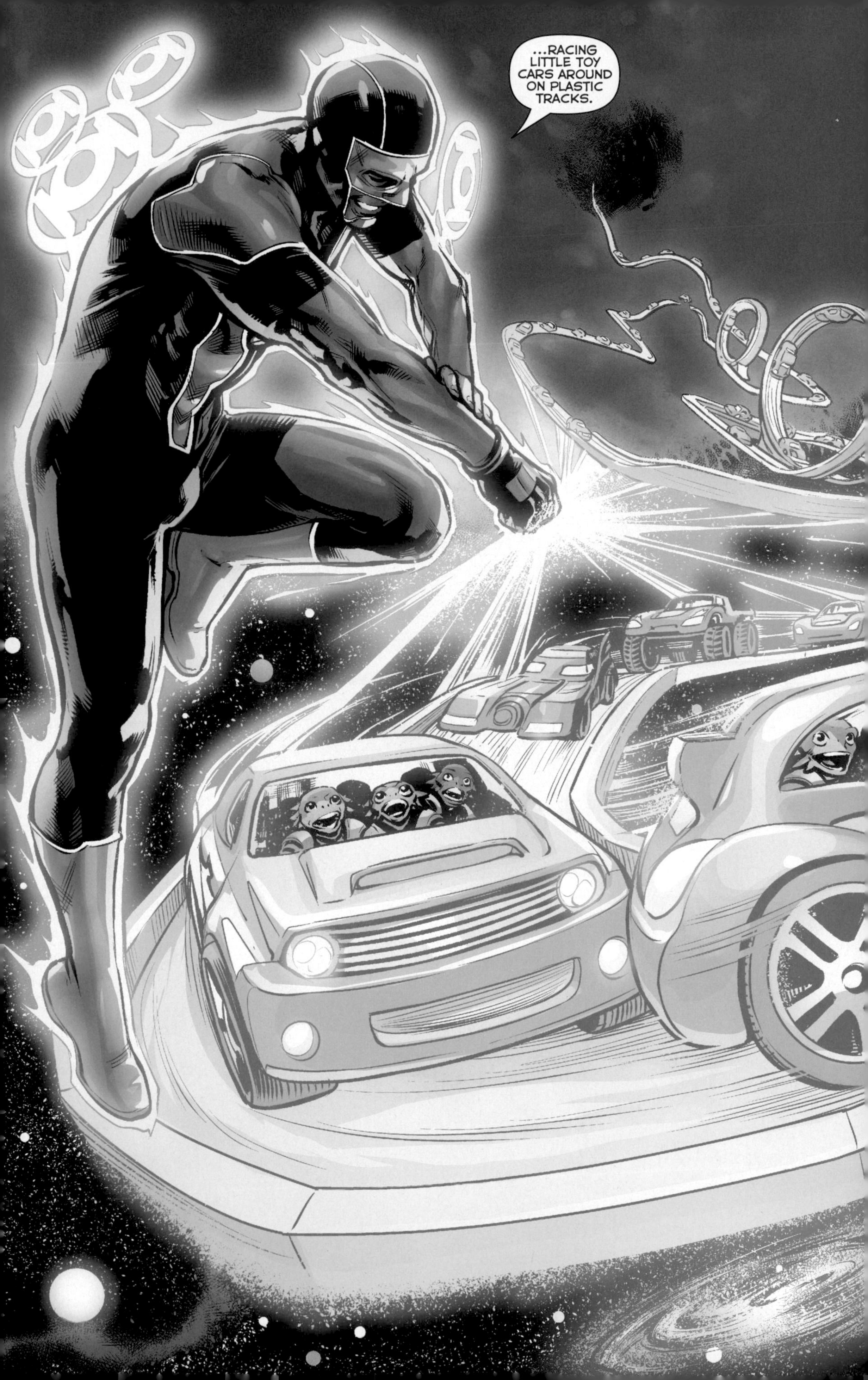
...RACING LITTLE TOY CARS AROUND ON PLASTIC TRACKS.

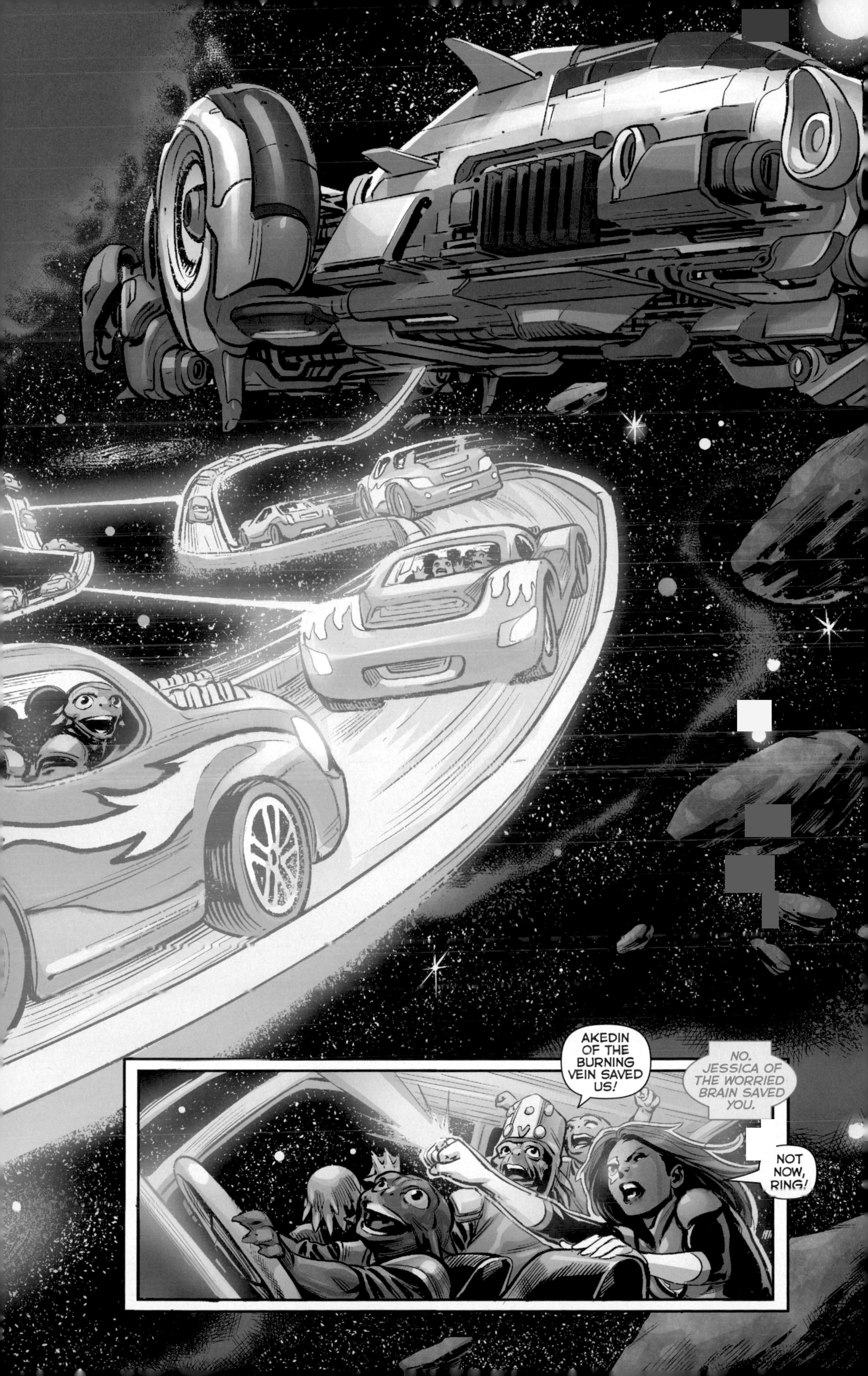
AKEDIN OF THE BURNING VEIN SAVED US!
NO. JESSICA OF THE WORRIED BRAIN SAVED YOU.
NOT NOW, RING!

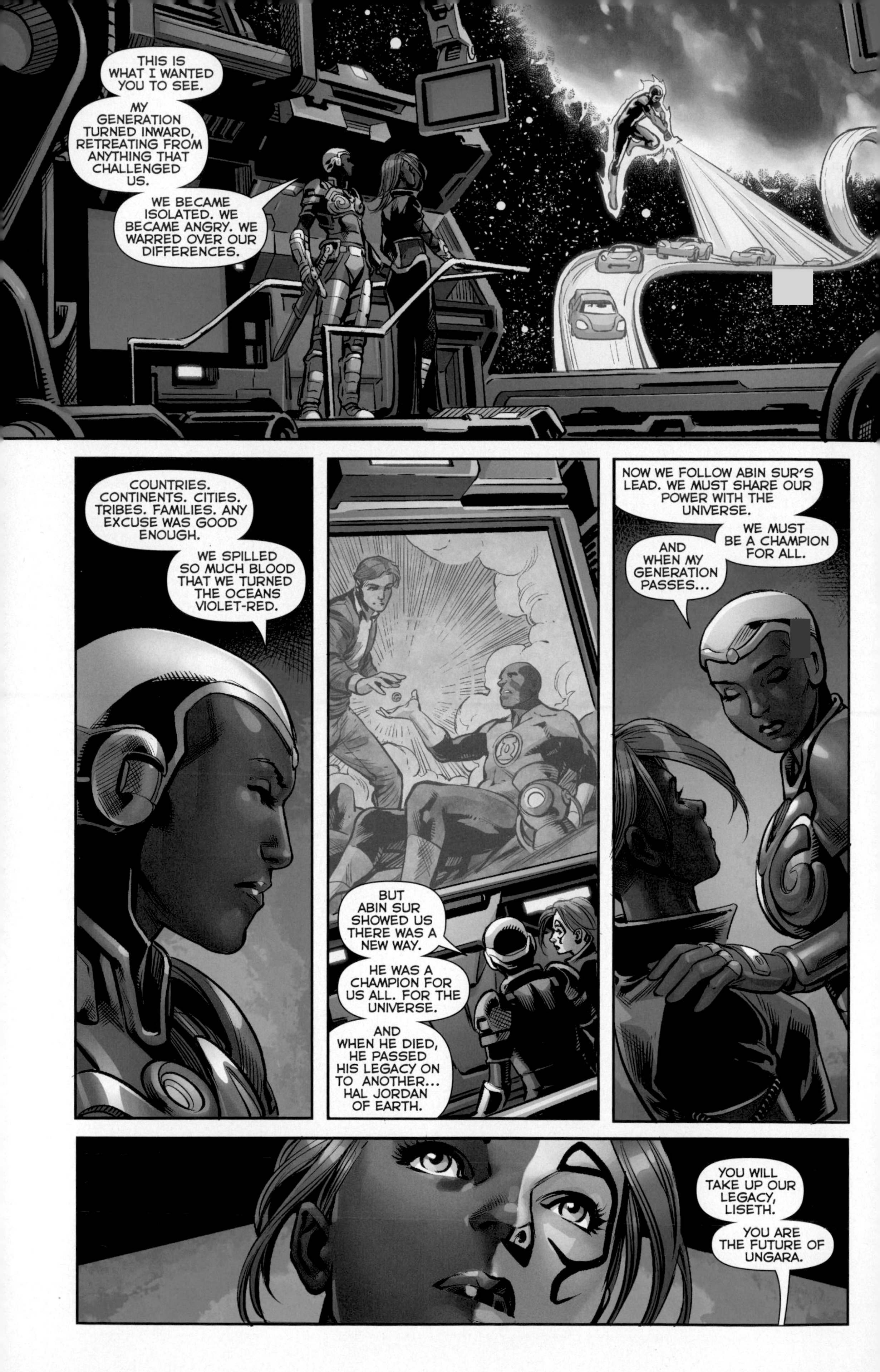
THIS IS WHAT I WANTED YOU TO SEE.
MY GENERATION TURNED INWARD, RETREATING FROM ANYTHING THAT CHALLENGED US.
WE BECAME ISOLATED. WE BECAME ANGRY. WE WARRED OVER OUR DIFFERENCES.
COUNTRIES. CONTINENTS. CITIES. TRIBES. FAMILIES. ANY EXCUSE WAS GOOD ENOUGH.
WE SPILLED SO MUCH BLOOD THAT WE TURNED THE OCEANS VIOLET-RED.
BUT ABIN SUR SHOWED US THERE WAS A NEW WAY.
HE WAS A CHAMPION FOR US ALL. FOR THE UNIVERSE.
AND WHEN HE DIED, HE PASSED HIS LEGACY ON TO ANOTHER... HAL JORDAN OF EARTH.
NOW WE FOLLOW ABIN SUR'S LEAD. WE MUST SHARE OUR POWER WITH THE UNIVERSE.
WE MUST BE A CHAMPION FOR ALL.
AND WHEN MY GENERATION PASSES...
YOU WILL TAKE UP OUR LEGACY, LISETH.
YOU ARE THE FUTURE OF UNGARA.

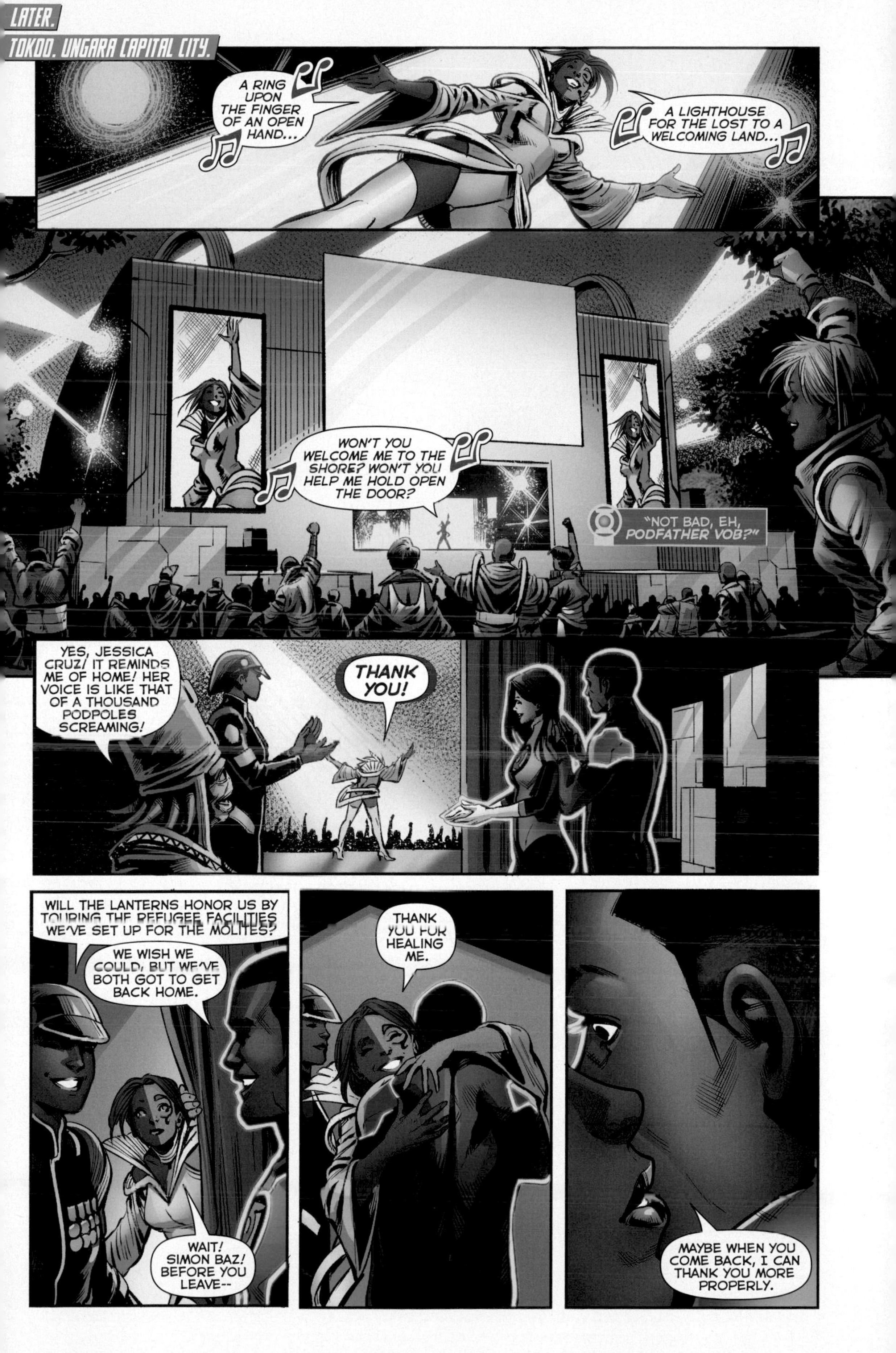
LATER.
TOKOO. UNGARA CAPITAL CITY.
A RING UPON THE FINGER OF AN OPEN HAND...
A LIGHTHOUSE FOR THE LOST TO A WELCOMING LAND...
WON'T YOU WELCOME ME TO THE SHORE? WON'T YOU HELP ME HOLD OPEN THE DOOR?
"NOT BAD, EH, PODFATHER VOB?"
YES, JESSICA CRUZ! IT REMINDS ME OF HOME! HER VOICE IS LIKE THAT OF A THOUSAND PODPOLES SCREAMING!
THANK YOU!
WILL THE LANTERNS HONOR US BY TOURING THE REFUGEE FACILITIES WE'VE SET UP FOR THE MOLITES?
WE WISH WE COULD, BUT WE'VE BOTH GOT TO GET BACK HOME.
WAIT! SIMON BAZ! BEFORE YOU LEAVE--
THANK YOU FOR HEALING ME.
MAYBE WHEN YOU COME BACK, I CAN THANK YOU MORE PROPERLY.

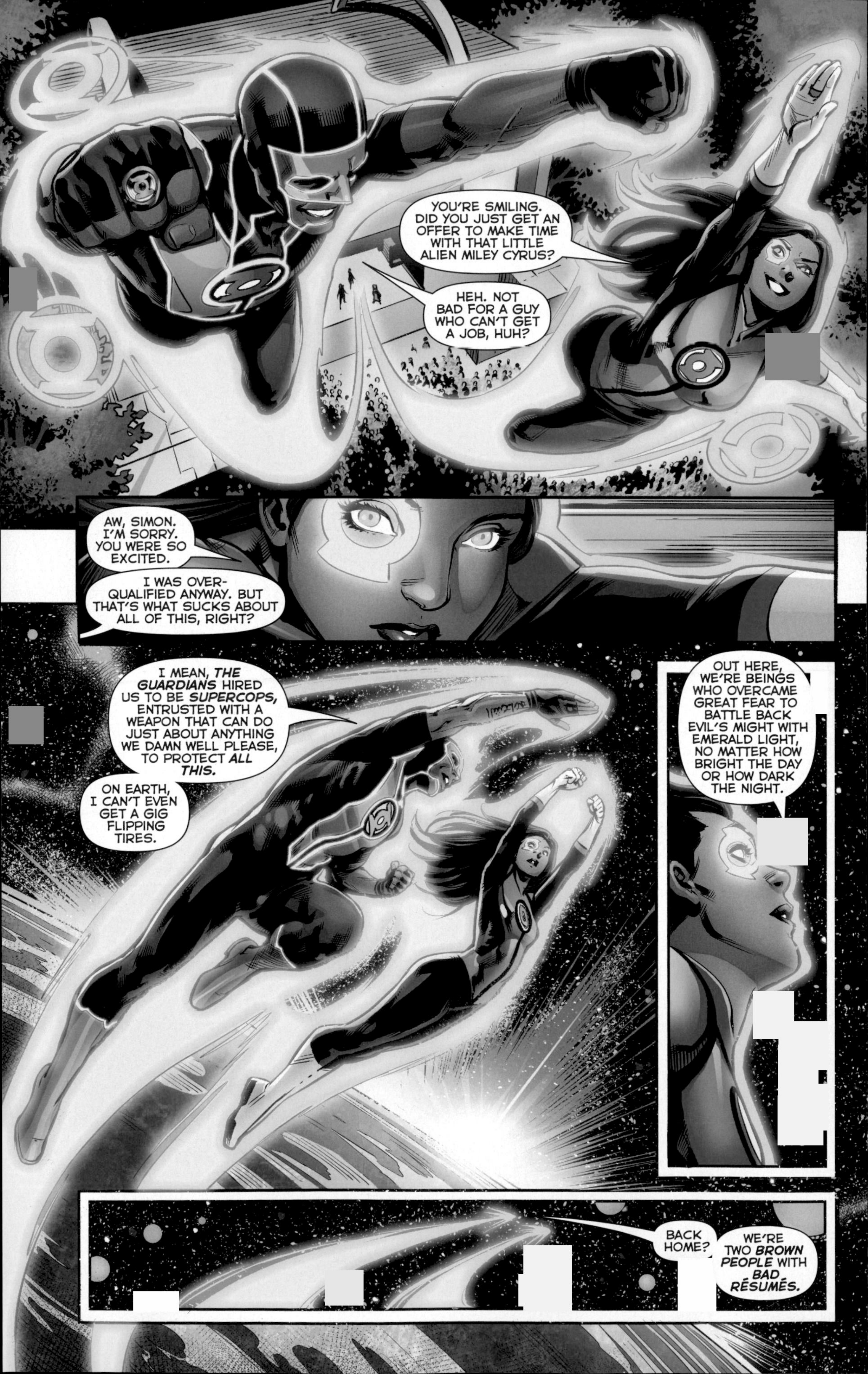

YOU'RE SMILING. DID YOU JUST GET AN OFFER TO MAKE TIME WITH THAT LITTLE ALIEN MILEY CYRUS?
HEH. NOT BAD FOR A GUY WHO CAN'T GET A JOB, HUH?
AW, SIMON. I'M SORRY. YOU WERE SO EXCITED.
I WAS OVER-QUALIFIED ANYWAY. BUT THAT'S WHAT SUCKS ABOUT ALL OF THIS, RIGHT?
I MEAN, THE GUARDIANS HIRED US TO BE SUPERCOPS, ENTRUSTED WITH A WEAPON THAT CAN DO JUST ABOUT ANYTHING WE DAMN WELL PLEASE, TO PROTECT ALL THIS.
ON EARTH, I CAN'T EVEN GET A GIG FLIPPING TIRES.
OUT HERE, WE'RE BEINGS WHO OVERCAME GREAT FEAR TO BATTLE BACK EVIL'S MIGHT WITH EMERALD LIGHT, NO MATTER HOW BRIGHT THE DAY OR HOW DARK THE NIGHT.
BACK HOME?
WE'RE TWO BROWN PEOPLE WITH BAD RÉSUMÉS.

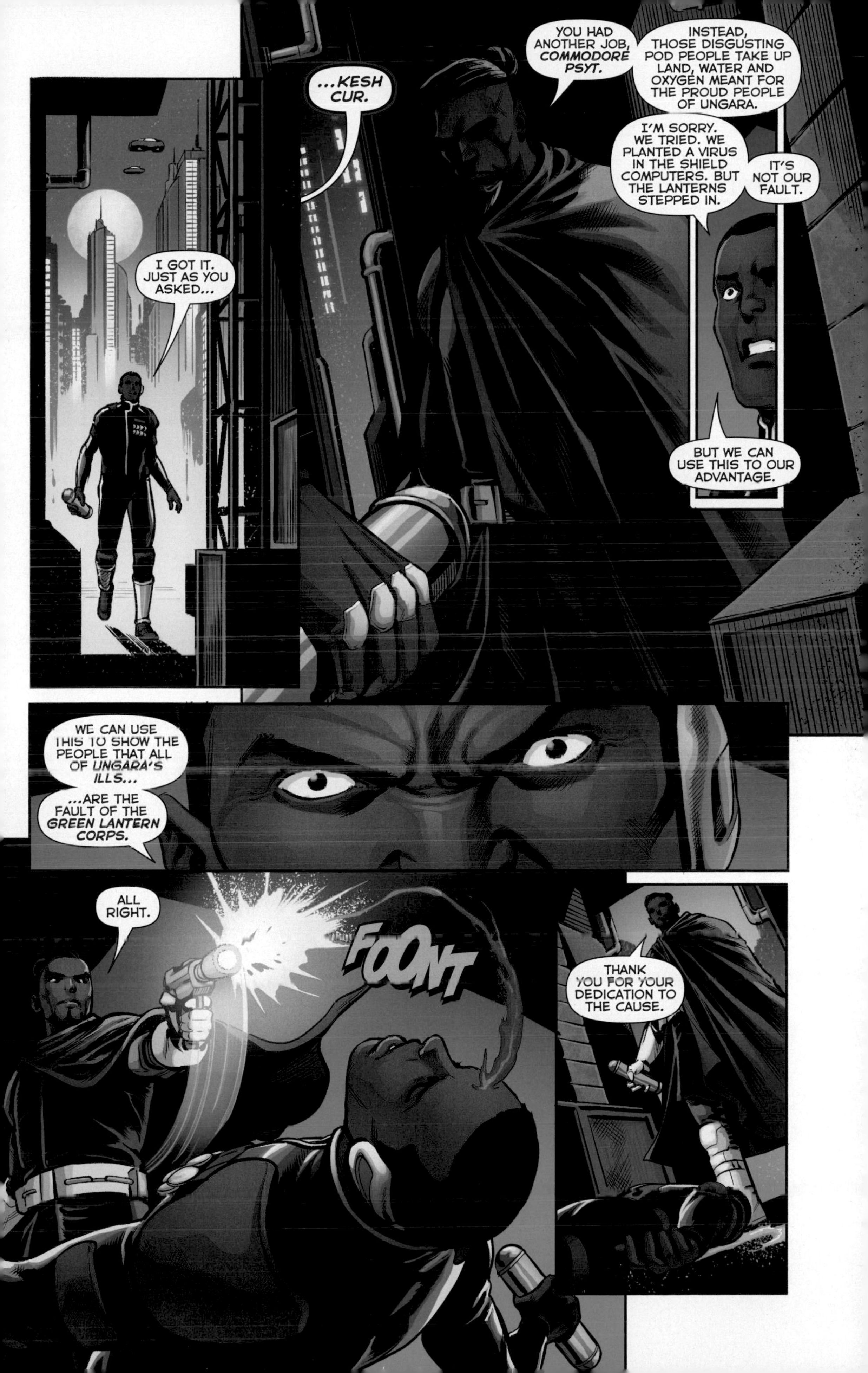
I GOT IT. JUST AS YOU ASKED...
...KESH CUR.
YOU HAD ANOTHER JOB, COMMODORE PSYT.
INSTEAD, THOSE DISGUSTING POD PEOPLE TAKE UP LAND, WATER AND OXYGEN MEANT FOR THE PROUD PEOPLE OF UNGARA.
I'M SORRY. WE TRIED. WE PLANTED A VIRUS IN THE SHIELD COMPUTERS. BUT THE LANTERNS STEPPED IN.
IT'S NOT OUR FAULT.
BUT WE CAN USE THIS TO OUR ADVANTAGE.
WE CAN USE THIS TO SHOW THE PEOPLE THAT ALL OF UNGARA'S ILLS...
...ARE THE FAULT OF THE GREEN LANTERN CORPS.
ALL RIGHT.
FOONT
THANK YOU FOR YOUR DEDICATION TO THE CAUSE.

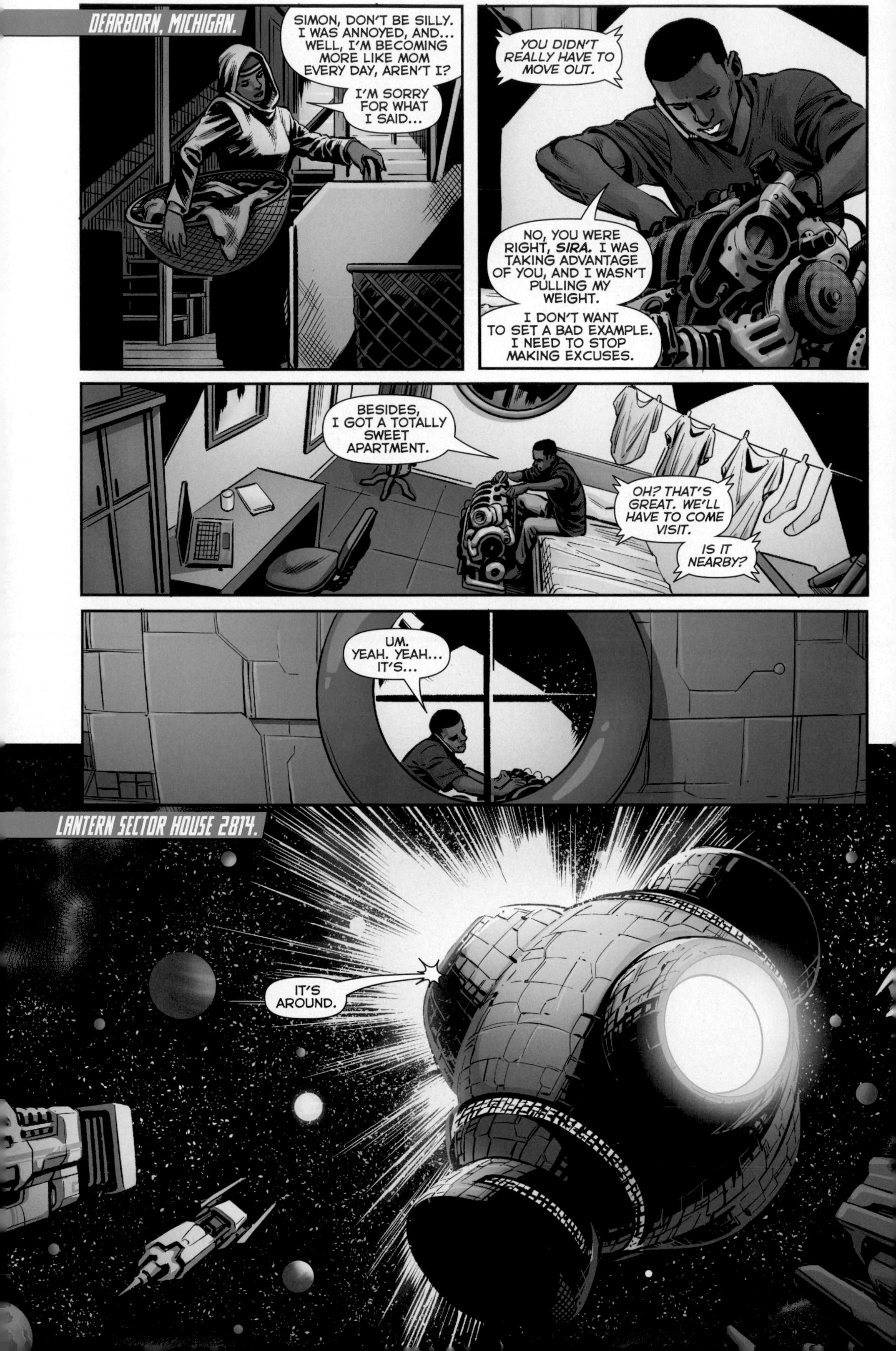
DEARBORN, MICHIGAN.
SIMON, DON'T BE SILLY. I WAS ANNOYED, AND... WELL, I'M BECOMING MORE LIKE MOM EVERY DAY, AREN'T I?
I'M SORRY FOR WHAT I SAID...
YOU DIDN'T REALLY HAVE TO MOVE OUT.
NO, YOU WERE RIGHT, SIRA. I WAS TAKING ADVANTAGE OF YOU, AND I WASN'T PULLING MY WEIGHT.
I DON'T WANT TO SET A BAD EXAMPLE. I NEED TO STOP MAKING EXCUSES.
BESIDES, I GOT A TOTALLY SWEET APARTMENT.
OH? THAT'S GREAT. WE'LL HAVE TO COME VISIT.
IS IT NEARBY?
UM. YEAH. YEAH... IT'S...
LANTERN SECTOR HOUSE 2814.
IT'S AROUND.

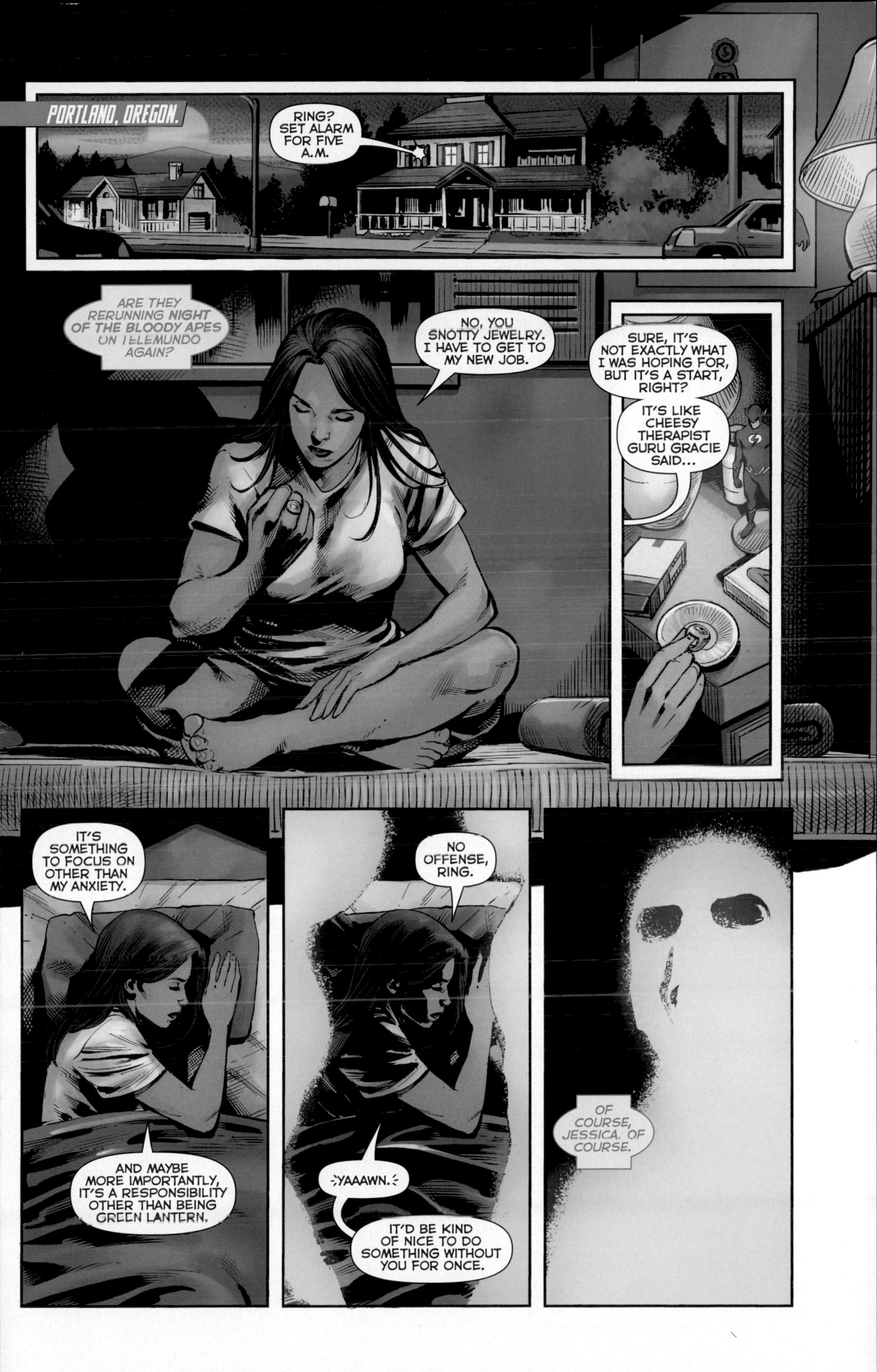
PORTLAND, OREGON.
RING? SET ALARM FOR FIVE A.M.
ARE THEY RERUNNING NIGHT OF THE BLOODY APES ON TELEMUNDO AGAIN?
NO, YOU SNOTTY JEWELRY. I HAVE TO GET TO MY NEW JOB.
SURE, IT'S NOT EXACTLY WHAT I WAS HOPING FOR, BUT IT'S A START, RIGHT?
IT'S LIKE CHEESY THERAPIST GURU GRACIE SAID...
IT'S SOMETHING TO FOCUS ON OTHER THAN MY ANXIETY.
AND MAYBE MORE IMPORTANTLY, IT'S A RESPONSIBILITY OTHER THAN BEING GREEN LANTERN.
NO OFFENSE, RING.
YAAAWN.
IT'D BE KIND OF NICE TO DO SOMETHING WITHOUT YOU FOR ONCE.
OF COURSE, JESSICA. OF COURSE.

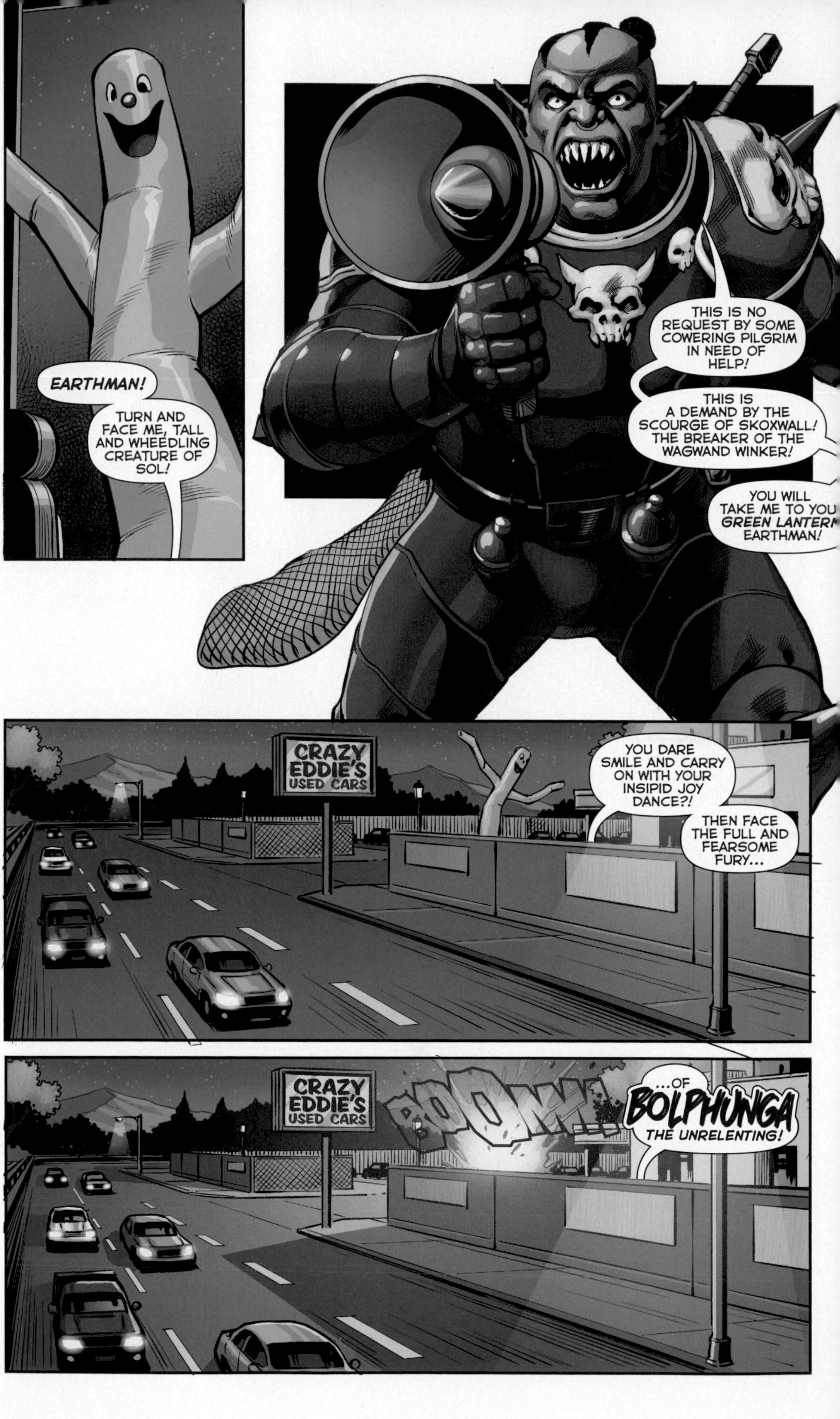
EARTHMAN!
TURN AND FACE ME, TALL AND WHEEDLING CREATURE OF SOL!
THIS IS NO REQUEST BY SOME COWERING PILGRIM IN NEED OF HELP!
THIS IS A DEMAND BY THE SCOURGE OF SKOXWALL! THE BREAKER OF THE WAGWAND WINKER!
YOU WILL TAKE ME TO YOU GREEN LANTER EARTHMAN!
CRAZY EDDIE'S USED CARS
YOU DARE SMILE AND CARRY ON WITH YOUR INSIPID JOY DANCE?!
THEN FACE THE FULL AND FEARSOME FURY...
CRAZY EDDIE'S USED CARS
BOOOM!
...OF BOLPHUNGA THE UNRELENTING!

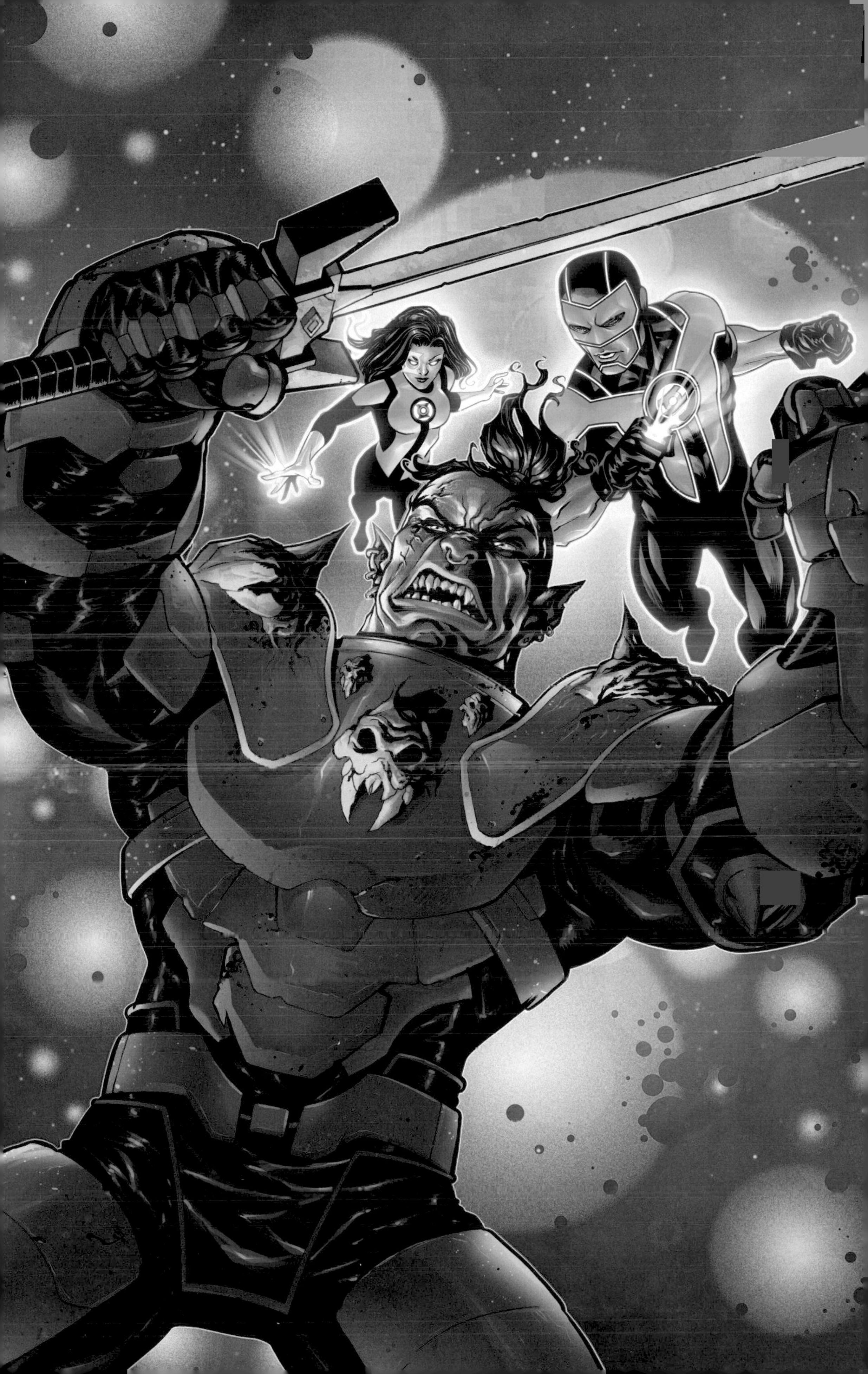

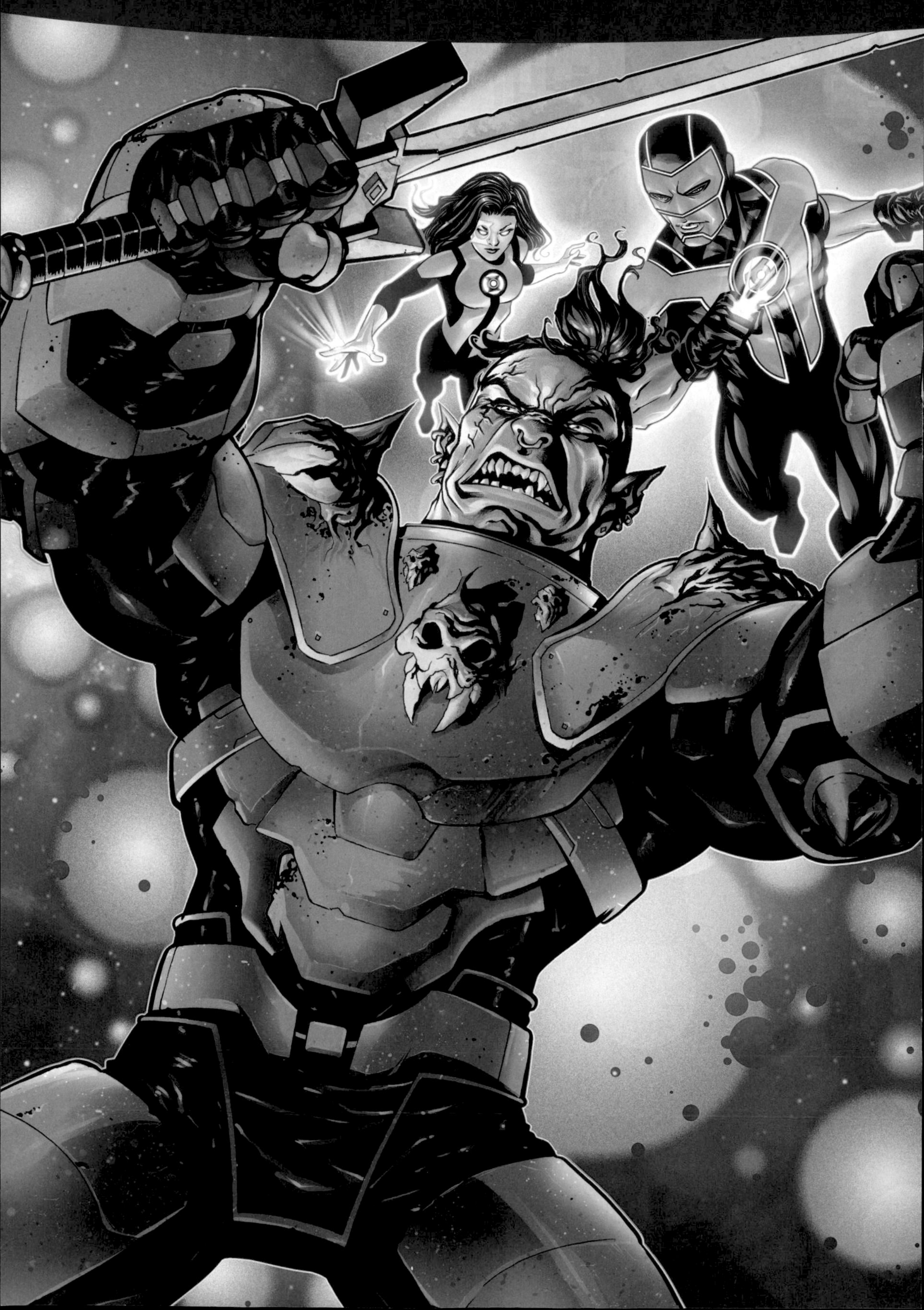

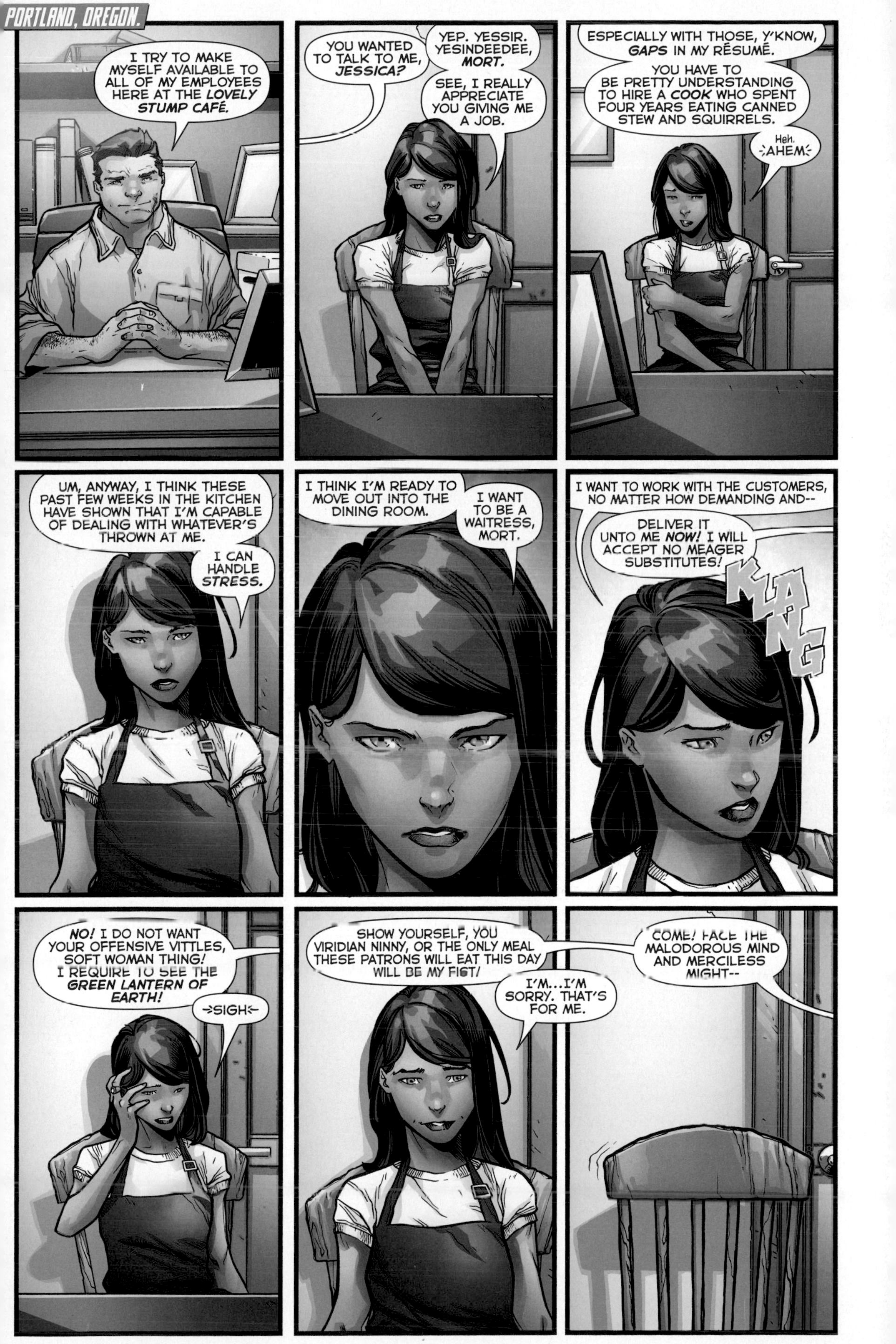
PORTLAND, OREGON.
I TRY TO MAKE MYSELF AVAILABLE TO ALL OF MY EMPLOYEES HERE AT THE LOVELY STUMP CAFÉ.
YOU WANTED TO TALK TO ME, JESSICA?
YEP. YESSIR. YESINDEEDEE, MORT.
SEE, I REALLY APPRECIATE YOU GIVING ME A JOB.
ESPECIALLY WITH THOSE, Y'KNOW, GAPS IN MY RÉSUMÉ.
YOU HAVE TO BE PRETTY UNDERSTANDING TO HIRE A COOK WHO SPENT FOUR YEARS EATING CANNED STEW AND SQUIRRELS.
Heh. AHEM
UM, ANYWAY, I THINK THESE PAST FEW WEEKS IN THE KITCHEN HAVE SHOWN THAT I'M CAPABLE OF DEALING WITH WHATEVER'S THROWN AT ME.
I CAN HANDLE STRESS.
I THINK I'M READY TO MOVE OUT INTO THE DINING ROOM.
I WANT TO BE A WAITRESS, MORT.
I WANT TO WORK WITH THE CUSTOMERS, NO MATTER HOW DEMANDING AND--
DELIVER IT UNTO ME NOW! I WILL ACCEPT NO MEAGER SUBSTITUTES!
KLANG
NO! I DO NOT WANT YOUR OFFENSIVE VITTLES, SOFT WOMAN THING! I REQUIRE TO SEE THE GREEN LANTERN OF EARTH!
SIGH
SHOW YOURSELF, YOU VIRIDIAN NINNY, OR THE ONLY MEAL THESE PATRONS WILL EAT THIS DAY WILL BE MY FIST!
I'M...I'M SORRY. THAT'S FOR ME.
COME! FACE THE MALODOROUS MIND AND MERCILESS MIGHT--

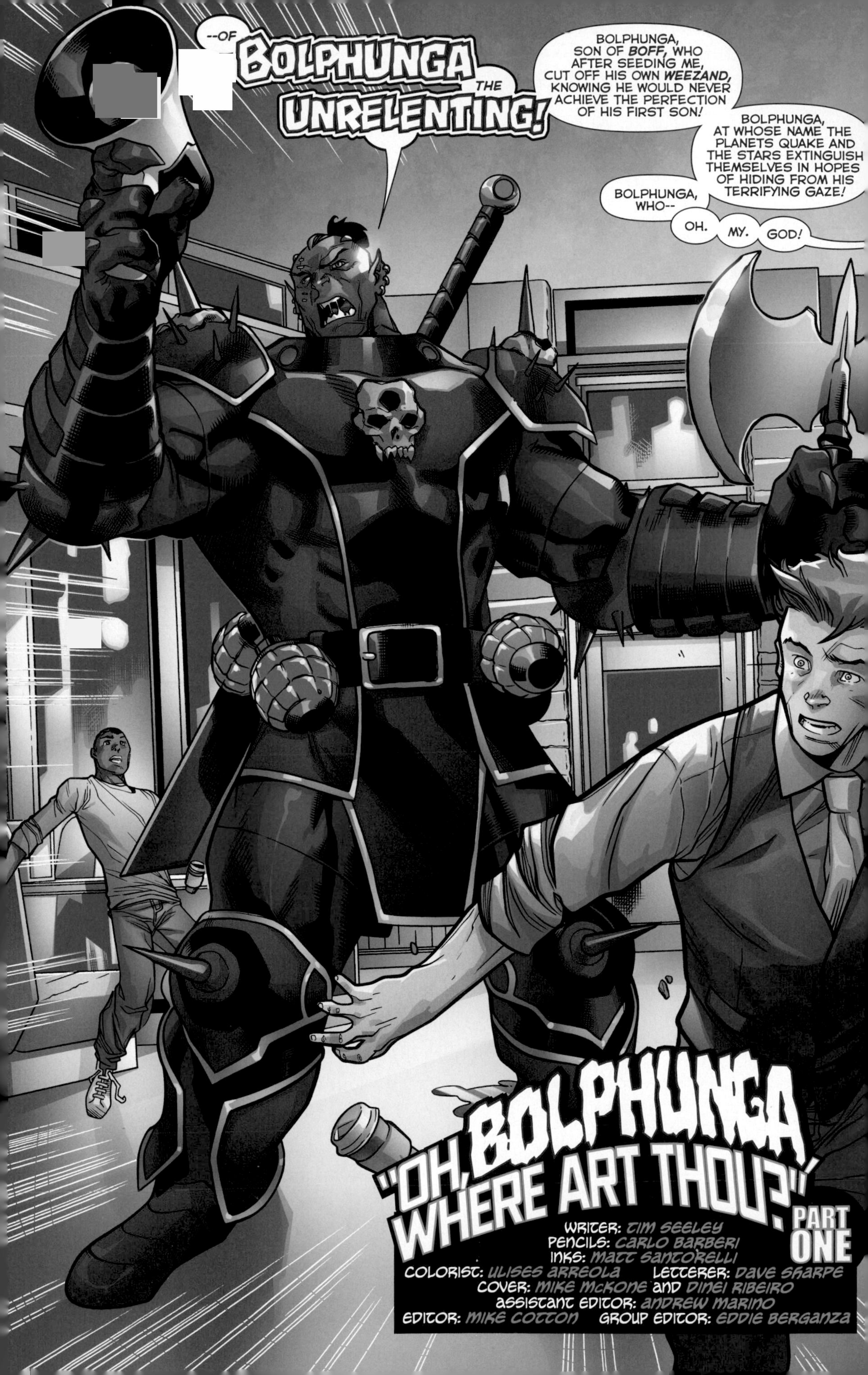
--OF BOLPHUNGA THE UNRELENTING!
BOLPHUNGA, SON OF BOFF, WHO AFTER SEEDING ME, CUT OFF HIS OWN WEEZAND, KNOWING HE WOULD NEVER ACHIEVE THE PERFECTION OF HIS FIRST SON!
BOLPHUNGA, AT WHOSE NAME THE PLANETS QUAKE AND THE STARS EXTINGUISH THEMSELVES IN HOPES OF HIDING FROM HIS TERRIFYING GAZE!
BOLPHUNGA, WHO--
OH.
MY.
GOD!
"OH, BOLPHUNGA WHERE ART THOU?"
PART ONE
WRITER: TIM SEELEY
PENCILS: CARLO BARBERI
INKS: MATT SANTORELLI
COLORIST: ULISES ARREOLA
LETTERER: DAVE SHARPE
COVER: MIKE McKONE and DINEI RIBEIRO
ASSISTANT EDITOR: ANDREW MARINO
EDITOR: MIKE COTTON
GROUP EDITOR: EDDIE BERGANZA

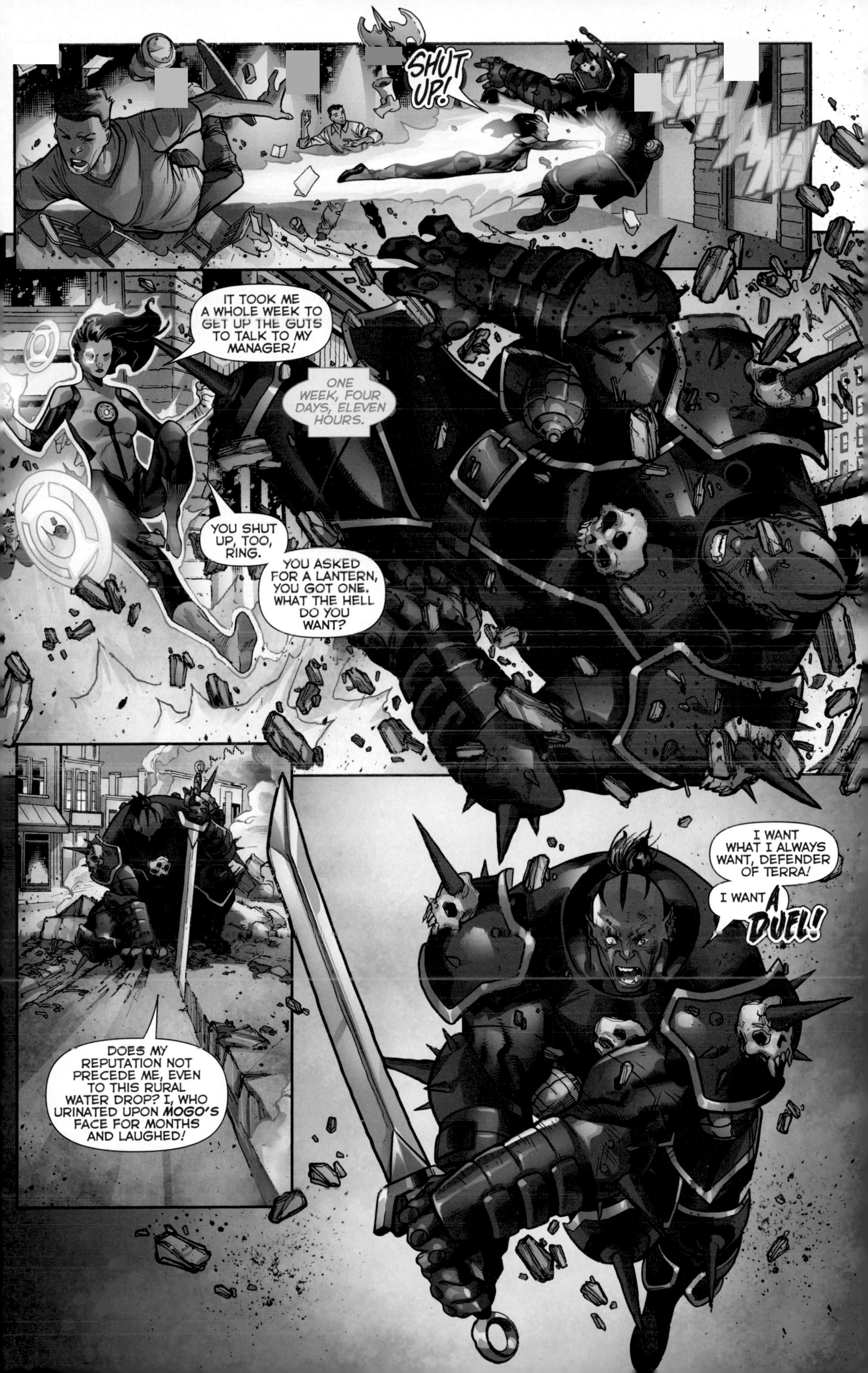
SHUT UP!
IT TOOK ME A WHOLE WEEK TO GET UP THE GUTS TO TALK TO MY MANAGER!
ONE WEEK, FOUR DAYS, ELEVEN HOURS.
YOU SHUT UP, TOO, RING.
YOU ASKED FOR A LANTERN, YOU GOT ONE. WHAT THE HELL DO YOU WANT?
DOES MY REPUTATION NOT PRECEDE ME, EVEN TO THIS RURAL WATER DROP? I, WHO URINATED UPON MOGO'S FACE FOR MONTHS AND LAUGHED!
I WANT WHAT I ALWAYS WANT, DEFENDER OF TERRA!
I WANT A DUEL!

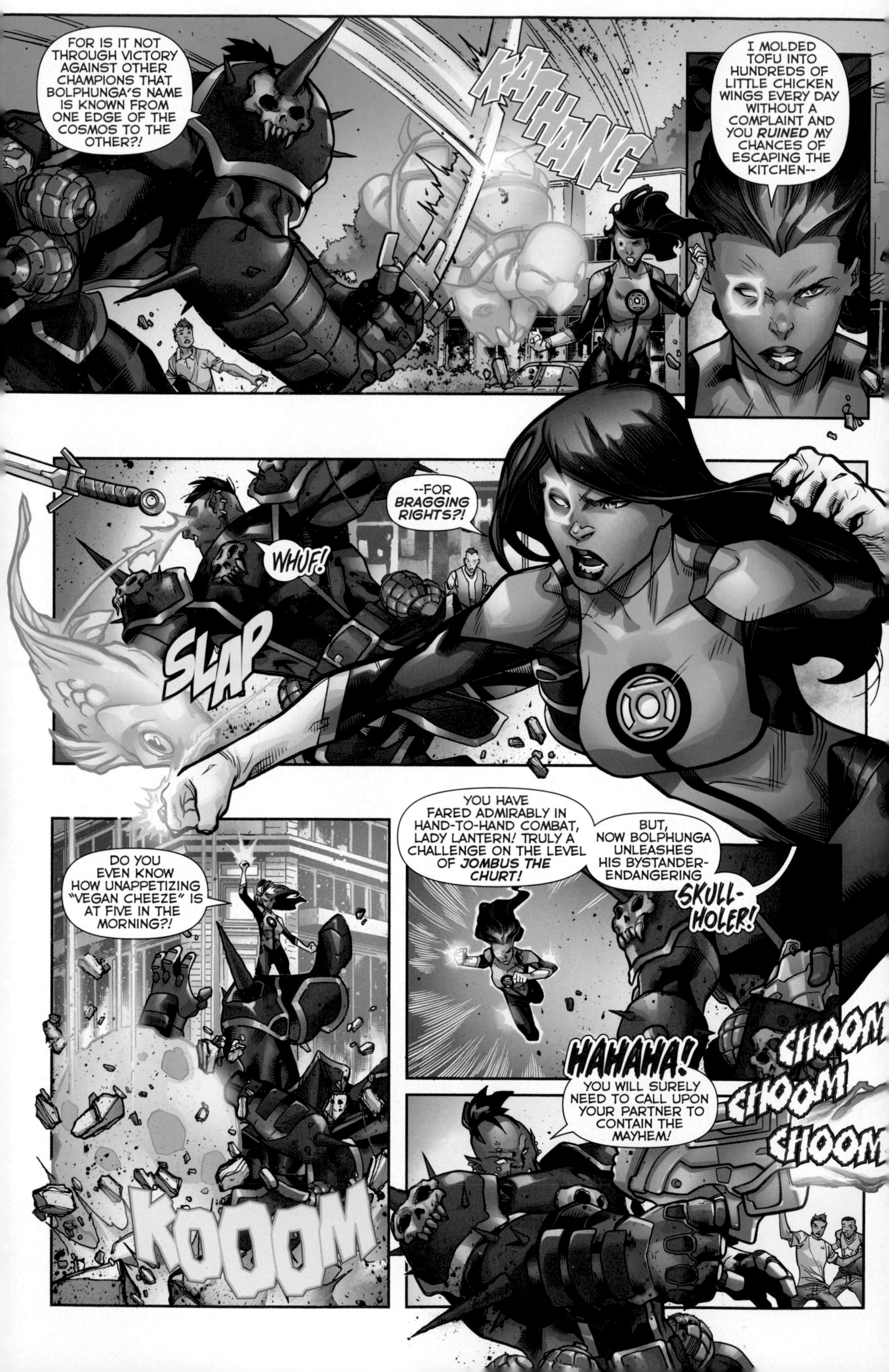
FOR IS IT NOT THROUGH VICTORY AGAINST OTHER CHAMPIONS THAT BOLPHUNGA'S NAME IS KNOWN FROM ONE EDGE OF THE COSMOS TO THE OTHER?!
KATHANG
I MOLDED TOFU INTO HUNDREDS OF LITTLE CHICKEN WINGS EVERY DAY WITHOUT A COMPLAINT AND YOU RUINED MY CHANCES OF ESCAPING THE KITCHEN--
--FOR BRAGGING RIGHTS?!
WHUF!
SLAP
DO YOU EVEN KNOW HOW UNAPPETIZING "VEGAN CHEEZE" IS AT FIVE IN THE MORNING?!
KOOOM
YOU HAVE FARED ADMIRABLY IN HAND-TO-HAND COMBAT, LADY LANTERN! TRULY A CHALLENGE ON THE LEVEL OF JOMBUS THE CHURT!
BUT, NOW BOLPHUNGA UNLEASHES HIS BYSTANDER-ENDANGERING SKULL-HOLER!
HAHAHA!
YOU WILL SURELY NEED TO CALL UPON YOUR PARTNER TO CONTAIN THE MAYHEM!
CHOOM
CHOOM
CHOOM

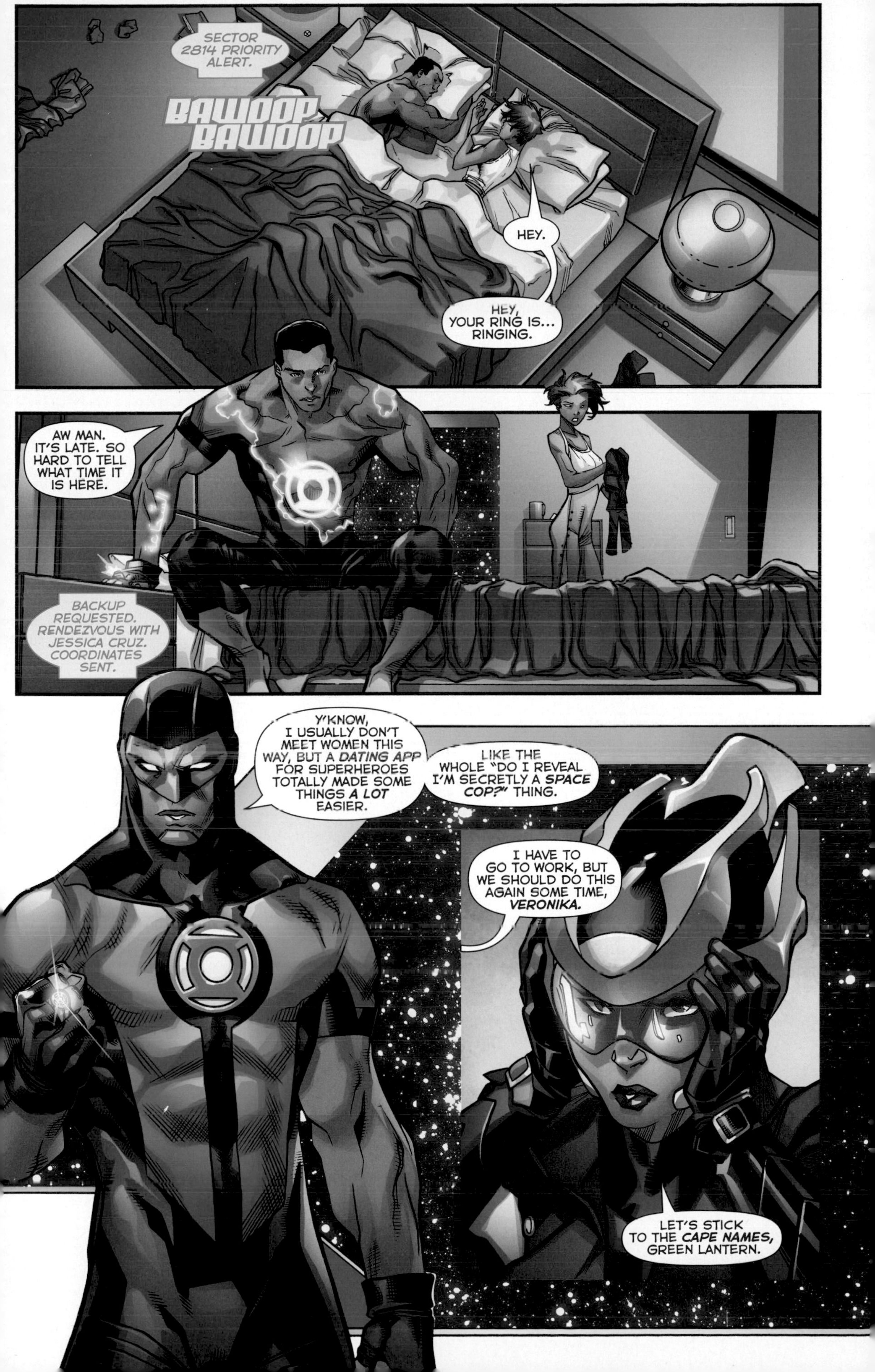
SECTOR 2814 PRIORITY ALERT.
BAWOOP BAWOOP
HEY.
HEY, YOUR RING IS... RINGING.
AW MAN. IT'S LATE. SO HARD TO TELL WHAT TIME IT IS HERE.
BACKUP REQUESTED. RENDEZVOUS WITH JESSICA CRUZ. COORDINATES SENT.
Y'KNOW, I USUALLY DON'T MEET WOMEN THIS WAY, BUT A DATING APP FOR SUPERHEROES TOTALLY MADE SOME THINGS A LOT EASIER.
LIKE THE WHOLE "DO I REVEAL I'M SECRETLY A SPACE COP?" THING.
I HAVE TO GO TO WORK, BUT WE SHOULD DO THIS AGAIN SOME TIME, VERONIKA.
LET'S STICK TO THE CAPE NAMES, GREEN LANTERN.

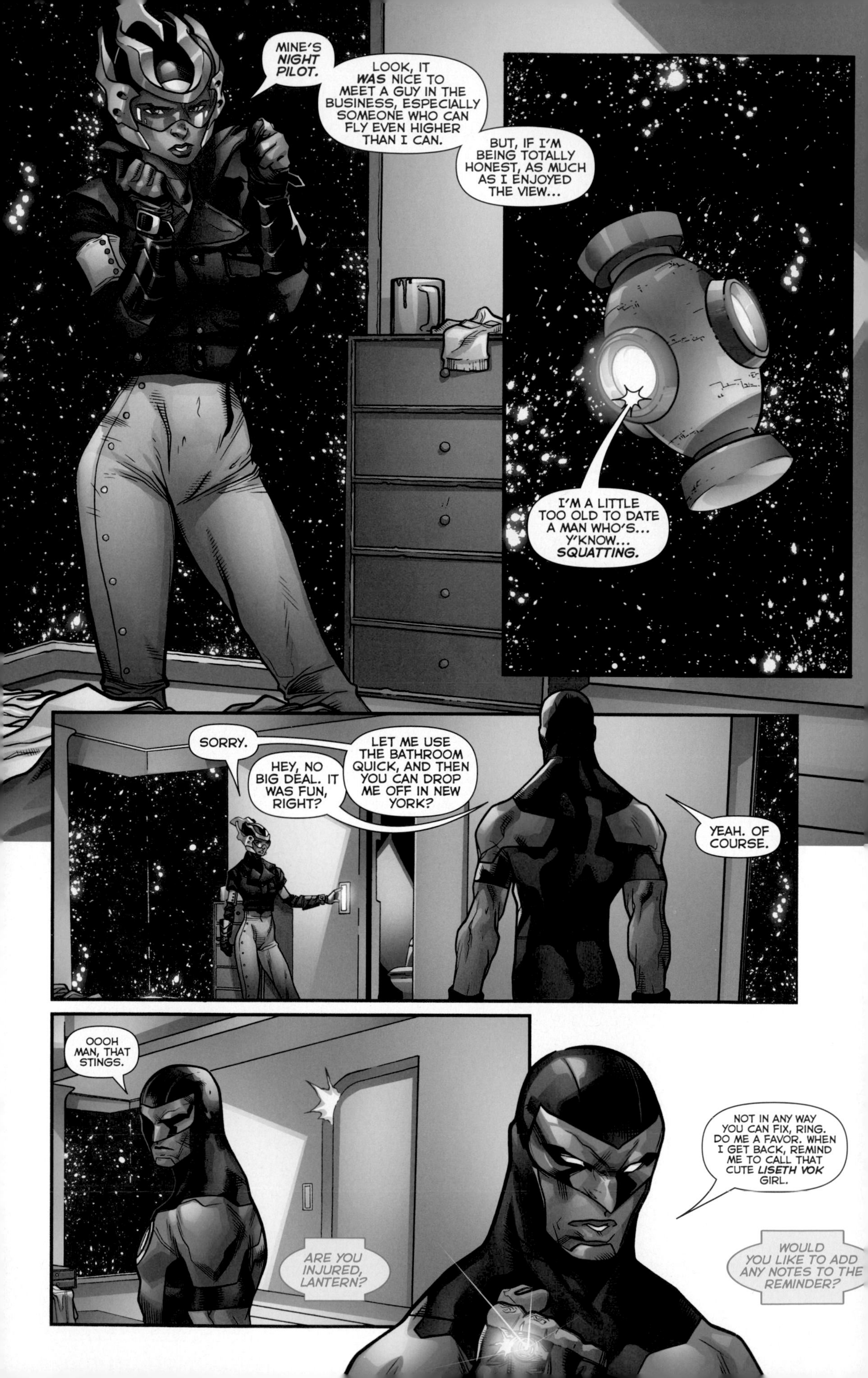
MINE'S NIGHT PILOT.
LOOK, IT WAS NICE TO MEET A GUY IN THE BUSINESS, ESPECIALLY SOMEONE WHO CAN FLY EVEN HIGHER THAN I CAN.
BUT, IF I'M BEING TOTALLY HONEST, AS MUCH AS I ENJOYED THE VIEW...
I'M A LITTLE TOO OLD TO DATE A MAN WHO'S... Y'KNOW... SQUATTING.
SORRY.
HEY, NO BIG DEAL. IT WAS FUN, RIGHT?
LET ME USE THE BATHROOM QUICK, AND THEN YOU CAN DROP ME OFF IN NEW YORK?
YEAH. OF COURSE.
OOOH MAN, THAT STINGS.
ARE YOU INJURED, LANTERN?
NOT IN ANY WAY YOU CAN FIX, RING. DO ME A FAVOR. WHEN I GET BACK, REMIND ME TO CALL THAT CUTE LISETH VOK GIRL.
WOULD YOU LIKE TO ADD ANY NOTES TO THE REMINDER?

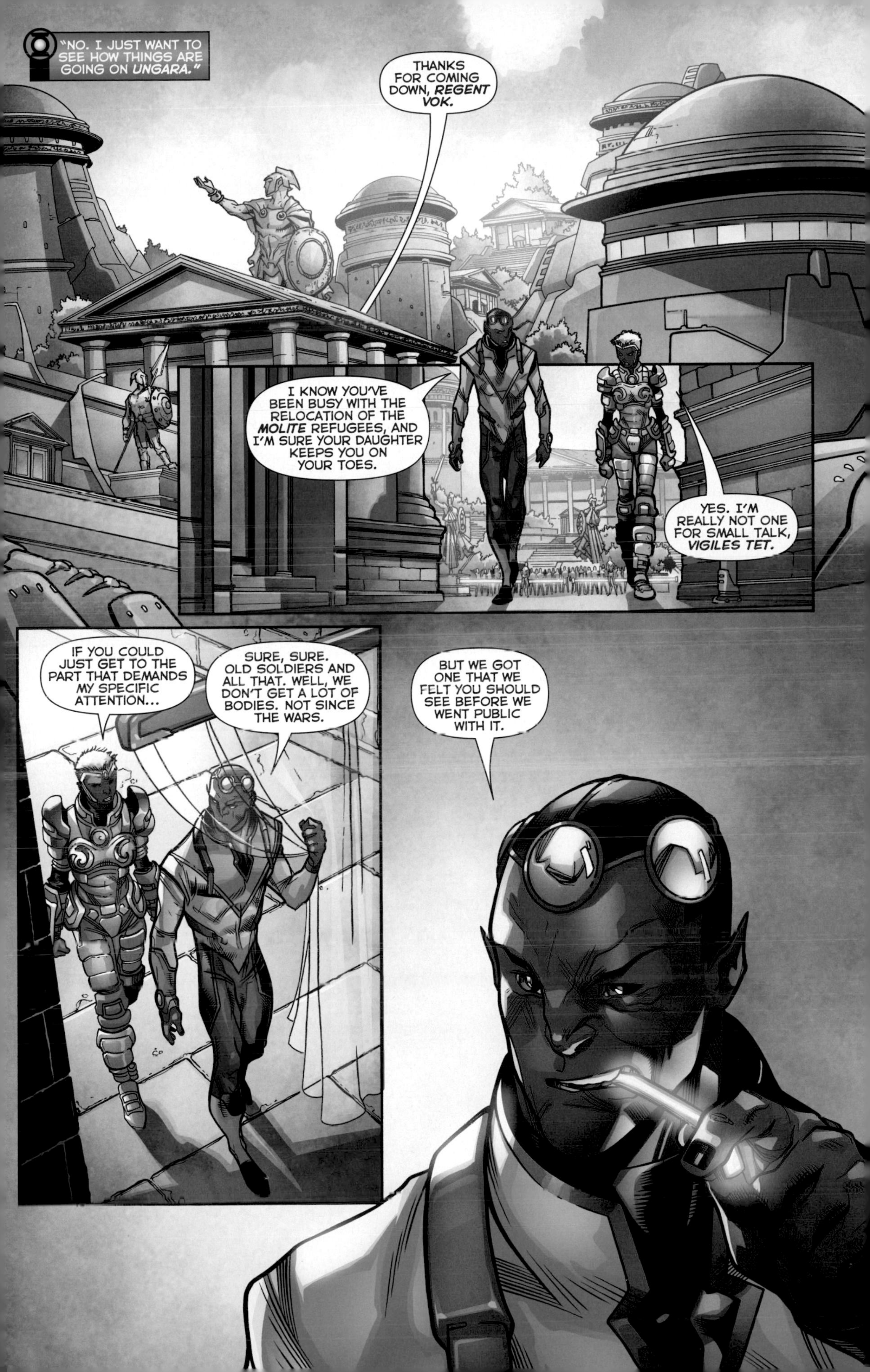
"NO. I JUST WANT TO SEE HOW THINGS ARE GOING ON *UNGARA*."
THANKS FOR COMING DOWN, ***REGENT VOK.***
I KNOW YOU'VE BEEN BUSY WITH THE RELOCATION OF THE ***MOLITE*** REFUGEES, AND I'M SURE YOUR DAUGHTER KEEPS YOU ON YOUR TOES.
YES. I'M REALLY NOT ONE FOR SMALL TALK, ***VIGILES TET.***
IF YOU COULD JUST GET TO THE PART THAT DEMANDS MY SPECIFIC ATTENTION...
SURE, SURE. OLD SOLDIERS AND ALL THAT. WELL, WE DON'T GET A LOT OF BODIES. NOT SINCE THE WARS.
BUT WE GOT ONE THAT WE FELT YOU SHOULD SEE BEFORE WE WENT PUBLIC WITH IT.

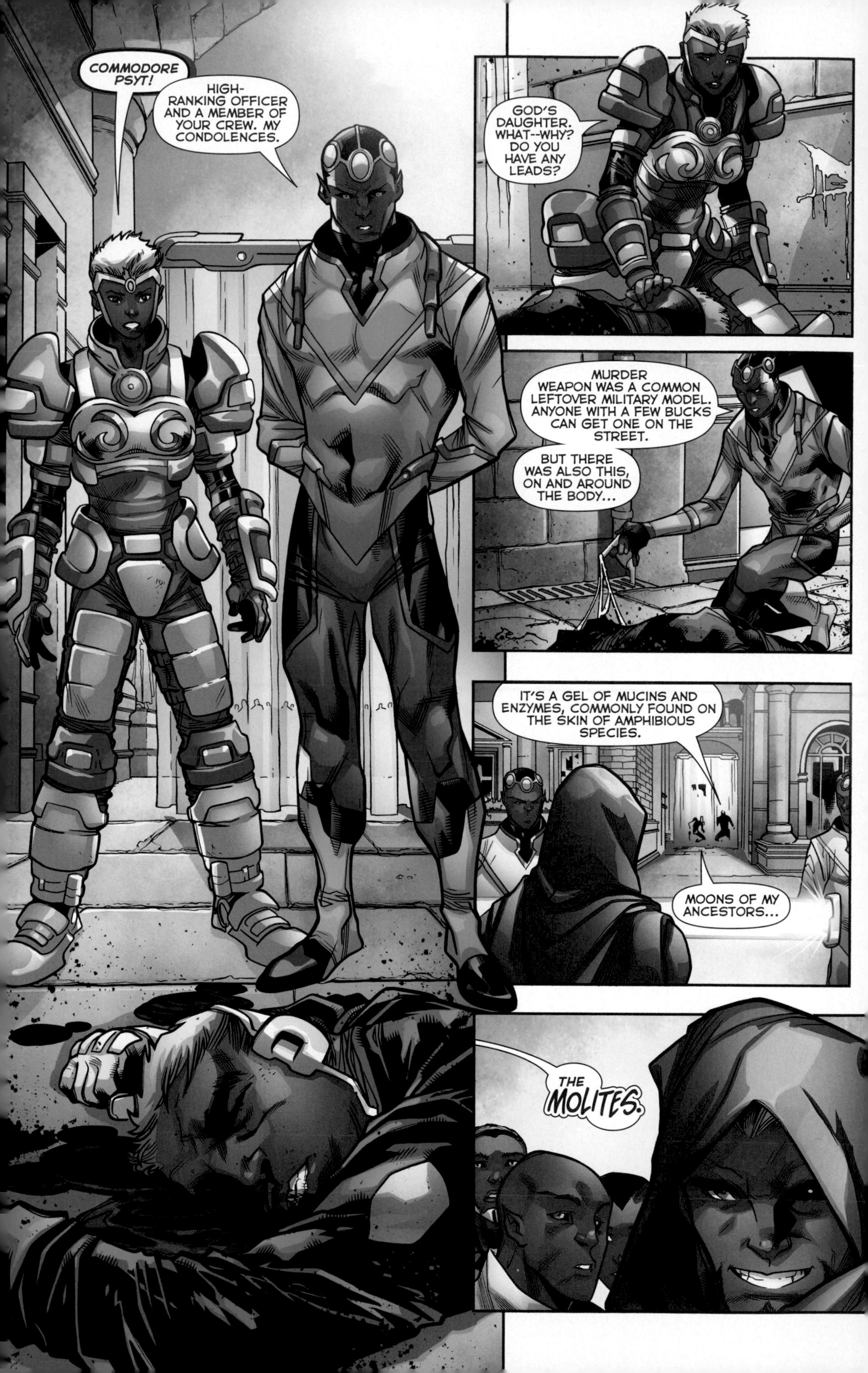
COMMODORE PSYT!
HIGH-RANKING OFFICER AND A MEMBER OF YOUR CREW. MY CONDOLENCES.
GOD'S DAUGHTER. WHAT--WHY? DO YOU HAVE ANY LEADS?
MURDER WEAPON WAS A COMMON LEFTOVER MILITARY MODEL. ANYONE WITH A FEW BUCKS CAN GET ONE ON THE STREET.
BUT THERE WAS ALSO THIS, ON AND AROUND THE BODY...
IT'S A GEL OF MUCINS AND ENZYMES, COMMONLY FOUND ON THE SKIN OF AMPHIBIOUS SPECIES.
MOONS OF MY ANCESTORS...
THE MOLITES.

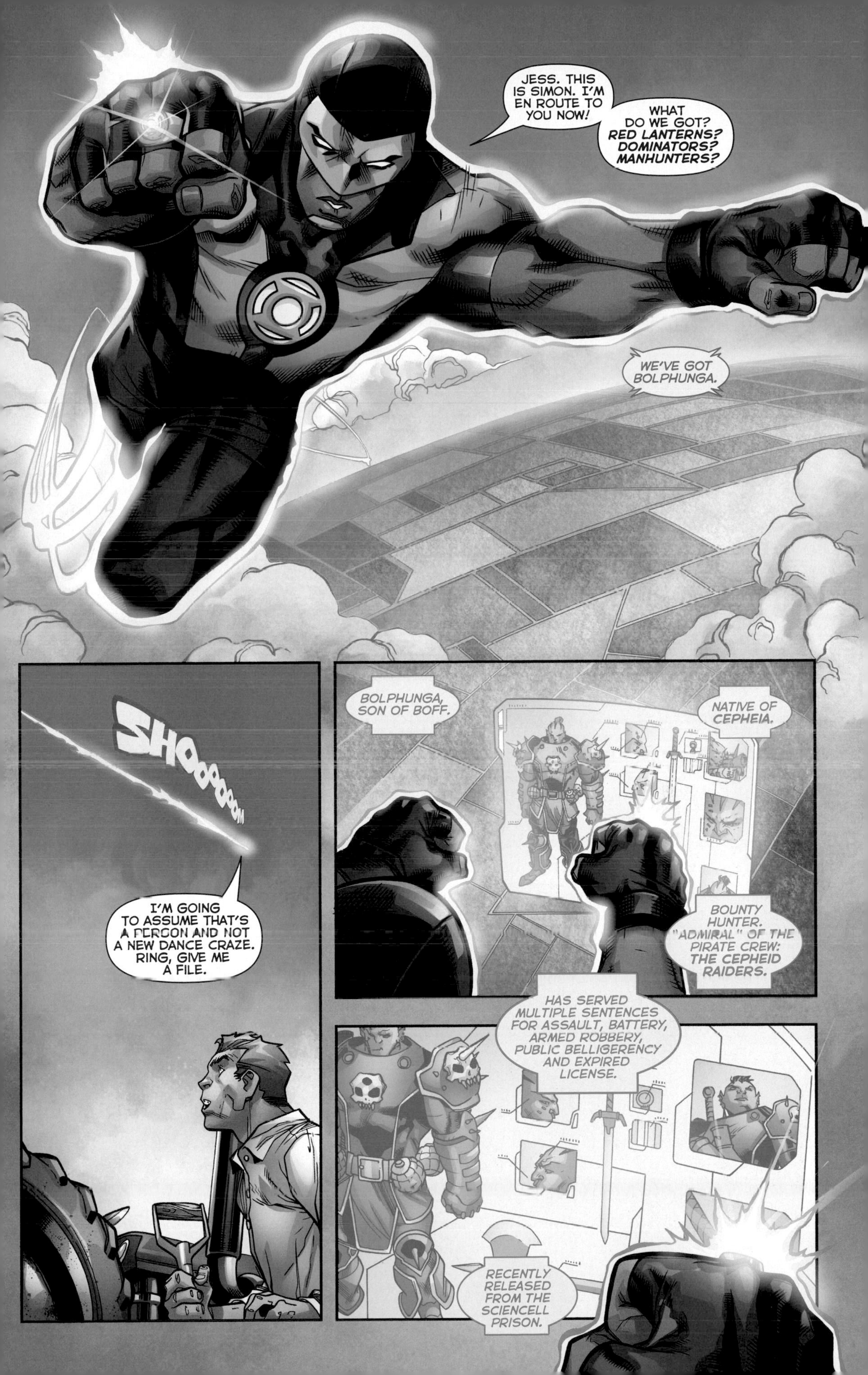
JESS. THIS IS SIMON. I'M EN ROUTE TO YOU NOW!
WHAT DO WE GOT? *RED LANTERNS? DOMINATORS? MANHUNTERS?*
WE'VE GOT BOLPHUNGA.
SHOOOOOOM
I'M GOING TO ASSUME THAT'S A PERSON AND NOT A NEW DANCE CRAZE. RING, GIVE ME A FILE.
BOLPHUNGA, SON OF BOFF.
NATIVE OF CEPHEIA.
BOUNTY HUNTER. "ADMIRAL" OF THE PIRATE CREW: THE CEPHEID RAIDERS.
HAS SERVED MULTIPLE SENTENCES FOR ASSAULT, BATTERY, ARMED ROBBERY, PUBLIC BELLIGERENCY AND EXPIRED LICENSE.
RECENTLY RELEASED FROM THE SCIENCELL PRISON.

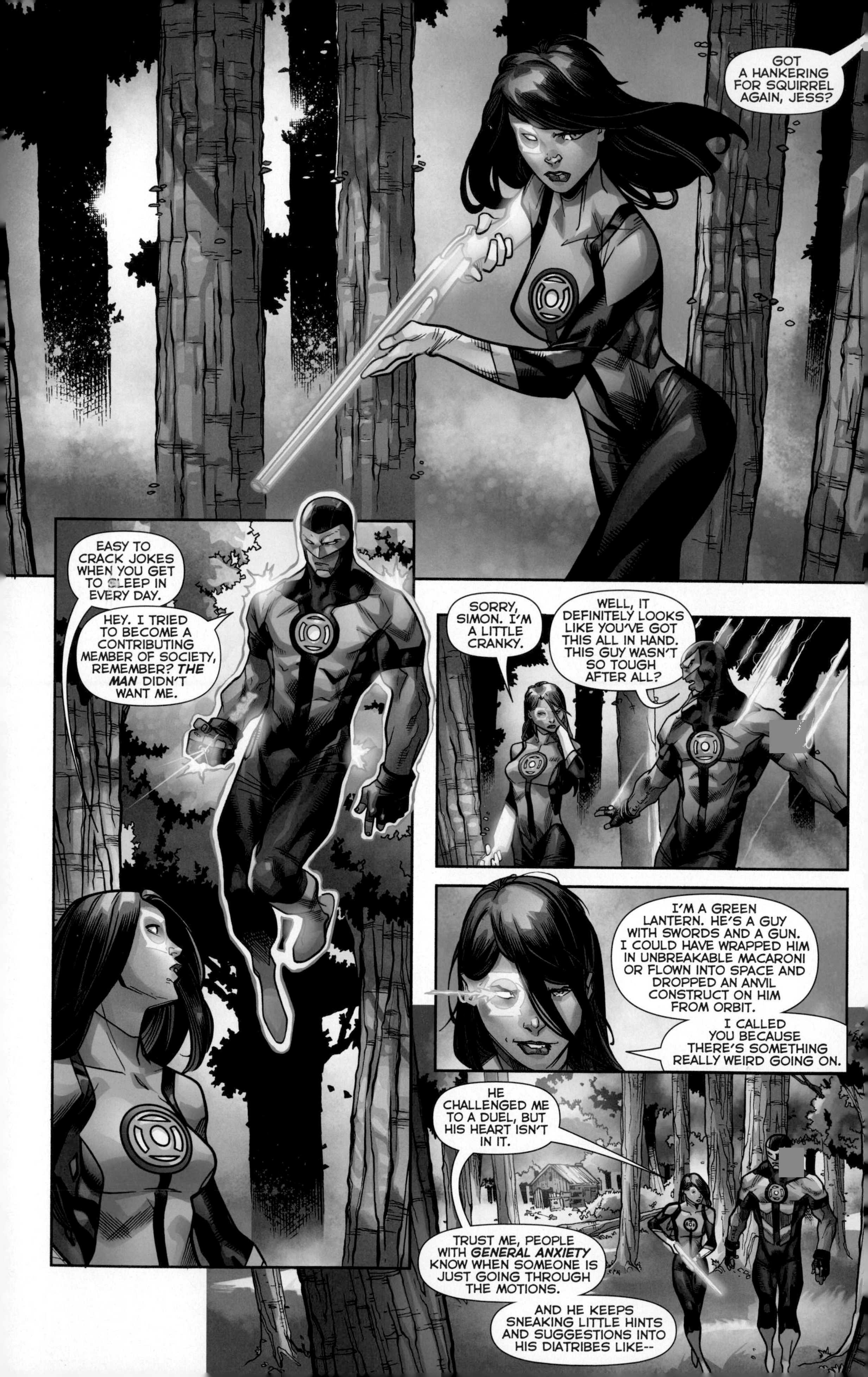
GOT A HANKERING FOR SQUIRREL AGAIN, JESS?
EASY TO CRACK JOKES WHEN YOU GET TO SLEEP IN EVERY DAY.
HEY. I TRIED TO BECOME A CONTRIBUTING MEMBER OF SOCIETY, REMEMBER? THE MAN DIDN'T WANT ME.
SORRY, SIMON. I'M A LITTLE CRANKY.
WELL, IT DEFINITELY LOOKS LIKE YOU'VE GOT THIS ALL IN HAND. THIS GUY WASN'T SO TOUGH AFTER ALL?
I'M A GREEN LANTERN. HE'S A GUY WITH SWORDS AND A GUN. I COULD HAVE WRAPPED HIM IN UNBREAKABLE MACARONI OR FLOWN INTO SPACE AND DROPPED AN ANVIL CONSTRUCT ON HIM FROM ORBIT.
I CALLED YOU BECAUSE THERE'S SOMETHING REALLY WEIRD GOING ON.
HE CHALLENGED ME TO A DUEL, BUT HIS HEART ISN'T IN IT.
TRUST ME, PEOPLE WITH GENERAL ANXIETY KNOW WHEN SOMEONE IS JUST GOING THROUGH THE MOTIONS.
AND HE KEEPS SNEAKING LITTLE HINTS AND SUGGESTIONS INTO HIS DIATRIBES LIKE--

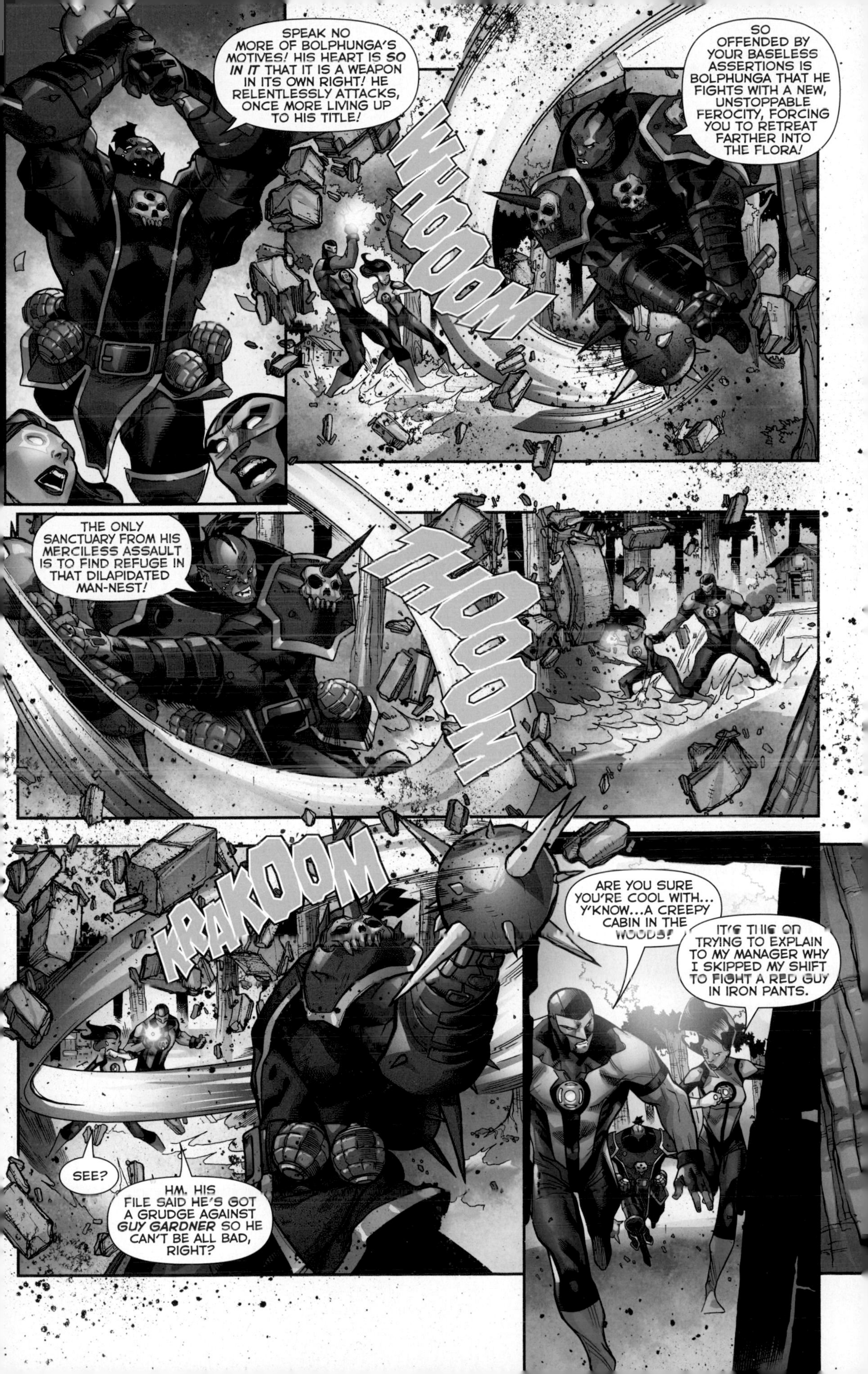
SPEAK NO MORE OF BOLPHUNGA'S MOTIVES! HIS HEART IS *SO IN IT* THAT IT IS A WEAPON IN ITS OWN RIGHT! HE RELENTLESSLY ATTACKS, ONCE MORE LIVING UP TO HIS TITLE!
WHOOOOM
SO OFFENDED BY YOUR BASELESS ASSERTIONS IS BOLPHUNGA THAT HE FIGHTS WITH A NEW, UNSTOPPABLE FEROCITY, FORCING YOU TO RETREAT FARTHER INTO THE FLORA!
THE ONLY SANCTUARY FROM HIS MERCILESS ASSAULT IS TO FIND REFUGE IN THAT DILAPIDATED MAN-NEST!
THOOOOM
KRAKOOM
SEE?
HM. HIS FILE SAID HE'S GOT A GRUDGE AGAINST *GUY GARDNER* SO HE CAN'T BE ALL BAD, RIGHT?
ARE YOU SURE YOU'RE COOL WITH... Y'KNOW...A CREEPY CABIN IN THE WOODS?
IT'S THIS OR TRYING TO EXPLAIN TO MY MANAGER WHY I SKIPPED MY SHIFT TO FIGHT A RED GUY IN IRON PANTS.

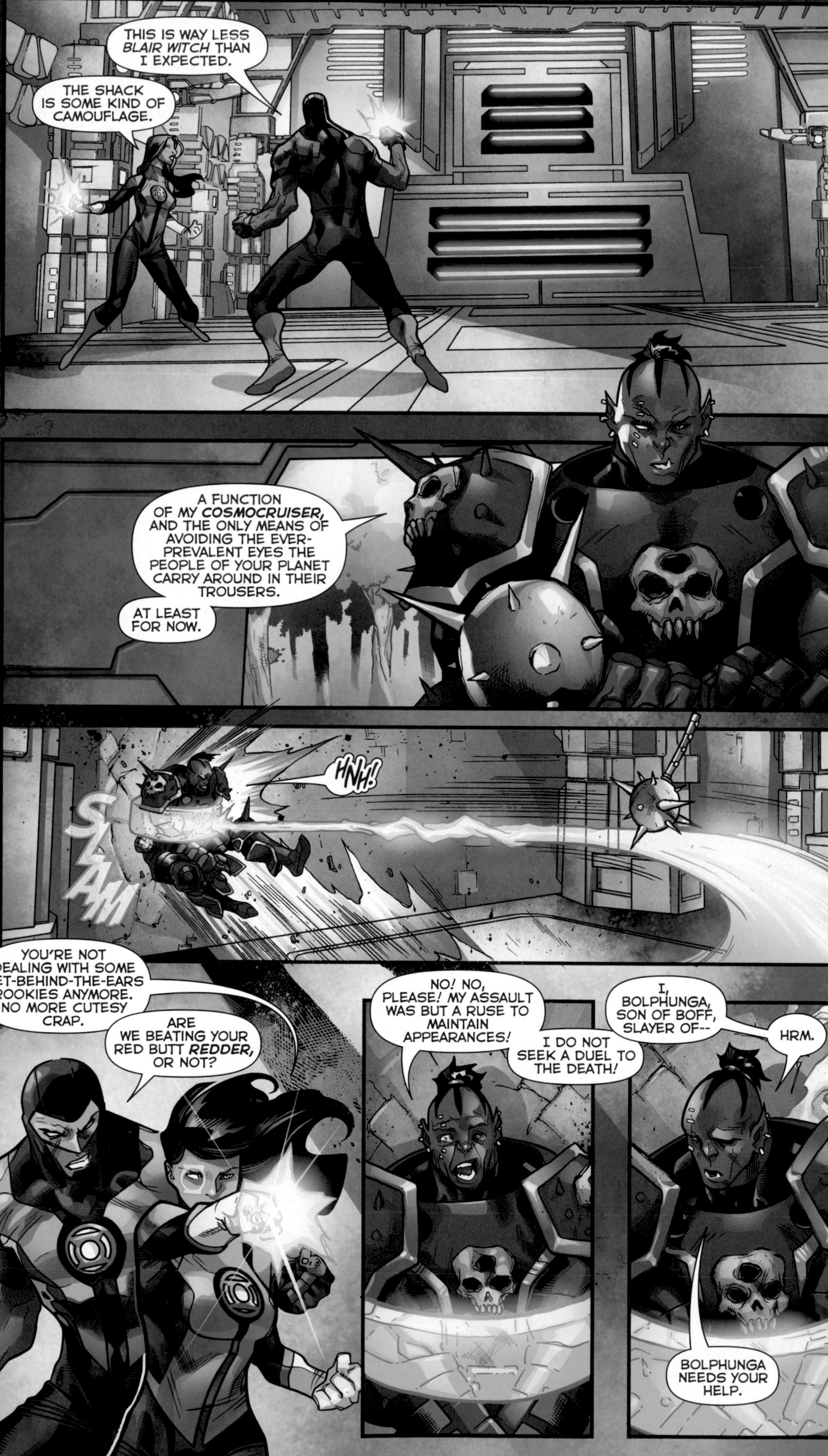
THIS IS WAY LESS *BLAIR WITCH* THAN I EXPECTED.
THE SHACK IS SOME KIND OF CAMOUFLAGE.
A FUNCTION OF MY **COSMOCRUISER,** AND THE ONLY MEANS OF AVOIDING THE EVER-PREVALENT EYES THE PEOPLE OF YOUR PLANET CARRY AROUND IN THEIR TROUSERS.
AT LEAST FOR NOW.
SLAM
HNH!
YOU'RE NOT DEALING WITH SOME WET-BEHIND-THE-EARS ROOKIES ANYMORE. NO MORE CUTESY CRAP.
ARE WE BEATING YOUR RED BUTT *REDDER,* OR NOT?
NO! NO, PLEASE! MY ASSAULT WAS BUT A RUSE TO MAINTAIN APPEARANCES!
I DO NOT SEEK A DUEL TO THE DEATH!
I, BOLPHUNGA, SON OF BOFF, SLAYER OF--
HRM.
BOLPHUNGA NEEDS YOUR HELP.

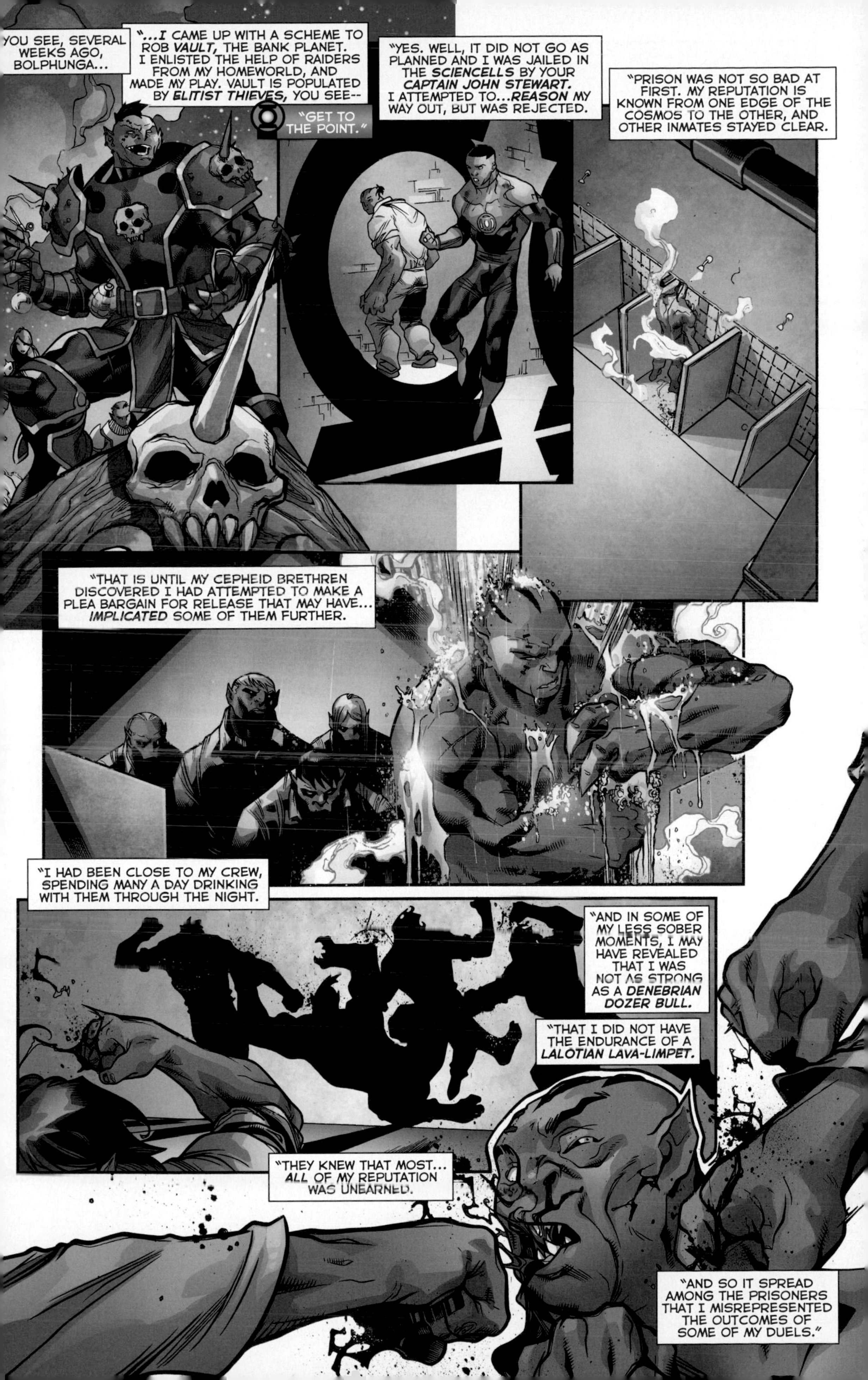
YOU SEE, SEVERAL WEEKS AGO, BOLPHUNGA...
"...I CAME UP WITH A SCHEME TO ROB VAULT, THE BANK PLANET. I ENLISTED THE HELP OF RAIDERS FROM MY HOMEWORLD, AND MADE MY PLAY. VAULT IS POPULATED BY ELITIST THIEVES, YOU SEE--
"GET TO THE POINT."
"YES. WELL, IT DID NOT GO AS PLANNED AND I WAS JAILED IN THE SCIENCELLS BY YOUR CAPTAIN JOHN STEWART. I ATTEMPTED TO...REASON MY WAY OUT, BUT WAS REJECTED.
"PRISON WAS NOT SO BAD AT FIRST. MY REPUTATION IS KNOWN FROM ONE EDGE OF THE COSMOS TO THE OTHER, AND OTHER INMATES STAYED CLEAR.
"THAT IS UNTIL MY CEPHEID BRETHREN DISCOVERED I HAD ATTEMPTED TO MAKE A PLEA BARGAIN FOR RELEASE THAT MAY HAVE... IMPLICATED SOME OF THEM FURTHER.
"I HAD BEEN CLOSE TO MY CREW, SPENDING MANY A DAY DRINKING WITH THEM THROUGH THE NIGHT.
"AND IN SOME OF MY LESS SOBER MOMENTS, I MAY HAVE REVEALED THAT I WAS NOT AS STRONG AS A DENEBRIAN DOZER BULL.
"THAT I DID NOT HAVE THE ENDURANCE OF A LALOTIAN LAVA-LIMPET.
"THEY KNEW THAT MOST... ALL OF MY REPUTATION WAS UNEARNED.
"AND SO IT SPREAD AMONG THE PRISONERS THAT I MISREPRESENTED THE OUTCOMES OF SOME OF MY DUELS."

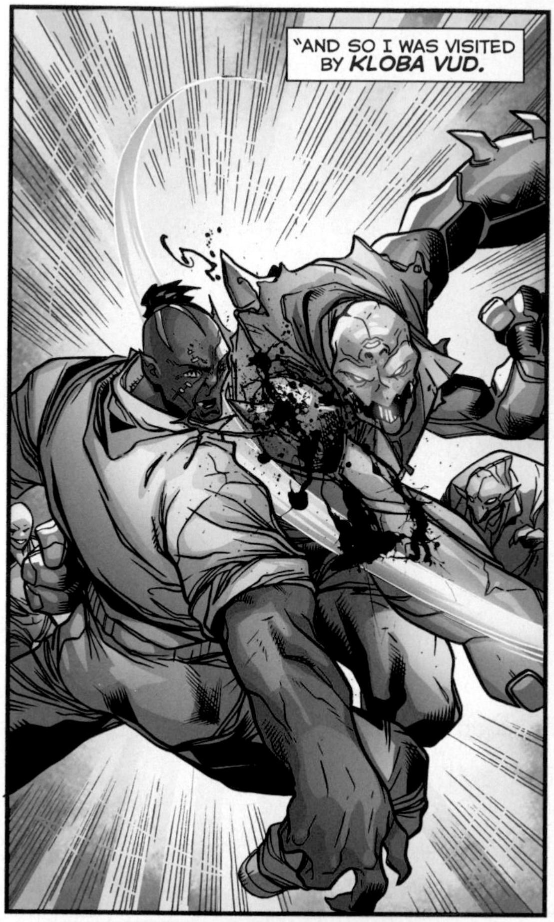
"AND SO I WAS VISITED BY KLOBA VUD.
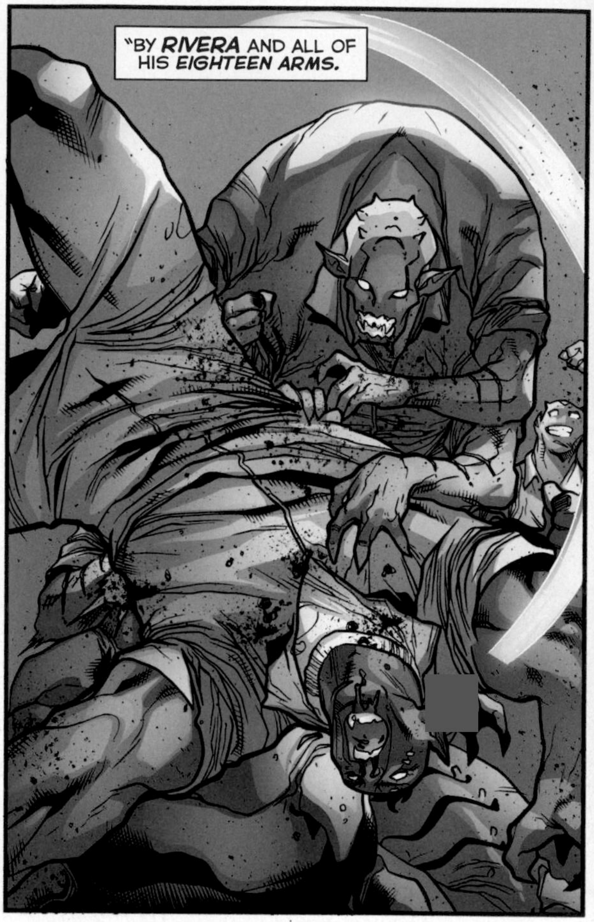
"BY RIVERA AND ALL OF HIS EIGHTEEN ARMS.
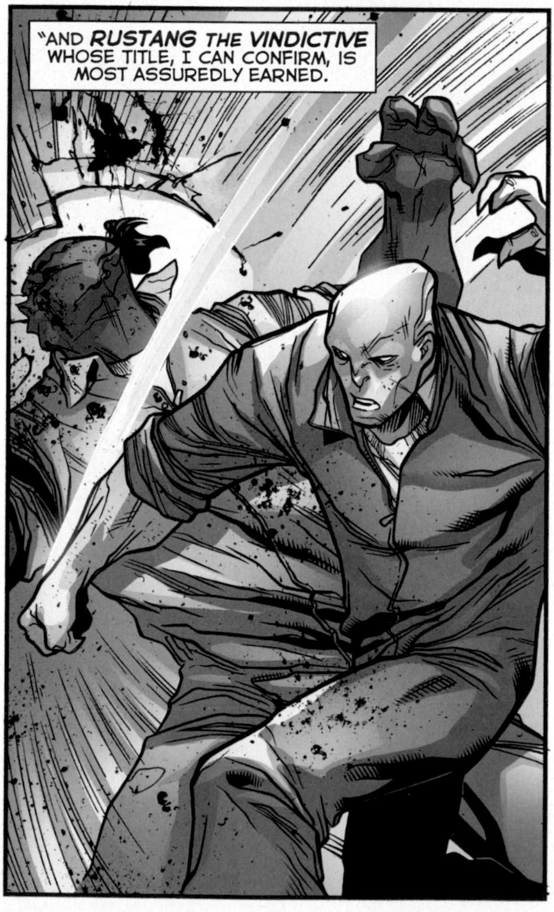
"AND RUSTANG THE VINDICTIVE WHOSE TITLE, I CAN CONFIRM, IS MOST ASSUREDLY EARNED.
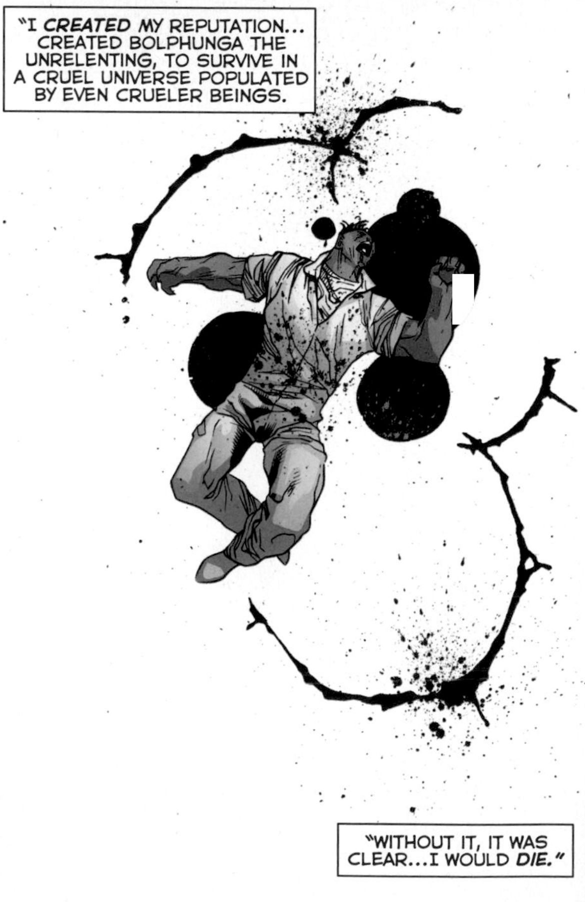
"I CREATED MY REPUTATION... CREATED BOLPHUNGA THE UNRELENTING, TO SURVIVE IN A CRUEL UNIVERSE POPULATED BY EVEN CRUELER BEINGS.
"WITHOUT IT, IT WAS CLEAR...I WOULD DIE."

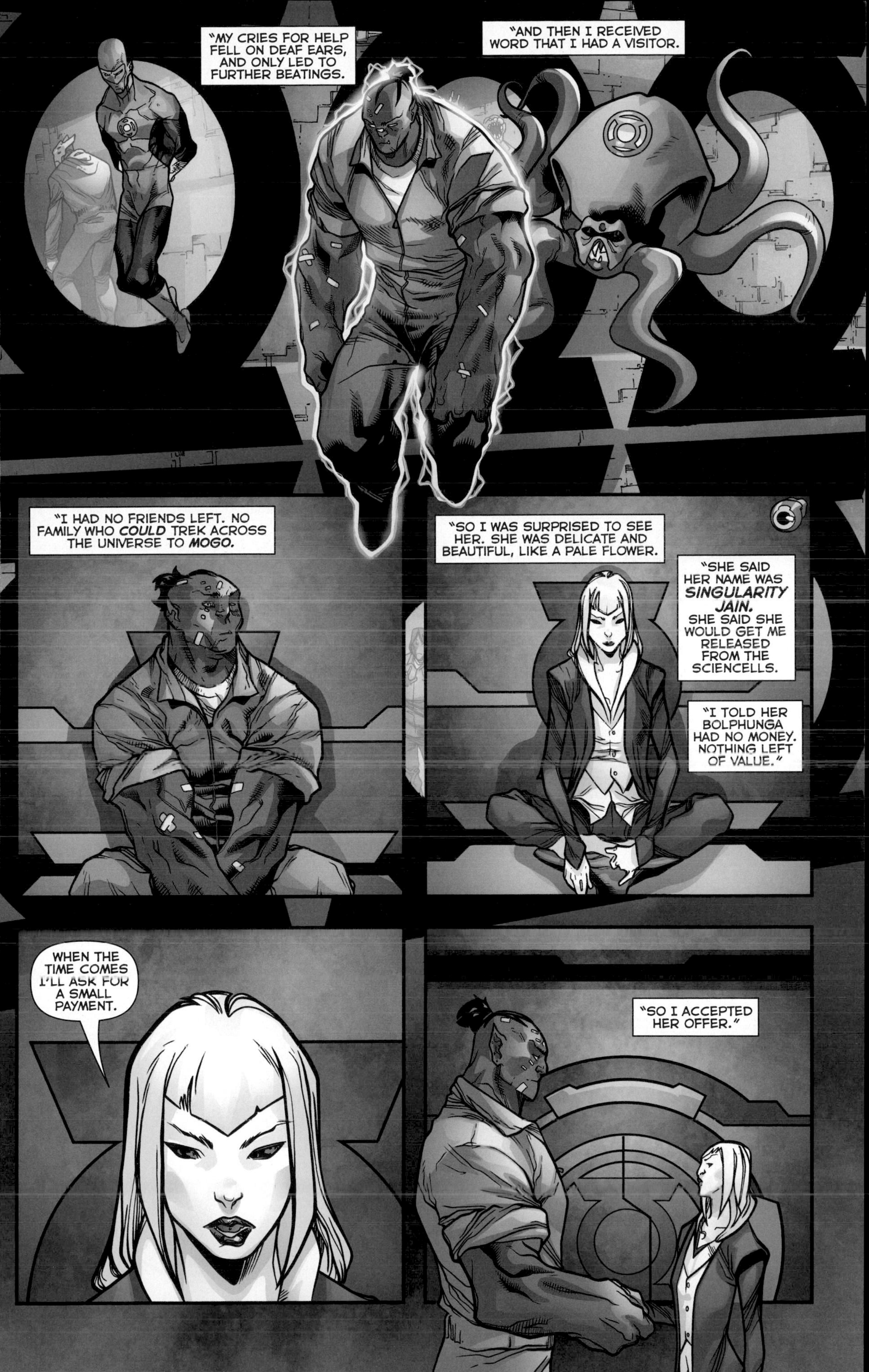
"MY CRIES FOR HELP FELL ON DEAF EARS, AND ONLY LED TO FURTHER BEATINGS.
"AND THEN I RECEIVED WORD THAT I HAD A VISITOR.
"I HAD NO FRIENDS LEFT. NO FAMILY WHO COULD TREK ACROSS THE UNIVERSE TO MOGO.
"SO I WAS SURPRISED TO SEE HER. SHE WAS DELICATE AND BEAUTIFUL, LIKE A PALE FLOWER.
"SHE SAID HER NAME WAS SINGULARITY JAIN. SHE SAID SHE WOULD GET ME RELEASED FROM THE SCIENCELLS.
"I TOLD HER BOLPHUNGA HAD NO MONEY. NOTHING LEFT OF VALUE."
WHEN THE TIME COMES I'LL ASK FOR A SMALL PAYMENT.
"SO I ACCEPTED HER OFFER."

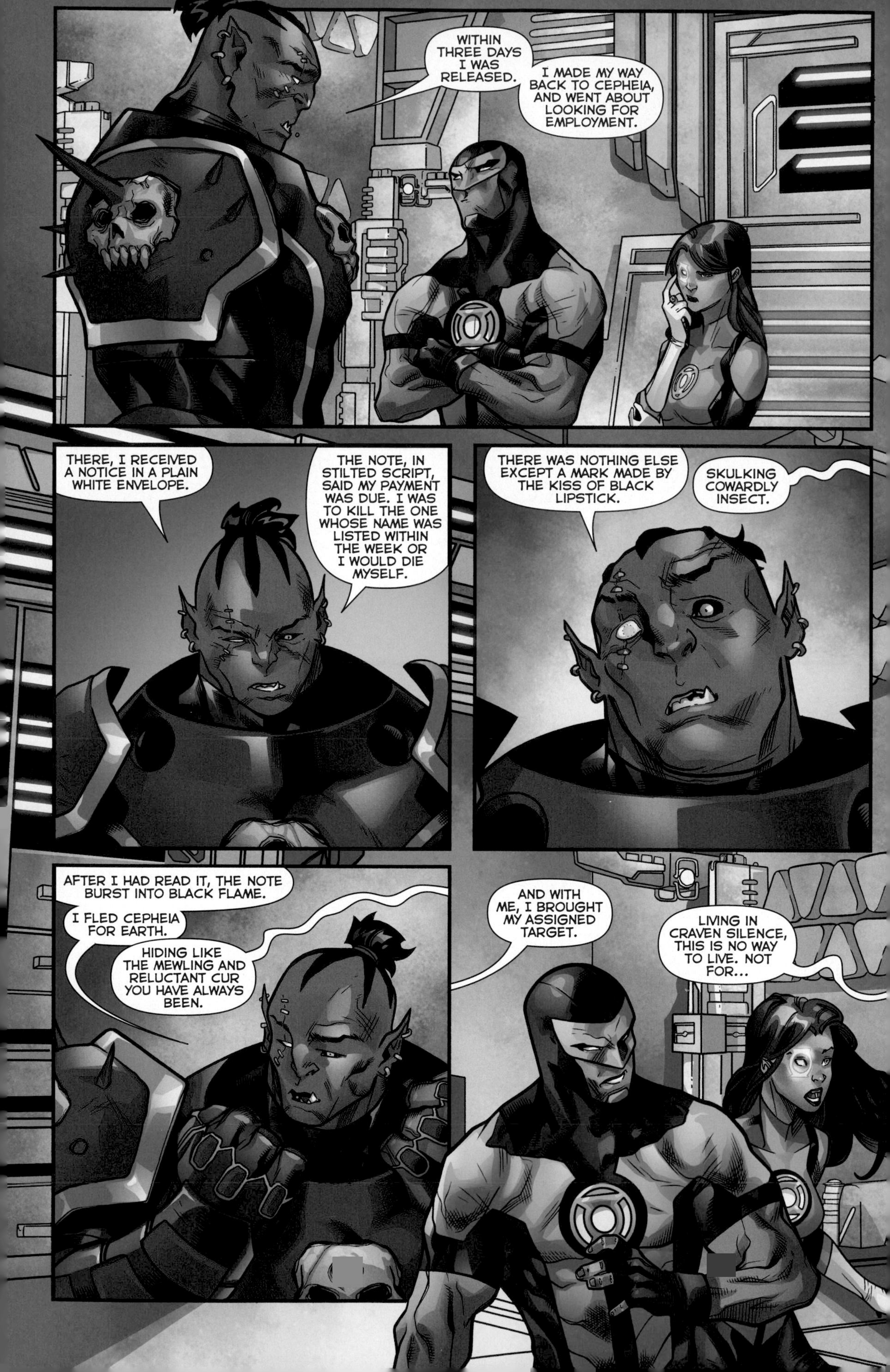
WITHIN THREE DAYS I WAS RELEASED.
I MADE MY WAY BACK TO CEPHEIA, AND WENT ABOUT LOOKING FOR EMPLOYMENT.
THERE, I RECEIVED A NOTICE IN A PLAIN WHITE ENVELOPE.
THE NOTE, IN STILTED SCRIPT, SAID MY PAYMENT WAS DUE. I WAS TO KILL THE ONE WHOSE NAME WAS LISTED WITHIN THE WEEK OR I WOULD DIE MYSELF.
THERE WAS NOTHING ELSE EXCEPT A MARK MADE BY THE KISS OF BLACK LIPSTICK.
SKULKING COWARDLY INSECT.
AFTER I HAD READ IT, THE NOTE BURST INTO BLACK FLAME.
I FLED CEPHEIA FOR EARTH.
HIDING LIKE THE MEWLING AND RELUCTANT CUR YOU HAVE ALWAYS BEEN.
AND WITH ME, I BROUGHT MY ASSIGNED TARGET.
LIVING IN CRAVEN SILENCE, THIS IS NO WAY TO LIVE. NOT FOR...

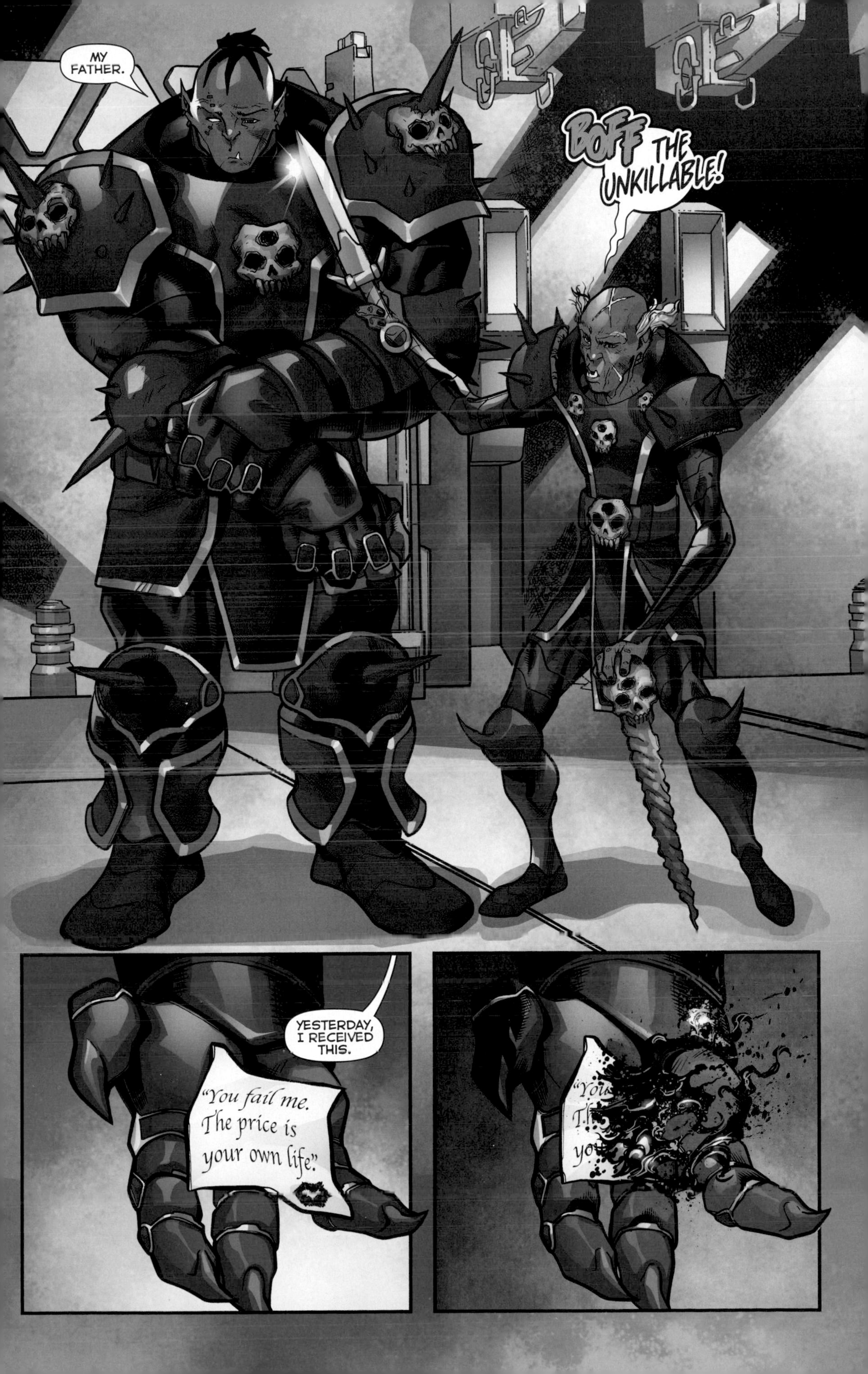
MY FATHER.
BOFF THE UNKILLABLE!
YESTERDAY, I RECEIVED THIS.
"You fail me. The price is your own life."

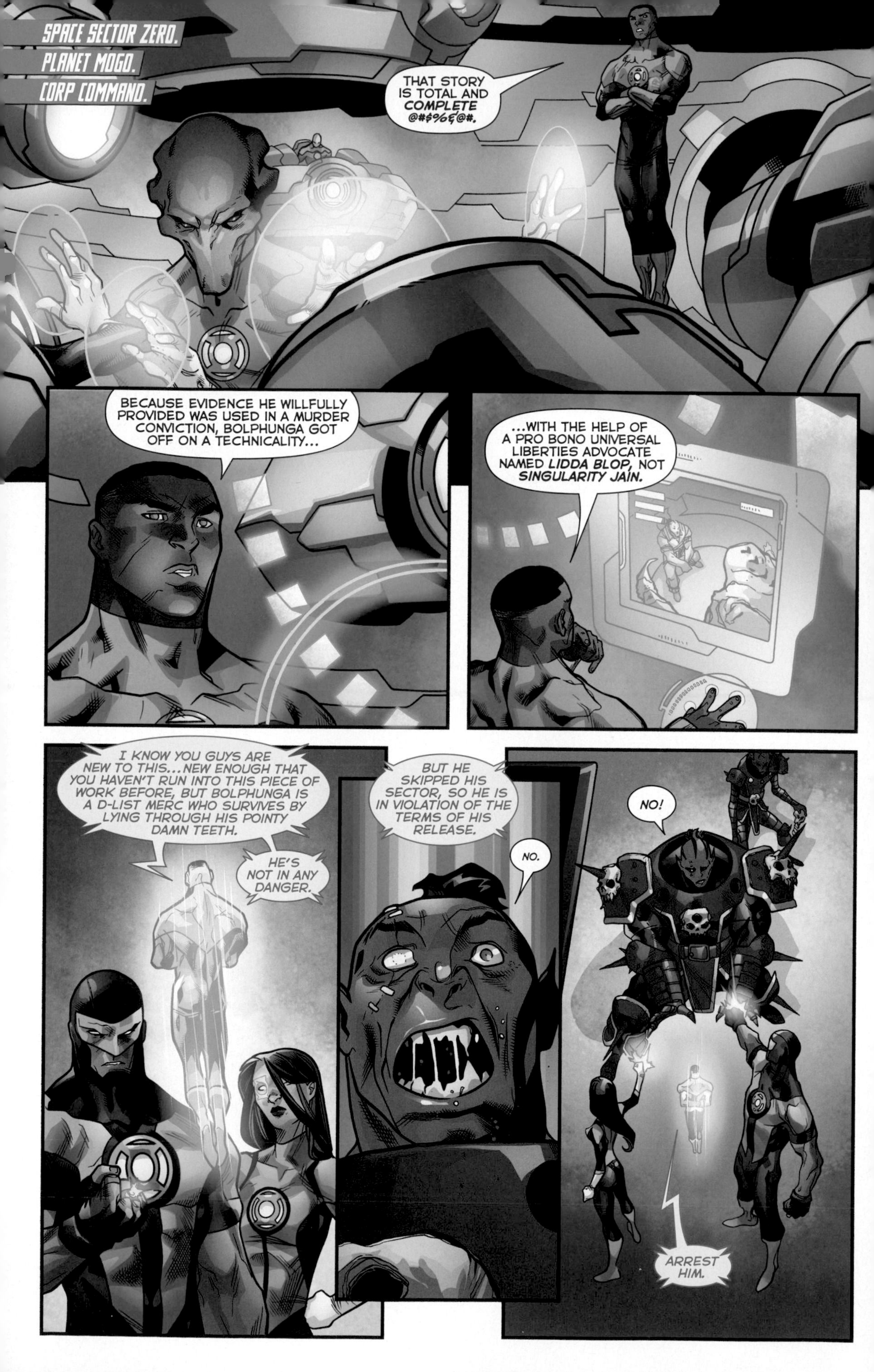
SPACE SECTOR ZERO.
PLANET MOGO.
CORP COMMAND.
THAT STORY IS TOTAL AND COMPLETE @#$%&@#.
BECAUSE EVIDENCE HE WILLFULLY PROVIDED WAS USED IN A MURDER CONVICTION, BOLPHUNGA GOT OFF ON A TECHNICALITY...
...WITH THE HELP OF A PRO BONO UNIVERSAL LIBERTIES ADVOCATE NAMED LIDDA BLOP, NOT SINGULARITY JAIN.
I KNOW YOU GUYS ARE NEW TO THIS...NEW ENOUGH THAT YOU HAVEN'T RUN INTO THIS PIECE OF WORK BEFORE, BUT BOLPHUNGA IS A D-LIST MERC WHO SURVIVES BY LYING THROUGH HIS POINTY DAMN TEETH.
HE'S NOT IN ANY DANGER.
BUT HE SKIPPED HIS SECTOR, SO HE IS IN VIOLATION OF THE TERMS OF HIS RELEASE.
NO.
NO!
ARREST HIM.

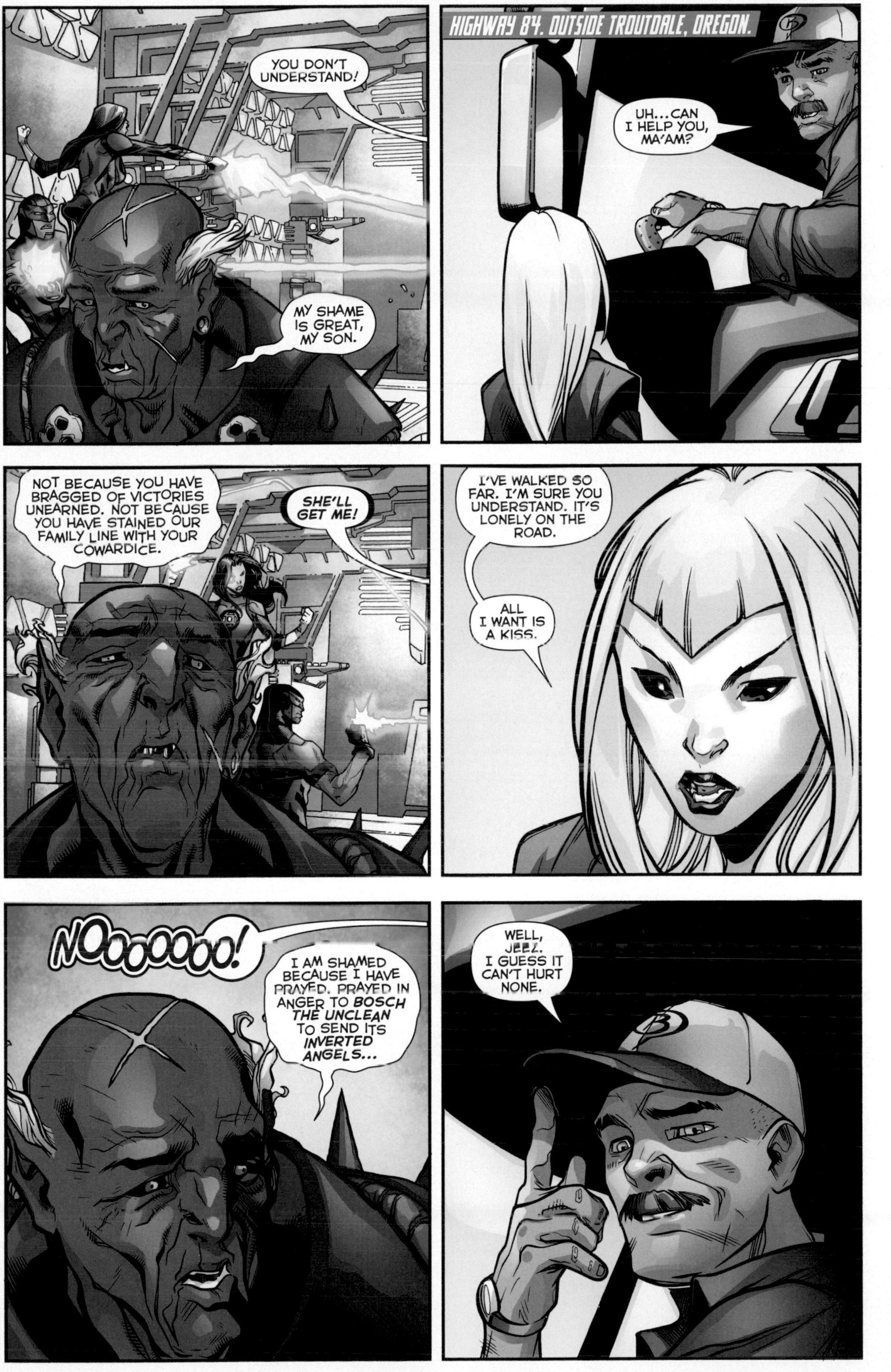
YOU DON'T UNDERSTAND!
MY SHAME IS GREAT, MY SON.
HIGHWAY 84. OUTSIDE TROUTDALE, OREGON.
UH...CAN I HELP YOU, MA'AM?
NOT BECAUSE YOU HAVE BRAGGED OF VICTORIES UNEARNED. NOT BECAUSE YOU HAVE STAINED OUR FAMILY LINE WITH YOUR COWARDICE.
SHE'LL GET ME!
I'VE WALKED SO FAR. I'M SURE YOU UNDERSTAND. IT'S LONELY ON THE ROAD.
ALL I WANT IS A KISS.
NOOOOOOO!
I AM SHAMED BECAUSE I HAVE PRAYED. PRAYED IN ANGER TO BOSCH THE UNCLEAN TO SEND ITS INVERTED ANGELS...
WELL, JEEZ. I GUESS IT CAN'T HURT NONE.

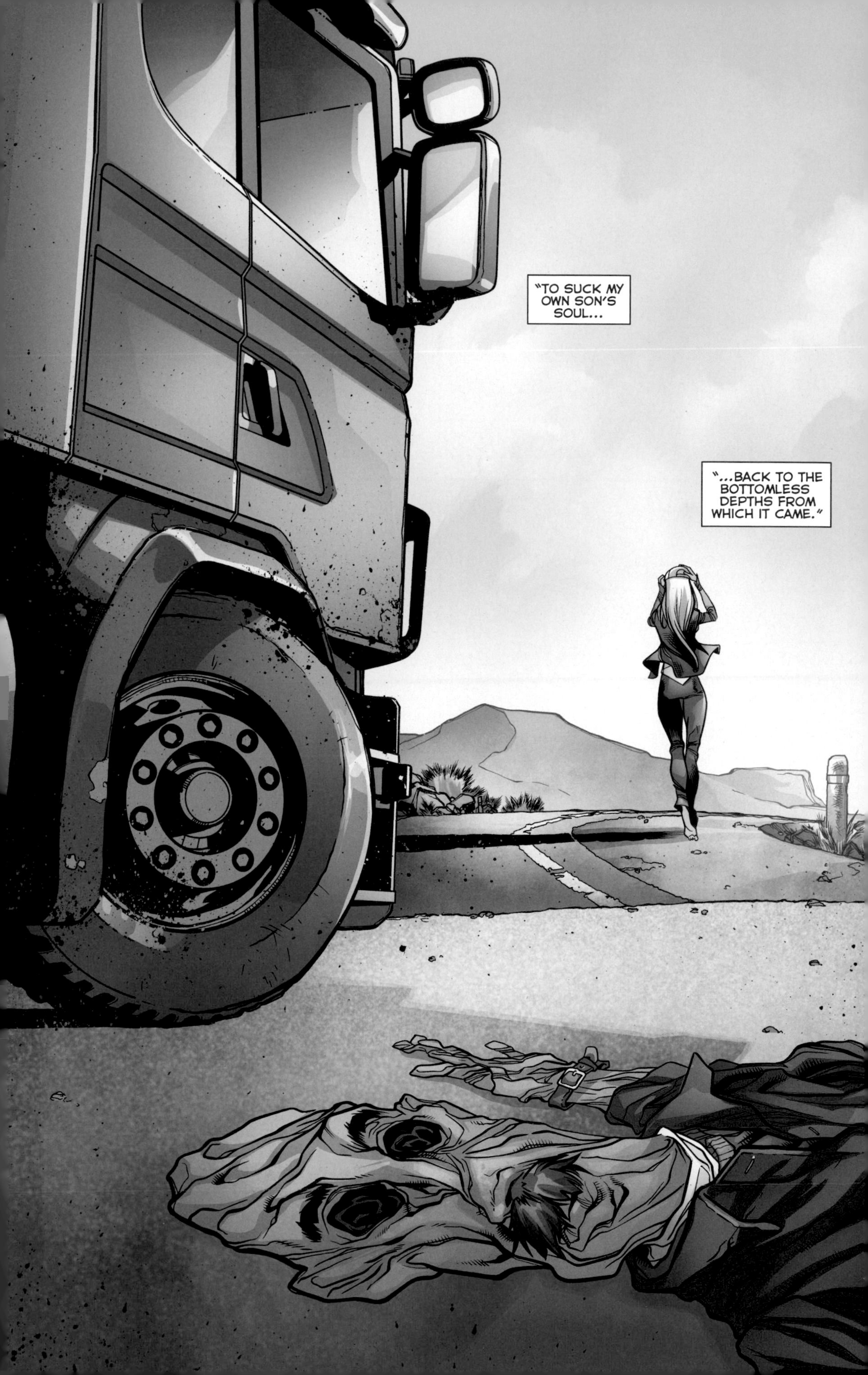
"TO SUCK MY OWN SON'S SOUL...
"...BACK TO THE BOTTOMLESS DEPTHS FROM WHICH IT CAME."

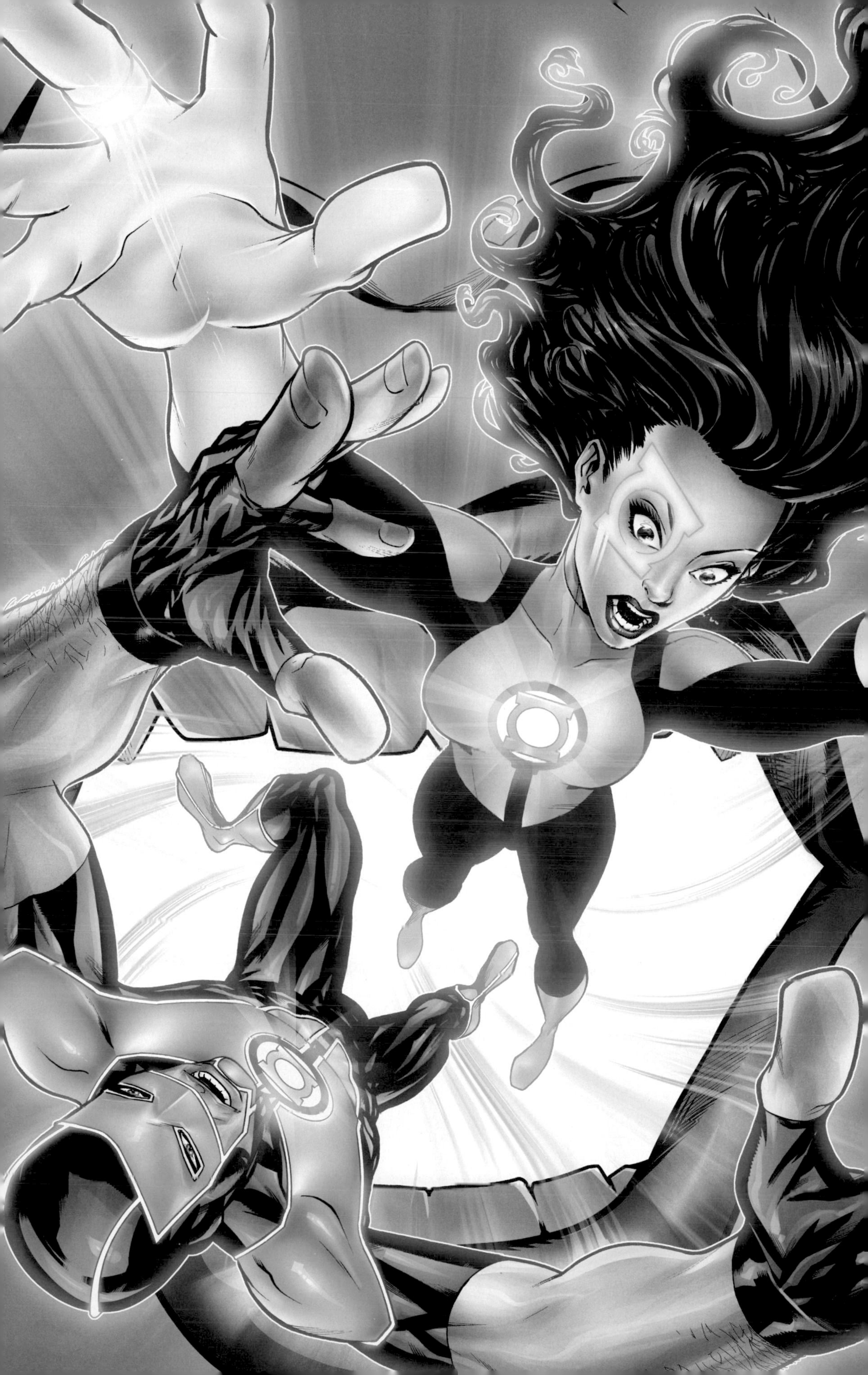

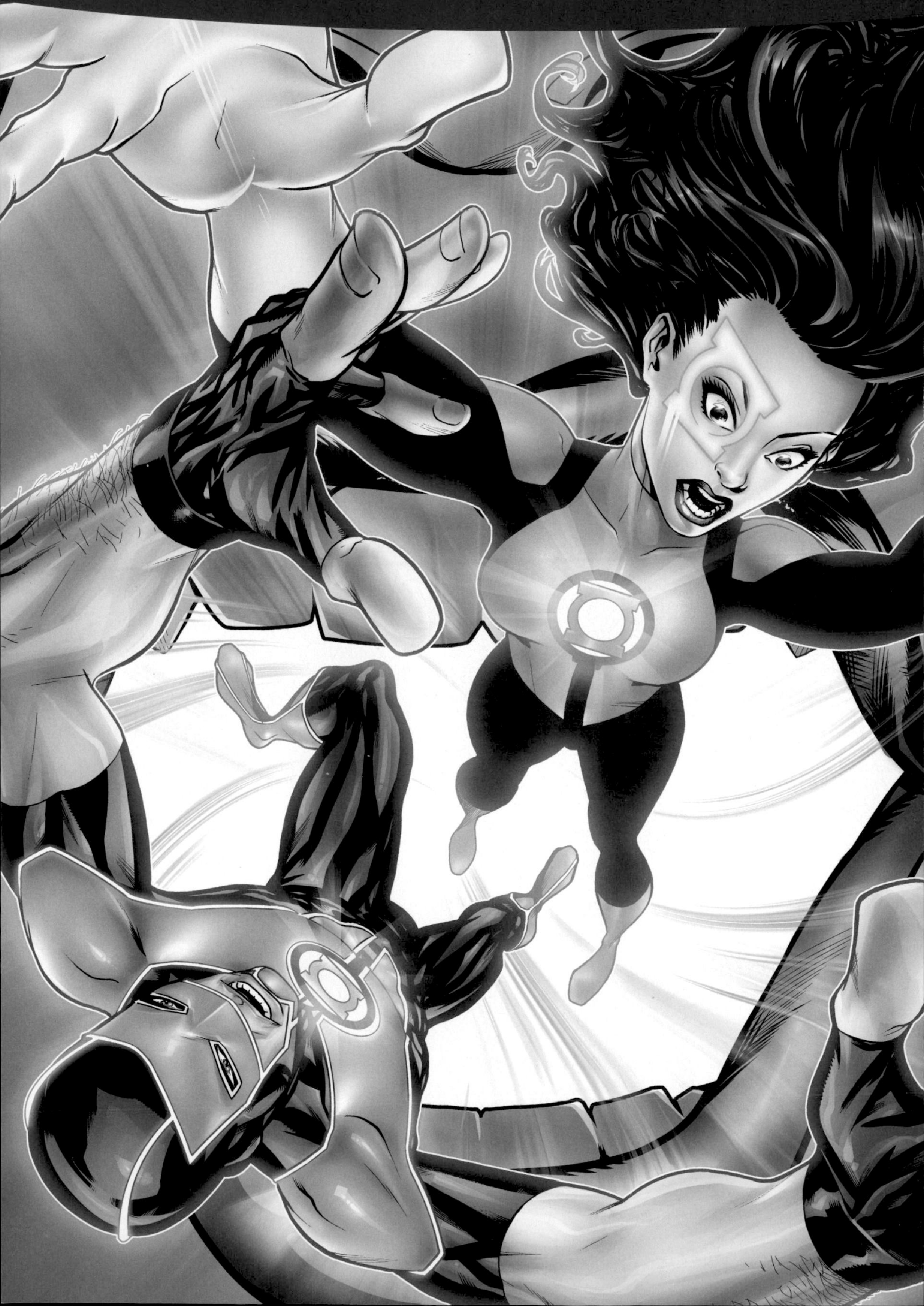

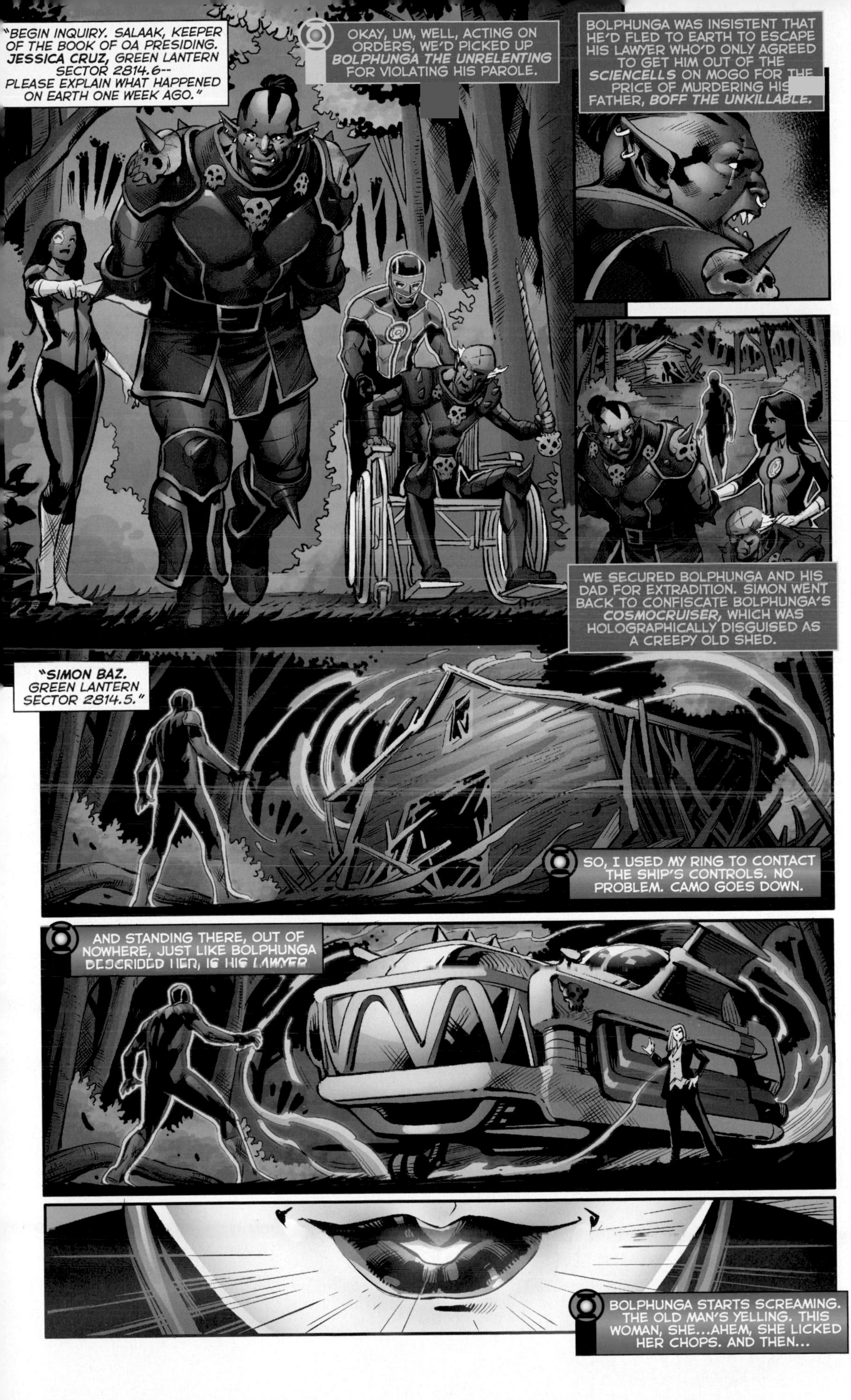
"BEGIN INQUIRY. SALAAK, KEEPER OF THE BOOK OF OA PRESIDING. JESSICA CRUZ, GREEN LANTERN SECTOR 2814.6-- PLEASE EXPLAIN WHAT HAPPENED ON EARTH ONE WEEK AGO."
OKAY, UM, WELL, ACTING ON ORDERS, WE'D PICKED UP BOLPHUNGA THE UNRELENTING FOR VIOLATING HIS PAROLE.
BOLPHUNGA WAS INSISTENT THAT HE'D FLED TO EARTH TO ESCAPE HIS LAWYER WHO'D ONLY AGREED TO GET HIM OUT OF THE SCIENCELLS ON MOGO FOR THE PRICE OF MURDERING HIS FATHER, BOFF THE UNKILLABLE.
WE SECURED BOLPHUNGA AND HIS DAD FOR EXTRADITION. SIMON WENT BACK TO CONFISCATE BOLPHUNGA'S COSMOCRUISER, WHICH WAS HOLOGRAPHICALLY DISGUISED AS A CREEPY OLD SHED.
"SIMON BAZ. GREEN LANTERN SECTOR 2814.5."
SO, I USED MY RING TO CONTACT THE SHIP'S CONTROLS. NO PROBLEM. CAMO GOES DOWN.
AND STANDING THERE, OUT OF NOWHERE, JUST LIKE BOLPHUNGA DESCRIBED HER, IS HIS LAWYER
BOLPHUNGA STARTS SCREAMING. THE OLD MAN'S YELLING. THIS WOMAN, SHE...AHEM, SHE LICKED HER CHOPS. AND THEN...

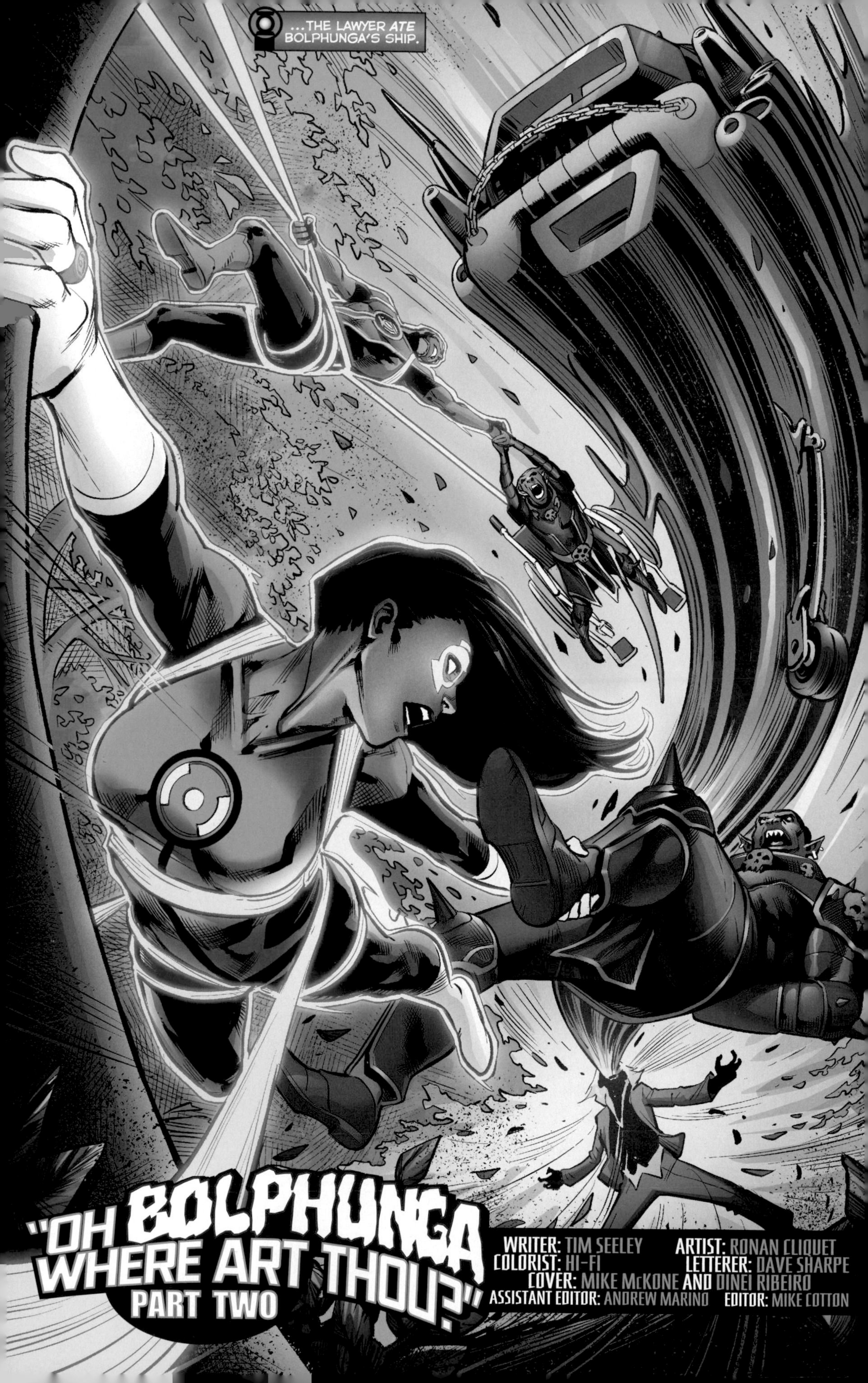
...THE LAWYER ATE BOLPHUNGA'S SHIP.
"OH BOLPHUNGA WHERE ART THOU?"
PART TWO
WRITER: TIM SEELEY ARTIST: RONAN CLIQUET
COLORIST: HI-FI LETTERER: DAVE SHARPE
COVER: MIKE McKONE AND DINEI RIBEIRO
ASSISTANT EDITOR: ANDREW MARINO EDITOR: MIKE COTTON

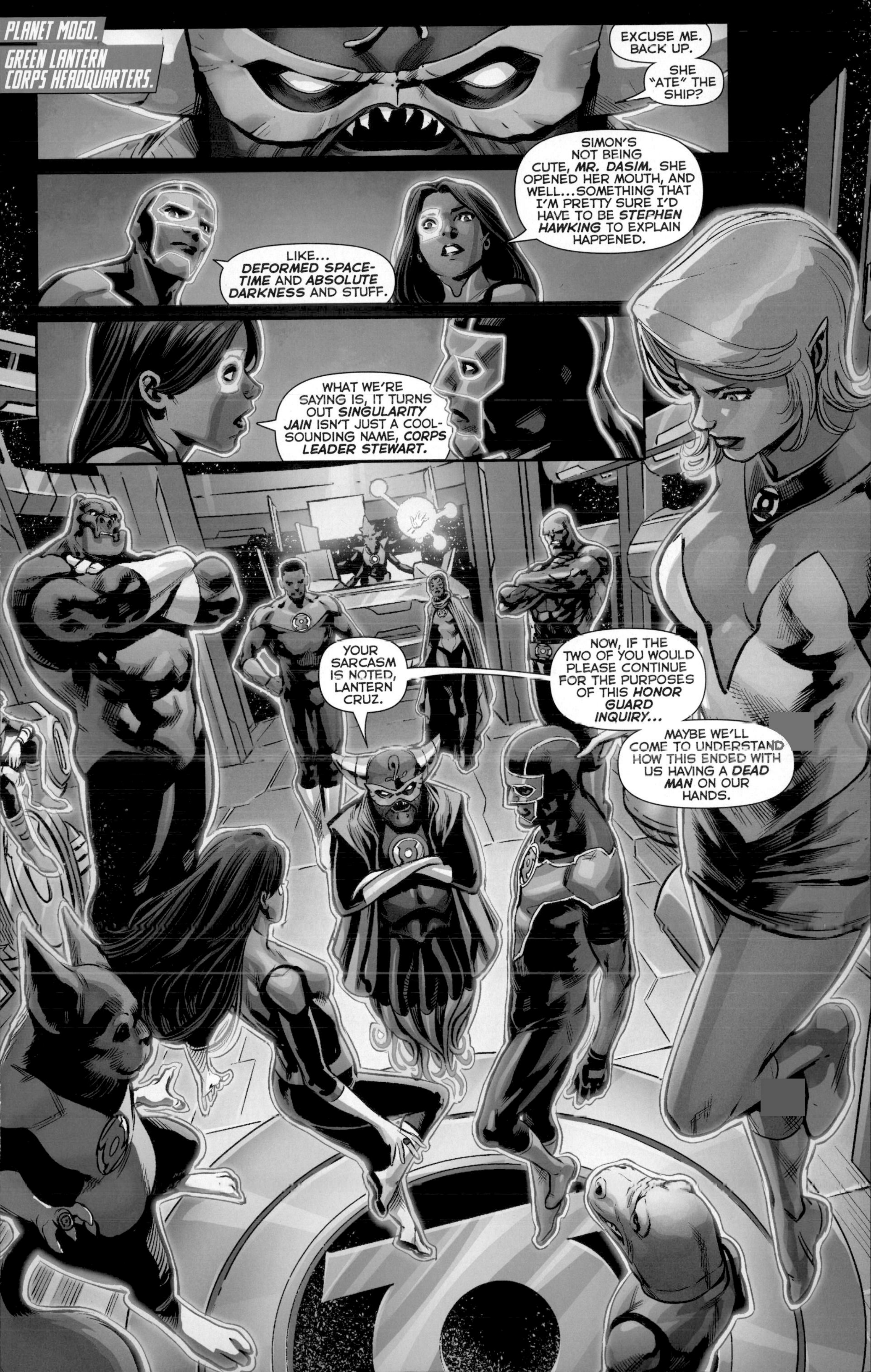
PLANET MOGO.
GREEN LANTERN CORPS HEADQUARTERS.
EXCUSE ME. BACK UP.
SHE "ATE" THE SHIP?
SIMON'S NOT BEING CUTE, MR. DASIM. SHE OPENED HER MOUTH, AND WELL...SOMETHING THAT I'M PRETTY SURE I'D HAVE TO BE STEPHEN HAWKING TO EXPLAIN HAPPENED.
LIKE... DEFORMED SPACE-TIME AND ABSOLUTE DARKNESS AND STUFF.
WHAT WE'RE SAYING IS, IT TURNS OUT SINGULARITY JAIN ISN'T JUST A COOL-SOUNDING NAME, CORPS LEADER STEWART.
YOUR SARCASM IS NOTED, LANTERN CRUZ.
NOW, IF THE TWO OF YOU WOULD PLEASE CONTINUE FOR THE PURPOSES OF THIS HONOR GUARD INQUIRY...
MAYBE WE'LL COME TO UNDERSTAND HOW THIS ENDED WITH US HAVING A DEAD MAN ON OUR HANDS.

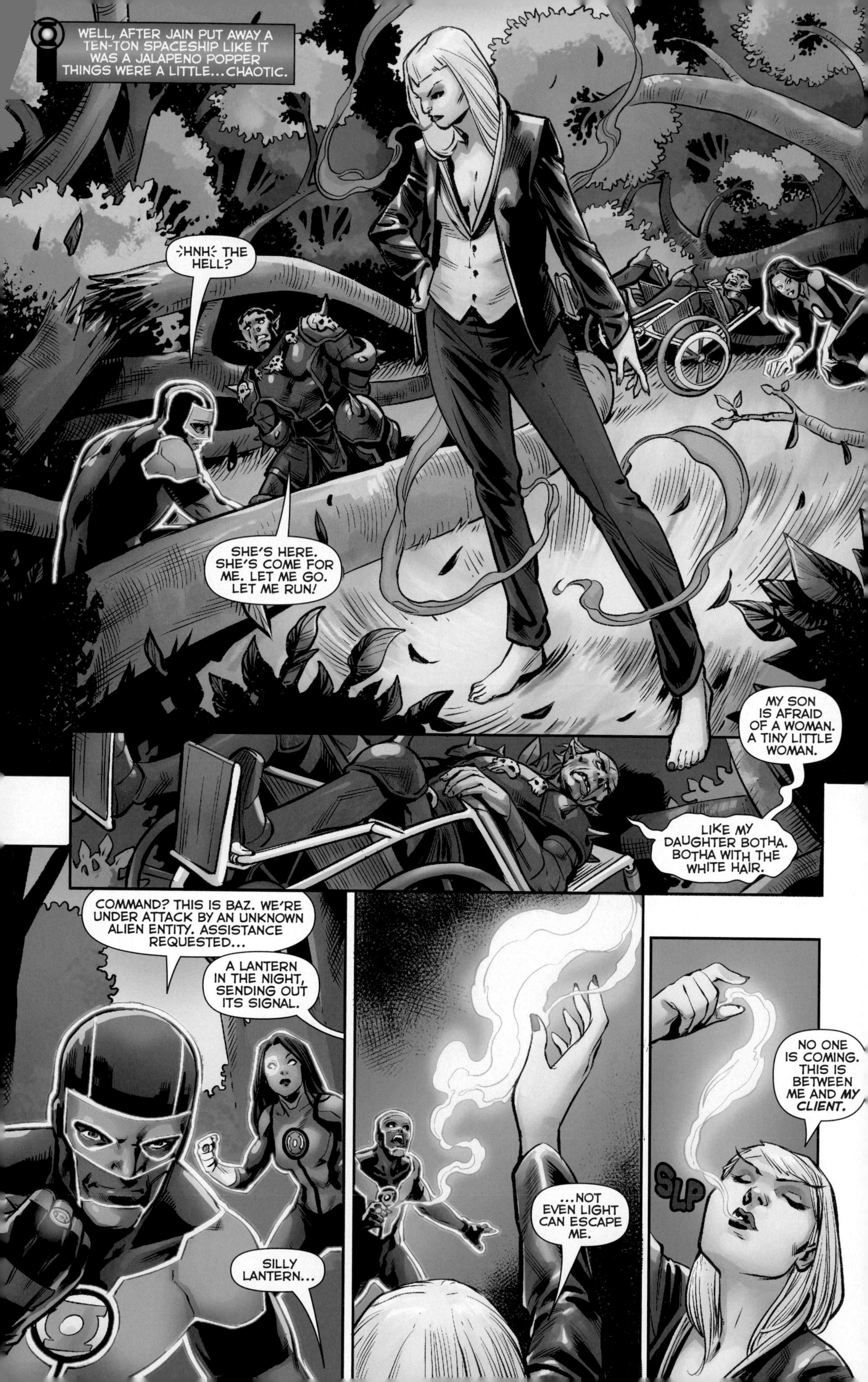
WELL, AFTER JAIN PUT AWAY A TEN-TON SPACESHIP LIKE IT WAS A JALAPENO POPPER THINGS WERE A LITTLE...CHAOTIC.
HNH THE HELL?
SHE'S HERE. SHE'S COME FOR ME. LET ME GO. LET ME RUN!
MY SON IS AFRAID OF A WOMAN. A TINY LITTLE WOMAN.
LIKE MY DAUGHTER BOTHA. BOTHA WITH THE WHITE HAIR.
COMMAND? THIS IS BAZ. WE'RE UNDER ATTACK BY AN UNKNOWN ALIEN ENTITY. ASSISTANCE REQUESTED...
A LANTERN IN THE NIGHT, SENDING OUT ITS SIGNAL.
SILLY LANTERN...
...NOT EVEN LIGHT CAN ESCAPE ME.
NO ONE IS COMING. THIS IS BETWEEN ME AND *MY CLIENT*.
SLP

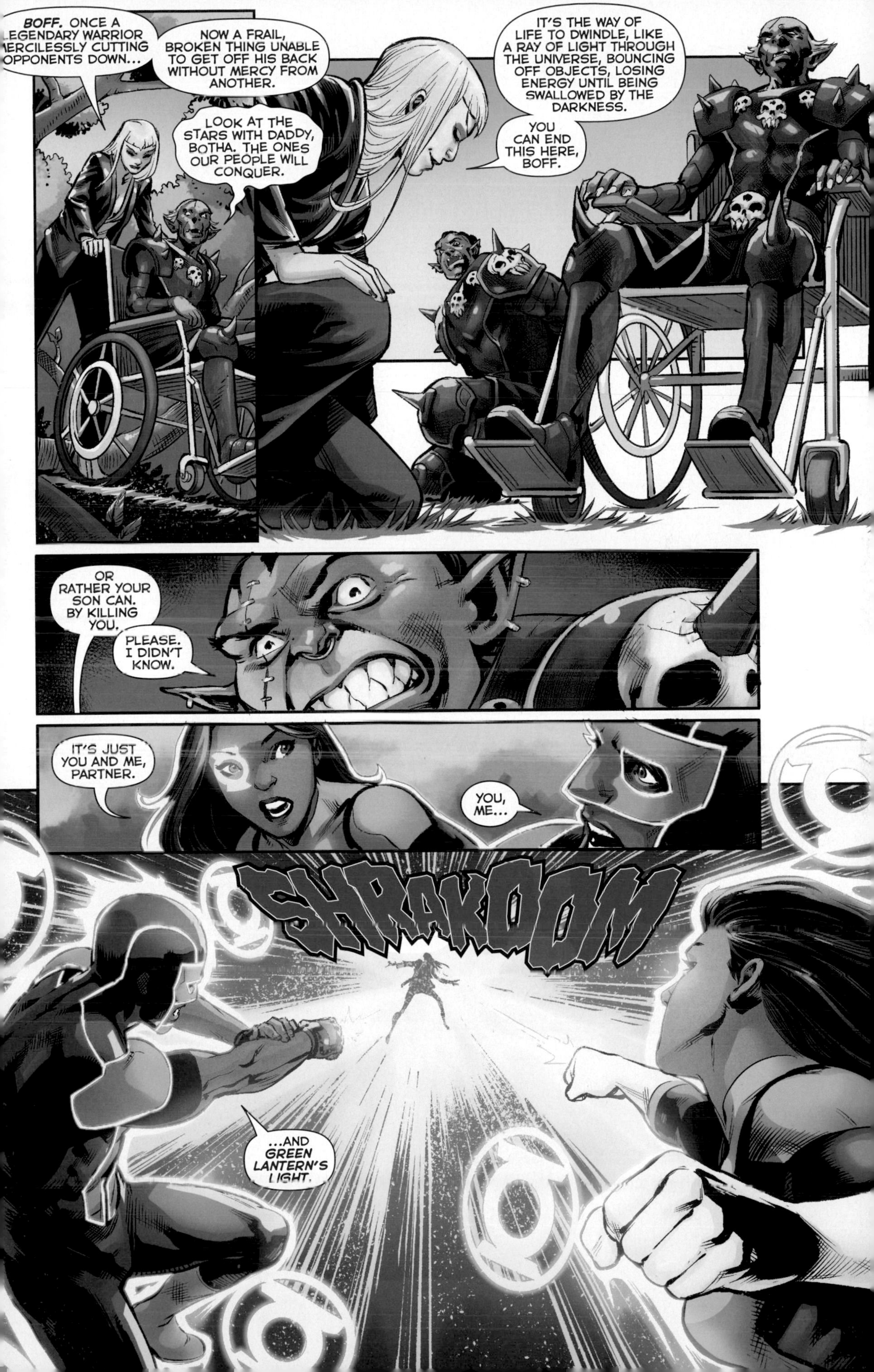
BOFF. ONCE A LEGENDARY WARRIOR MERCILESSLY CUTTING OPPONENTS DOWN...
NOW A FRAIL, BROKEN THING UNABLE TO GET OFF HIS BACK WITHOUT MERCY FROM ANOTHER.
LOOK AT THE STARS WITH DADDY, BOTHA. THE ONES OUR PEOPLE WILL CONQUER.
IT'S THE WAY OF LIFE TO DWINDLE, LIKE A RAY OF LIGHT THROUGH THE UNIVERSE, BOUNCING OFF OBJECTS, LOSING ENERGY UNTIL BEING SWALLOWED BY THE DARKNESS.
YOU CAN END THIS HERE, BOFF.
OR RATHER YOUR SON CAN. BY KILLING YOU.
PLEASE. I DIDN'T KNOW.
IT'S JUST YOU AND ME, PARTNER.
YOU, ME...
SHRAKOOM
...AND GREEN LANTERN'S LIGHT.

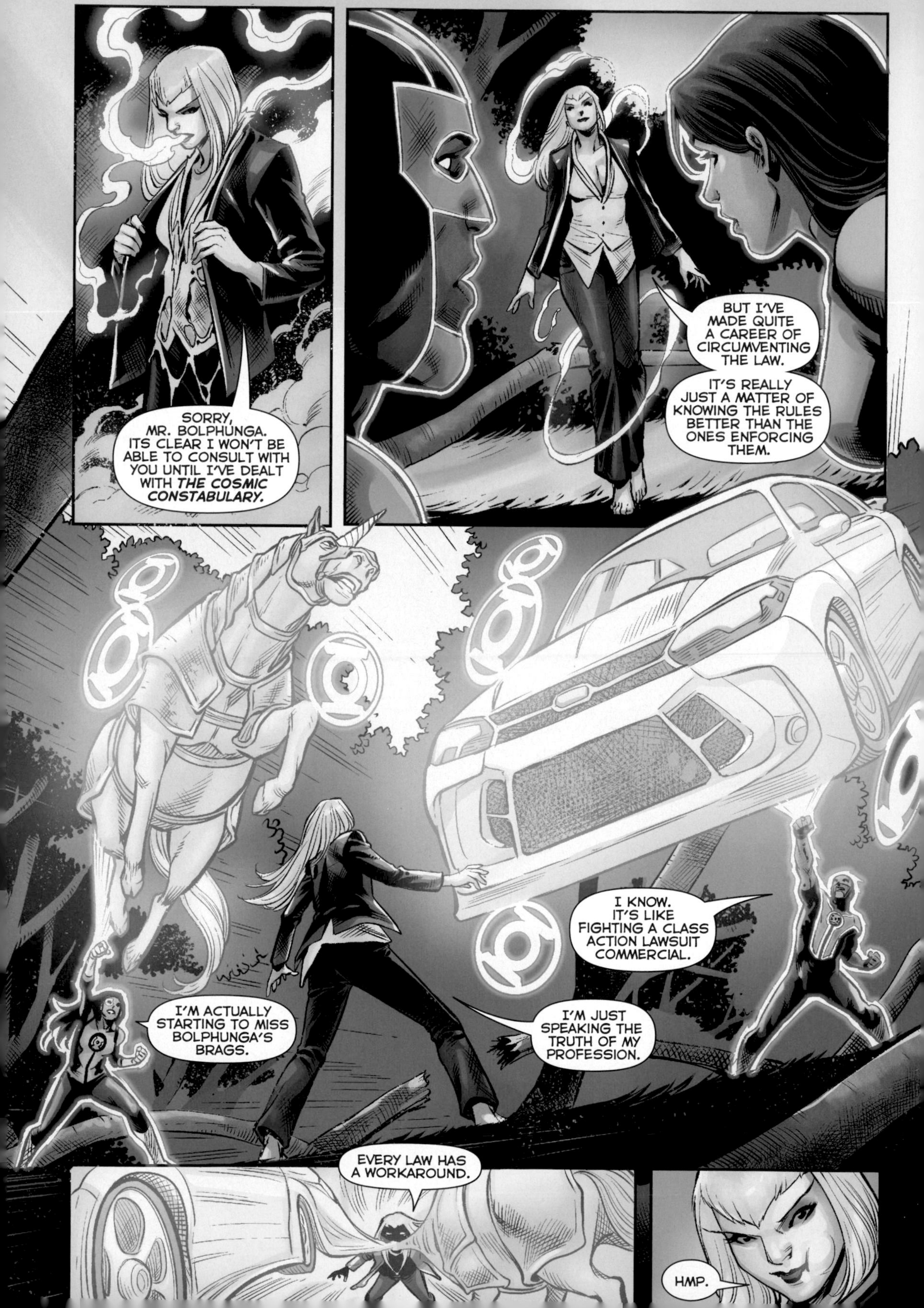
SORRY, MR. BOLPHUNGA. ITS CLEAR I WON'T BE ABLE TO CONSULT WITH YOU UNTIL I'VE DEALT WITH THE COSMIC CONSTABULARY.
BUT I'VE MADE QUITE A CAREER OF CIRCUMVENTING THE LAW.
IT'S REALLY JUST A MATTER OF KNOWING THE RULES BETTER THAN THE ONES ENFORCING THEM.
I KNOW. IT'S LIKE FIGHTING A CLASS ACTION LAWSUIT COMMERCIAL.
I'M ACTUALLY STARTING TO MISS BOLPHUNGA'S BRAGS.
I'M JUST SPEAKING THE TRUTH OF MY PROFESSION.
EVERY LAW HAS A WORKAROUND.
HMP.

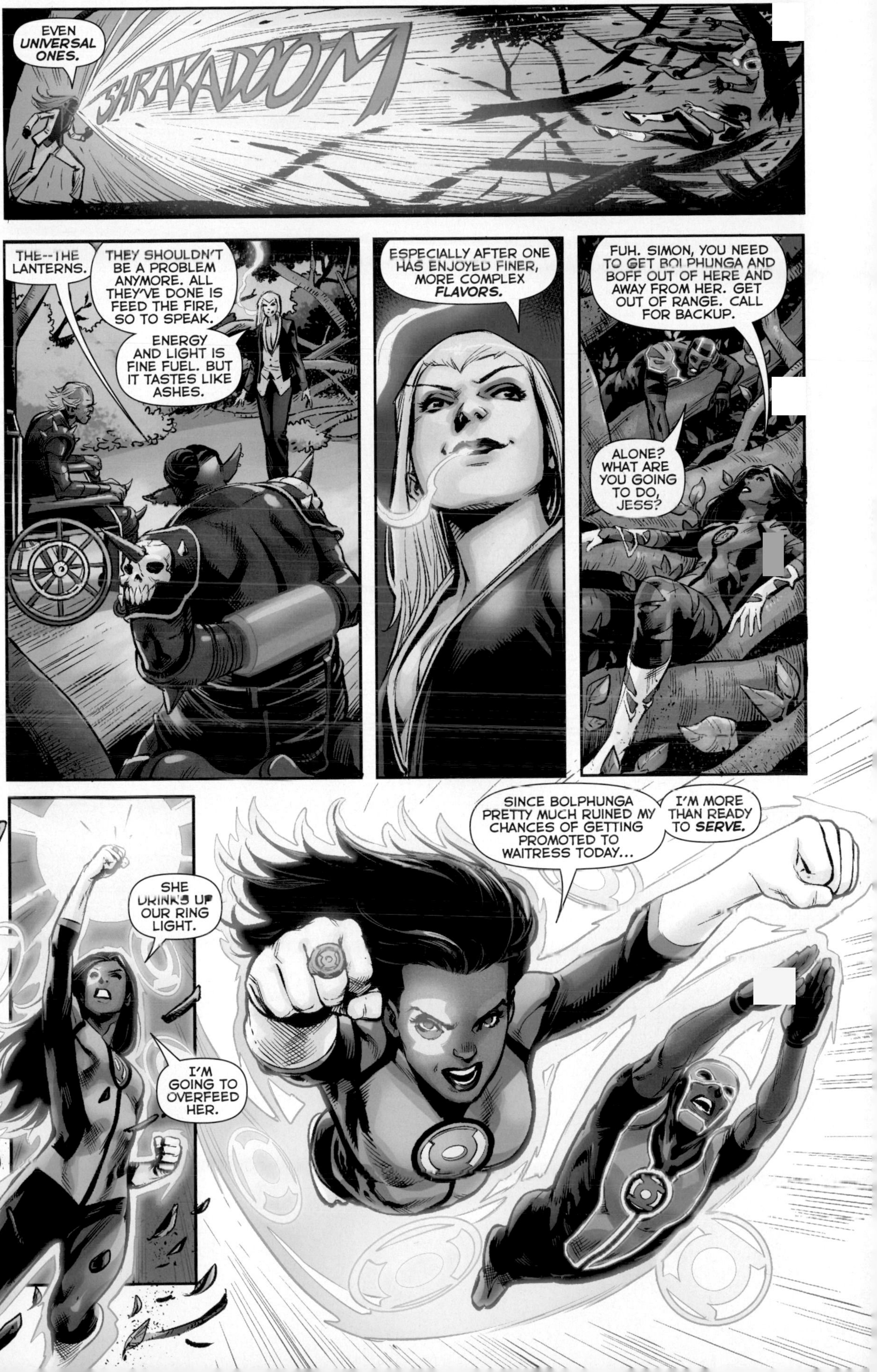
EVEN UNIVERSAL ONES.
SHRAKADOOM
THE--THE LANTERNS.
THEY SHOULDN'T BE A PROBLEM ANYMORE. ALL THEY'VE DONE IS FEED THE FIRE, SO TO SPEAK.
ENERGY AND LIGHT IS FINE FUEL. BUT IT TASTES LIKE ASHES.
ESPECIALLY AFTER ONE HAS ENJOYED FINER, MORE COMPLEX FLAVORS.
FUH. SIMON, YOU NEED TO GET BOLPHUNGA AND BOFF OUT OF HERE AND AWAY FROM HER. GET OUT OF RANGE. CALL FOR BACKUP.
ALONE? WHAT ARE YOU GOING TO DO, JESS?
SHE DRINKS UP OUR RING LIGHT.
I'M GOING TO OVERFEED HER.
SINCE BOLPHUNGA PRETTY MUCH RUINED MY CHANCES OF GETTING PROMOTED TO WAITRESS TODAY...
I'M MORE THAN READY TO SERVE.

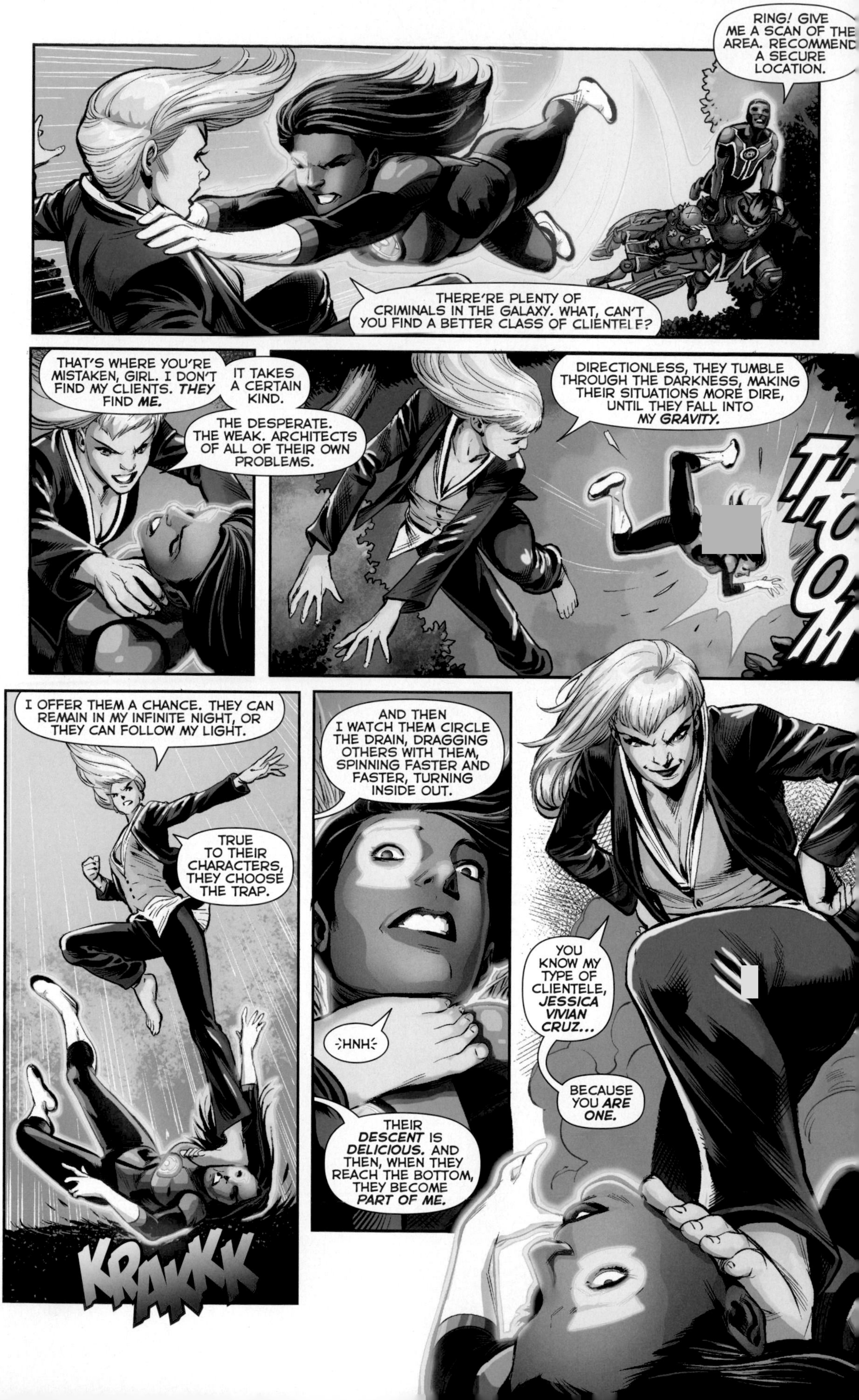
RING! GIVE ME A SCAN OF THE AREA. RECOMMEND A SECURE LOCATION.
THERE'RE PLENTY OF CRIMINALS IN THE GALAXY. WHAT, CAN'T YOU FIND A BETTER CLASS OF CLIENTELE?
THAT'S WHERE YOU'RE MISTAKEN, GIRL. I DON'T FIND MY CLIENTS. *THEY* FIND *ME.*
IT TAKES A CERTAIN KIND.
THE DESPERATE. THE WEAK. ARCHITECTS OF ALL OF THEIR OWN PROBLEMS.
DIRECTIONLESS, THEY TUMBLE THROUGH THE DARKNESS, MAKING THEIR SITUATIONS MORE DIRE, UNTIL THEY FALL INTO *MY GRAVITY.*
I OFFER THEM A CHANCE. THEY CAN REMAIN IN MY INFINITE NIGHT, OR THEY CAN FOLLOW MY LIGHT.
TRUE TO THEIR CHARACTERS, THEY CHOOSE THE TRAP.
KRAKKK
AND THEN I WATCH THEM CIRCLE THE DRAIN, DRAGGING OTHERS WITH THEM, SPINNING FASTER AND FASTER, TURNING INSIDE OUT.
HNH
THEIR *DESCENT* IS *DELICIOUS.* AND THEN, WHEN THEY REACH THE BOTTOM, THEY BECOME *PART OF ME.*
YOU KNOW MY TYPE OF CLIENTELE, *JESSICA VIVIAN CRUZ...*
BECAUSE YOU *ARE ONE.*

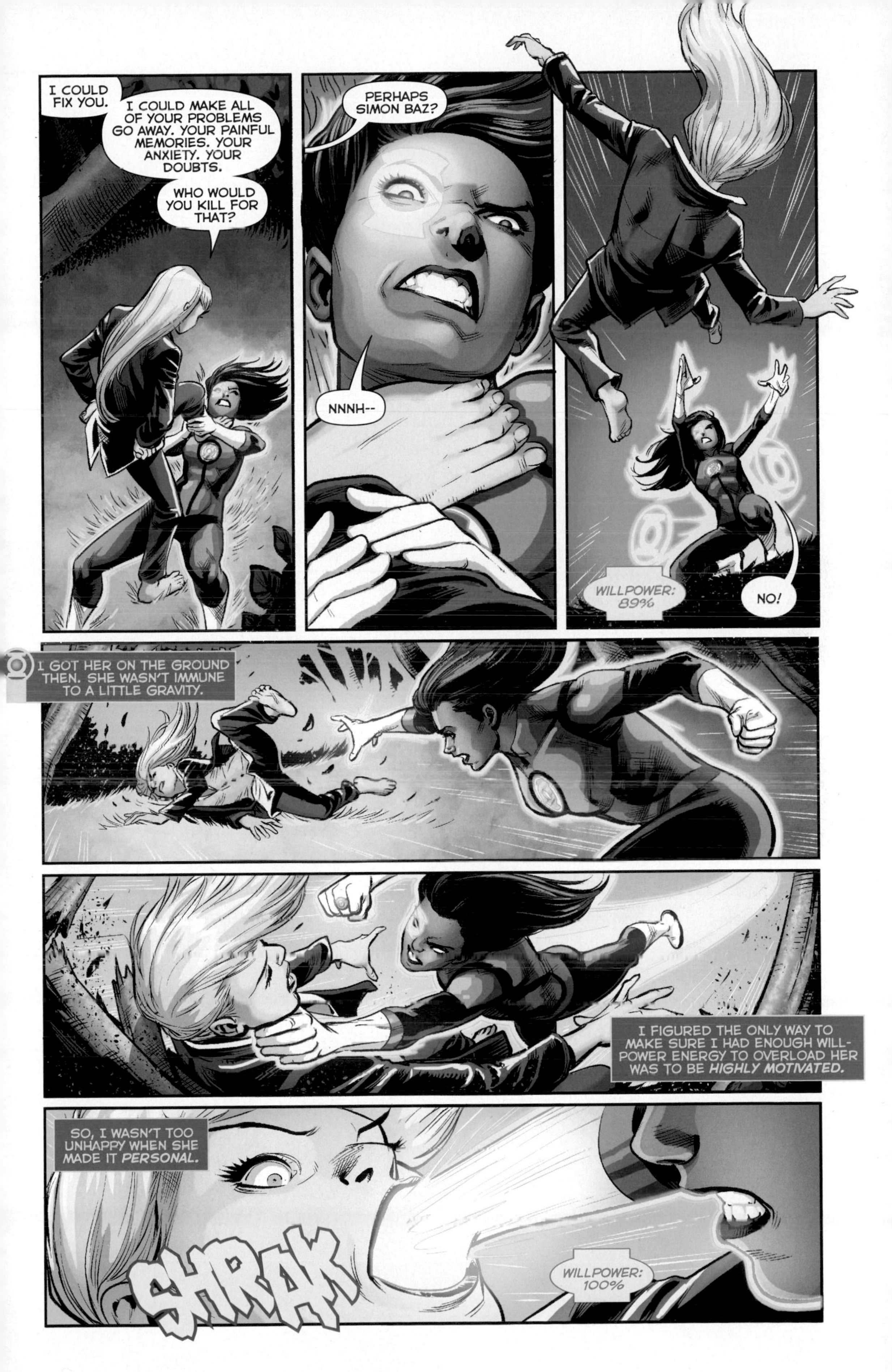
I COULD FIX YOU.
I COULD MAKE ALL OF YOUR PROBLEMS GO AWAY. YOUR PAINFUL MEMORIES. YOUR ANXIETY. YOUR DOUBTS.
WHO WOULD YOU KILL FOR THAT?
PERHAPS SIMON BAZ?
NNNH--
WILLPOWER: 89%
NO!
I GOT HER ON THE GROUND THEN. SHE WASN'T IMMUNE TO A LITTLE GRAVITY.
I FIGURED THE ONLY WAY TO MAKE SURE I HAD ENOUGH WILL-POWER ENERGY TO OVERLOAD HER WAS TO BE *HIGHLY MOTIVATED.*
SO, I WASN'T TOO UNHAPPY WHEN SHE MADE IT *PERSONAL.*
SHRAK
WILLPOWER: 100%

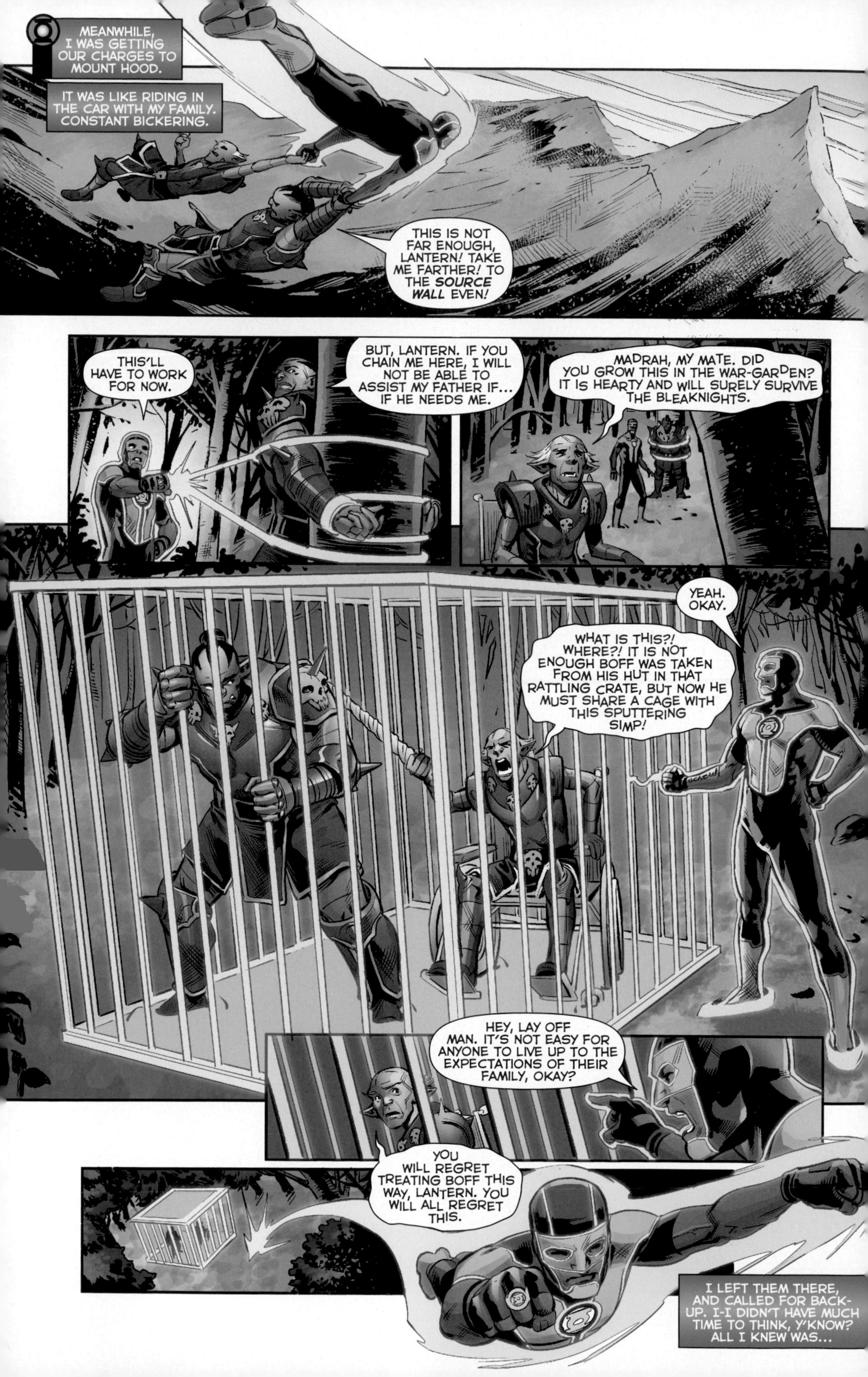
MEANWHILE, I WAS GETTING OUR CHARGES TO MOUNT HOOD.
IT WAS LIKE RIDING IN THE CAR WITH MY FAMILY. CONSTANT BICKERING.
THIS IS NOT FAR ENOUGH, LANTERN! TAKE ME FARTHER! TO THE SOURCE WALL EVEN!
THIS'LL HAVE TO WORK FOR NOW.
BUT, LANTERN. IF YOU CHAIN ME HERE, I WILL NOT BE ABLE TO ASSIST MY FATHER IF... IF HE NEEDS ME.
MADRAH, MY MATE. DID YOU GROW THIS IN THE WAR-GARDEN? IT IS HEARTY AND WILL SURELY SURVIVE THE BLEAKNIGHTS.
YEAH. OKAY.
WHAT IS THIS?! WHERE?! IT IS NOT ENOUGH BOFF WAS TAKEN FROM HIS HUT IN THAT RATTLING CRATE, BUT NOW HE MUST SHARE A CAGE WITH THIS SPUTTERING SIMP!
HEY, LAY OFF MAN. IT'S NOT EASY FOR ANYONE TO LIVE UP TO THE EXPECTATIONS OF THEIR FAMILY, OKAY?
YOU WILL REGRET TREATING BOFF THIS WAY, LANTERN. YOU WILL ALL REGRET THIS.
I LEFT THEM THERE, AND CALLED FOR BACK-UP. I-I DIDN'T HAVE MUCH TIME TO THINK, Y'KNOW? ALL I KNEW WAS...

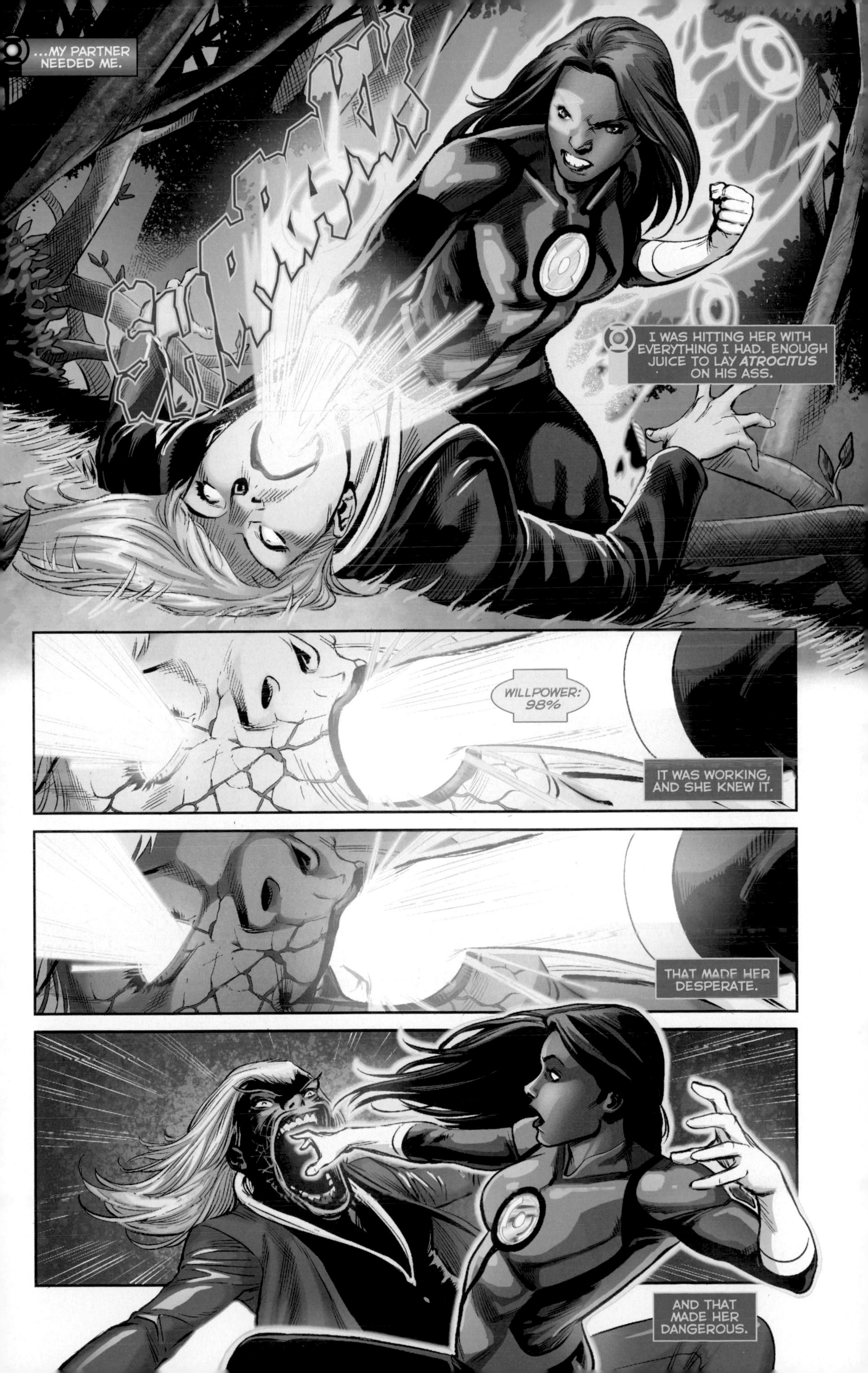
...MY PARTNER NEEDED ME.
SHRAKK!
I WAS HITTING HER WITH EVERYTHING I HAD. ENOUGH JUICE TO LAY *ATROCITUS* ON HIS ASS.
WILLPOWER: 98%
IT WAS WORKING, AND SHE KNEW IT.
THAT MADE HER DESPERATE.
AND THAT MADE HER DANGEROUS.

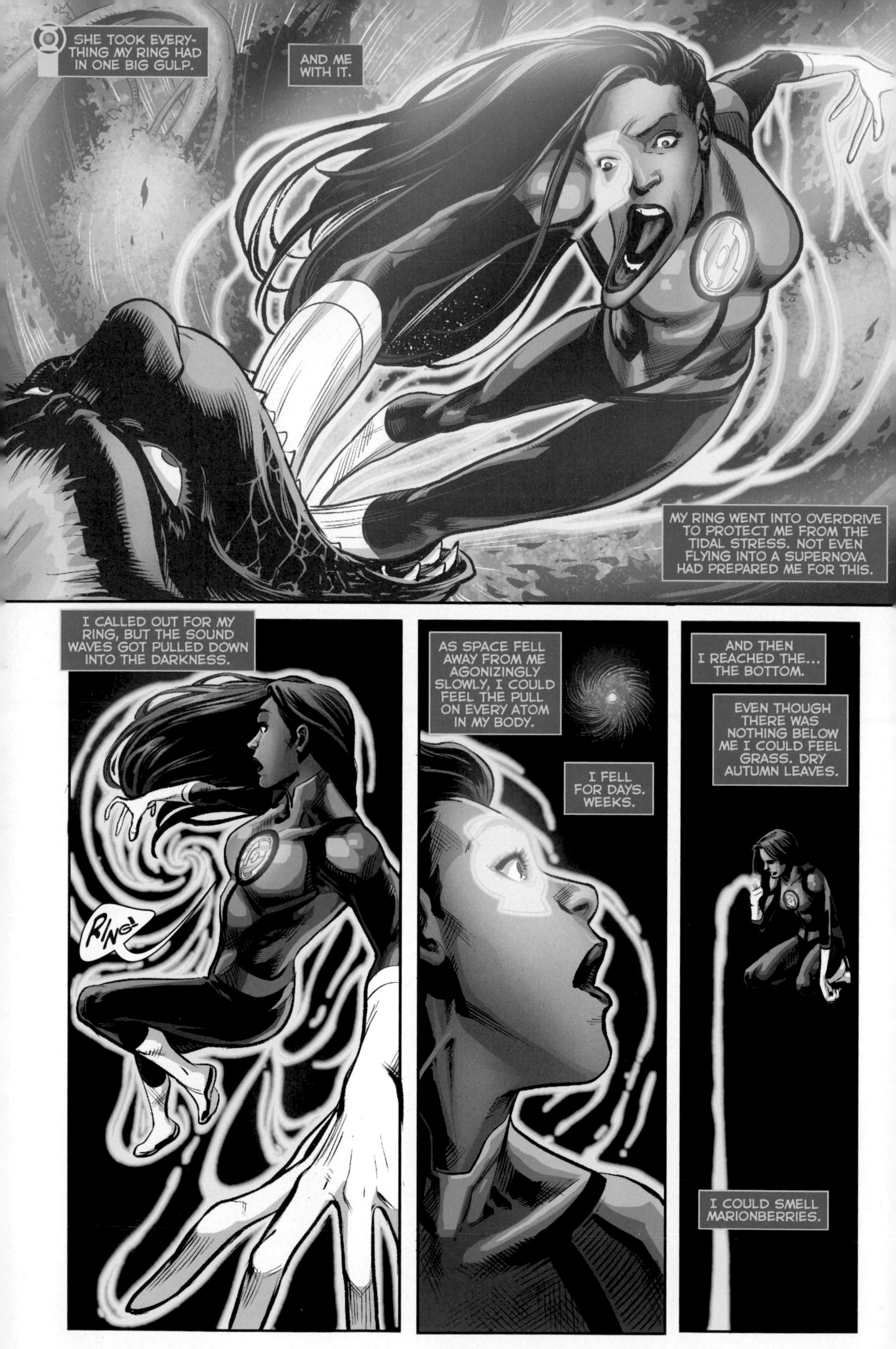
SHE TOOK EVERYTHING MY RING HAD IN ONE BIG GULP.
AND ME WITH IT.
MY RING WENT INTO OVERDRIVE TO PROTECT ME FROM THE TIDAL STRESS. NOT EVEN FLYING INTO A SUPERNOVA HAD PREPARED ME FOR THIS.
I CALLED OUT FOR MY RING, BUT THE SOUND WAVES GOT PULLED DOWN INTO THE DARKNESS.
RING!
AS SPACE FELL AWAY FROM ME AGONIZINGLY SLOWLY, I COULD FEEL THE PULL ON EVERY ATOM IN MY BODY.
I FELL FOR DAYS. WEEKS.
AND THEN I REACHED THE... THE BOTTOM.
EVEN THOUGH THERE WAS NOTHING BELOW ME I COULD FEEL GRASS. DRY AUTUMN LEAVES.
I COULD SMELL MARIONBERRIES.

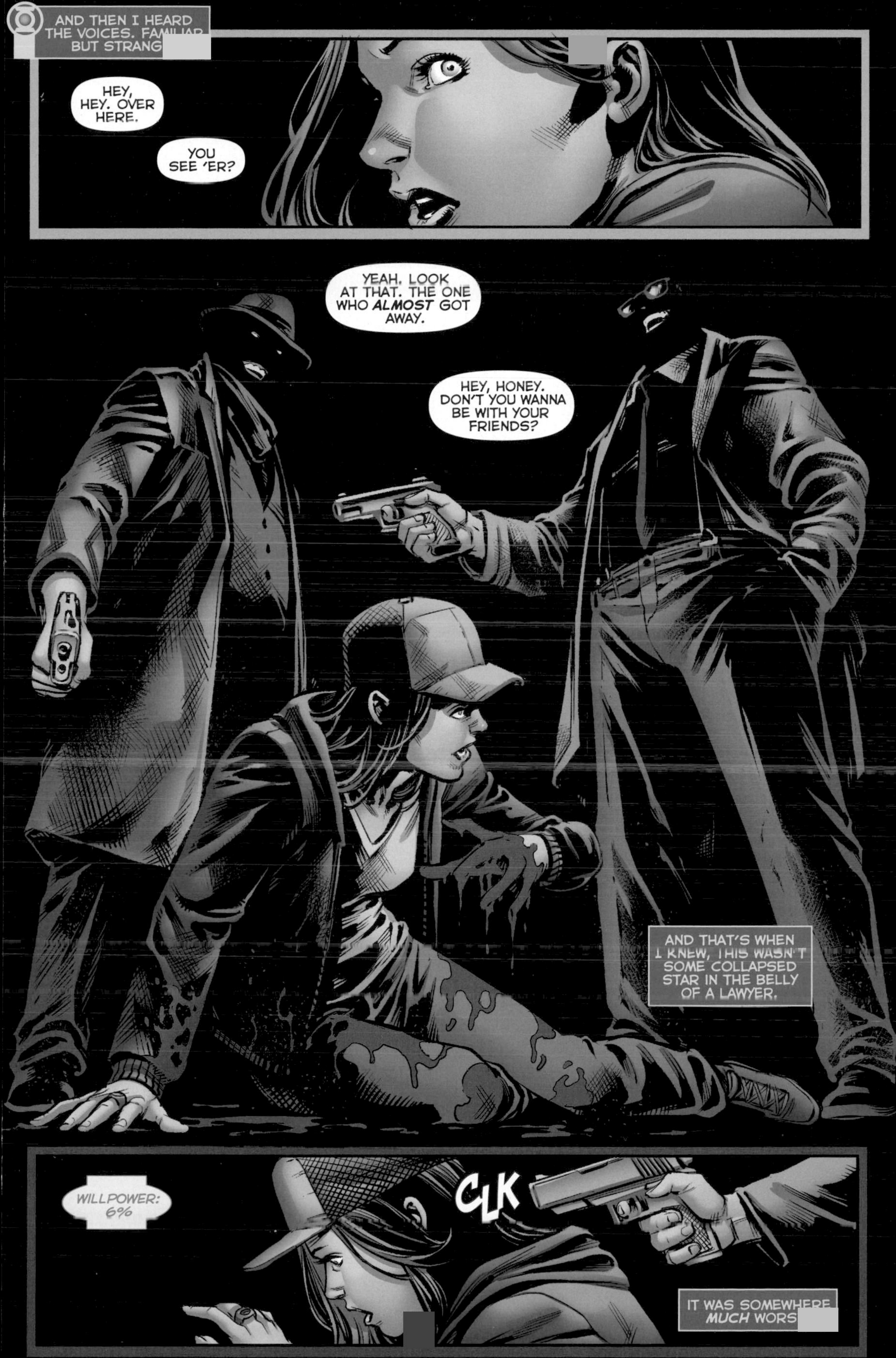

AND THEN I HEARD THE VOICES. FAMILIAR BUT STRANG
HEY, HEY. OVER HERE.
YOU SEE 'ER?
YEAH. LOOK AT THAT. THE ONE WHO *ALMOST* GOT AWAY.
HEY, HONEY. DON'T YOU WANNA BE WITH YOUR FRIENDS?
AND THAT'S WHEN I KNEW, THIS WASN'T SOME COLLAPSED STAR IN THE BELLY OF A LAWYER.
WILLPOWER: 6%
CLK
IT WAS SOMEWHERE *MUCH* WORS

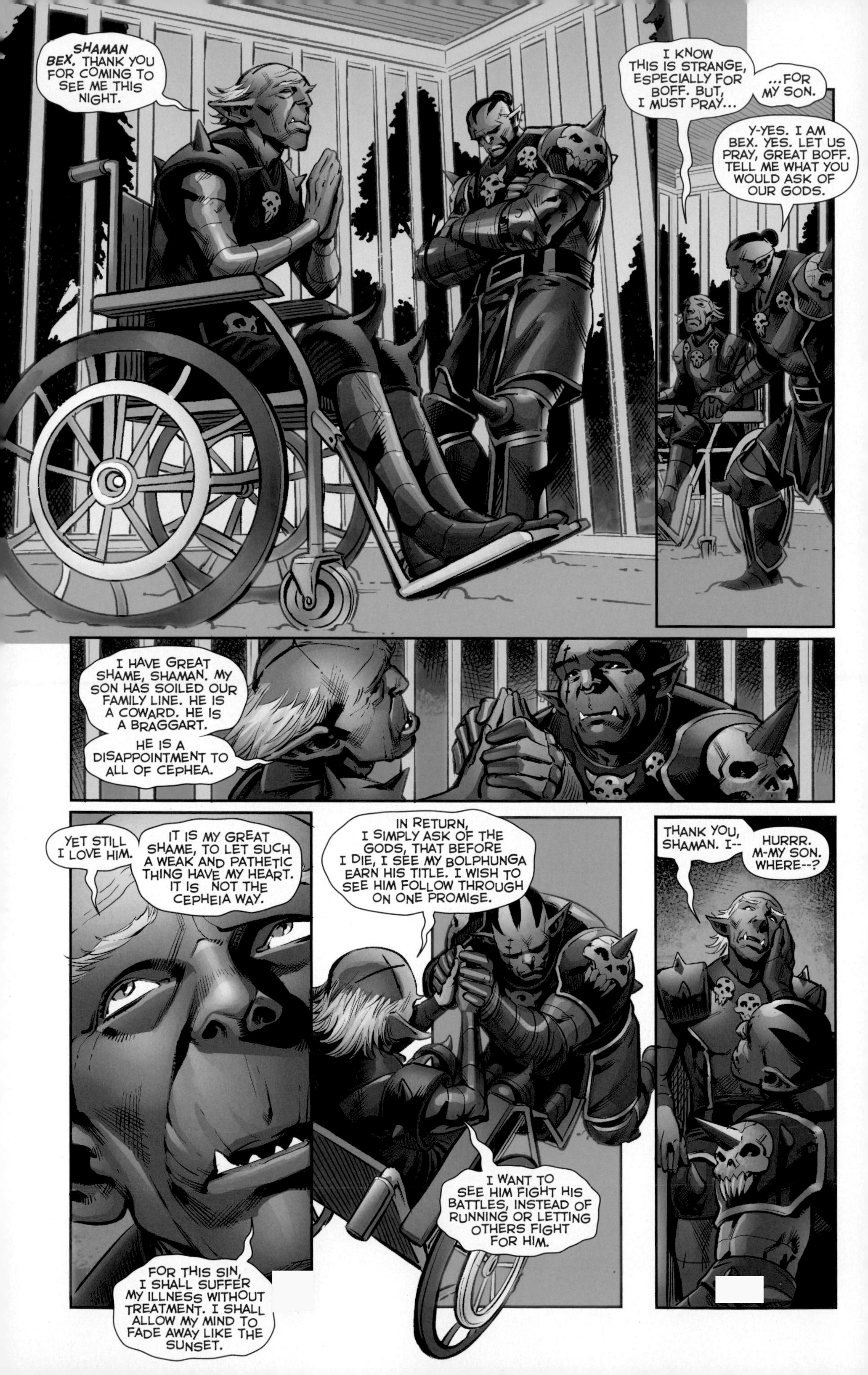
SHAMAN BEX. THANK YOU FOR COMING TO SEE ME THIS NIGHT.
I KNOW THIS IS STRANGE, ESPECIALLY FOR BOFF. BUT, I MUST PRAY...
...FOR MY SON.
Y-YES. I AM BEX. YES. LET US PRAY, GREAT BOFF. TELL ME WHAT YOU WOULD ASK OF OUR GODS.
I HAVE GREAT SHAME, SHAMAN. MY SON HAS SOILED OUR FAMILY LINE. HE IS A COWARD. HE IS A BRAGGART.
HE IS A DISAPPOINTMENT TO ALL OF CEPHEA.
YET STILL I LOVE HIM.
IT IS MY GREAT SHAME, TO LET SUCH A WEAK AND PATHETIC THING HAVE MY HEART. IT IS NOT THE CEPHEIA WAY.
FOR THIS SIN, I SHALL SUFFER MY ILLNESS WITHOUT TREATMENT. I SHALL ALLOW MY MIND TO FADE AWAY LIKE THE SUNSET.
IN RETURN, I SIMPLY ASK OF THE GODS, THAT BEFORE I DIE, I SEE MY BOLPHUNGA EARN HIS TITLE. I WISH TO SEE HIM FOLLOW THROUGH ON ONE PROMISE.
I WANT TO SEE HIM FIGHT HIS BATTLES, INSTEAD OF RUNNING OR LETTING OTHERS FIGHT FOR HIM.
THANK YOU, SHAMAN. I--
HURRR. M-MY SON. WHERE--?

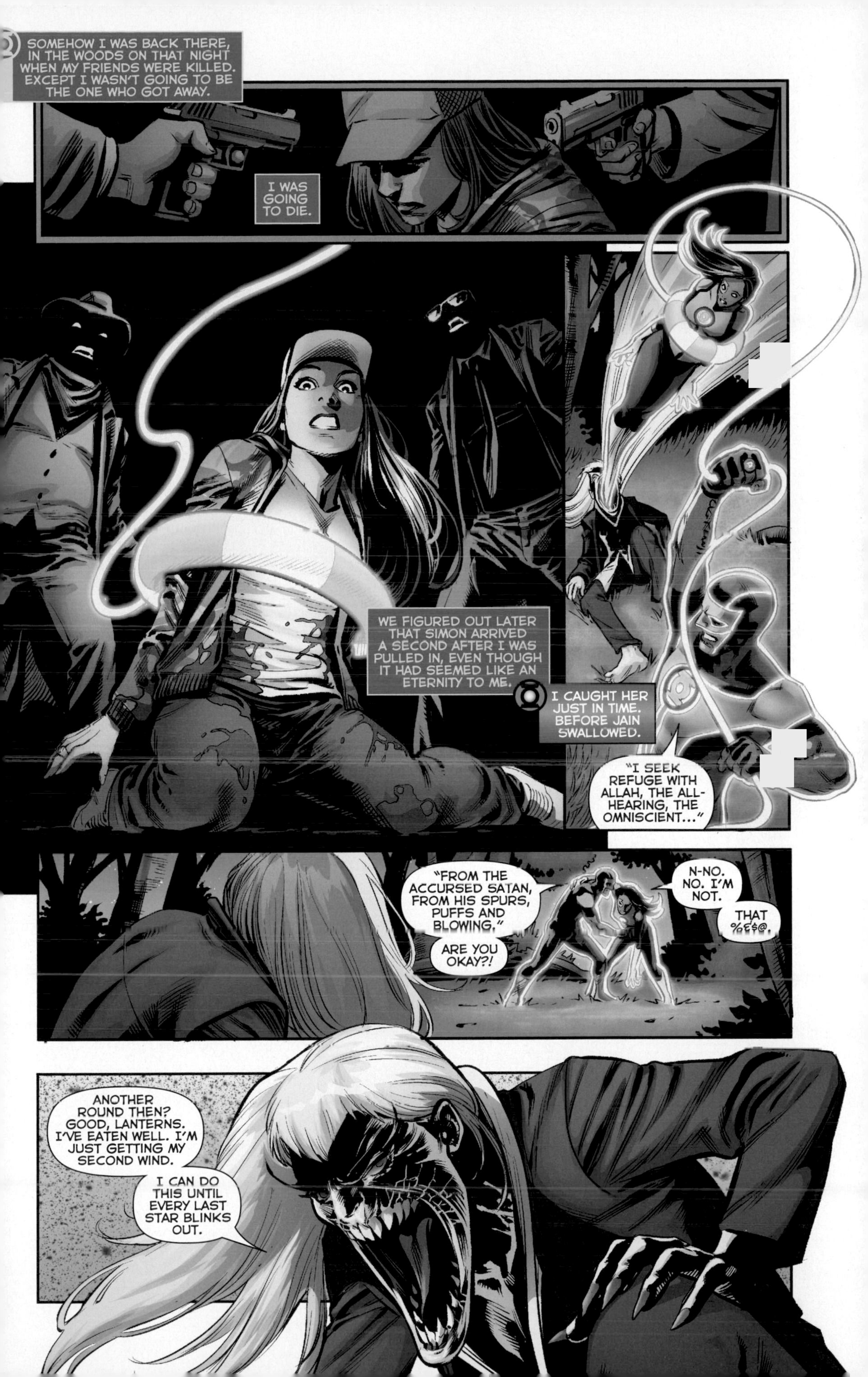
SOMEHOW I WAS BACK THERE, IN THE WOODS ON THAT NIGHT WHEN MY FRIENDS WERE KILLED. EXCEPT I WASN'T GOING TO BE THE ONE WHO GOT AWAY.
I WAS GOING TO DIE.
WE FIGURED OUT LATER THAT SIMON ARRIVED A SECOND AFTER I WAS PULLED IN, EVEN THOUGH IT HAD SEEMED LIKE AN ETERNITY TO ME.
I CAUGHT HER JUST IN TIME. BEFORE JAIN SWALLOWED.
"I SEEK REFUGE WITH ALLAH, THE ALL-HEARING, THE OMNISCIENT..."
"FROM THE ACCURSED SATAN, FROM HIS SPURS, PUFFS AND BLOWING."
ARE YOU OKAY?!
N-NO. NO. I'M NOT.
THAT %£$@.
ANOTHER ROUND THEN? GOOD, LANTERNS. I'VE EATEN WELL. I'M JUST GETTING MY SECOND WIND.
I CAN DO THIS UNTIL EVERY LAST STAR BLINKS OUT.

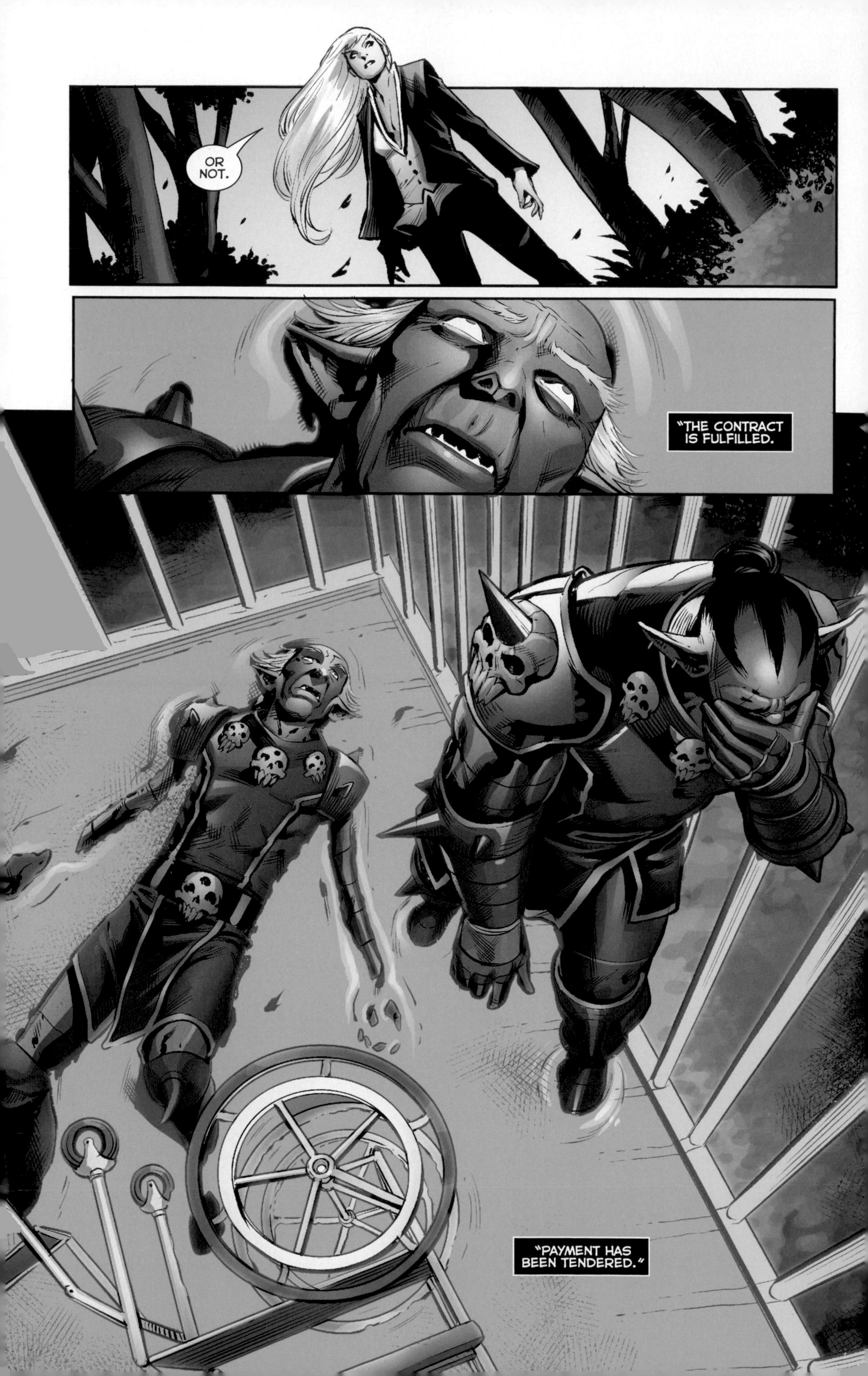
OR NOT.
"THE CONTRACT IS FULFILLED.
"PAYMENT HAS BEEN TENDERED."

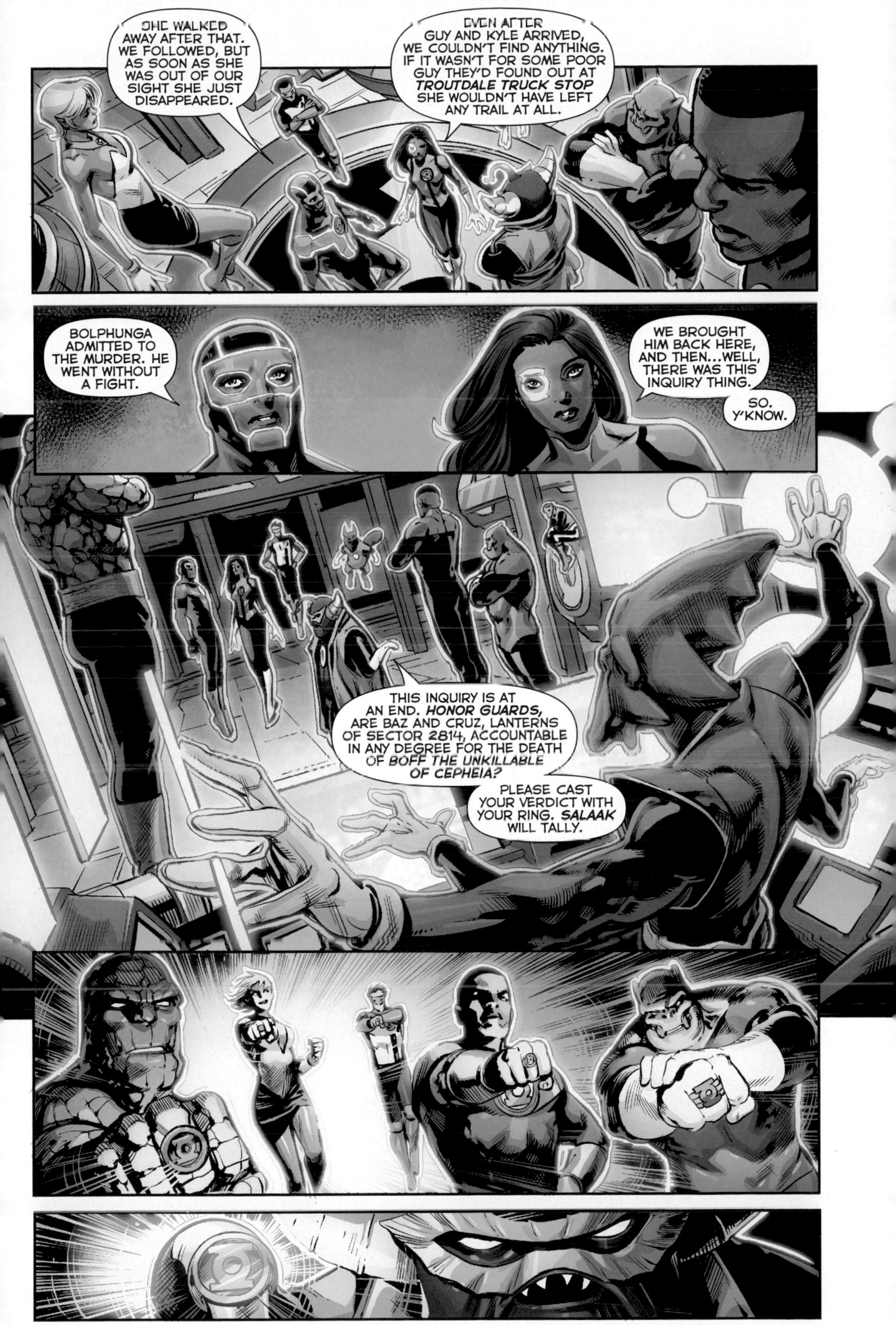
SHE WALKED AWAY AFTER THAT. WE FOLLOWED, BUT AS SOON AS SHE WAS OUT OF OUR SIGHT SHE JUST DISAPPEARED.
EVEN AFTER GUY AND KYLE ARRIVED, WE COULDN'T FIND ANYTHING. IF IT WASN'T FOR SOME POOR GUY THEY'D FOUND OUT AT TROUTDALE TRUCK STOP SHE WOULDN'T HAVE LEFT ANY TRAIL AT ALL.
BOLPHUNGA ADMITTED TO THE MURDER. HE WENT WITHOUT A FIGHT.
WE BROUGHT HIM BACK HERE, AND THEN...WELL, THERE WAS THIS INQUIRY THING.
SO. Y'KNOW.
THIS INQUIRY IS AT AN END. HONOR GUARDS, ARE BAZ AND CRUZ, LANTERNS OF SECTOR 2814, ACCOUNTABLE IN ANY DEGREE FOR THE DEATH OF BOFF THE UNKILLABLE OF CEPHEIA?
PLEASE CAST YOUR VERDICT WITH YOUR RING. SALAAK WILL TALLY.

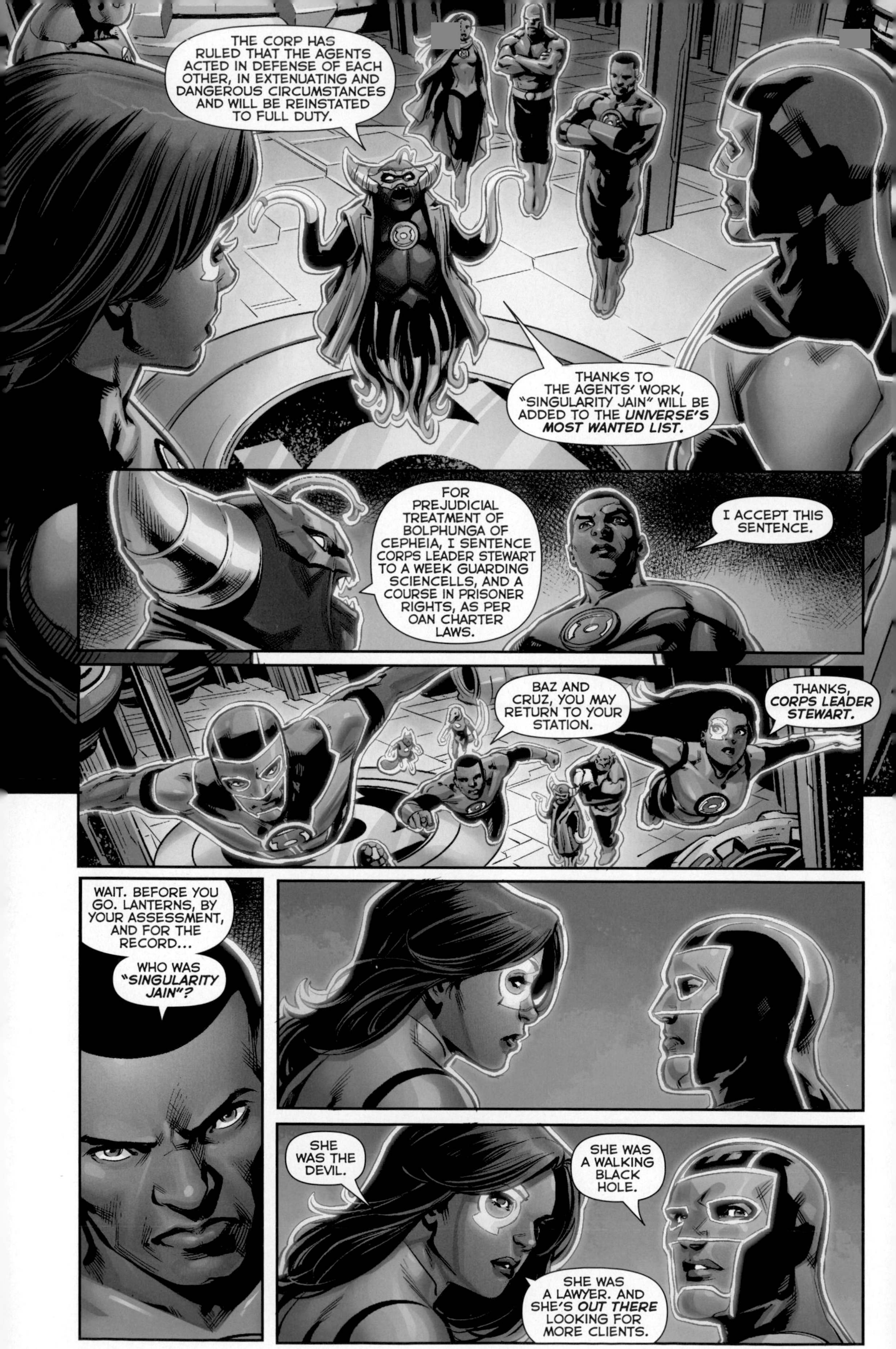
THE CORP HAS RULED THAT THE AGENTS ACTED IN DEFENSE OF EACH OTHER, IN EXTENUATING AND DANGEROUS CIRCUMSTANCES AND WILL BE REINSTATED TO FULL DUTY.
THANKS TO THE AGENTS' WORK, "SINGULARITY JAIN" WILL BE ADDED TO THE *UNIVERSE'S MOST WANTED LIST.*
FOR PREJUDICIAL TREATMENT OF BOLPHUNGA OF CEPHEIA, I SENTENCE CORPS LEADER STEWART TO A WEEK GUARDING SCIENCELLS, AND A COURSE IN PRISONER RIGHTS, AS PER OAN CHARTER LAWS.
I ACCEPT THIS SENTENCE.
BAZ AND CRUZ, YOU MAY RETURN TO YOUR STATION.
THANKS, *CORPS LEADER STEWART.*
WAIT. BEFORE YOU GO. LANTERNS, BY YOUR ASSESSMENT, AND FOR THE RECORD...
WHO WAS *"SINGULARITY JAIN"?*
SHE WAS THE DEVIL.
SHE WAS A WALKING BLACK HOLE.
SHE WAS A LAWYER. AND SHE'S *OUT THERE* LOOKING FOR MORE CLIENTS.

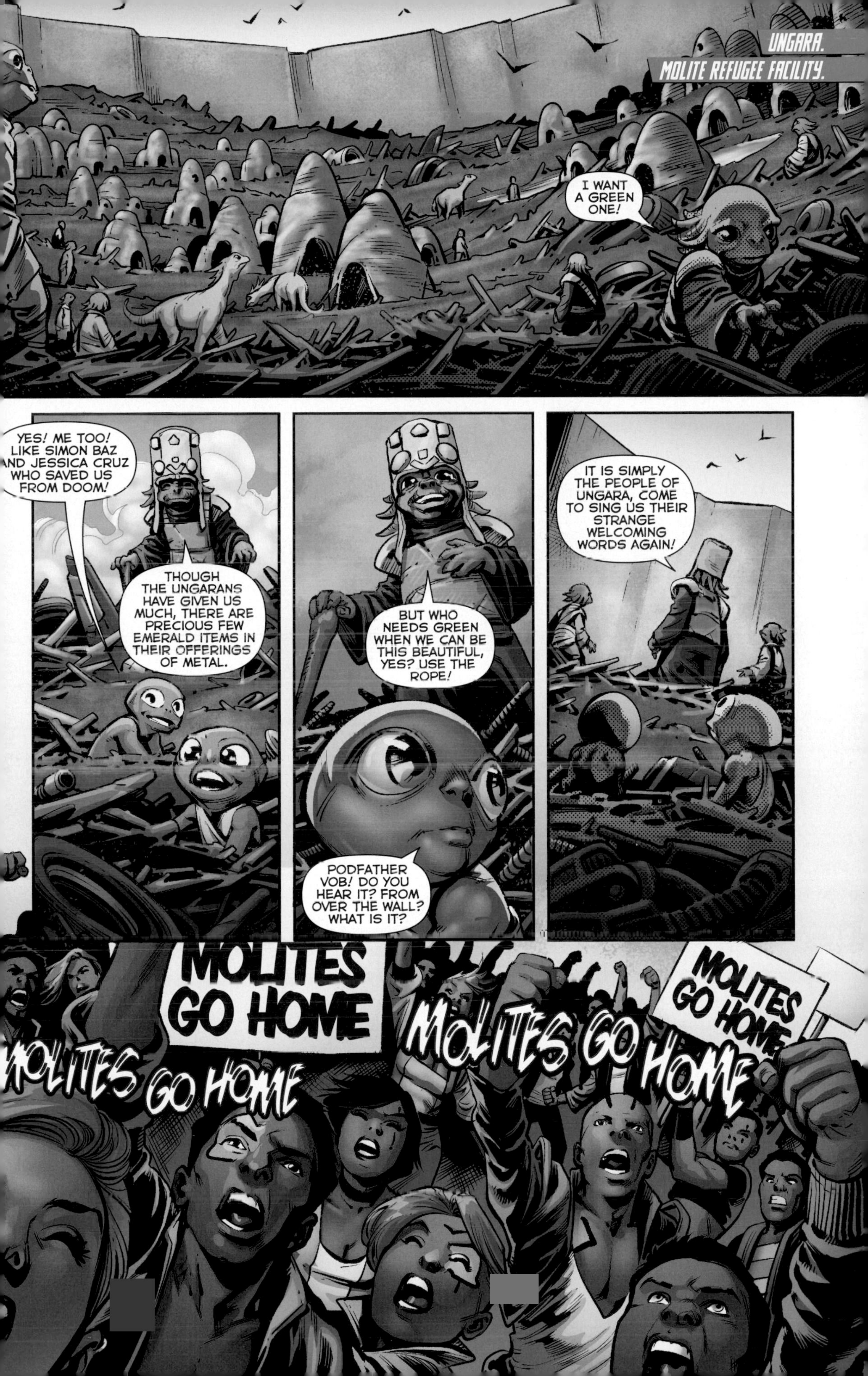
UNGARA.
MOLITE REFUGEE FACILITY.
I WANT A GREEN ONE!
YES! ME TOO! LIKE SIMON BAZ AND JESSICA CRUZ WHO SAVED US FROM DOOM!
THOUGH THE UNGARANS HAVE GIVEN US MUCH, THERE ARE PRECIOUS FEW EMERALD ITEMS IN THEIR OFFERINGS OF METAL.
BUT WHO NEEDS GREEN WHEN WE CAN BE THIS BEAUTIFUL, YES? USE THE ROPE!
PODFATHER VOB! DO YOU HEAR IT? FROM OVER THE WALL? WHAT IS IT?
IT IS SIMPLY THE PEOPLE OF UNGARA, COME TO SING US THEIR STRANGE WELCOMING WORDS AGAIN!
MOLITES GO HOME
MOLITES GO HOME
MOLITES GO HOME
MOLITES GO HOME

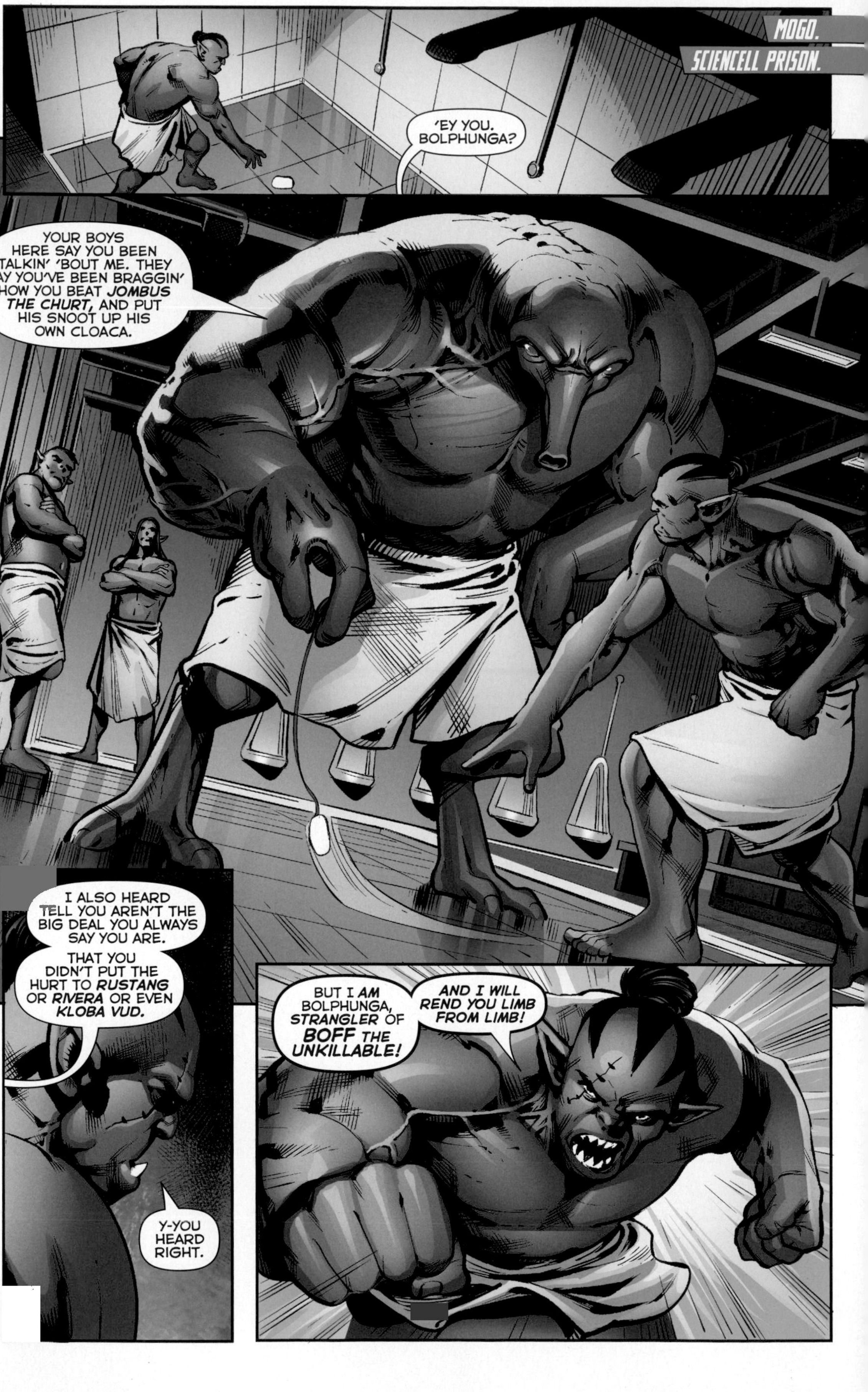
MOGO.
SCIENCELL PRISON.
'EY YOU. BOLPHUNGA?
YOUR BOYS HERE SAY YOU BEEN TALKIN' 'BOUT ME. THEY SAY YOU'VE BEEN BRAGGIN' HOW YOU BEAT JOMBUS THE CHURT, AND PUT HIS SNOOT UP HIS OWN CLOACA.
I ALSO HEARD TELL YOU AREN'T THE BIG DEAL YOU ALWAYS SAY YOU ARE.
THAT YOU DIDN'T PUT THE HURT TO RUSTANG OR RIVERA OR EVEN KLOBA VUD.
Y-YOU HEARD RIGHT.
BUT I AM BOLPHUNGA, STRANGLER OF BOFF THE UNKILLABLE!
AND I WILL REND YOU LIMB FROM LIMB!

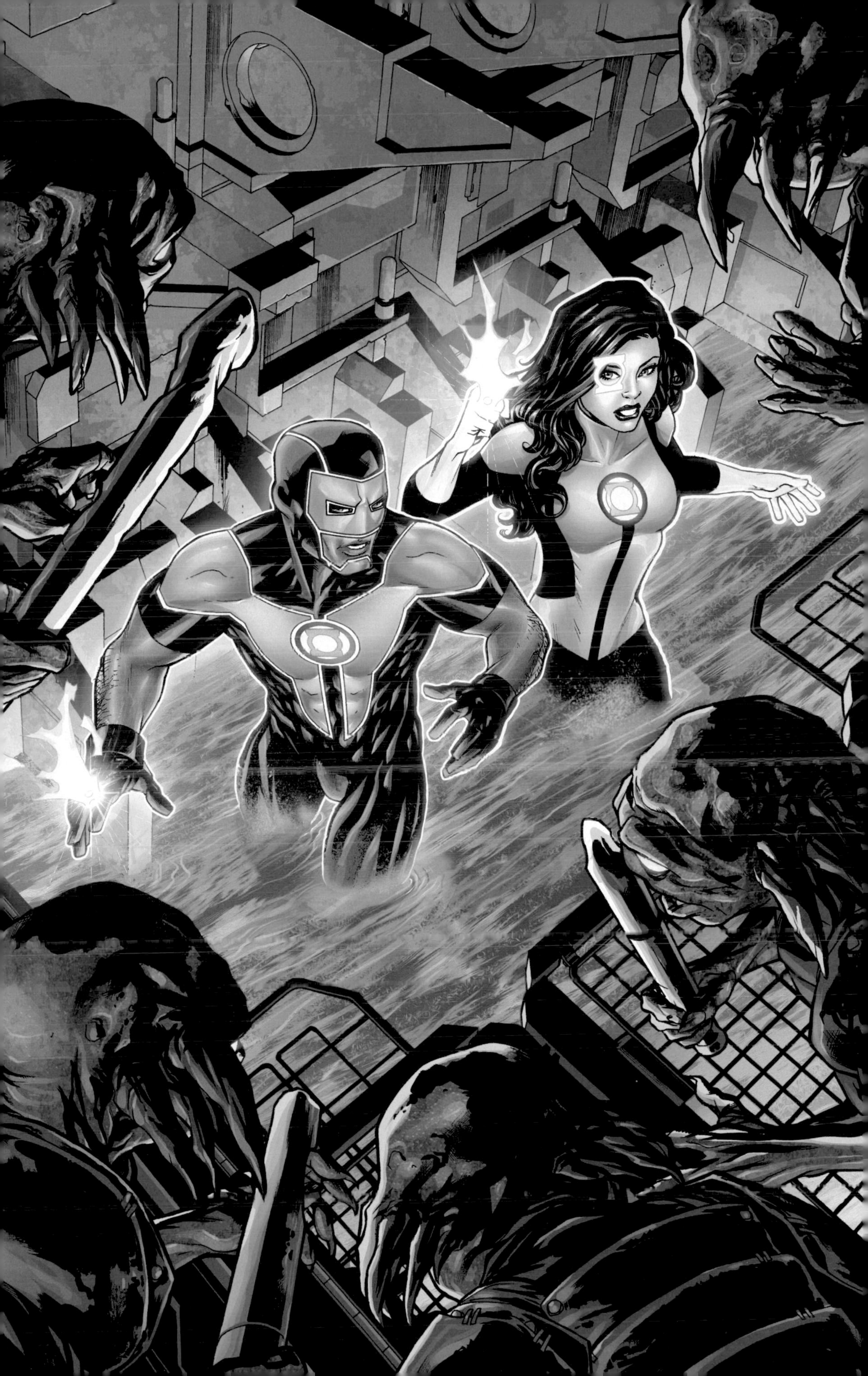

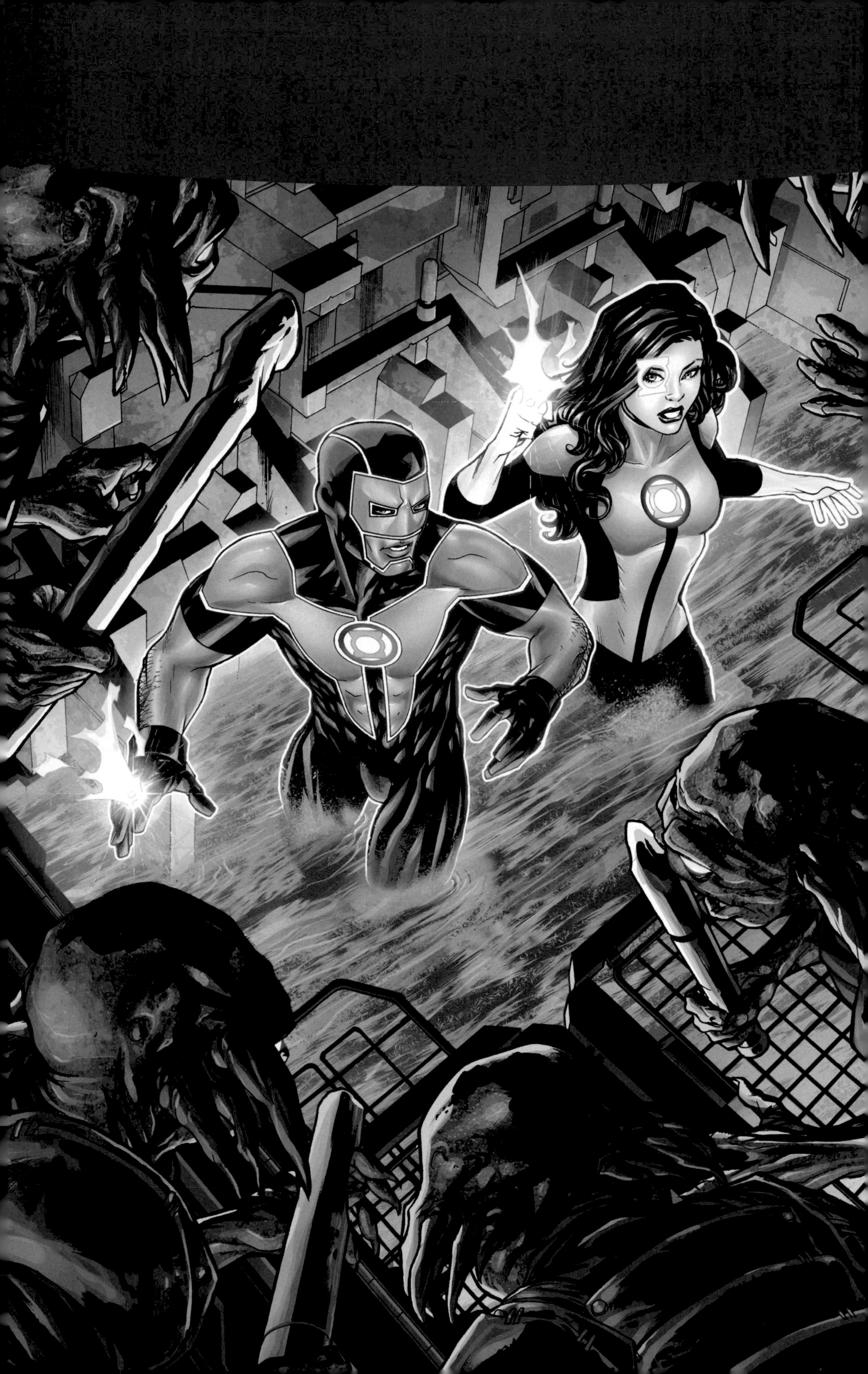

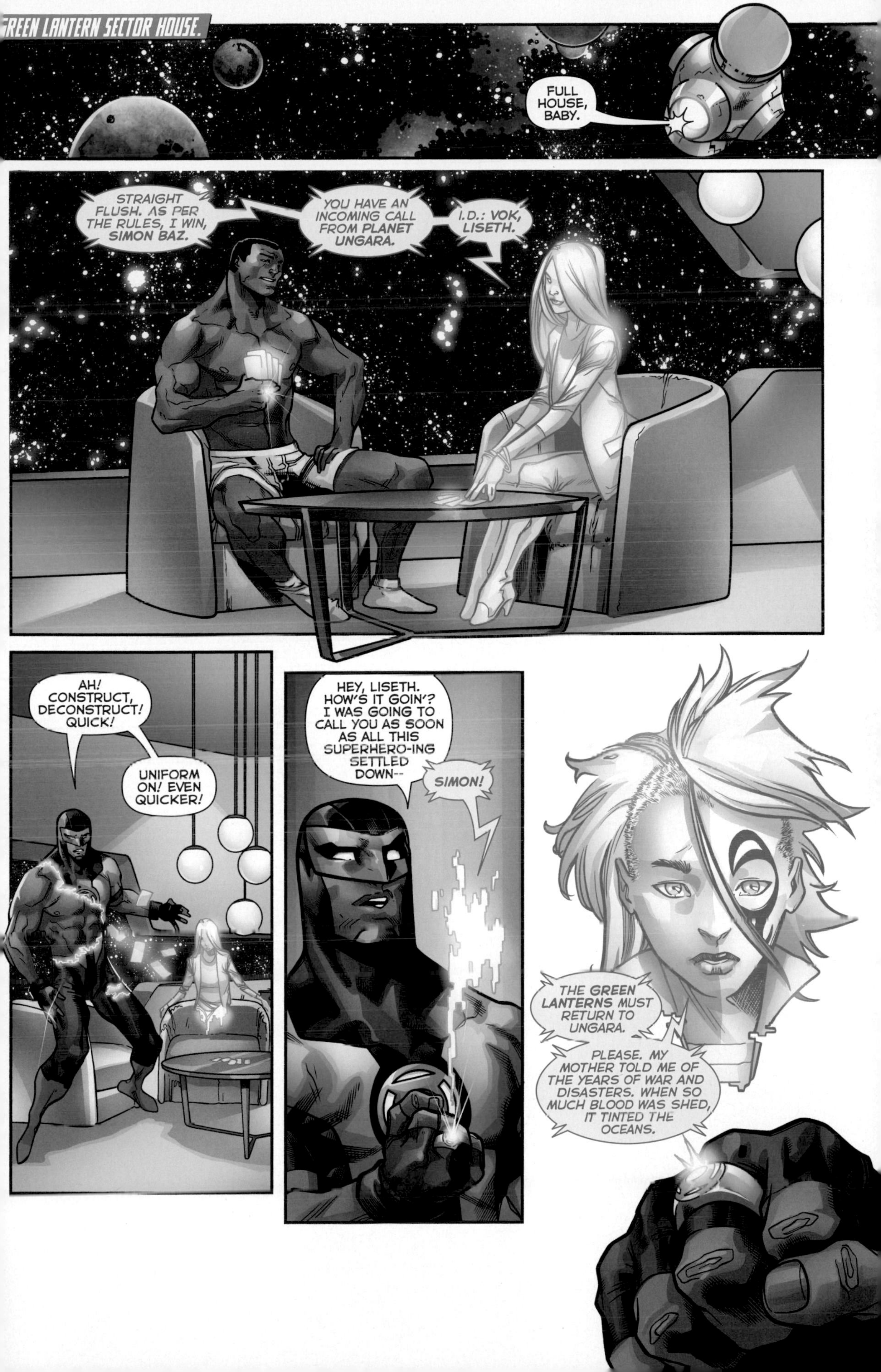
GREEN LANTERN SECTOR HOUSE.
FULL HOUSE, BABY.
STRAIGHT FLUSH. AS PER THE RULES, I WIN, SIMON BAZ.
YOU HAVE AN INCOMING CALL FROM PLANET UNGARA.
I.D.: VOK, LISETH.
AH! CONSTRUCT, DECONSTRUCT! QUICK!
UNIFORM ON! EVEN QUICKER!
HEY, LISETH. HOW'S IT GOIN'? I WAS GOING TO CALL YOU AS SOON AS ALL THIS SUPERHERO-ING SETTLED DOWN--
SIMON!
THE GREEN LANTERNS MUST RETURN TO UNGARA.
PLEASE. MY MOTHER TOLD ME OF THE YEARS OF WAR AND DISASTERS. WHEN SO MUCH BLOOD WAS SHED, IT TINTED THE OCEANS.

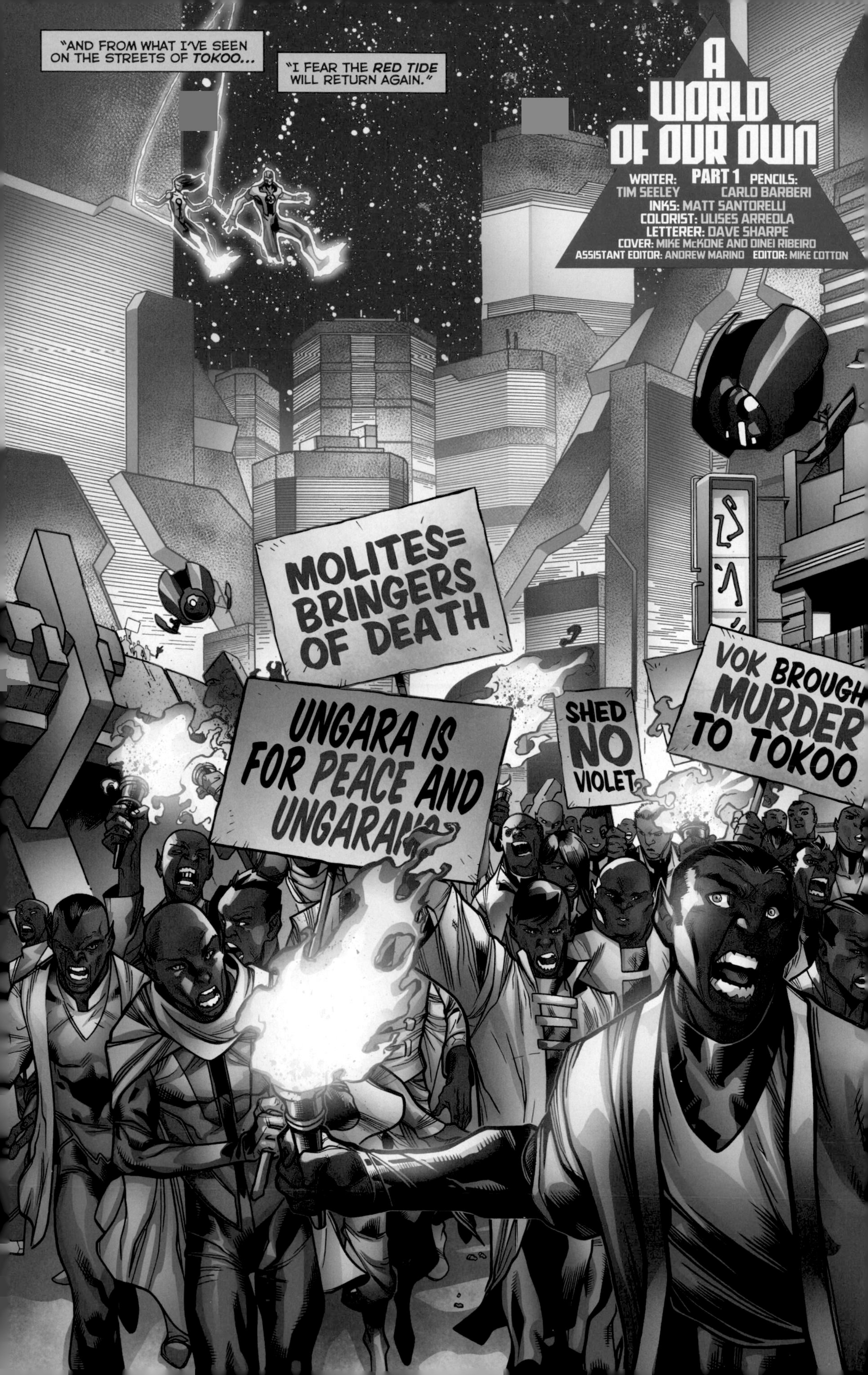
"AND FROM WHAT I'VE SEEN ON THE STREETS OF TOKOO...
"I FEAR THE RED TIDE WILL RETURN AGAIN."
A WORLD OF OUR OWN
PART 1
WRITER: TIM SEELEY PENCILS: CARLO BARBERI
INKS: MATT SANTORELLI
COLORIST: ULISES ARREOLA
LETTERER: DAVE SHARPE
COVER: MIKE McKONE AND DINEI RIBEIRO
ASSISTANT EDITOR: ANDREW MARINO EDITOR: MIKE COTTON
MOLITES= BRINGERS OF DEATH
UNGARA IS FOR PEACE AND UNGARAN
SHED NO VIOLET
VOK BROUGH MURDER TO TOKOO

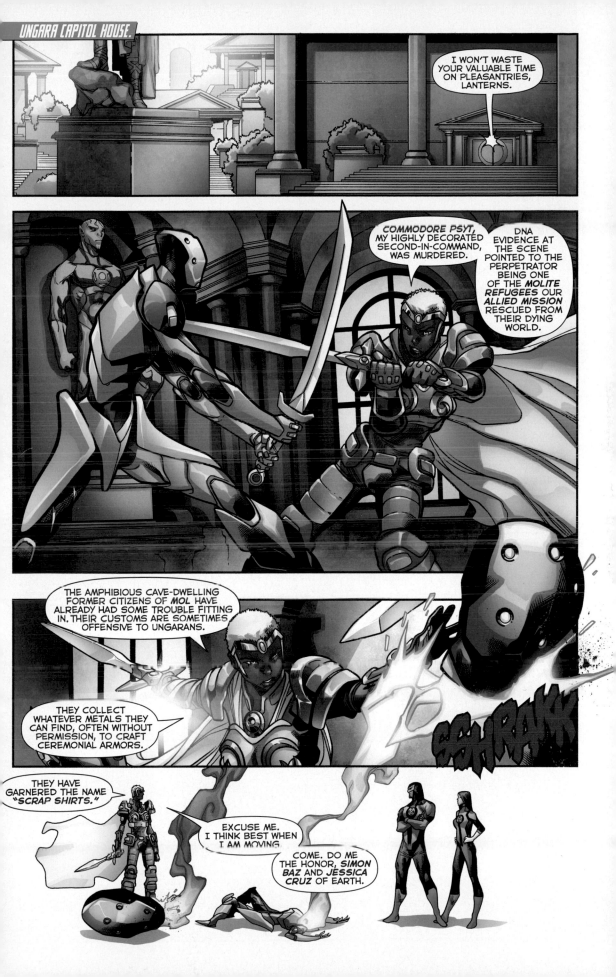

UNGARA CAPITOL HOUSE.

I WON'T WASTE YOUR VALUABLE TIME ON PLEASANTRIES, LANTERNS.

COMMODORE PSYT, MY HIGHLY DECORATED SECOND-IN-COMMAND, WAS MURDERED.

DNA EVIDENCE AT THE SCENE POINTED TO THE PERPETRATOR BEING ONE OF THE *MOLITE REFUGEES* OUR *ALLIED MISSION* RESCUED FROM THEIR DYING WORLD.

THE AMPHIBIOUS CAVE-DWELLING FORMER CITIZENS OF *MOL* HAVE ALREADY HAD SOME TROUBLE FITTING IN. THEIR CUSTOMS ARE SOMETIMES OFFENSIVE TO UNGARANS.

THEY COLLECT WHATEVER METALS THEY CAN FIND, OFTEN WITHOUT PERMISSION, TO CRAFT CEREMONIAL ARMORS.

SSHRAKK

THEY HAVE GARNERED THE NAME *"SCRAP SHIRTS."*

EXCUSE ME. I THINK BEST WHEN I AM MOVING.

COME. DO ME THE HONOR, *SIMON BAZ* AND *JESSICA CRUZ* OF EARTH.

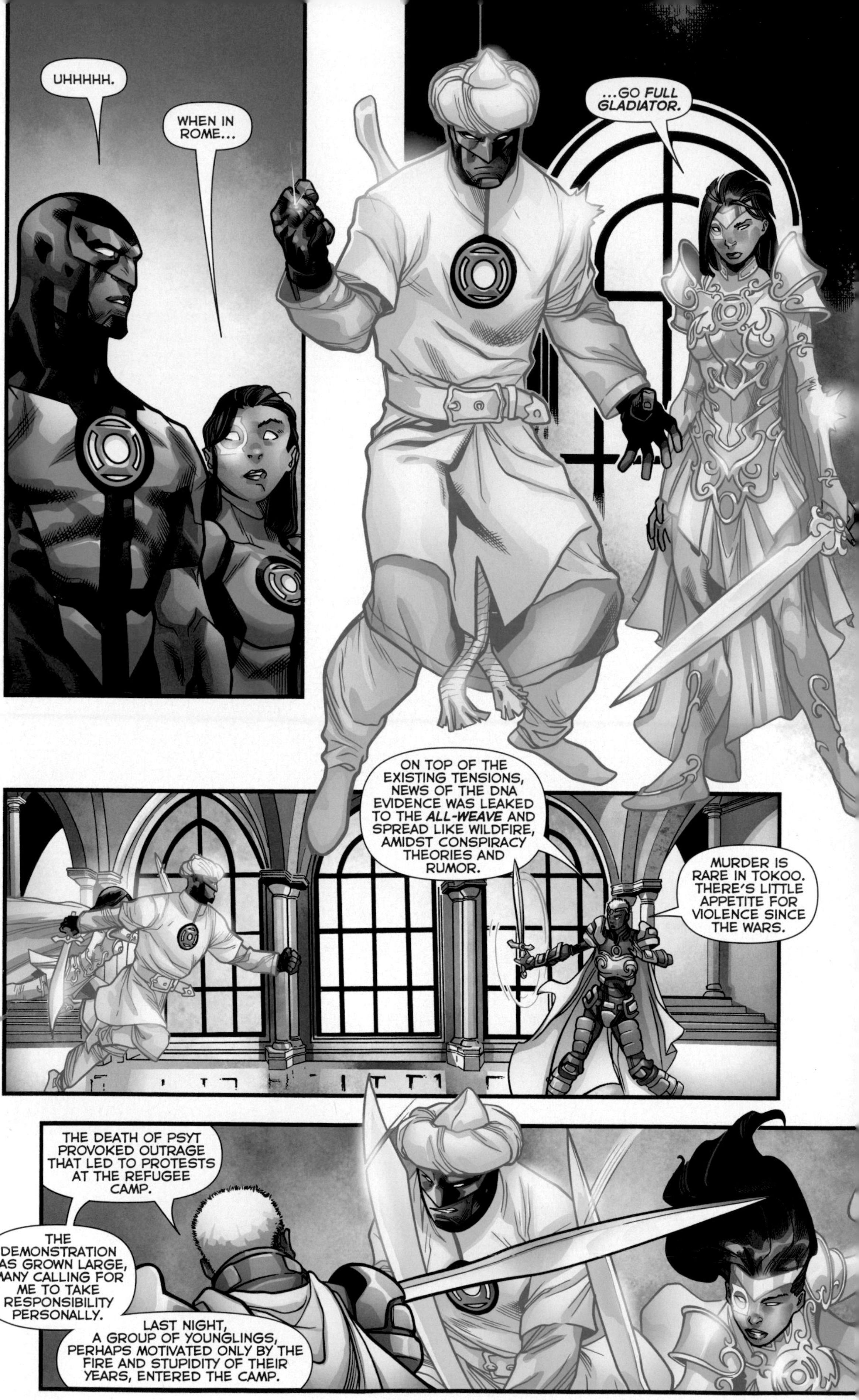
UHHHHH.
WHEN IN ROME...
...GO FULL GLADIATOR.
ON TOP OF THE EXISTING TENSIONS, NEWS OF THE DNA EVIDENCE WAS LEAKED TO THE ALL-WEAVE AND SPREAD LIKE WILDFIRE, AMIDST CONSPIRACY THEORIES AND RUMOR.
MURDER IS RARE IN TOKOO. THERE'S LITTLE APPETITE FOR VIOLENCE SINCE THE WARS.
THE DEATH OF PSYT PROVOKED OUTRAGE THAT LED TO PROTESTS AT THE REFUGEE CAMP.
THE DEMONSTRATION HAS GROWN LARGE, MANY CALLING FOR ME TO TAKE RESPONSIBILITY PERSONALLY.
LAST NIGHT, A GROUP OF YOUNGLINGS, PERHAPS MOTIVATED ONLY BY THE FIRE AND STUPIDITY OF THEIR YEARS, ENTERED THE CAMP.

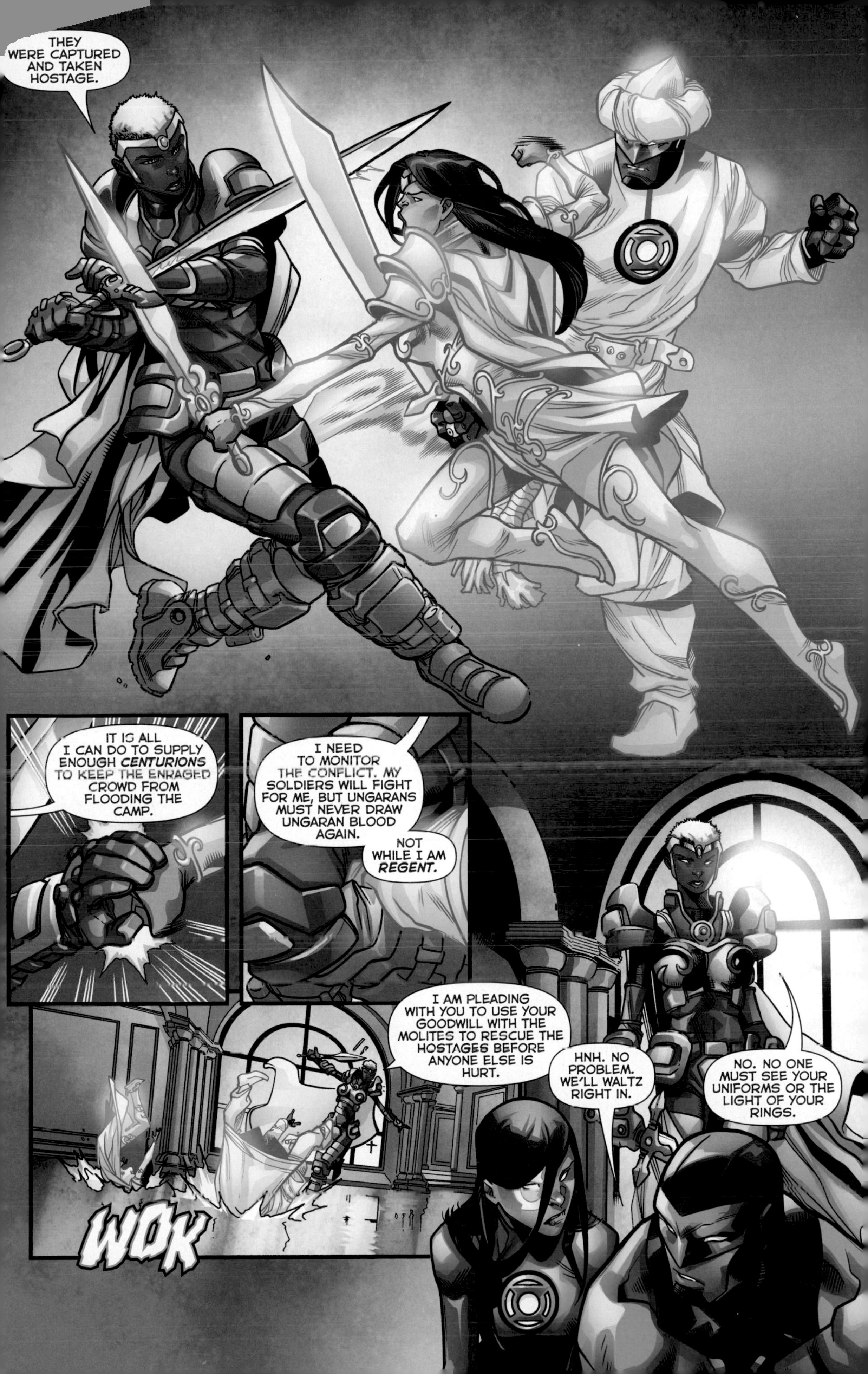
THEY WERE CAPTURED AND TAKEN HOSTAGE.
IT IS ALL I CAN DO TO SUPPLY ENOUGH *CENTURIONS* TO KEEP THE ENRAGED CROWD FROM FLOODING THE CAMP.
I NEED TO MONITOR THE CONFLICT. MY SOLDIERS WILL FIGHT FOR ME, BUT UNGARANS MUST NEVER DRAW UNGARAN BLOOD AGAIN.
NOT WHILE I AM *REGENT.*
WOK
I AM PLEADING WITH YOU TO USE YOUR GOODWILL WITH THE MOLITES TO RESCUE THE HOSTAGES BEFORE ANYONE ELSE IS HURT.
HNH. NO PROBLEM. WE'LL WALTZ RIGHT IN.
NO. NO ONE MUST SEE YOUR UNIFORMS OR THE LIGHT OF YOUR RINGS.

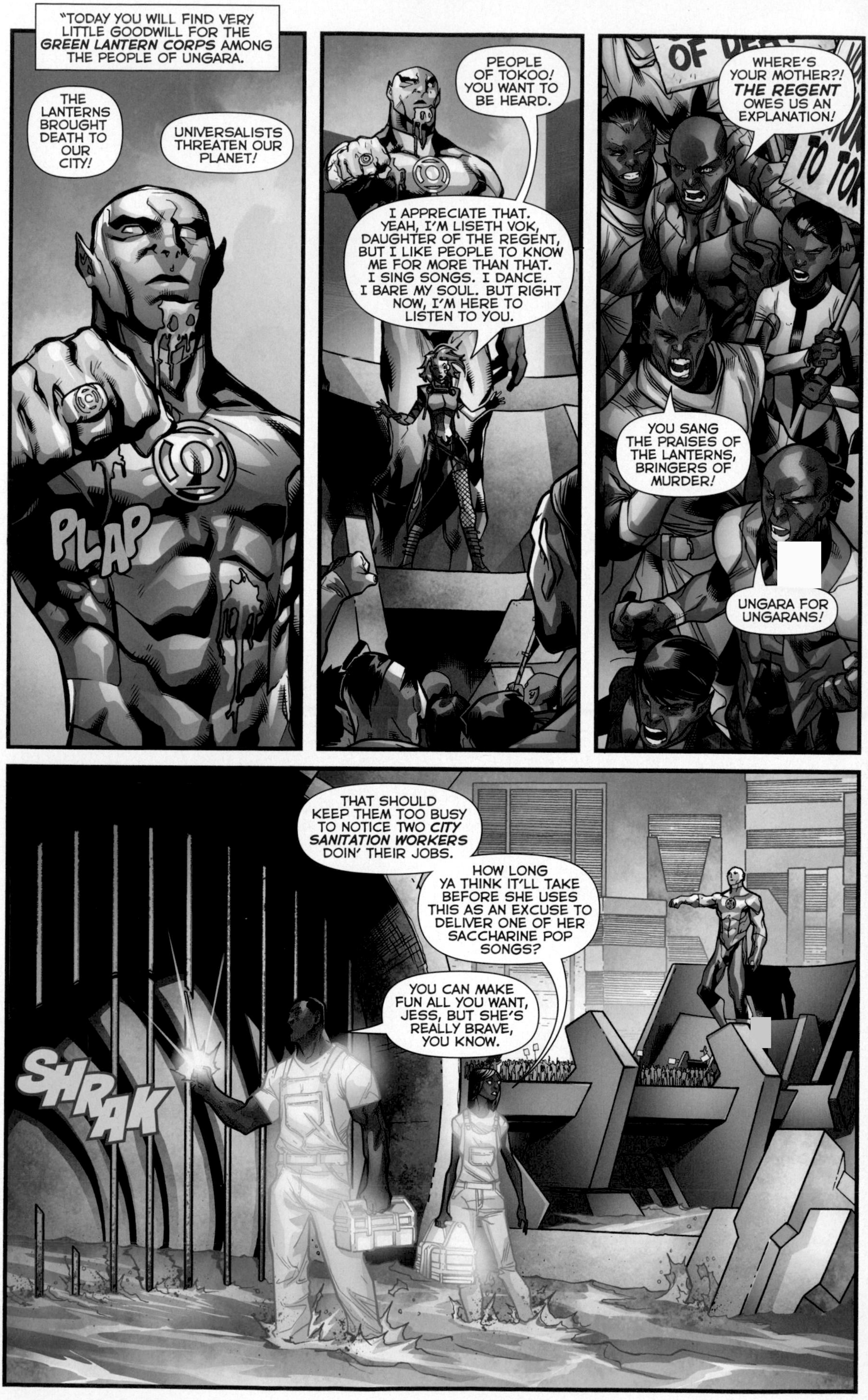
"TODAY YOU WILL FIND VERY LITTLE GOODWILL FOR THE GREEN LANTERN CORPS AMONG THE PEOPLE OF UNGARA.
THE LANTERNS BROUGHT DEATH TO OUR CITY!
UNIVERSALISTS THREATEN OUR PLANET!
PLAP
PEOPLE OF TOKOO! YOU WANT TO BE HEARD.
I APPRECIATE THAT. YEAH, I'M LISETH VOK, DAUGHTER OF THE REGENT, BUT I LIKE PEOPLE TO KNOW ME FOR MORE THAN THAT. I SING SONGS. I DANCE. I BARE MY SOUL. BUT RIGHT NOW, I'M HERE TO LISTEN TO YOU.
OF DE
WHERE'S YOUR MOTHER?! THE REGENT OWES US AN EXPLANATION!
TO TOR
YOU SANG THE PRAISES OF THE LANTERNS, BRINGERS OF MURDER!
UNGARA FOR UNGARANS!
THAT SHOULD KEEP THEM TOO BUSY TO NOTICE TWO CITY SANITATION WORKERS DOIN' THEIR JOBS.
HOW LONG YA THINK IT'LL TAKE BEFORE SHE USES THIS AS AN EXCUSE TO DELIVER ONE OF HER SACCHARINE POP SONGS?
YOU CAN MAKE FUN ALL YOU WANT, JESS, BUT SHE'S REALLY BRAVE, YOU KNOW.
SHRAK

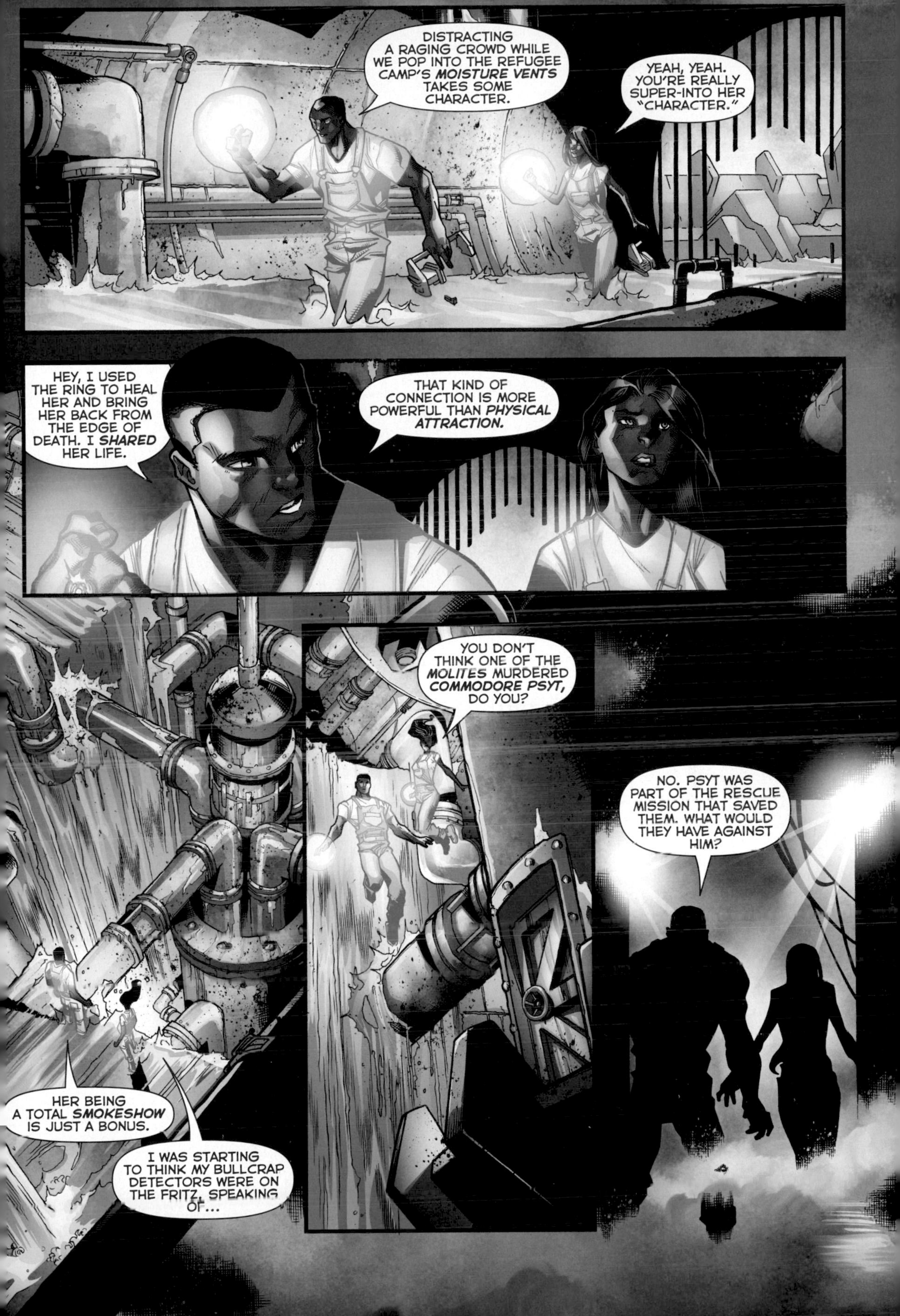
DISTRACTING A RAGING CROWD WHILE WE POP INTO THE REFUGEE CAMP'S MOISTURE VENTS TAKES SOME CHARACTER.
YEAH, YEAH. YOU'RE REALLY SUPER-INTO HER "CHARACTER."
HEY, I USED THE RING TO HEAL HER AND BRING HER BACK FROM THE EDGE OF DEATH. I SHARED HER LIFE.
THAT KIND OF CONNECTION IS MORE POWERFUL THAN PHYSICAL ATTRACTION.
HER BEING A TOTAL SMOKESHOW IS JUST A BONUS.
I WAS STARTING TO THINK MY BULLCRAP DETECTORS WERE ON THE FRITZ. SPEAKING OF...
YOU DON'T THINK ONE OF THE MOLITES MURDERED COMMODORE PSYT, DO YOU?
NO. PSYT WAS PART OF THE RESCUE MISSION THAT SAVED THEM. WHAT WOULD THEY HAVE AGAINST HIM?

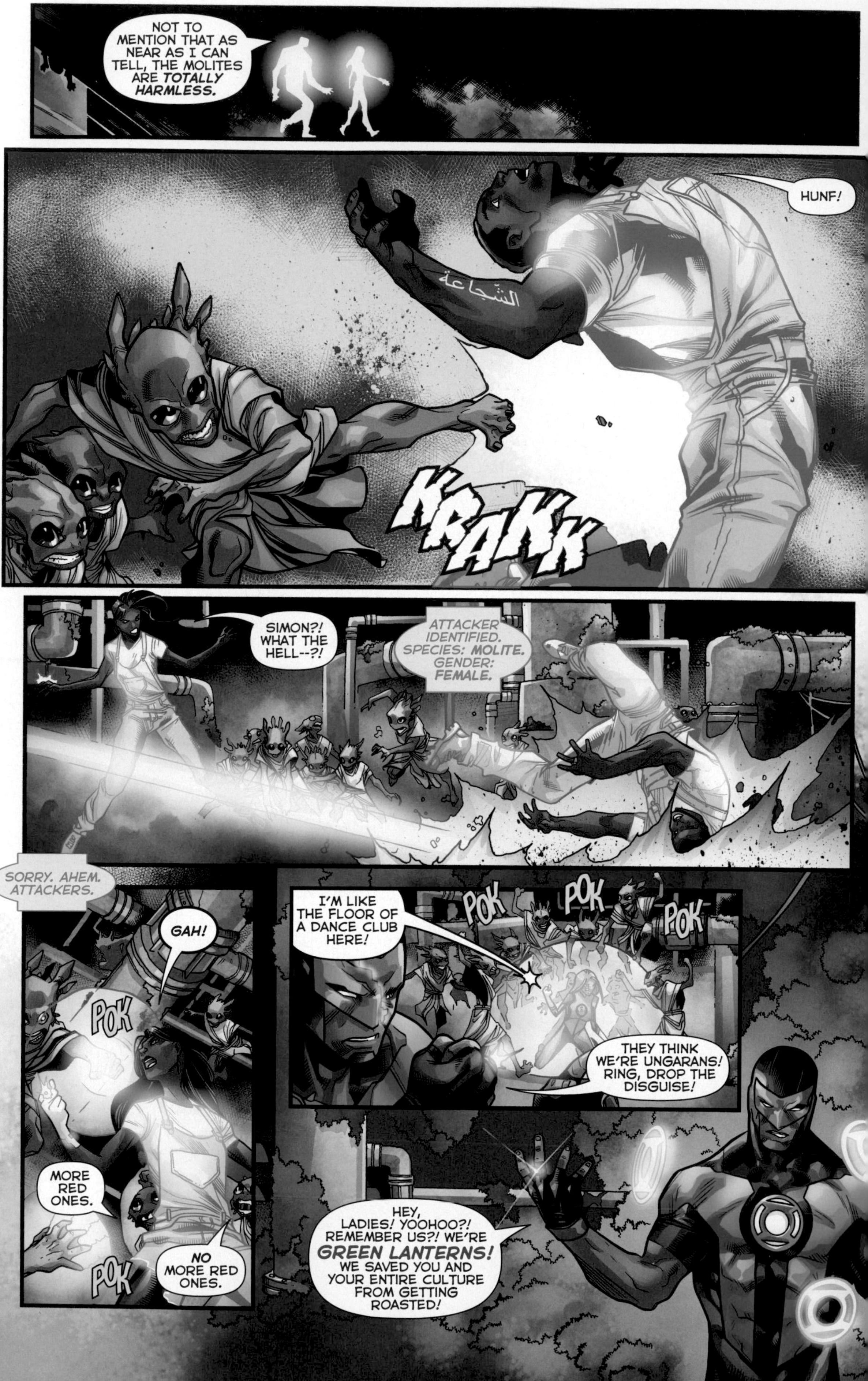
NOT TO MENTION THAT AS NEAR AS I CAN TELL, THE MOLITES ARE TOTALLY HARMLESS.
HUNF!
الشجاعة
KRAKK
SIMON?! WHAT THE HELL--?!
ATTACKER IDENTIFIED. SPECIES: MOLITE. GENDER: FEMALE.
SORRY. AHEM. ATTACKERS.
GAH!
POK
MORE RED ONES.
NO MORE RED ONES.
POK
I'M LIKE THE FLOOR OF A DANCE CLUB HERE!
POK
POK
POK
THEY THINK WE'RE UNGARANS! RING, DROP THE DISGUISE!
HEY, LADIES! YOOHOO?! REMEMBER US?! WE'RE GREEN LANTERNS! WE SAVED YOU AND YOUR ENTIRE CULTURE FROM GETTING ROASTED!

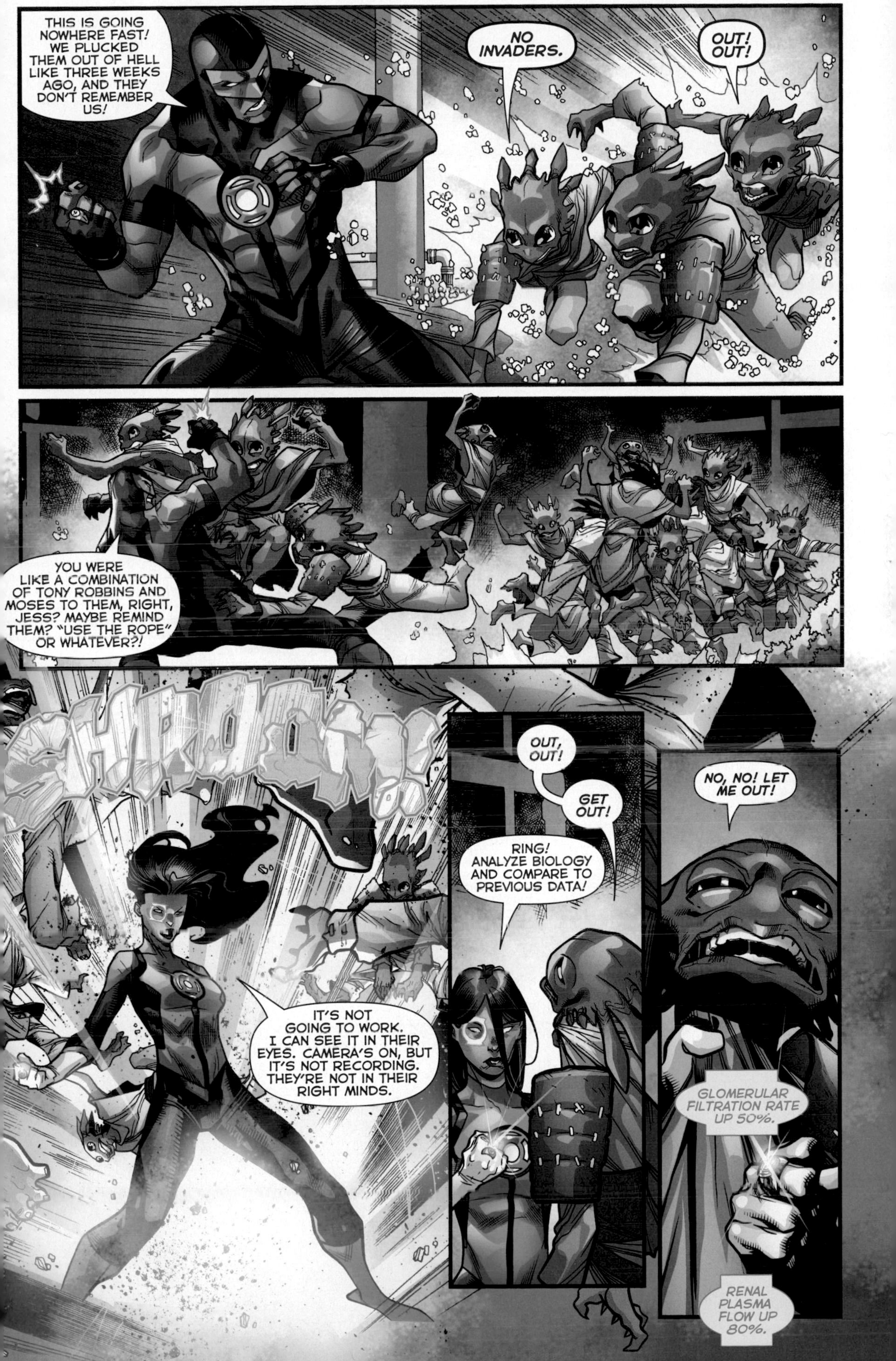
THIS IS GOING NOWHERE FAST! WE PLUCKED THEM OUT OF HELL LIKE THREE WEEKS AGO, AND THEY DON'T REMEMBER US!
NO INVADERS.
OUT! OUT!
YOU WERE LIKE A COMBINATION OF TONY ROBBINS AND MOSES TO THEM, RIGHT, JESS? MAYBE REMIND THEM? "USE THE ROPE" OR WHATEVER?!
SHROOM!
IT'S NOT GOING TO WORK. I CAN SEE IT IN THEIR EYES. CAMERA'S ON, BUT IT'S NOT RECORDING. THEY'RE NOT IN THEIR RIGHT MINDS.
OUT, OUT!
GET OUT!
RING! ANALYZE BIOLOGY AND COMPARE TO PREVIOUS DATA!
NO, NO! LET ME OUT!
GLOMERULAR FILTRATION RATE UP 50%.
RENAL PLASMA FLOW UP 80%.

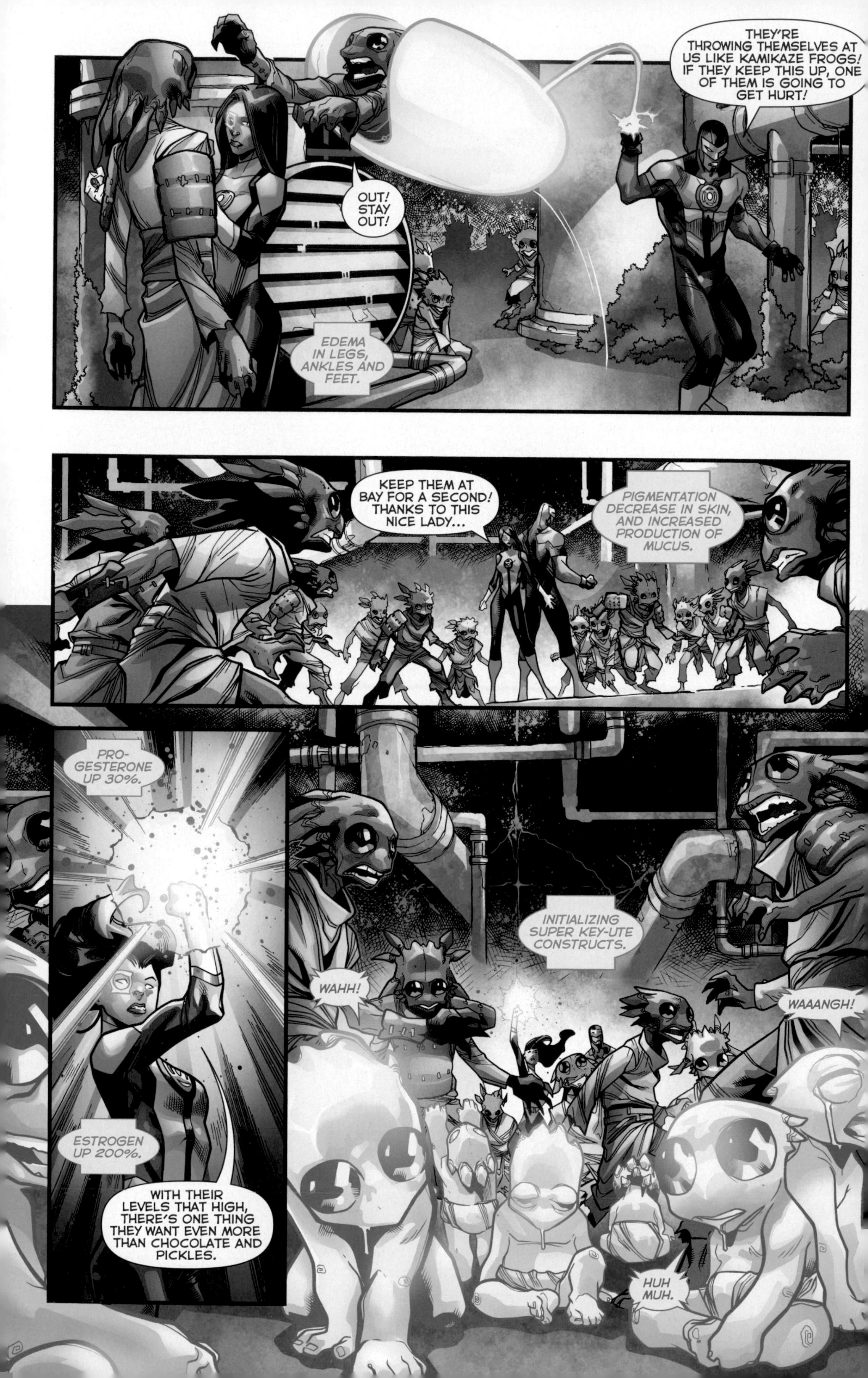
THEY'RE THROWING THEMSELVES AT US LIKE KAMIKAZE FROGS! IF THEY KEEP THIS UP, ONE OF THEM IS GOING TO GET HURT!
OUT! STAY OUT!
EDEMA IN LEGS, ANKLES AND FEET.
KEEP THEM AT BAY FOR A SECOND! THANKS TO THIS NICE LADY...
PIGMENTATION DECREASE IN SKIN, AND INCREASED PRODUCTION OF MUCUS.
PRO-GESTERONE UP 30%.
ESTROGEN UP 200%.
WITH THEIR LEVELS THAT HIGH, THERE'S ONE THING THEY WANT EVEN MORE THAN CHOCOLATE AND PICKLES.
INITIALIZING SUPER KEY-UTE CONSTRUCTS.
WAHH!
WAAANGH!
HUH MUH.

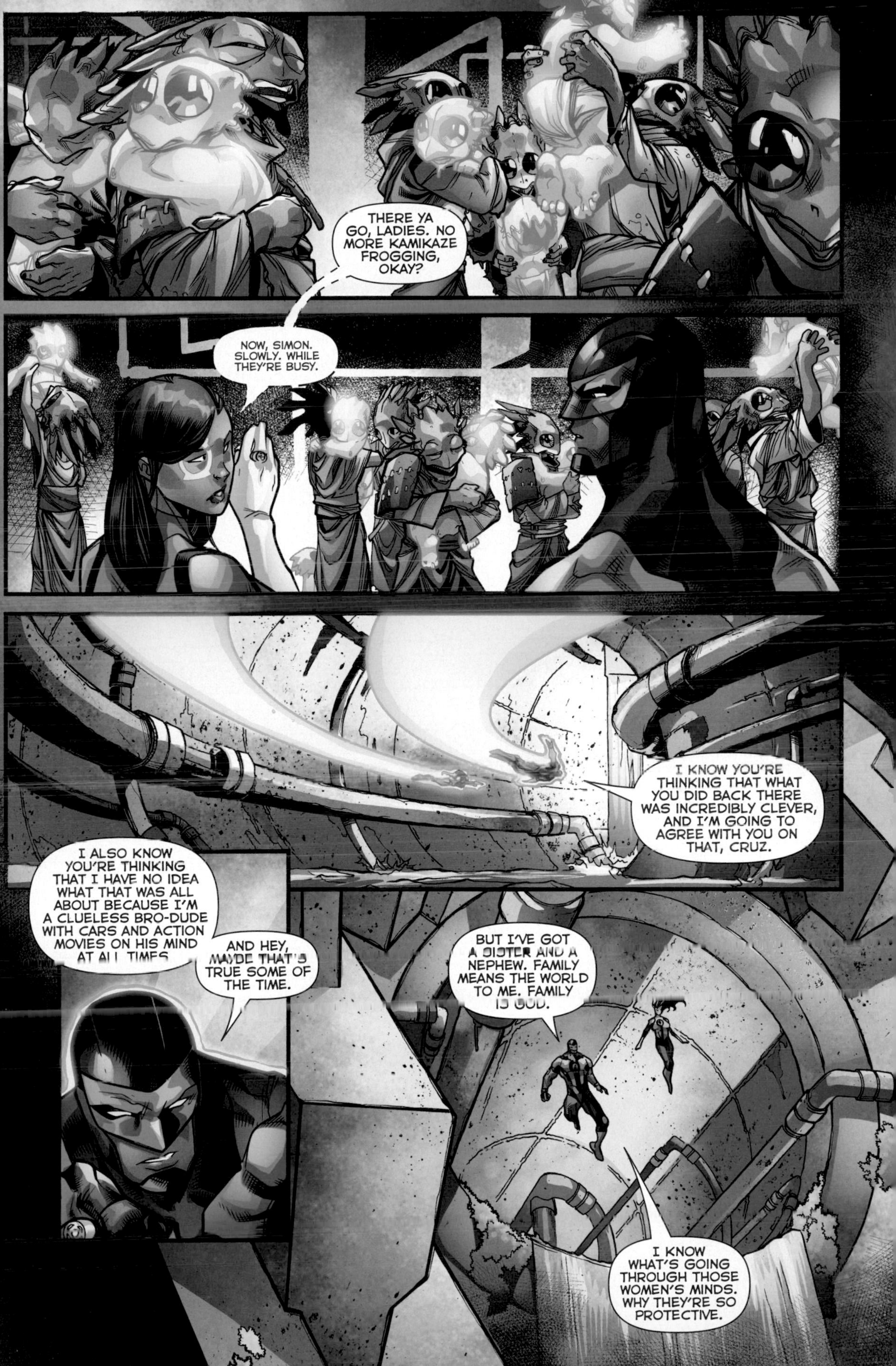
THERE YA GO, LADIES. NO MORE KAMIKAZE FROGGING, OKAY?
NOW, SIMON. SLOWLY. WHILE THEY'RE BUSY.
I KNOW YOU'RE THINKING THAT WHAT YOU DID BACK THERE WAS INCREDIBLY CLEVER, AND I'M GOING TO AGREE WITH YOU ON THAT, CRUZ.
I ALSO KNOW YOU'RE THINKING THAT I HAVE NO IDEA WHAT THAT WAS ALL ABOUT BECAUSE I'M A CLUELESS BRO-DUDE WITH CARS AND ACTION MOVIES ON HIS MIND AT ALL TIMES.
AND HEY, MAYBE THAT'S TRUE SOME OF THE TIME.
BUT I'VE GOT A SISTER AND A NEPHEW. FAMILY MEANS THE WORLD TO ME. FAMILY IS GOD.
I KNOW WHAT'S GOING THROUGH THOSE WOMEN'S MINDS. WHY THEY'RE SO PROTECTIVE.

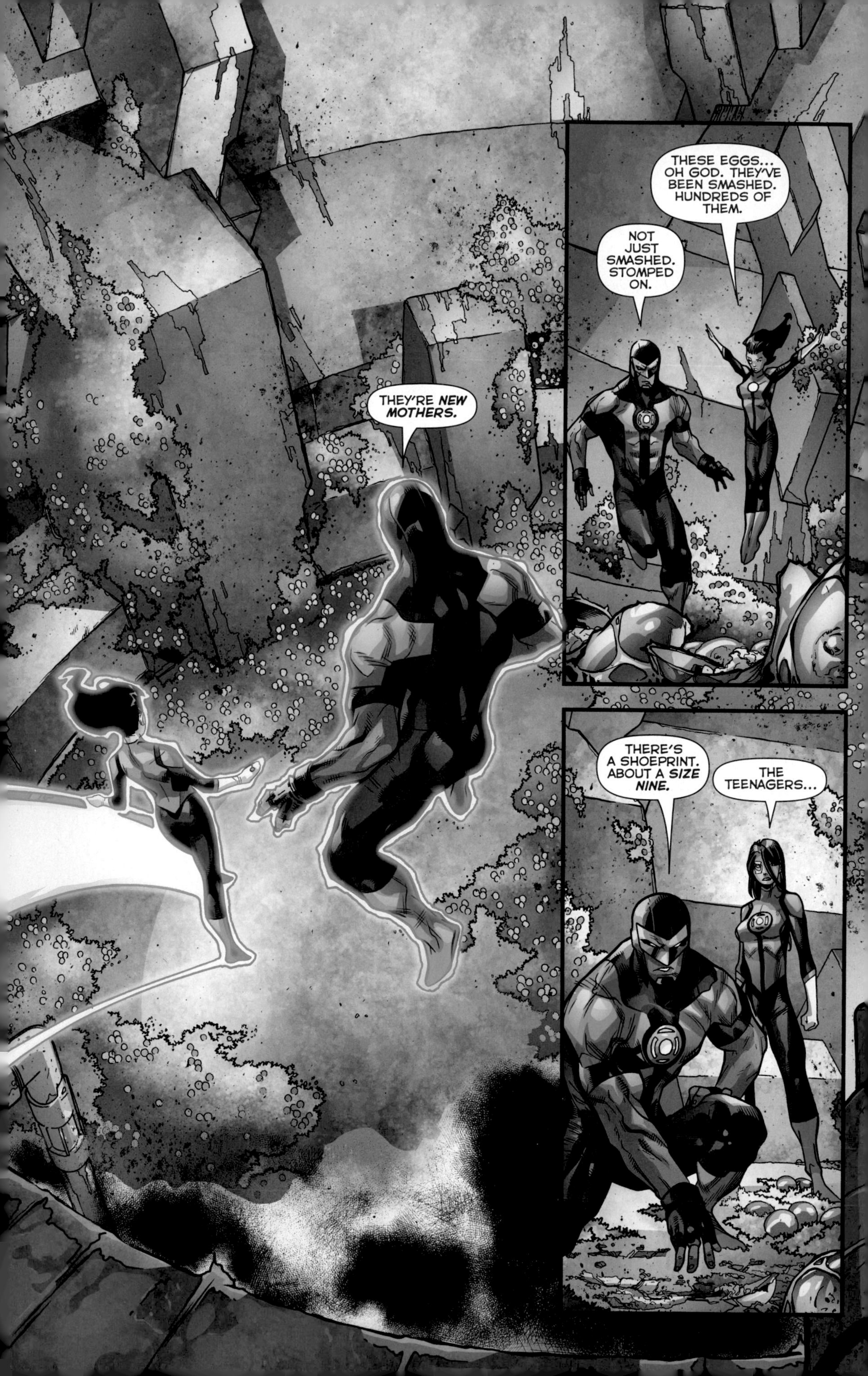
THEY'RE *NEW MOTHERS.*
THESE EGGS... OH GOD. THEY'VE BEEN SMASHED. HUNDREDS OF THEM.
NOT JUST SMASHED. STOMPED ON.
THERE'S A SHOEPRINT. ABOUT A *SIZE NINE.*
THE TEENAGERS...

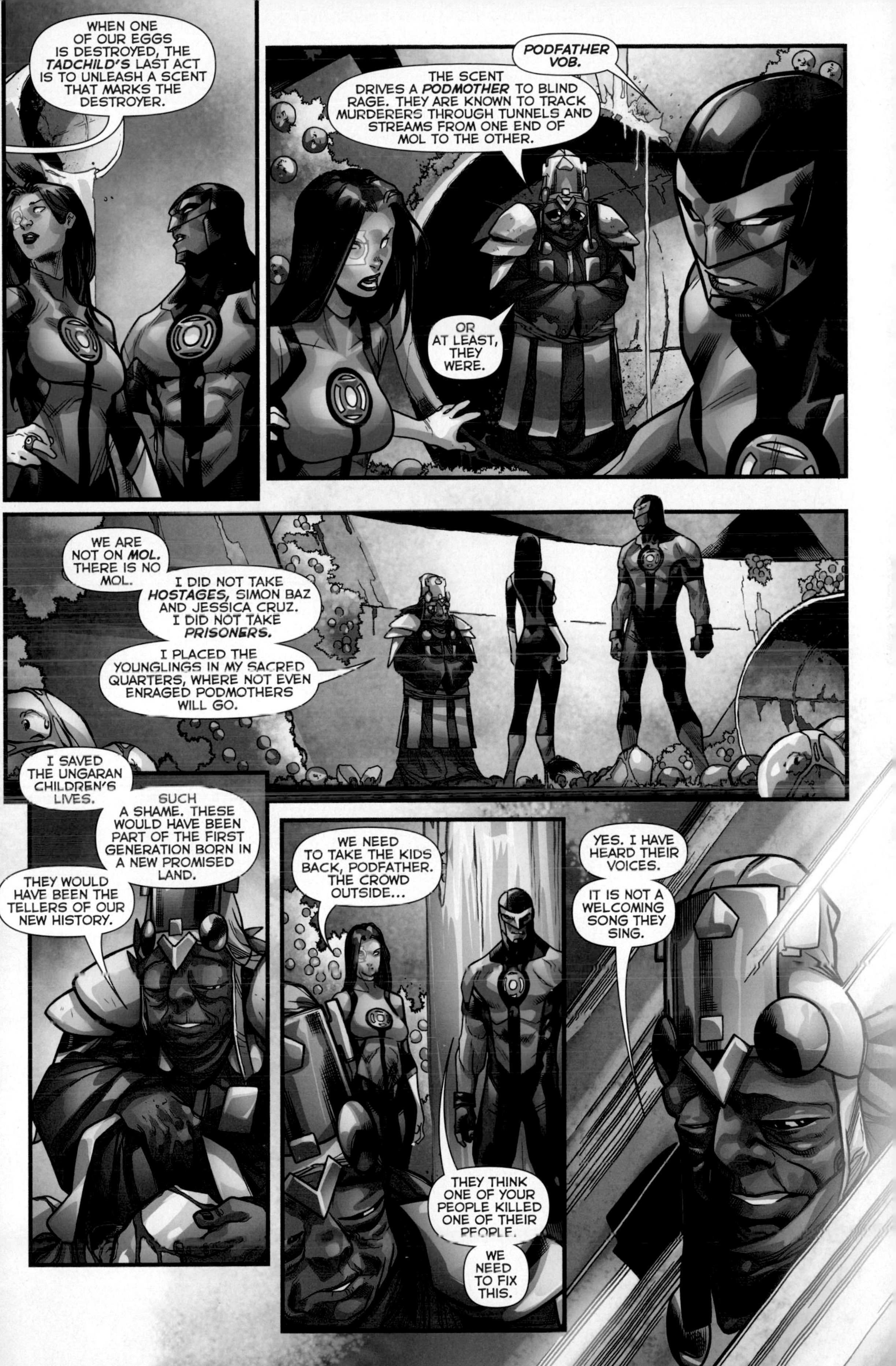
WHEN ONE OF OUR EGGS IS DESTROYED, THE TADCHILD'S LAST ACT IS TO UNLEASH A SCENT THAT MARKS THE DESTROYER.
PODFATHER VOB.
THE SCENT DRIVES A PODMOTHER TO BLIND RAGE. THEY ARE KNOWN TO TRACK MURDERERS THROUGH TUNNELS AND STREAMS FROM ONE END OF MOL TO THE OTHER.
OR AT LEAST, THEY WERE.
WE ARE NOT ON MOL. THERE IS NO MOL.
I DID NOT TAKE HOSTAGES, SIMON BAZ AND JESSICA CRUZ. I DID NOT TAKE PRISONERS.
I PLACED THE YOUNGLINGS IN MY SACRED QUARTERS, WHERE NOT EVEN ENRAGED PODMOTHERS WILL GO.
I SAVED THE UNGARAN CHILDREN'S LIVES.
SUCH A SHAME. THESE WOULD HAVE BEEN PART OF THE FIRST GENERATION BORN IN A NEW PROMISED LAND.
THEY WOULD HAVE BEEN THE TELLERS OF OUR NEW HISTORY.
WE NEED TO TAKE THE KIDS BACK, PODFATHER. THE CROWD OUTSIDE...
THEY THINK ONE OF YOUR PEOPLE KILLED ONE OF THEIR PEOPLE.
WE NEED TO FIX THIS.
YES. I HAVE HEARD THEIR VOICES.
IT IS NOT A WELCOMING SONG THEY SING.

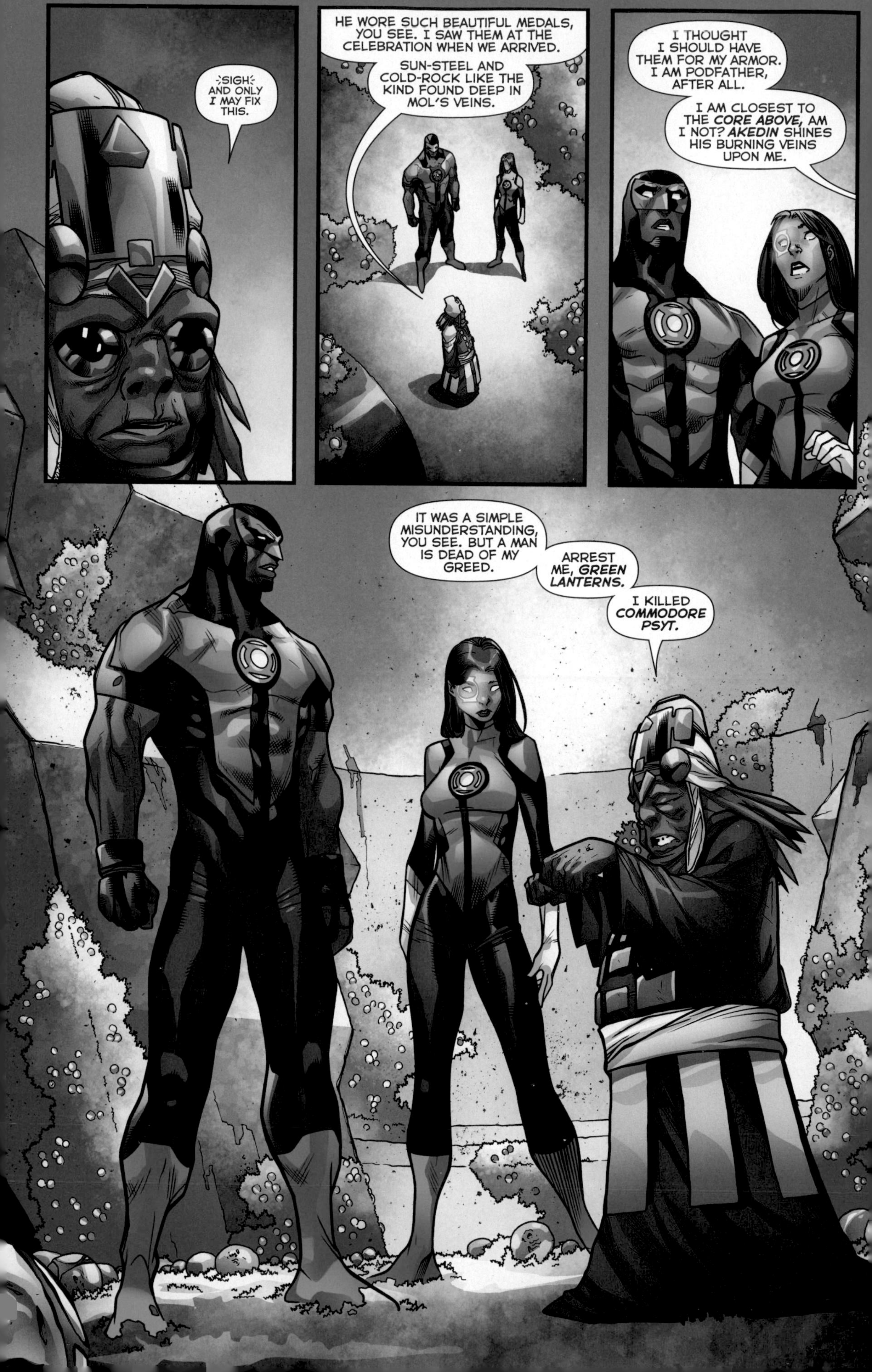

SIGH AND ONLY I MAY FIX THIS.
HE WORE SUCH BEAUTIFUL MEDALS, YOU SEE. I SAW THEM AT THE CELEBRATION WHEN WE ARRIVED.
SUN-STEEL AND COLD-ROCK LIKE THE KIND FOUND DEEP IN MOL'S VEINS.
I THOUGHT I SHOULD HAVE THEM FOR MY ARMOR. I AM PODFATHER, AFTER ALL.
I AM CLOSEST TO THE CORE ABOVE, AM I NOT? AKEDIN SHINES HIS BURNING VEINS UPON ME.
IT WAS A SIMPLE MISUNDERSTANDING, YOU SEE. BUT A MAN IS DEAD OF MY GREED.
ARREST ME, GREEN LANTERNS.
I KILLED COMMODORE PSYT.

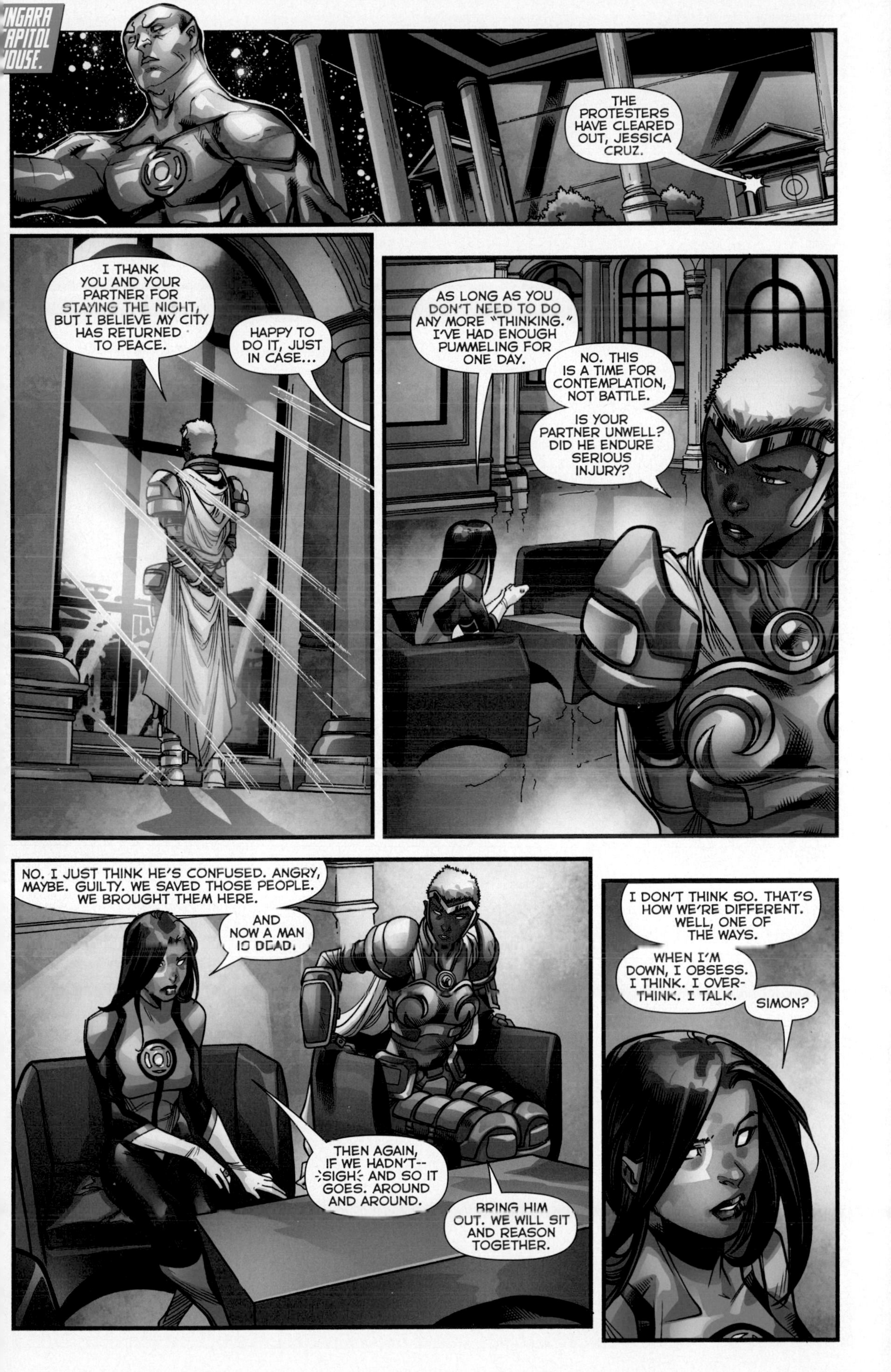
NGARA
APITOL
OUSE.
THE PROTESTERS HAVE CLEARED OUT, JESSICA CRUZ.
I THANK YOU AND YOUR PARTNER FOR STAYING THE NIGHT, BUT I BELIEVE MY CITY HAS RETURNED TO PEACE.
HAPPY TO DO IT, JUST IN CASE...
AS LONG AS YOU DON'T NEED TO DO ANY MORE "THINKING." I'VE HAD ENOUGH PUMMELING FOR ONE DAY.
NO. THIS IS A TIME FOR CONTEMPLATION, NOT BATTLE.
IS YOUR PARTNER UNWELL? DID HE ENDURE SERIOUS INJURY?
NO. I JUST THINK HE'S CONFUSED. ANGRY, MAYBE. GUILTY. WE SAVED THOSE PEOPLE. WE BROUGHT THEM HERE.
AND NOW A MAN IS DEAD.
THEN AGAIN, IF WE HADN'T-- SIGH AND SO IT GOES. AROUND AND AROUND.
BRING HIM OUT. WE WILL SIT AND REASON TOGETHER.
I DON'T THINK SO. THAT'S HOW WE'RE DIFFERENT. WELL, ONE OF THE WAYS.
WHEN I'M DOWN, I OBSESS. I THINK. I OVER-THINK. I TALK.
SIMON?

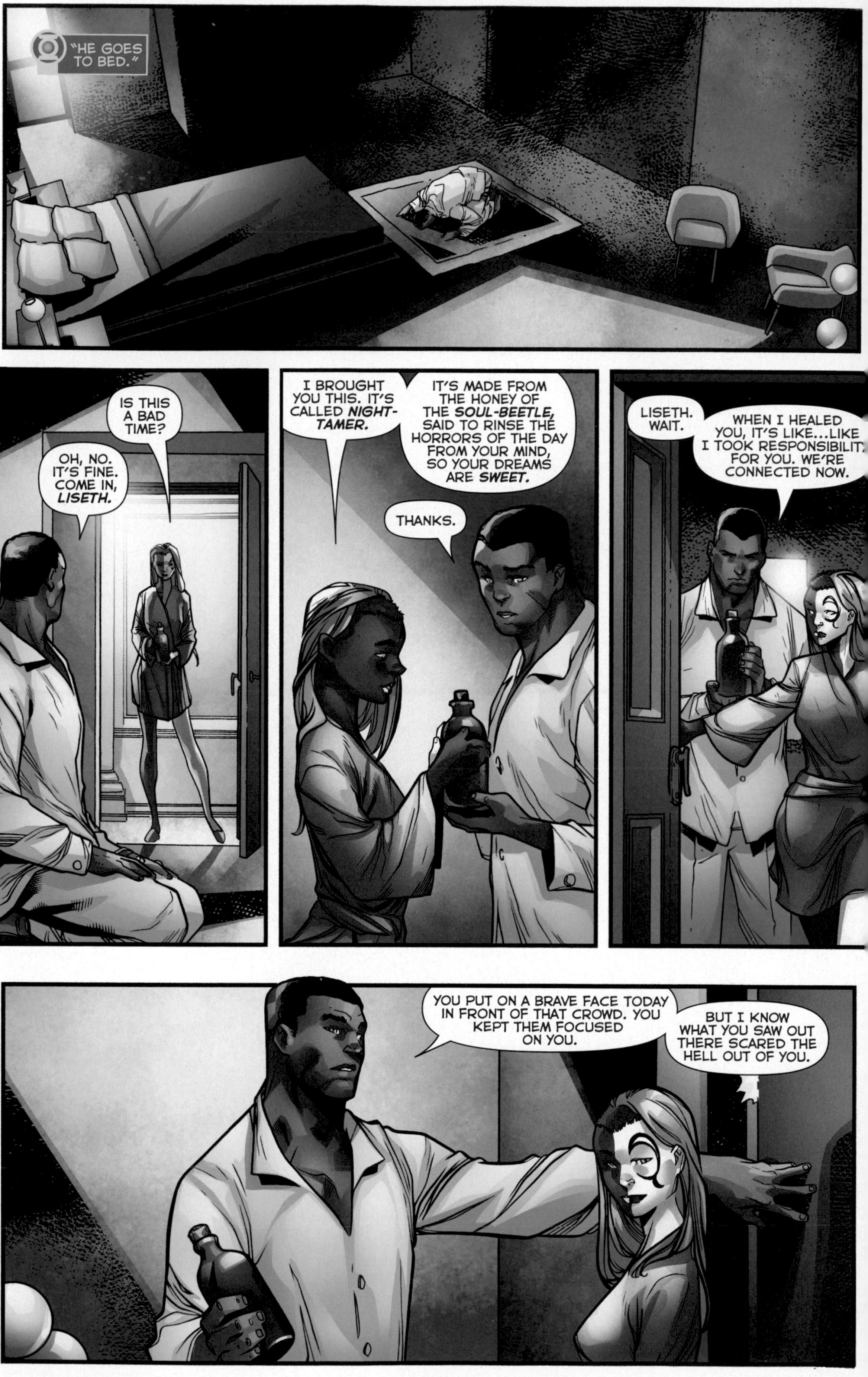
"HE GOES TO BED."
IS THIS A BAD TIME?
OH, NO. IT'S FINE. COME IN, LISETH.
I BROUGHT YOU THIS. IT'S CALLED NIGHT-TAMER.
IT'S MADE FROM THE HONEY OF THE SOUL-BEETLE, SAID TO RINSE THE HORRORS OF THE DAY FROM YOUR MIND, SO YOUR DREAMS ARE SWEET.
THANKS.
LISETH. WAIT.
WHEN I HEALED YOU, IT'S LIKE...LIKE I TOOK RESPONSIBILIT FOR YOU. WE'RE CONNECTED NOW.
YOU PUT ON A BRAVE FACE TODAY IN FRONT OF THAT CROWD. YOU KEPT THEM FOCUSED ON YOU.
BUT I KNOW WHAT YOU SAW OUT THERE SCARED THE HELL OUT OF YOU.

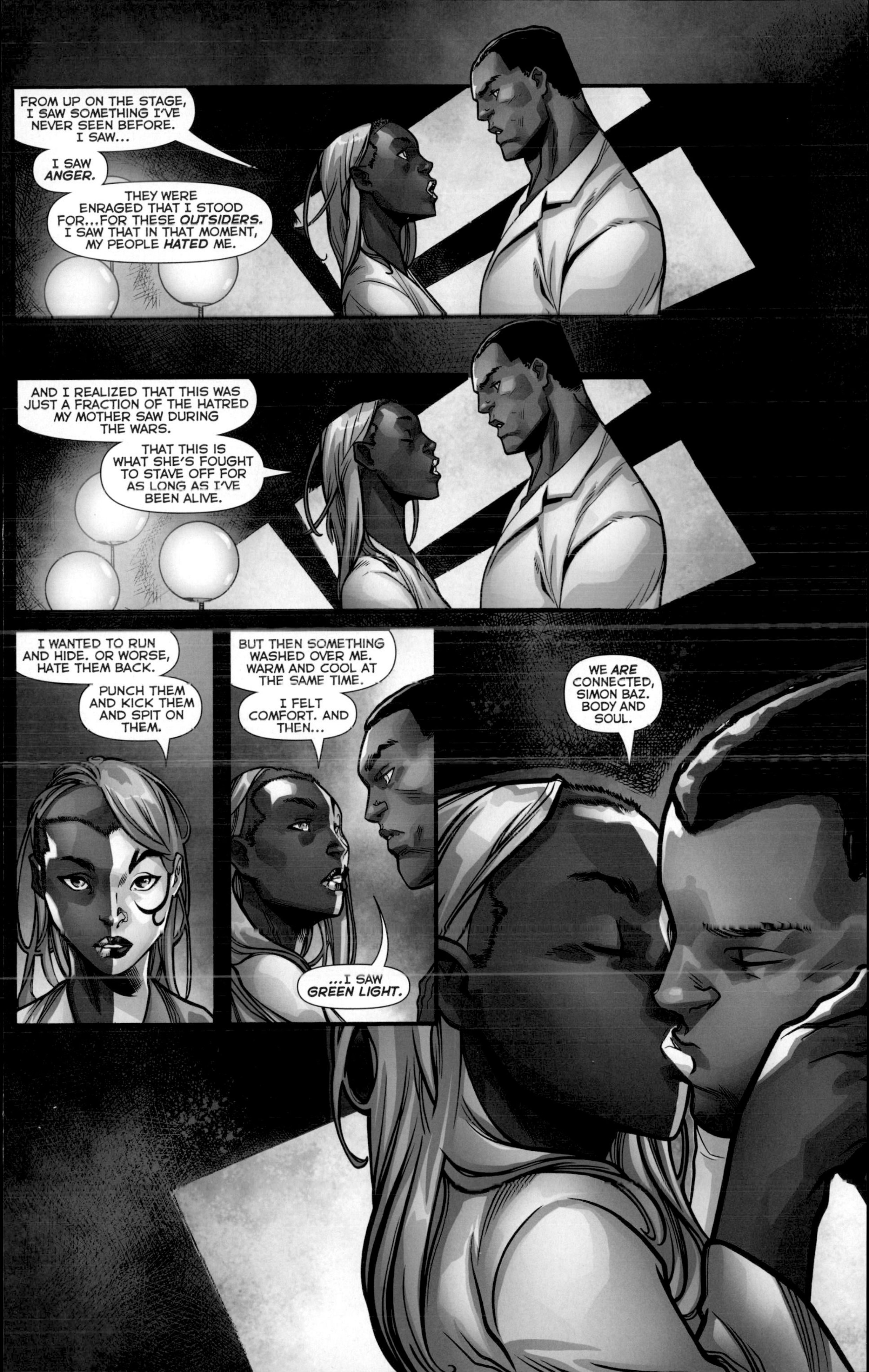

FROM UP ON THE STAGE, I SAW SOMETHING I'VE NEVER SEEN BEFORE. I SAW...
I SAW ANGER.
THEY WERE ENRAGED THAT I STOOD FOR...FOR THESE OUTSIDERS. I SAW THAT IN THAT MOMENT, MY PEOPLE HATED ME.
AND I REALIZED THAT THIS WAS JUST A FRACTION OF THE HATRED MY MOTHER SAW DURING THE WARS.
THAT THIS IS WHAT SHE'S FOUGHT TO STAVE OFF FOR AS LONG AS I'VE BEEN ALIVE.
I WANTED TO RUN AND HIDE. OR WORSE, HATE THEM BACK.
PUNCH THEM AND KICK THEM AND SPIT ON THEM.
BUT THEN SOMETHING WASHED OVER ME. WARM AND COOL AT THE SAME TIME.
I FELT COMFORT. AND THEN...
...I SAW GREEN LIGHT.
WE ARE CONNECTED, SIMON BAZ. BODY AND SOUL.

HOW DO YOU DO IT?

WHAT DO YOU MEAN?

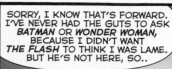

SORRY, I KNOW THAT'S FORWARD. I'VE NEVER HAD THE GUTS TO ASK *BATMAN* OR *WONDER WOMAN*, BECAUSE I DIDN'T WANT *THE FLASH* TO THINK I WAS LAME. BUT HE'S NOT HERE, SO..

WHAT I MEAN IS, EVERYTHING YOU STAND FOR COULD HAVE FALLEN APART. YOUR WORLD NEARLY CRUMBLED IN FRONT OF YOU. HOW DO YOU FACE IT ALL LIKE THIS? THIS COOL?

I'M A SOLDIER, JESSICA CRUZ. I AM A *GENERAL.*

WORRY IS IN THE DETAILS. TO LEAD MILLIONS TO WAR, AND CLAIM VICTORY, SOME... *DETAILS* HAVE TO BE LOST.

THE ONLY WAY I KNOW TO WIN IS TO FOCUS ON THE WAR AND NOT THE BATTLES.

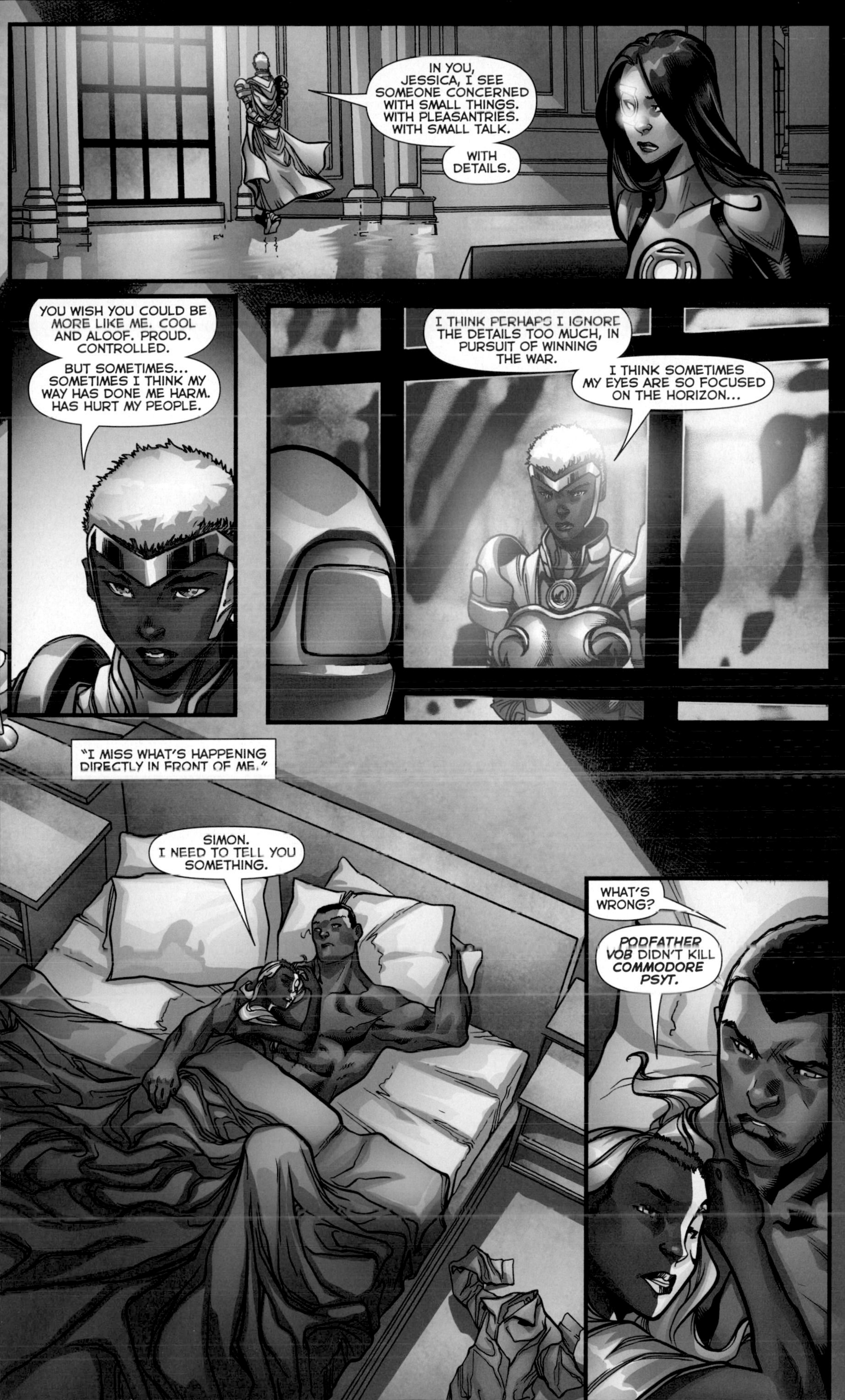
IN YOU, JESSICA, I SEE SOMEONE CONCERNED WITH SMALL THINGS. WITH PLEASANTRIES. WITH SMALL TALK.
WITH DETAILS.
YOU WISH YOU COULD BE MORE LIKE ME. COOL AND ALOOF. PROUD. CONTROLLED.
BUT SOMETIMES... SOMETIMES I THINK MY WAY HAS DONE ME HARM. HAS HURT MY PEOPLE.
I THINK PERHAPS I IGNORE THE DETAILS TOO MUCH, IN PURSUIT OF WINNING THE WAR.
I THINK SOMETIMES MY EYES ARE SO FOCUSED ON THE HORIZON...
"I MISS WHAT'S HAPPENING DIRECTLY IN FRONT OF ME."
SIMON. I NEED TO TELL YOU SOMETHING.
WHAT'S WRONG?
PODFATHER VOB DIDN'T KILL COMMODORE PSYT.

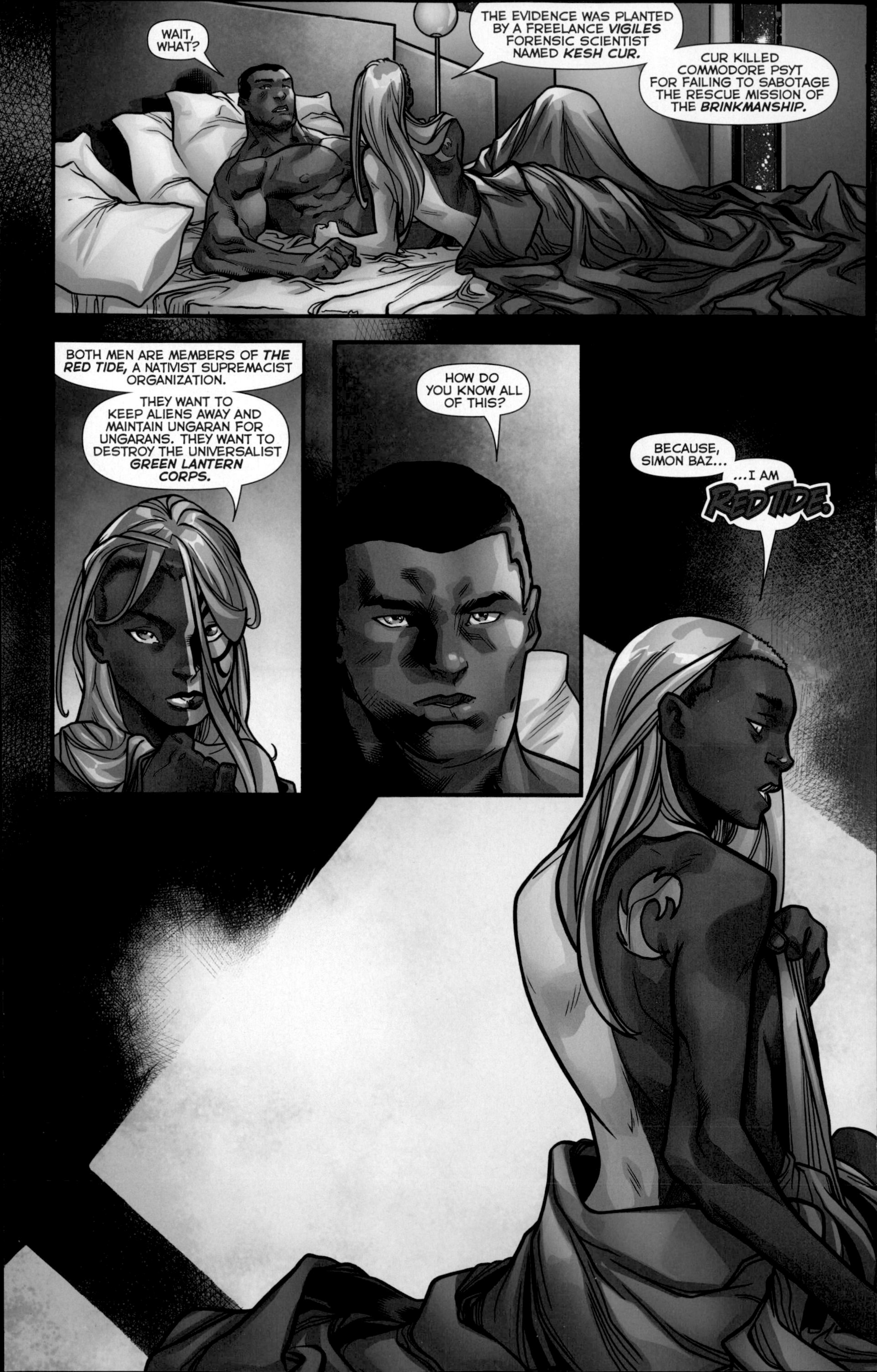

WAIT, WHAT?
THE EVIDENCE WAS PLANTED BY A FREELANCE VIGILES FORENSIC SCIENTIST NAMED KESH CUR.
CUR KILLED COMMODORE PSYT FOR FAILING TO SABOTAGE THE RESCUE MISSION OF THE BRINKMANSHIP.
BOTH MEN ARE MEMBERS OF THE RED TIDE, A NATIVIST SUPREMACIST ORGANIZATION.
THEY WANT TO KEEP ALIENS AWAY AND MAINTAIN UNGARAN FOR UNGARANS. THEY WANT TO DESTROY THE UNIVERSALIST GREEN LANTERN CORPS.
HOW DO YOU KNOW ALL OF THIS?
BECAUSE, SIMON BAZ...
...I AM RED TIDE.

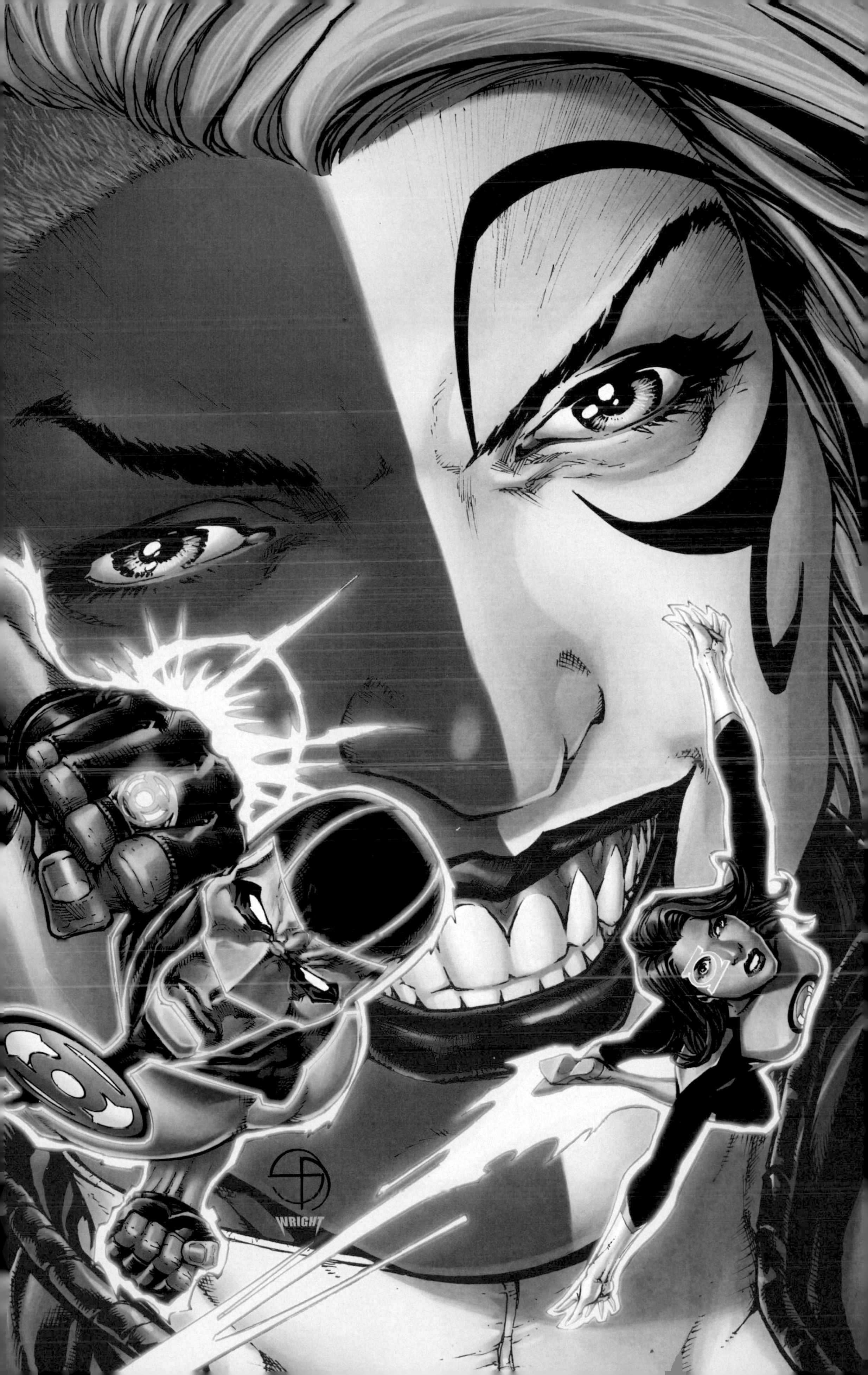
WRIGHT

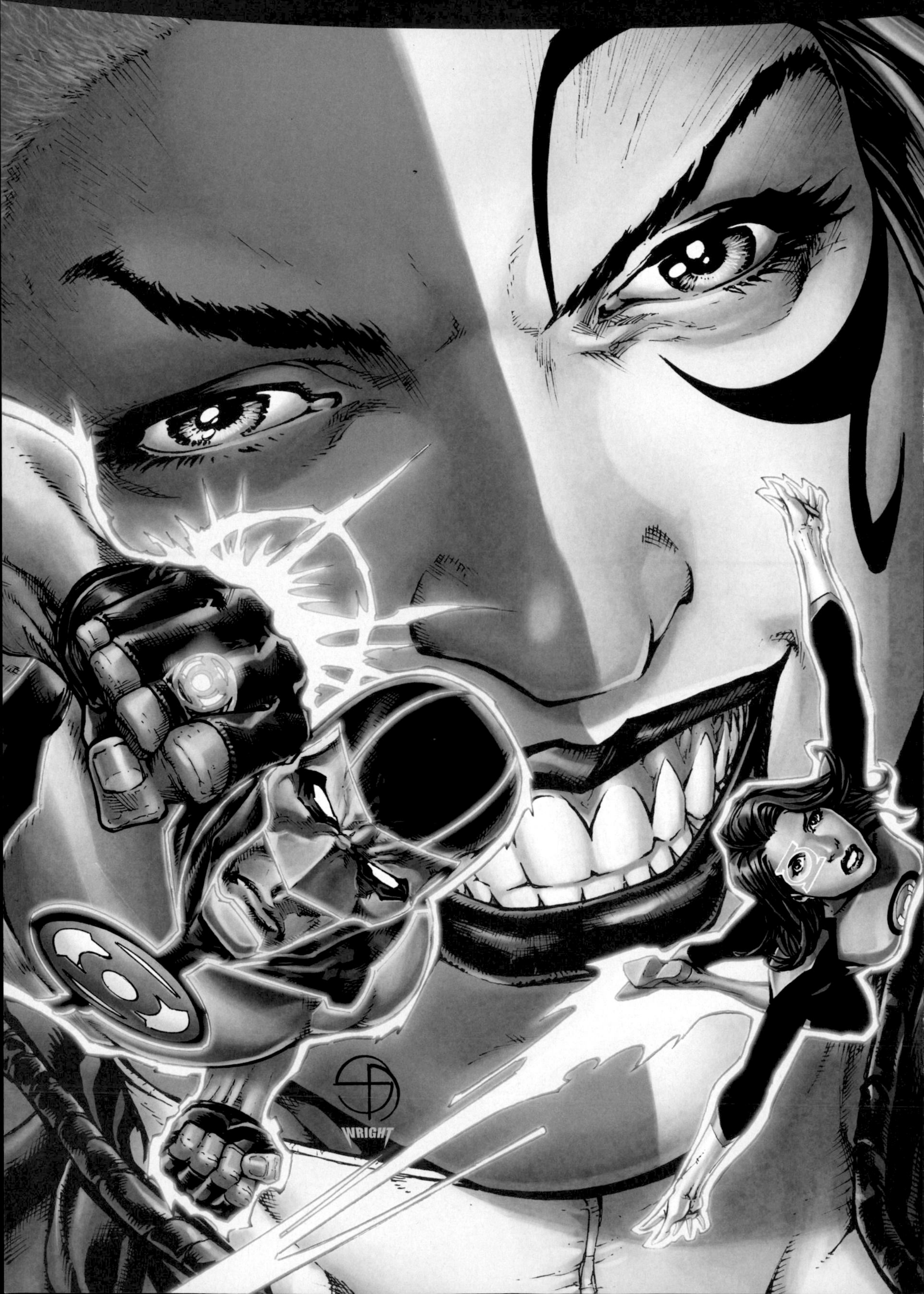
WRIGHT

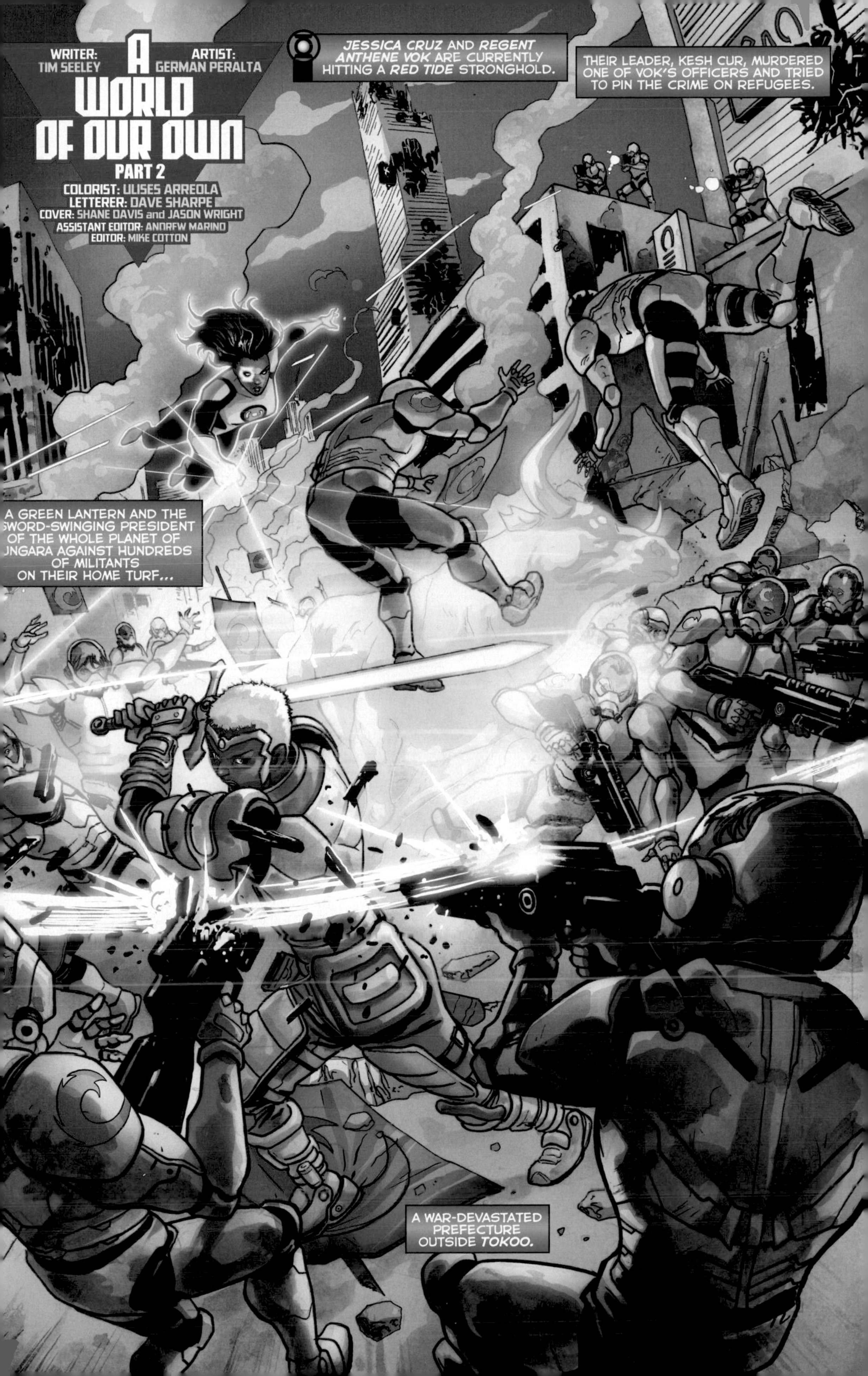

WRITER: TIM SEELEY
A WORLD OF OUR OWN
ARTIST: GERMAN PERALTA
PART 2
COLORIST: ULISES ARREOLA
LETTERER: DAVE SHARPE
COVER: SHANE DAVIS and JASON WRIGHT
ASSISTANT EDITOR: ANDREW MARINO
EDITOR: MIKE COTTON
JESSICA CRUZ AND REGENT ANTHENE VOK ARE CURRENTLY HITTING A RED TIDE STRONGHOLD.
THEIR LEADER, KESH CUR, MURDERED ONE OF VOK'S OFFICERS AND TRIED TO PIN THE CRIME ON REFUGEES.
A GREEN LANTERN AND THE SWORD-SWINGING PRESIDENT OF THE WHOLE PLANET OF UNGARA AGAINST HUNDREDS OF MILITANTS ON THEIR HOME TURF...
A WAR-DEVASTATED PREFECTURE OUTSIDE TOKOO.

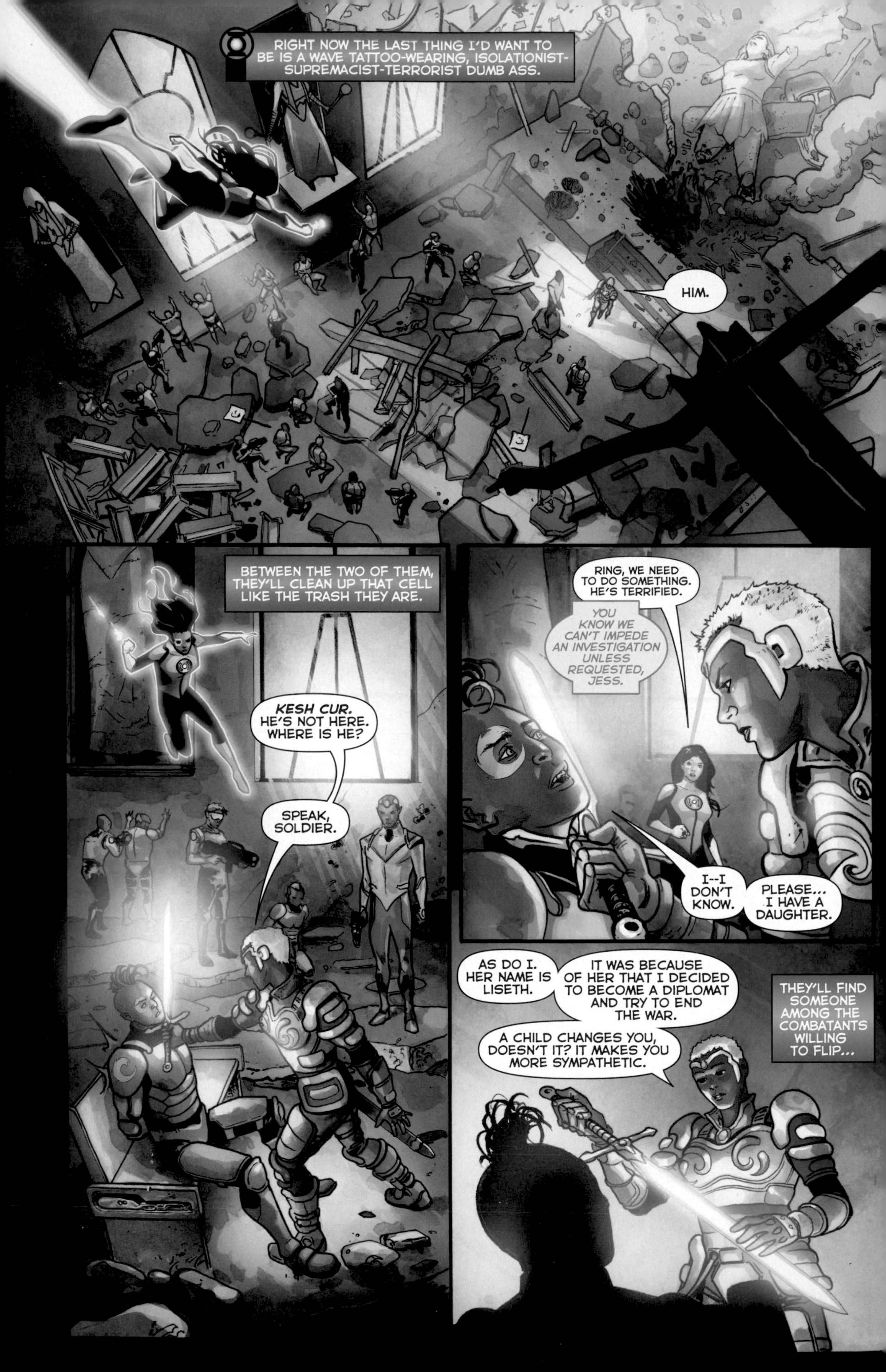
RIGHT NOW THE LAST THING I'D WANT TO BE IS A WAVE TATTOO-WEARING, ISOLATIONIST-SUPREMACIST-TERRORIST DUMB ASS.
HIM.
BETWEEN THE TWO OF THEM, THEY'LL CLEAN UP THAT CELL LIKE THE TRASH THEY ARE.
KESH CUR. HE'S NOT HERE. WHERE IS HE?
SPEAK, SOLDIER.
RING, WE NEED TO DO SOMETHING. HE'S TERRIFIED.
YOU KNOW WE CAN'T IMPEDE AN INVESTIGATION UNLESS REQUESTED, JESS.
I--I DON'T KNOW.
PLEASE... I HAVE A DAUGHTER.
AS DO I. HER NAME IS LISETH.
IT WAS BECAUSE OF HER THAT I DECIDED TO BECOME A DIPLOMAT AND TRY TO END THE WAR.
A CHILD CHANGES YOU, DOESN'T IT? IT MAKES YOU MORE SYMPATHETIC.
THEY'LL FIND SOMEONE AMONG THE COMBATANTS WILLING TO FLIP...

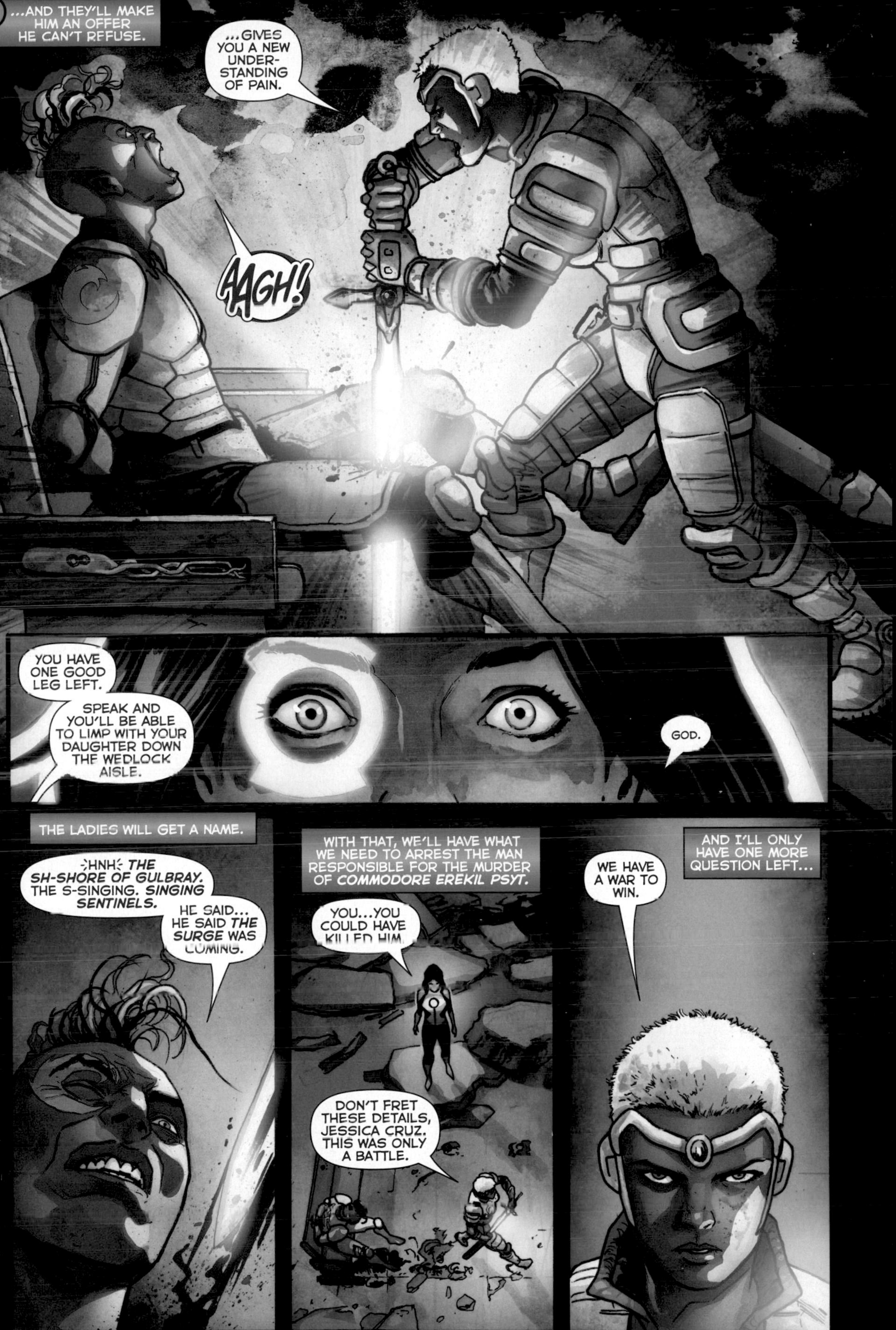
...AND THEY'LL MAKE HIM AN OFFER HE CAN'T REFUSE.
...GIVES YOU A NEW UNDER-STANDING OF PAIN.
AAGH!
YOU HAVE ONE GOOD LEG LEFT.
SPEAK AND YOU'LL BE ABLE TO LIMP WITH YOUR DAUGHTER DOWN THE WEDLOCK AISLE.
GOD.
THE LADIES WILL GET A NAME.
HNH THE SH-SHORE OF GULBRAY. THE S-SINGING. SINGING SENTINELS.
HE SAID... HE SAID THE SURGE WAS COMING.
WITH THAT, WE'LL HAVE WHAT WE NEED TO ARREST THE MAN RESPONSIBLE FOR THE MURDER OF COMMODORE EREKIL PSYT.
YOU...YOU COULD HAVE KILLED HIM.
DON'T FRET THESE DETAILS, JESSICA CRUZ. THIS WAS ONLY A BATTLE.
AND I'LL ONLY HAVE ONE MORE QUESTION LEFT...
WE HAVE A WAR TO WIN.

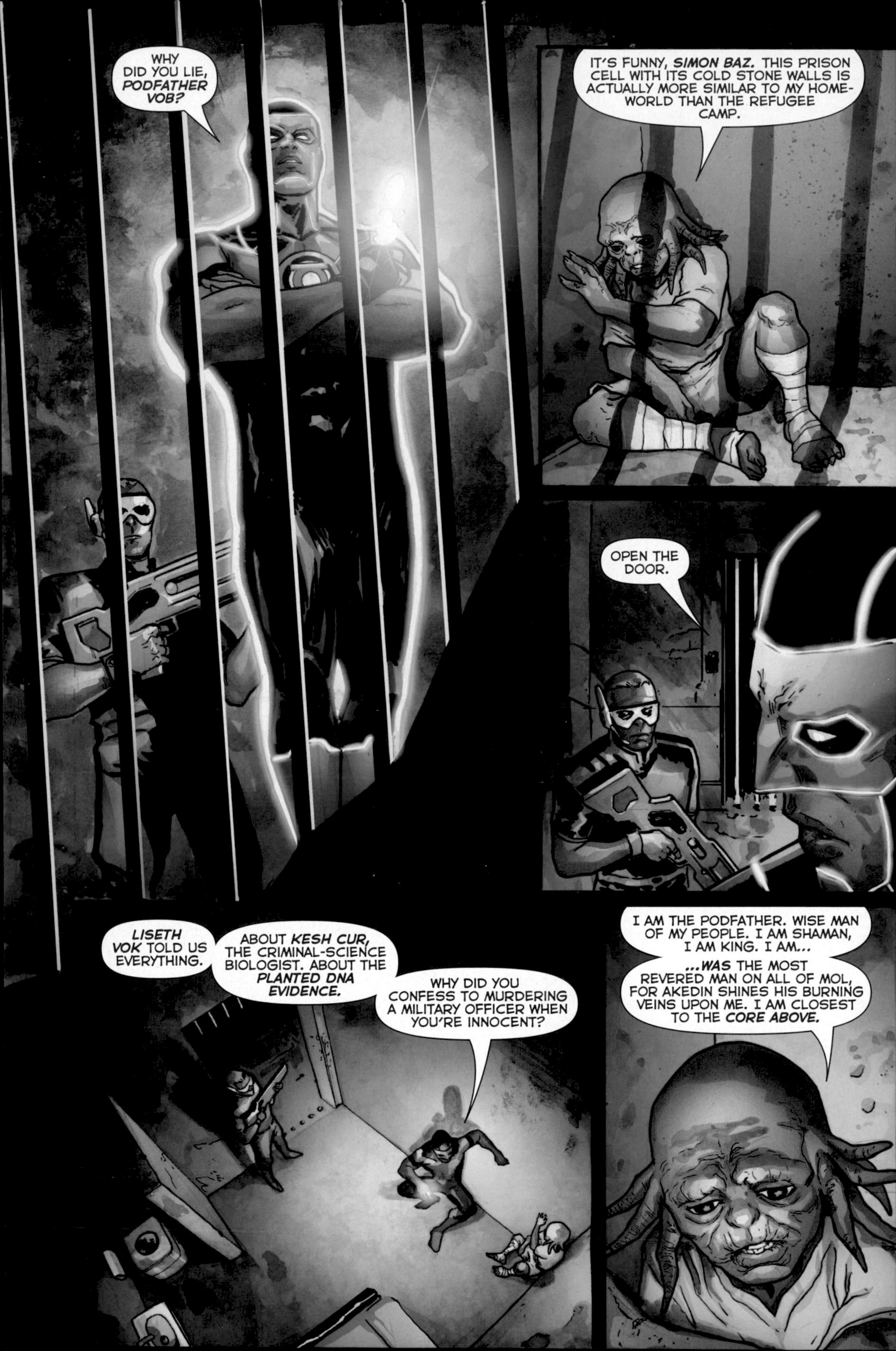
WHY DID YOU LIE, PODFATHER VOB?
IT'S FUNNY, SIMON BAZ. THIS PRISON CELL WITH ITS COLD STONE WALLS IS ACTUALLY MORE SIMILAR TO MY HOME-WORLD THAN THE REFUGEE CAMP.
OPEN THE DOOR.
LISETH VOK TOLD US EVERYTHING.
ABOUT KESH CUR, THE CRIMINAL-SCIENCE BIOLOGIST. ABOUT THE PLANTED DNA EVIDENCE.
WHY DID YOU CONFESS TO MURDERING A MILITARY OFFICER WHEN YOU'RE INNOCENT?
I AM THE PODFATHER. WISE MAN OF MY PEOPLE. I AM SHAMAN, I AM KING. I AM...
...WAS THE MOST REVERED MAN ON ALL OF MOL, FOR AKEDIN SHINES HIS BURNING VEINS UPON ME. I AM CLOSEST TO THE CORE ABOVE.

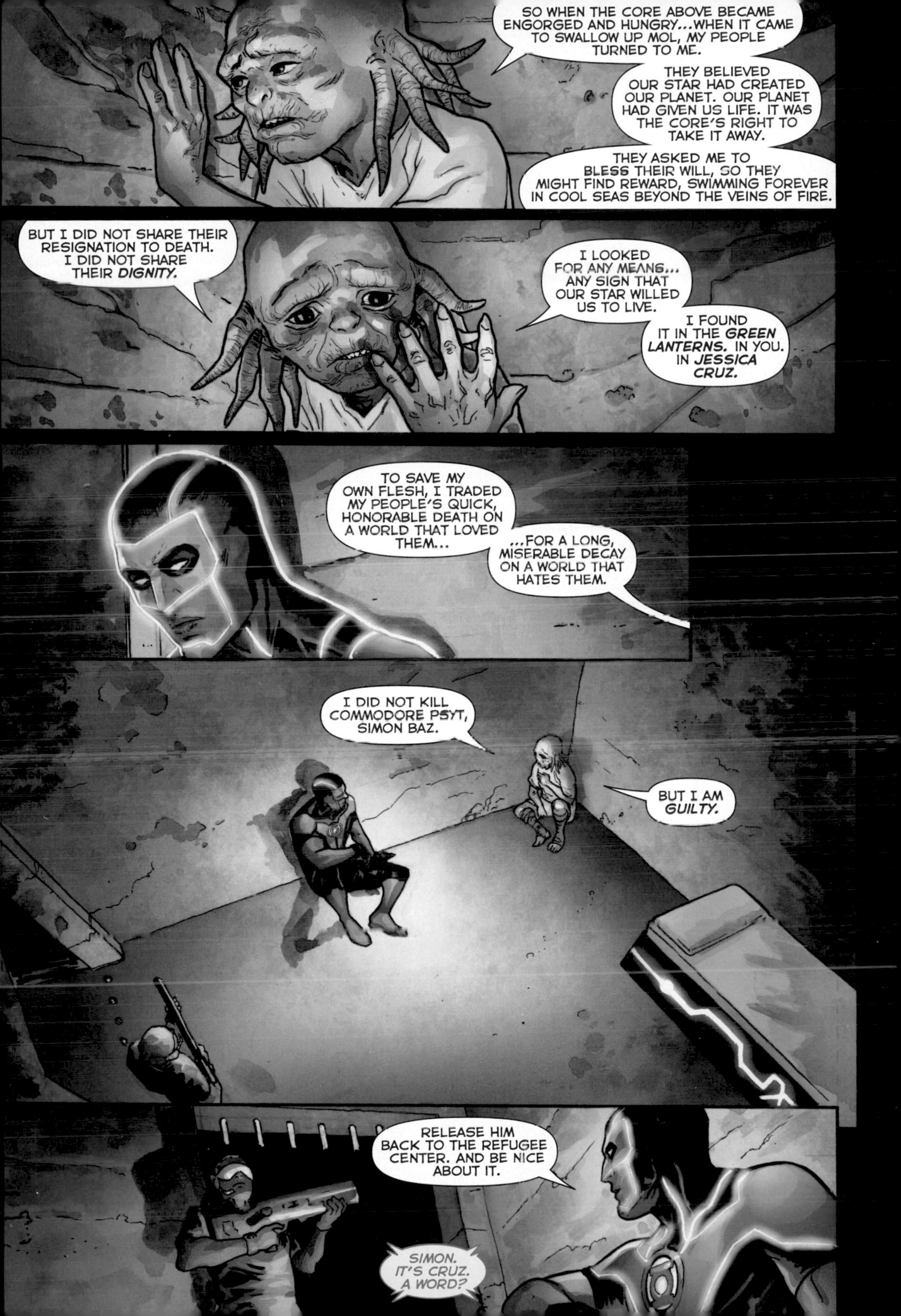
SO WHEN THE CORE ABOVE BECAME ENGORGED AND HUNGRY...WHEN IT CAME TO SWALLOW UP MOL, MY PEOPLE TURNED TO ME.
THEY BELIEVED OUR STAR HAD CREATED OUR PLANET. OUR PLANET HAD GIVEN US LIFE. IT WAS THE CORE'S RIGHT TO TAKE IT AWAY.
THEY ASKED ME TO BLESS THEIR WILL, SO THEY MIGHT FIND REWARD, SWIMMING FOREVER IN COOL SEAS BEYOND THE VEINS OF FIRE.
BUT I DID NOT SHARE THEIR RESIGNATION TO DEATH. I DID NOT SHARE THEIR *DIGNITY.*
I LOOKED FOR ANY MEANS... ANY SIGN THAT OUR STAR WILLED US TO LIVE.
I FOUND IT IN THE *GREEN LANTERNS.* IN YOU. IN *JESSICA CRUZ.*
TO SAVE MY OWN FLESH, I TRADED MY PEOPLE'S QUICK, HONORABLE DEATH ON A WORLD THAT LOVED THEM...
...FOR A LONG, MISERABLE DECAY ON A WORLD THAT HATES THEM.
I DID NOT KILL COMMODORE PSYT, SIMON BAZ.
BUT I AM *GUILTY.*
RELEASE HIM BACK TO THE REFUGEE CENTER. AND BE NICE ABOUT IT.
SIMON. IT'S CRUZ. A WORD?

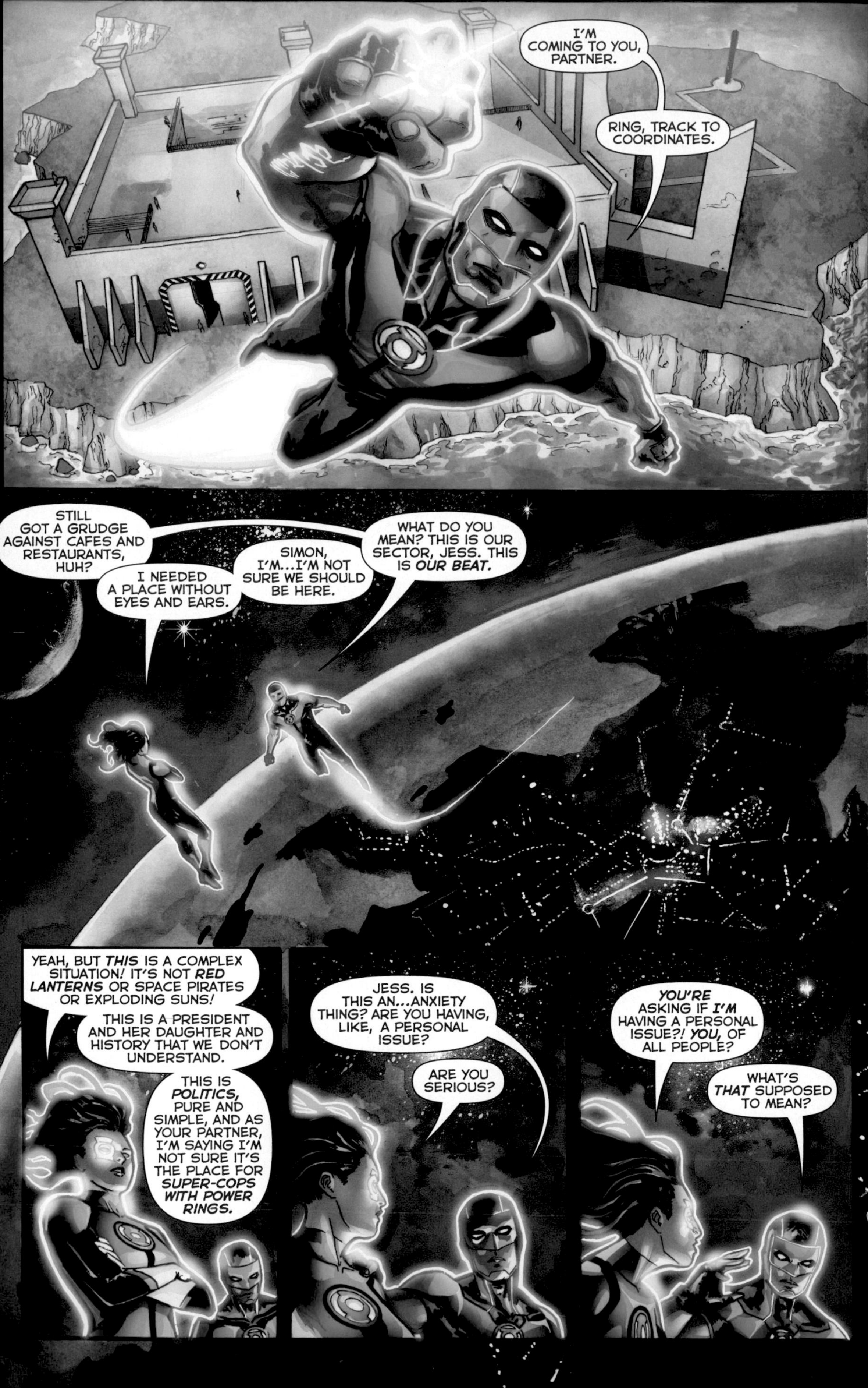

I'M COMING TO YOU, PARTNER.
RING, TRACK TO COORDINATES.
STILL GOT A GRUDGE AGAINST CAFES AND RESTAURANTS, HUH?
I NEEDED A PLACE WITHOUT EYES AND EARS.
SIMON, I'M...I'M NOT SURE WE SHOULD BE HERE.
WHAT DO YOU MEAN? THIS IS OUR SECTOR, JESS. THIS IS *OUR BEAT.*
YEAH, BUT *THIS* IS A COMPLEX SITUATION! IT'S NOT *RED LANTERNS* OR SPACE PIRATES OR EXPLODING SUNS!
THIS IS A PRESIDENT AND HER DAUGHTER AND HISTORY THAT WE DON'T UNDERSTAND.
THIS IS *POLITICS,* PURE AND SIMPLE, AND AS YOUR PARTNER, I'M SAYING I'M NOT SURE IT'S THE PLACE FOR *SUPER-COPS WITH POWER RINGS.*
JESS. IS THIS AN...ANXIETY THING? ARE YOU HAVING, LIKE, A PERSONAL ISSUE?
ARE YOU SERIOUS?
YOU'RE ASKING IF *I'M* HAVING A PERSONAL ISSUE?! *YOU,* OF ALL PEOPLE?
WHAT'S *THAT* SUPPOSED TO MEAN?

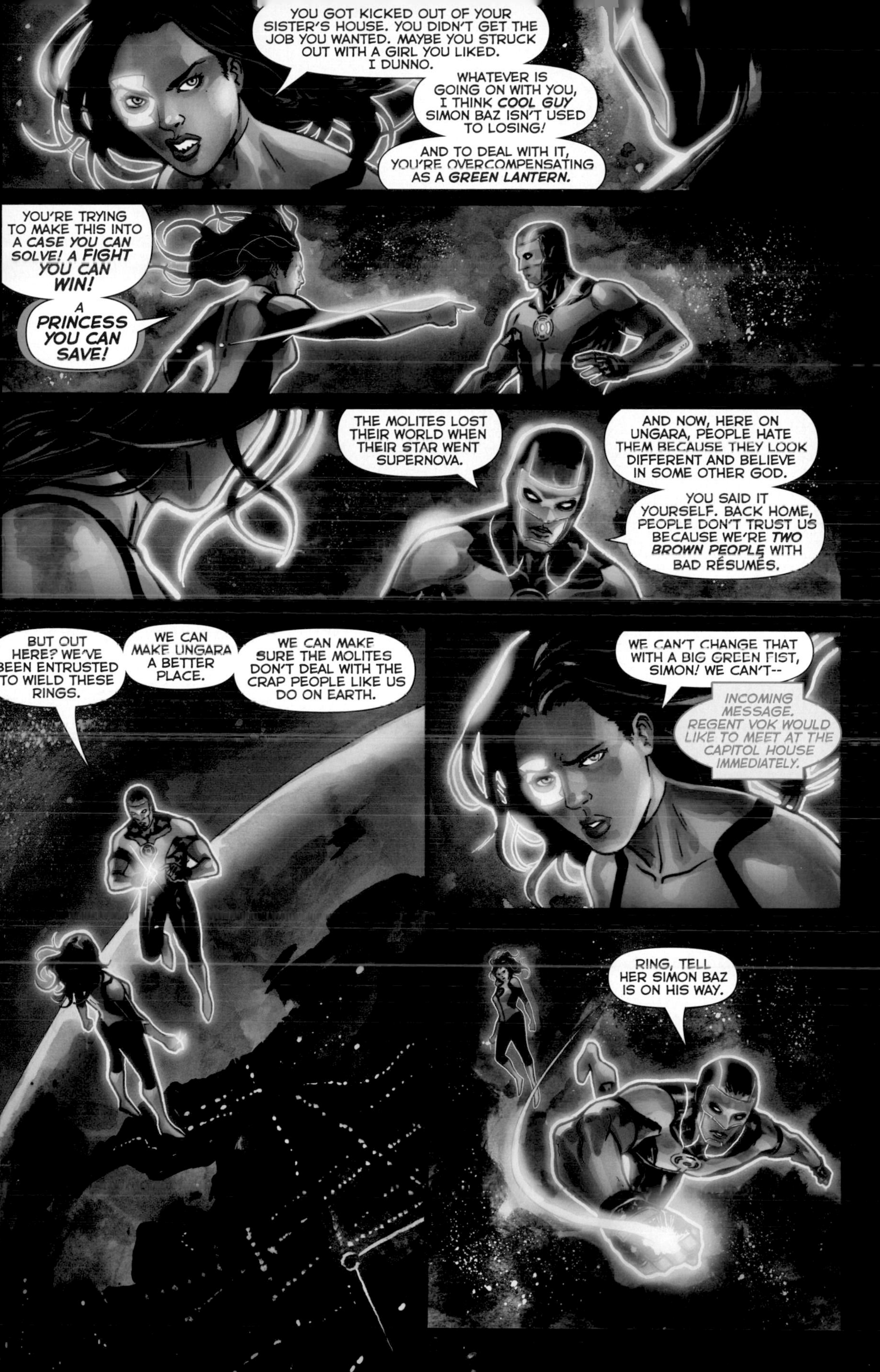

YOU GOT KICKED OUT OF YOUR SISTER'S HOUSE. YOU DIDN'T GET THE JOB YOU WANTED. MAYBE YOU STRUCK OUT WITH A GIRL YOU LIKED. I DUNNO.
WHATEVER IS GOING ON WITH YOU, I THINK COOL GUY SIMON BAZ ISN'T USED TO LOSING!
AND TO DEAL WITH IT, YOU'RE OVERCOMPENSATING AS A GREEN LANTERN.
YOU'RE TRYING TO MAKE THIS INTO A CASE YOU CAN SOLVE! A FIGHT YOU CAN WIN!
A PRINCESS YOU CAN SAVE!
THE MOLITES LOST THEIR WORLD WHEN THEIR STAR WENT SUPERNOVA.
AND NOW, HERE ON UNGARA, PEOPLE HATE THEM BECAUSE THEY LOOK DIFFERENT AND BELIEVE IN SOME OTHER GOD.
YOU SAID IT YOURSELF. BACK HOME, PEOPLE DON'T TRUST US BECAUSE WE'RE TWO BROWN PEOPLE WITH BAD RÉSUMÉS.
BUT OUT HERE? WE'VE BEEN ENTRUSTED TO WIELD THESE RINGS.
WE CAN MAKE UNGARA A BETTER PLACE.
WE CAN MAKE SURE THE MOLITES DON'T DEAL WITH THE CRAP PEOPLE LIKE US DO ON EARTH.
WE CAN'T CHANGE THAT WITH A BIG GREEN FIST, SIMON! WE CAN'T--
INCOMING MESSAGE. REGENT VOK WOULD LIKE TO MEET AT THE CAPITOL HOUSE IMMEDIATELY.
RING, TELL HER SIMON BAZ IS ON HIS WAY.

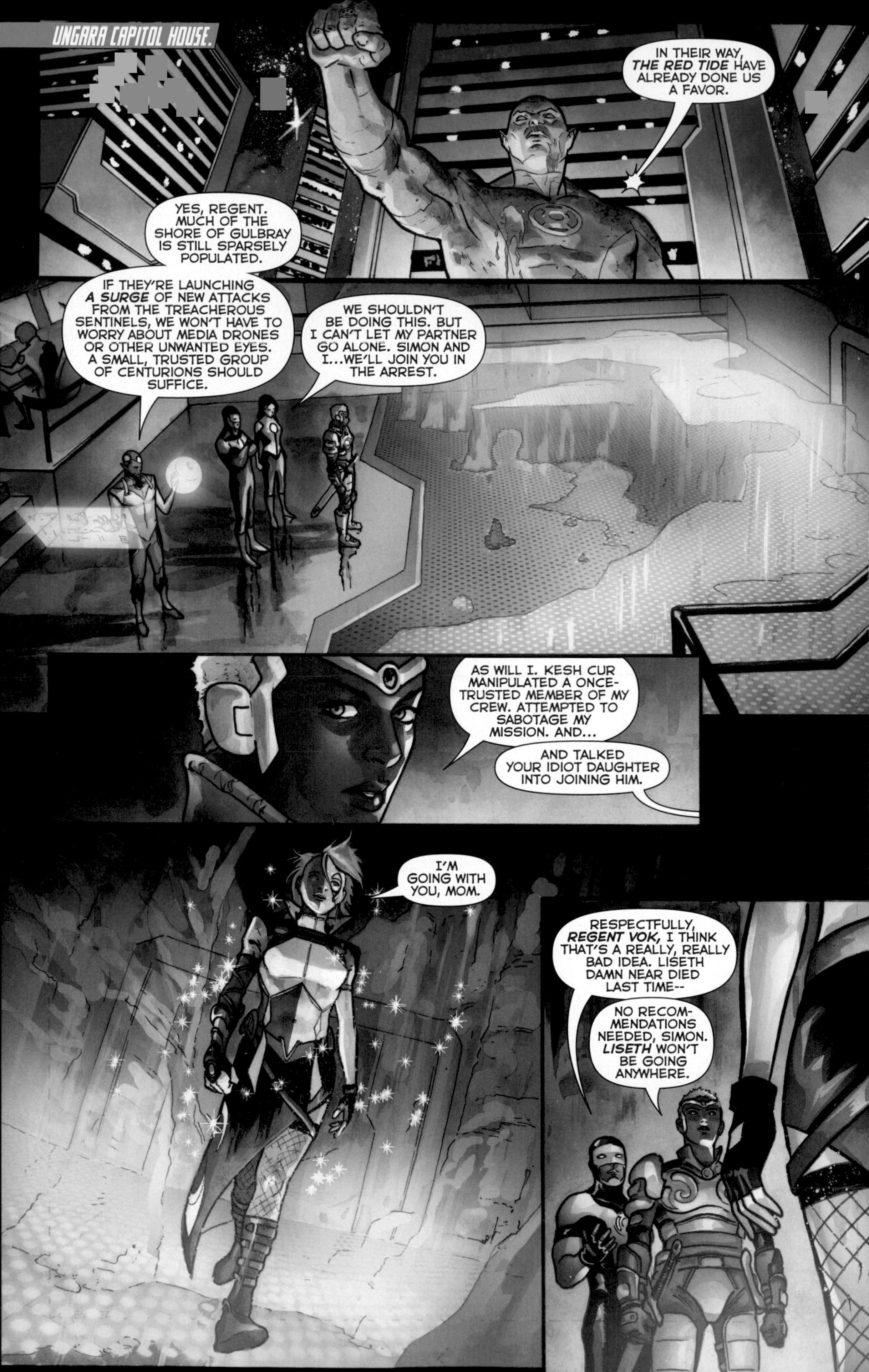
UNGARA CAPITOL HOUSE.
IN THEIR WAY, THE RED TIDE HAVE ALREADY DONE US A FAVOR.
YES, REGENT. MUCH OF THE SHORE OF GULBRAY IS STILL SPARSELY POPULATED.
IF THEY'RE LAUNCHING A SURGE OF NEW ATTACKS FROM THE TREACHEROUS SENTINELS, WE WON'T HAVE TO WORRY ABOUT MEDIA DRONES OR OTHER UNWANTED EYES. A SMALL, TRUSTED GROUP OF CENTURIONS SHOULD SUFFICE.
WE SHOULDN'T BE DOING THIS. BUT I CAN'T LET MY PARTNER GO ALONE. SIMON AND I...WE'LL JOIN YOU IN THE ARREST.
AS WILL I. KESH CUR MANIPULATED A ONCE-TRUSTED MEMBER OF MY CREW. ATTEMPTED TO SABOTAGE MY MISSION. AND...
AND TALKED YOUR IDIOT DAUGHTER INTO JOINING HIM.
I'M GOING WITH YOU, MOM.
RESPECTFULLY, REGENT VOK, I THINK THAT'S A REALLY, REALLY BAD IDEA. LISETH DAMN NEAR DIED LAST TIME--
NO RECOM-MENDATIONS NEEDED, SIMON. LISETH WON'T BE GOING ANYWHERE.

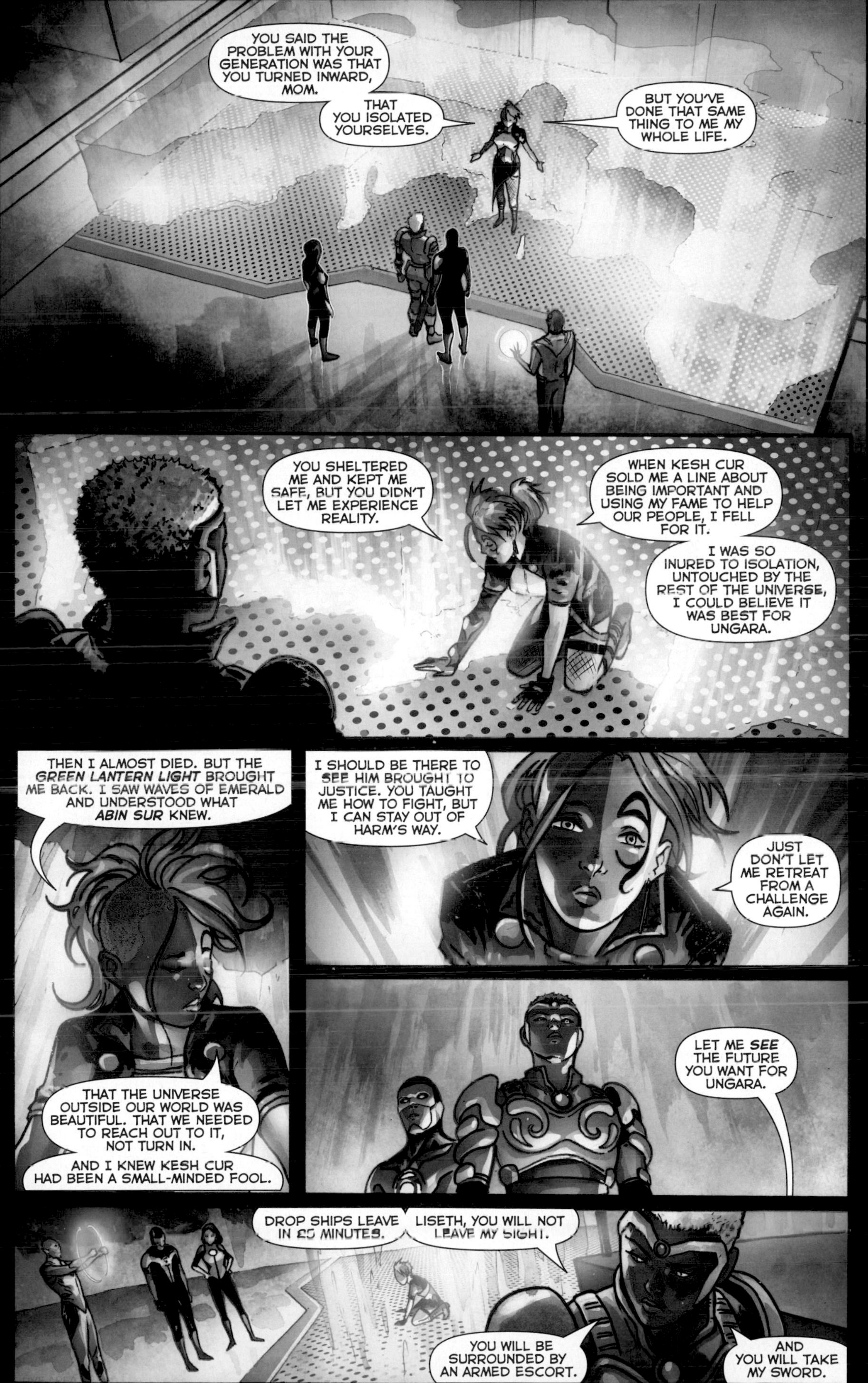
YOU SAID THE PROBLEM WITH YOUR GENERATION WAS THAT YOU TURNED INWARD, MOM.
THAT YOU ISOLATED YOURSELVES.
BUT YOU'VE DONE THAT SAME THING TO ME MY WHOLE LIFE.
YOU SHELTERED ME AND KEPT ME SAFE, BUT YOU DIDN'T LET ME EXPERIENCE REALITY.
WHEN KESH CUR SOLD ME A LINE ABOUT BEING IMPORTANT AND USING MY FAME TO HELP OUR PEOPLE, I FELL FOR IT.
I WAS SO INURED TO ISOLATION, UNTOUCHED BY THE REST OF THE UNIVERSE, I COULD BELIEVE IT WAS BEST FOR UNGARA.
THEN I ALMOST DIED. BUT THE *GREEN LANTERN LIGHT* BROUGHT ME BACK. I SAW WAVES OF EMERALD AND UNDERSTOOD WHAT **ABIN SUR** KNEW.
THAT THE UNIVERSE OUTSIDE OUR WORLD WAS BEAUTIFUL. THAT WE NEEDED TO REACH OUT TO IT, NOT TURN IN.
AND I KNEW KESH CUR HAD BEEN A SMALL-MINDED FOOL.
I SHOULD BE THERE TO SEE HIM BROUGHT TO JUSTICE. YOU TAUGHT ME HOW TO FIGHT, BUT I CAN STAY OUT OF HARM'S WAY.
JUST DON'T LET ME RETREAT FROM A CHALLENGE AGAIN.
LET ME **SEE** THE FUTURE YOU WANT FOR UNGARA.
DROP SHIPS LEAVE IN 25 MINUTES.
LISETH, YOU WILL NOT LEAVE MY SIGHT.
YOU WILL BE SURROUNDED BY AN ARMED ESCORT.
AND YOU WILL TAKE MY SWORD.

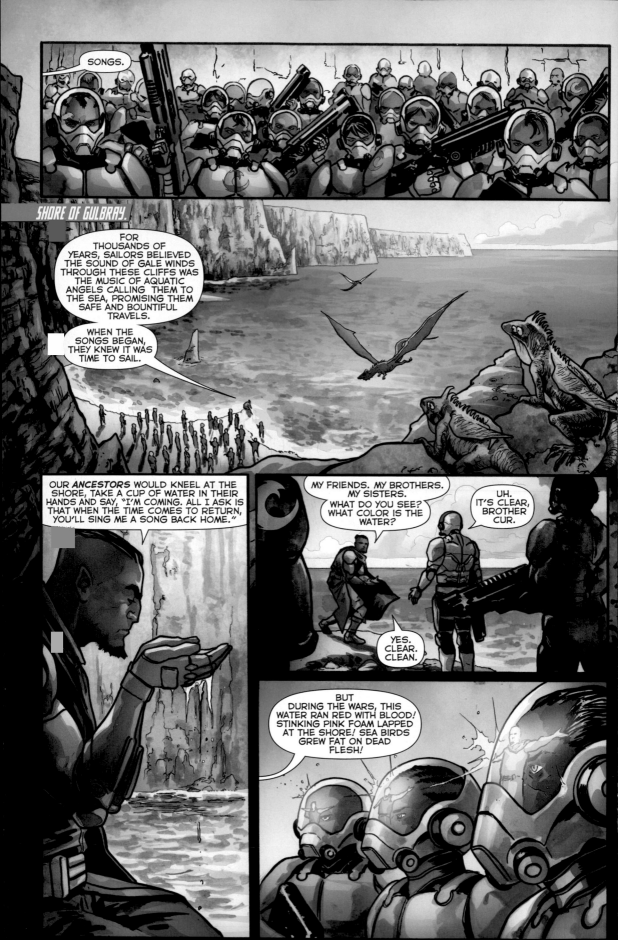

SONGS.

SHORE OF GULBRAY.

FOR THOUSANDS OF YEARS, SAILORS BELIEVED THE SOUND OF GALE WINDS THROUGH THESE CLIFFS WAS THE MUSIC OF AQUATIC ANGELS CALLING THEM TO THE SEA, PROMISING THEM SAFE AND BOUNTIFUL TRAVELS.

WHEN THE SONGS BEGAN, THEY KNEW IT WAS TIME TO SAIL.

OUR *ANCESTORS* WOULD KNEEL AT THE SHORE, TAKE A CUP OF WATER IN THEIR HANDS AND SAY, "I'M COMING. ALL I ASK IS THAT WHEN THE TIME COMES TO RETURN, YOU'LL SING ME A SONG BACK HOME."

MY FRIENDS. MY BROTHERS. MY SISTERS. WHAT DO YOU SEE? WHAT COLOR IS THE WATER?

UH. IT'S CLEAR, BROTHER CUR.

YES. CLEAR. CLEAN.

BUT DURING THE WARS, THIS WATER RAN RED WITH BLOOD! STINKING PINK FOAM LAPPED AT THE SHORE! SEA BIRDS GREW FAT ON DEAD FLESH!

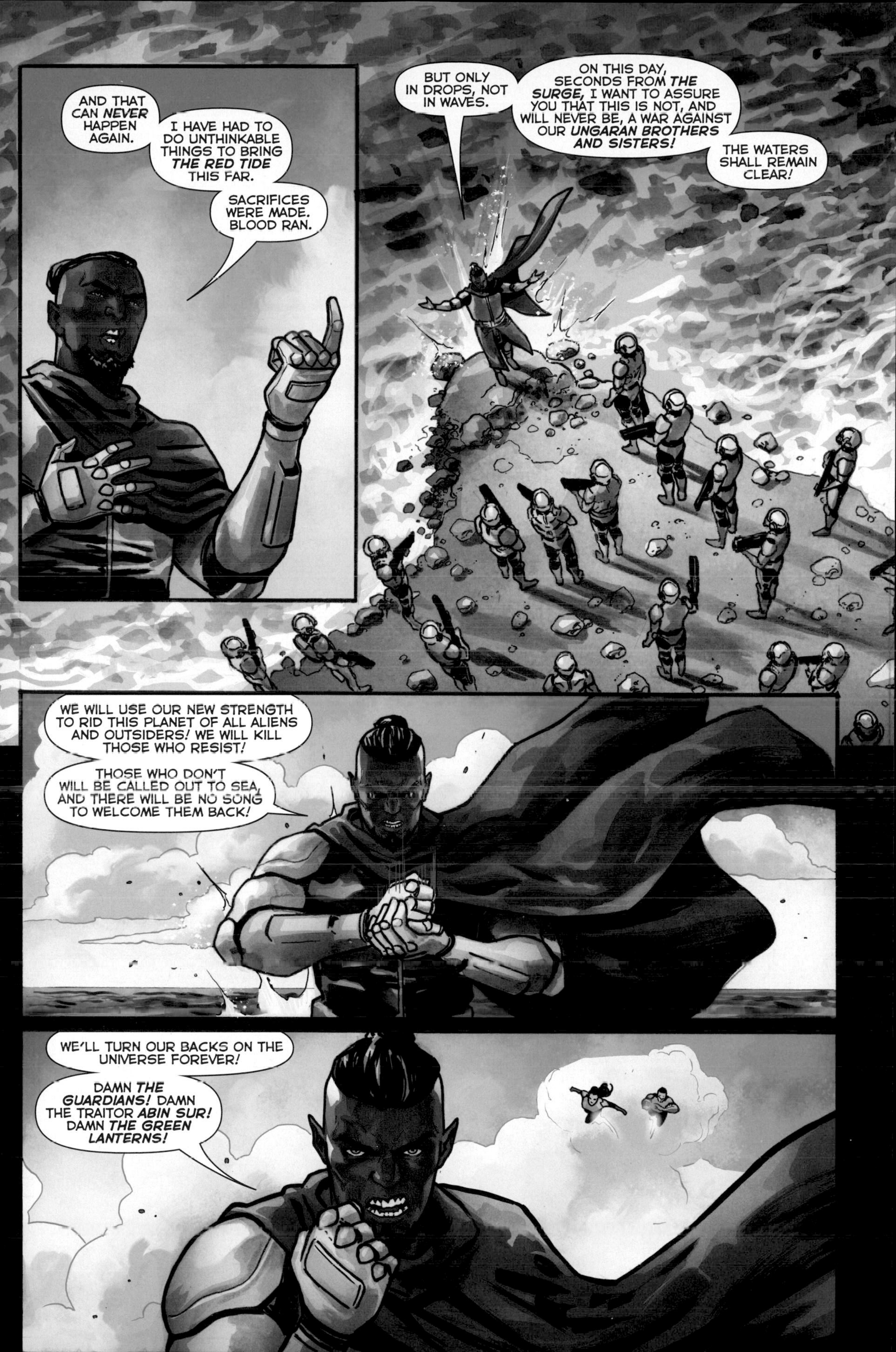
AND THAT CAN NEVER HAPPEN AGAIN.
I HAVE HAD TO DO UNTHINKABLE THINGS TO BRING THE RED TIDE THIS FAR.
SACRIFICES WERE MADE. BLOOD RAN.
BUT ONLY IN DROPS, NOT IN WAVES.
ON THIS DAY, SECONDS FROM THE SURGE, I WANT TO ASSURE YOU THAT THIS IS NOT, AND WILL NEVER BE, A WAR AGAINST OUR UNGARAN BROTHERS AND SISTERS!
THE WATERS SHALL REMAIN CLEAR!
WE WILL USE OUR NEW STRENGTH TO RID THIS PLANET OF ALL ALIENS AND OUTSIDERS! WE WILL KILL THOSE WHO RESIST!
THOSE WHO DON'T WILL BE CALLED OUT TO SEA, AND THERE WILL BE NO SONG TO WELCOME THEM BACK!
WE'LL TURN OUR BACKS ON THE UNIVERSE FOREVER!
DAMN THE GUARDIANS! DAMN THE TRAITOR ABIN SUR! DAMN THE GREEN LANTERNS!

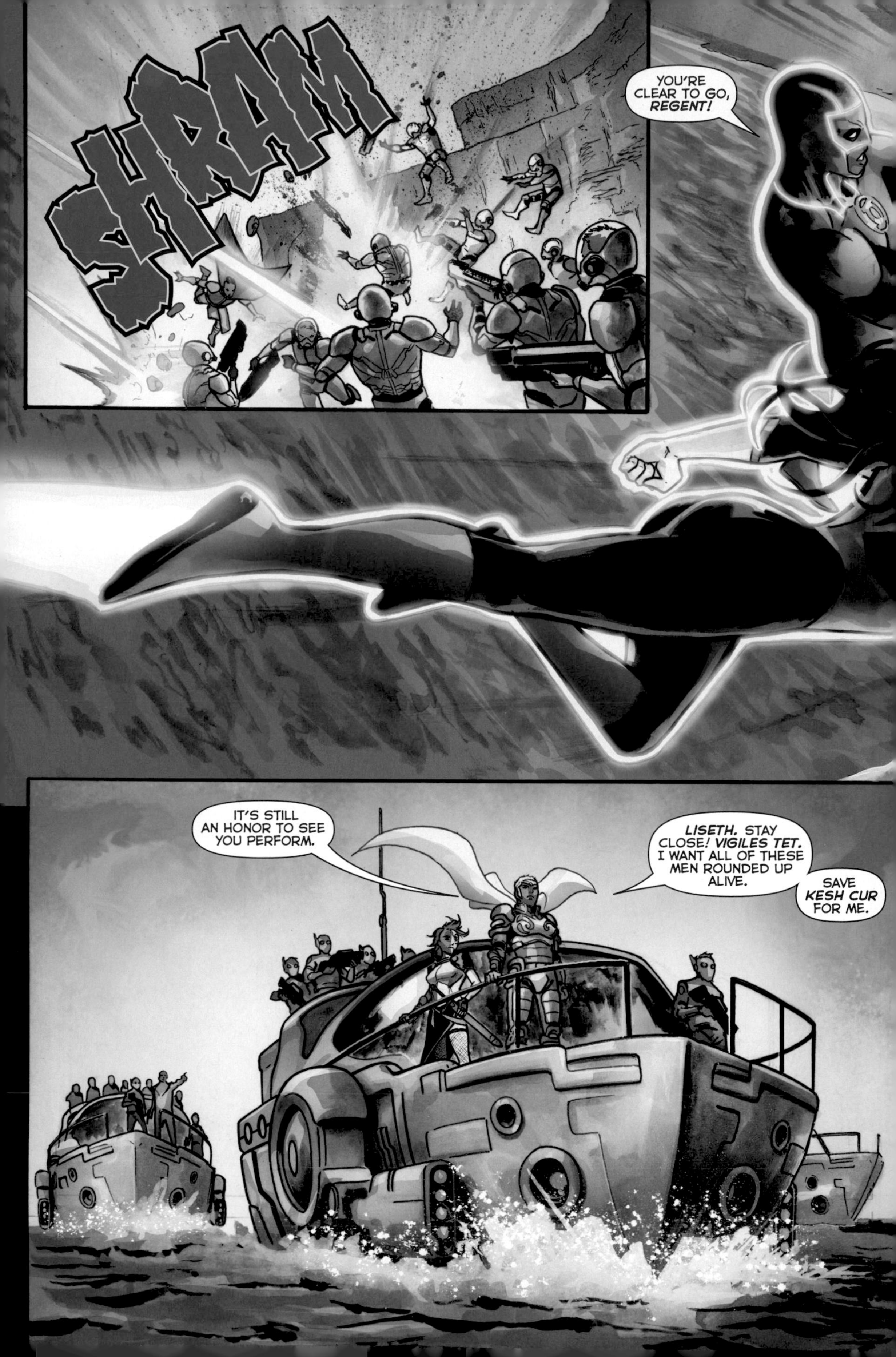
SHRAM
YOU'RE CLEAR TO GO, *REGENT!*
IT'S STILL AN HONOR TO SEE YOU PERFORM.
LISETH. STAY CLOSE! *VIGILES TET.* I WANT ALL OF THESE MEN ROUNDED UP ALIVE.
SAVE *KESH CUR* FOR ME.

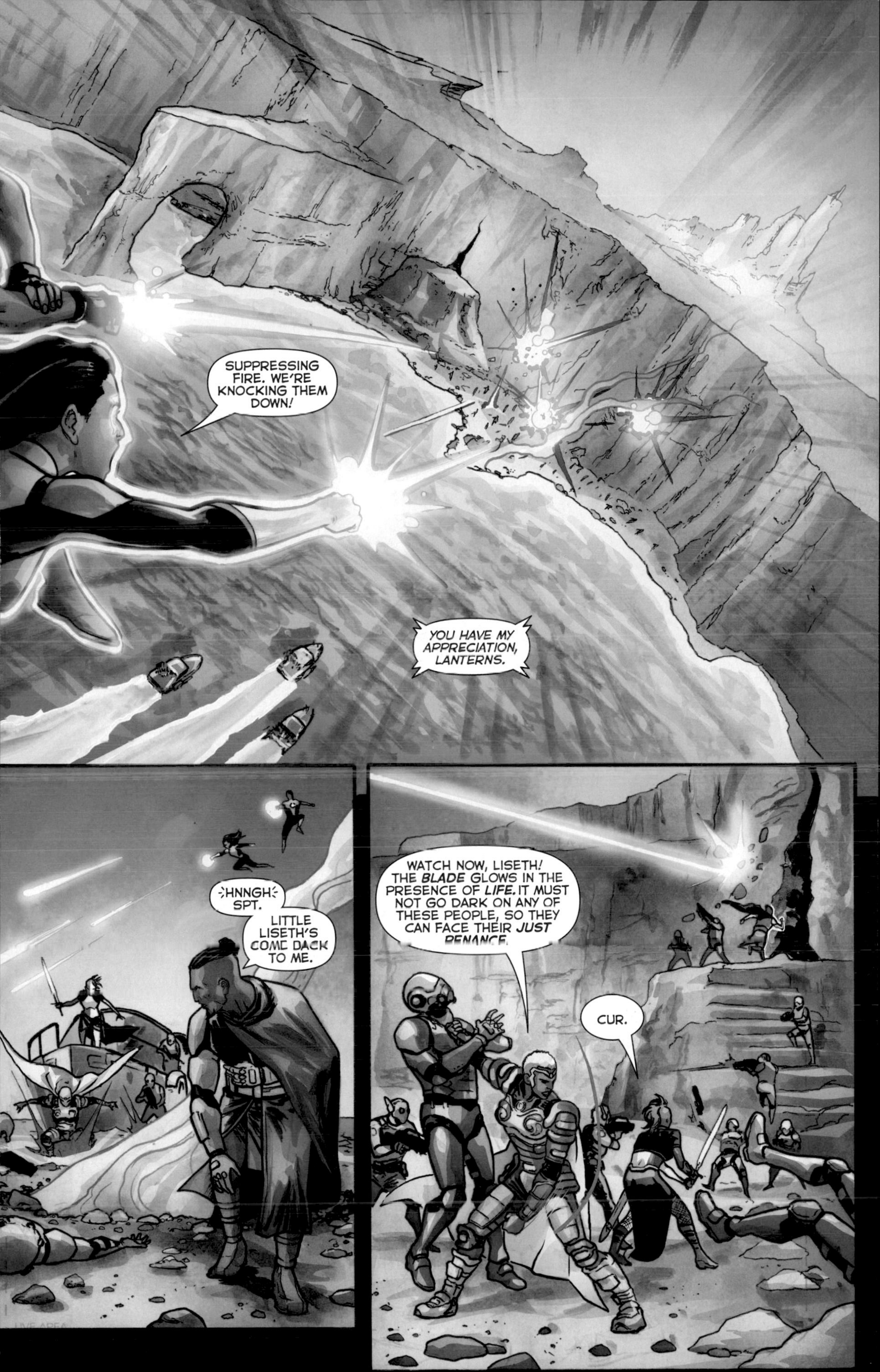
SUPPRESSING FIRE. WE'RE KNOCKING THEM DOWN!
YOU HAVE MY APPRECIATION, LANTERNS.
HNNGH SPT.
LITTLE LISETH'S COME BACK TO ME.
WATCH NOW, LISETH! THE BLADE GLOWS IN THE PRESENCE OF LIFE. IT MUST NOT GO DARK ON ANY OF THESE PEOPLE, SO THEY CAN FACE THEIR JUST PENANCE.
CUR.

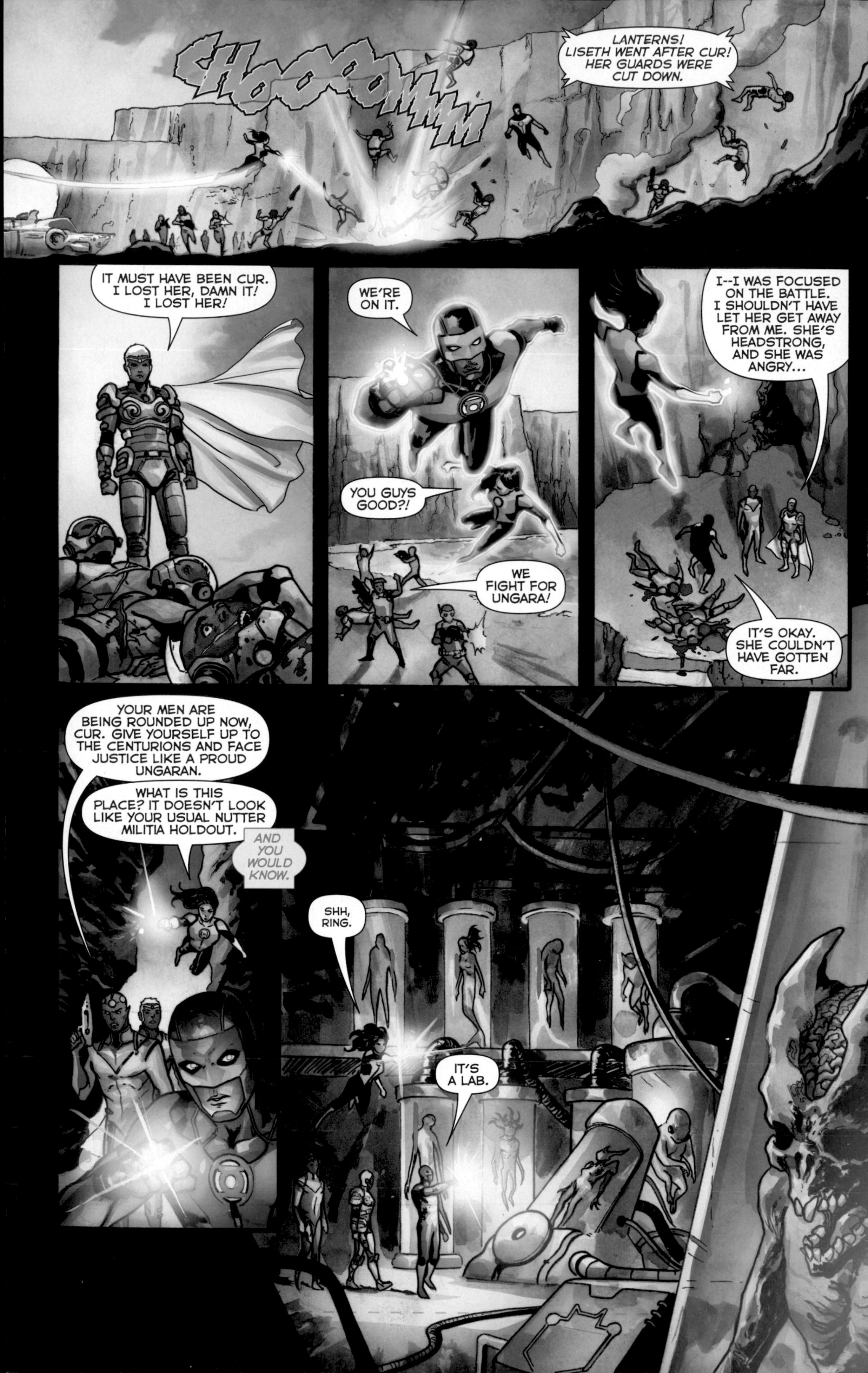
CHOOOOMMM
LANTERNS! LISETH WENT AFTER CUR! HER GUARDS WERE CUT DOWN.
IT MUST HAVE BEEN CUR. I LOST HER, DAMN IT! I LOST HER!
WE'RE ON IT.
YOU GUYS GOOD?!
WE FIGHT FOR UNGARA!
I--I WAS FOCUSED ON THE BATTLE. I SHOULDN'T HAVE LET HER GET AWAY FROM ME. SHE'S HEADSTRONG, AND SHE WAS ANGRY...
IT'S OKAY. SHE COULDN'T HAVE GOTTEN FAR.
YOUR MEN ARE BEING ROUNDED UP NOW, CUR. GIVE YOURSELF UP TO THE CENTURIONS AND FACE JUSTICE LIKE A PROUD UNGARAN.
WHAT IS THIS PLACE? IT DOESN'T LOOK LIKE YOUR USUAL NUTTER MILITIA HOLDOUT.
AND YOU WOULD KNOW.
SHH, RING.
IT'S A LAB.

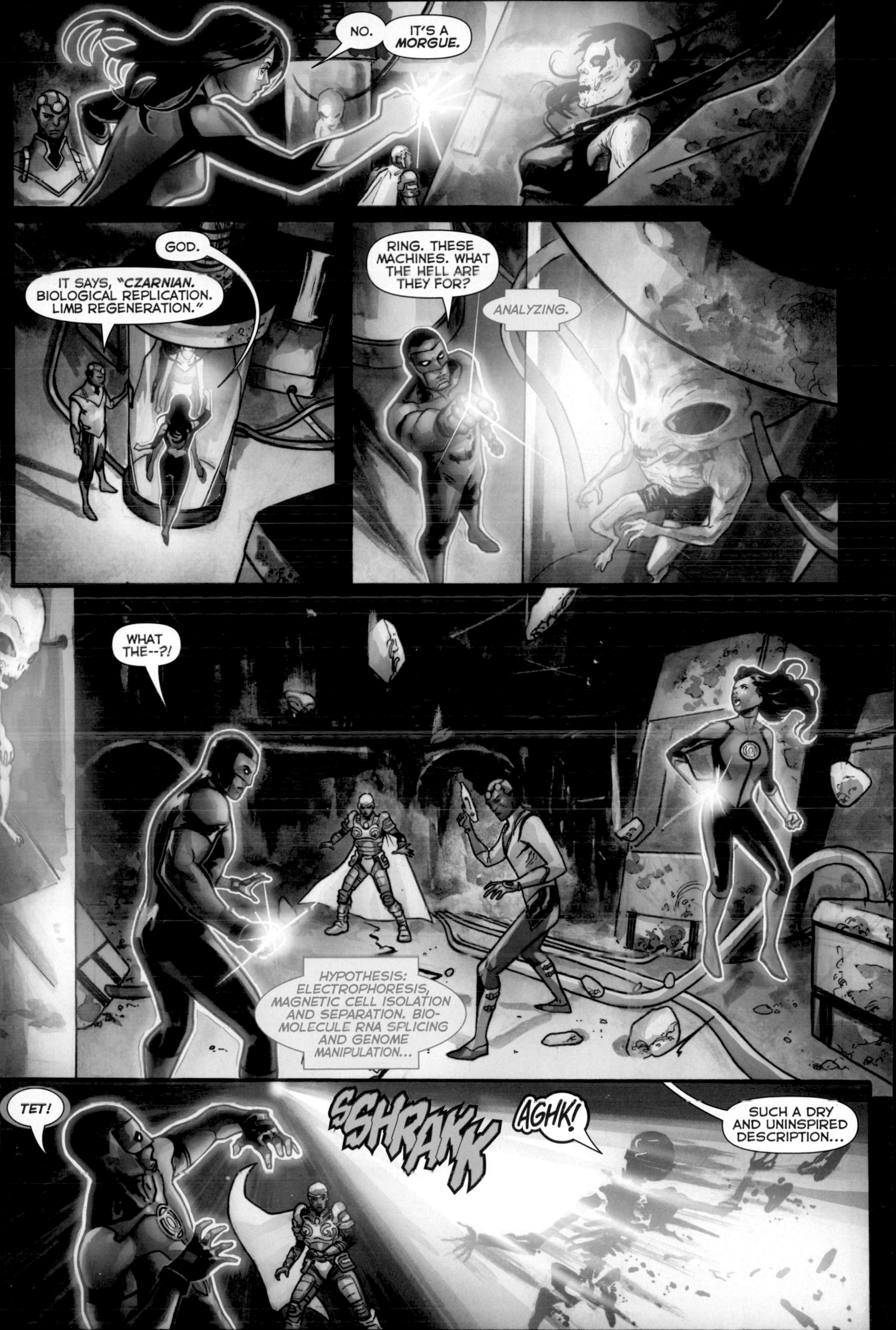
NO.
IT'S A MORGUE.
GOD.
IT SAYS, "CZARNIAN. BIOLOGICAL REPLICATION. LIMB REGENERATION."
RING. THESE MACHINES. WHAT THE HELL ARE THEY FOR?
ANALYZING.
WHAT THE--?!
HYPOTHESIS: ELECTROPHORESIS, MAGNETIC CELL ISOLATION AND SEPARATION. BIO-MOLECULE RNA SPLICING AND GENOME MANIPULATION...
TET!
SSHRAKK
AGHK!
SUCH A DRY AND UNINSPIRED DESCRIPTION...

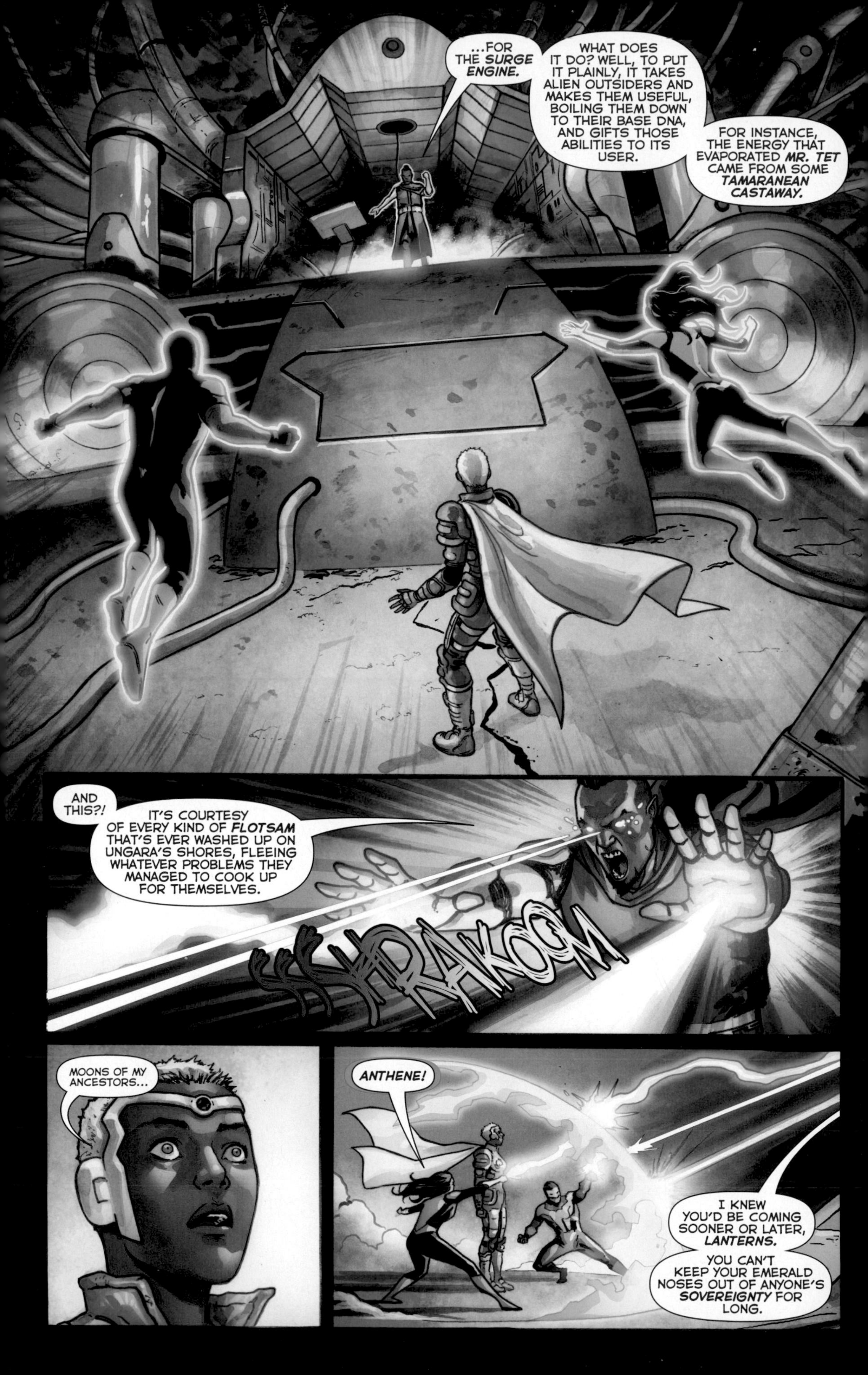

...FOR THE SURGE ENGINE.
WHAT DOES IT DO? WELL, TO PUT IT PLAINLY, IT TAKES ALIEN OUTSIDERS AND MAKES THEM USEFUL, BOILING THEM DOWN TO THEIR BASE DNA, AND GIFTS THOSE ABILITIES TO ITS USER.
FOR INSTANCE, THE ENERGY THAT EVAPORATED MR. TET CAME FROM SOME TAMARANEAN CASTAWAY.
AND THIS?!
IT'S COURTESY OF EVERY KIND OF FLOTSAM THAT'S EVER WASHED UP ON UNGARA'S SHORES, FLEEING WHATEVER PROBLEMS THEY MANAGED TO COOK UP FOR THEMSELVES.
SSSHRAKOOM
MOONS OF MY ANCESTORS...
ANTHENE!
I KNEW YOU'D BE COMING SOONER OR LATER, LANTERNS.
YOU CAN'T KEEP YOUR EMERALD NOSES OUT OF ANYONE'S SOVEREIGNTY FOR LONG.

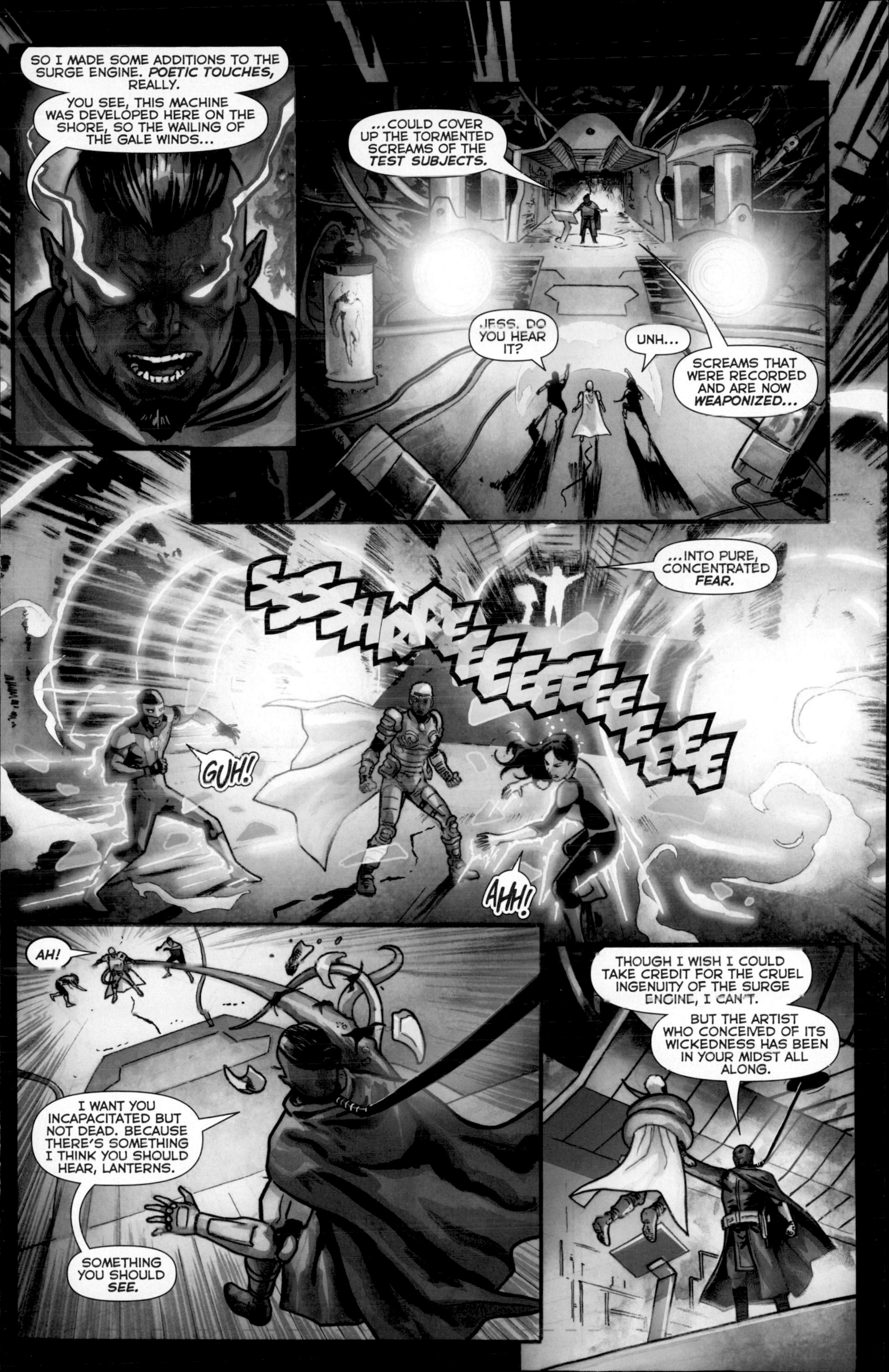

SO I MADE SOME ADDITIONS TO THE SURGE ENGINE. *POETIC TOUCHES,* REALLY.
YOU SEE, THIS MACHINE WAS DEVELOPED HERE ON THE SHORE, SO THE WAILING OF THE GALE WINDS...
...COULD COVER UP THE TORMENTED SCREAMS OF THE *TEST SUBJECTS.*
JESS. DO YOU HEAR IT?
UNH...
SCREAMS THAT WERE RECORDED AND ARE NOW *WEAPONIZED...*
...INTO PURE, CONCENTRATED *FEAR.*
SSSHREEEEEEEEEEEEEE
GUH!
AHH!
AH!
I WANT YOU INCAPACITATED BUT NOT DEAD. BECAUSE THERE'S SOMETHING I THINK YOU SHOULD HEAR, LANTERNS.
SOMETHING YOU SHOULD *SEE.*
THOUGH I WISH I COULD TAKE CREDIT FOR THE CRUEL INGENUITY OF THE SURGE ENGINE, I CAN'T.
BUT THE ARTIST WHO CONCEIVED OF ITS WICKEDNESS HAS BEEN IN YOUR MIDST ALL ALONG.

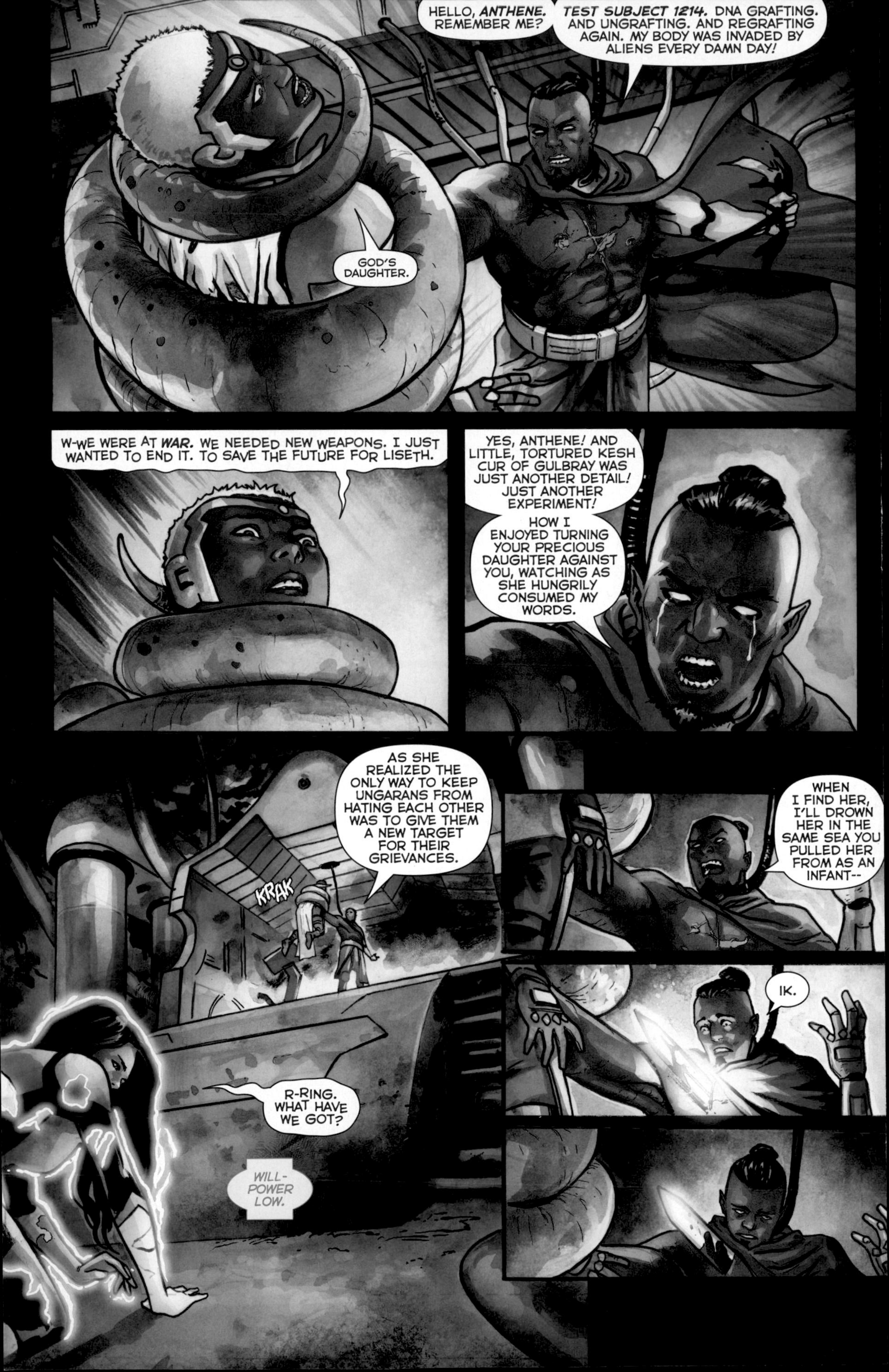
HELLO, ANTHENE. REMEMBER ME?
TEST SUBJECT 1214. DNA GRAFTING. AND UNGRAFTING. AND REGRAFTING AGAIN. MY BODY WAS INVADED BY ALIENS EVERY DAMN DAY!
GOD'S DAUGHTER.
W-WE WERE AT WAR. WE NEEDED NEW WEAPONS. I JUST WANTED TO END IT. TO SAVE THE FUTURE FOR LISETH.
YES, ANTHENE! AND LITTLE, TORTURED KESH CUR OF GULBRAY WAS JUST ANOTHER DETAIL! JUST ANOTHER EXPERIMENT!
HOW I ENJOYED TURNING YOUR PRECIOUS DAUGHTER AGAINST YOU, WATCHING AS SHE HUNGRILY CONSUMED MY WORDS.
AS SHE REALIZED THE ONLY WAY TO KEEP UNGARANS FROM HATING EACH OTHER WAS TO GIVE THEM A NEW TARGET FOR THEIR GRIEVANCES.
KRAK
WHEN I FIND HER, I'LL DROWN HER IN THE SAME SEA YOU PULLED HER FROM AS AN INFANT--
IK.
R-RING. WHAT HAVE WE GOT?
WILL-POWER LOW.

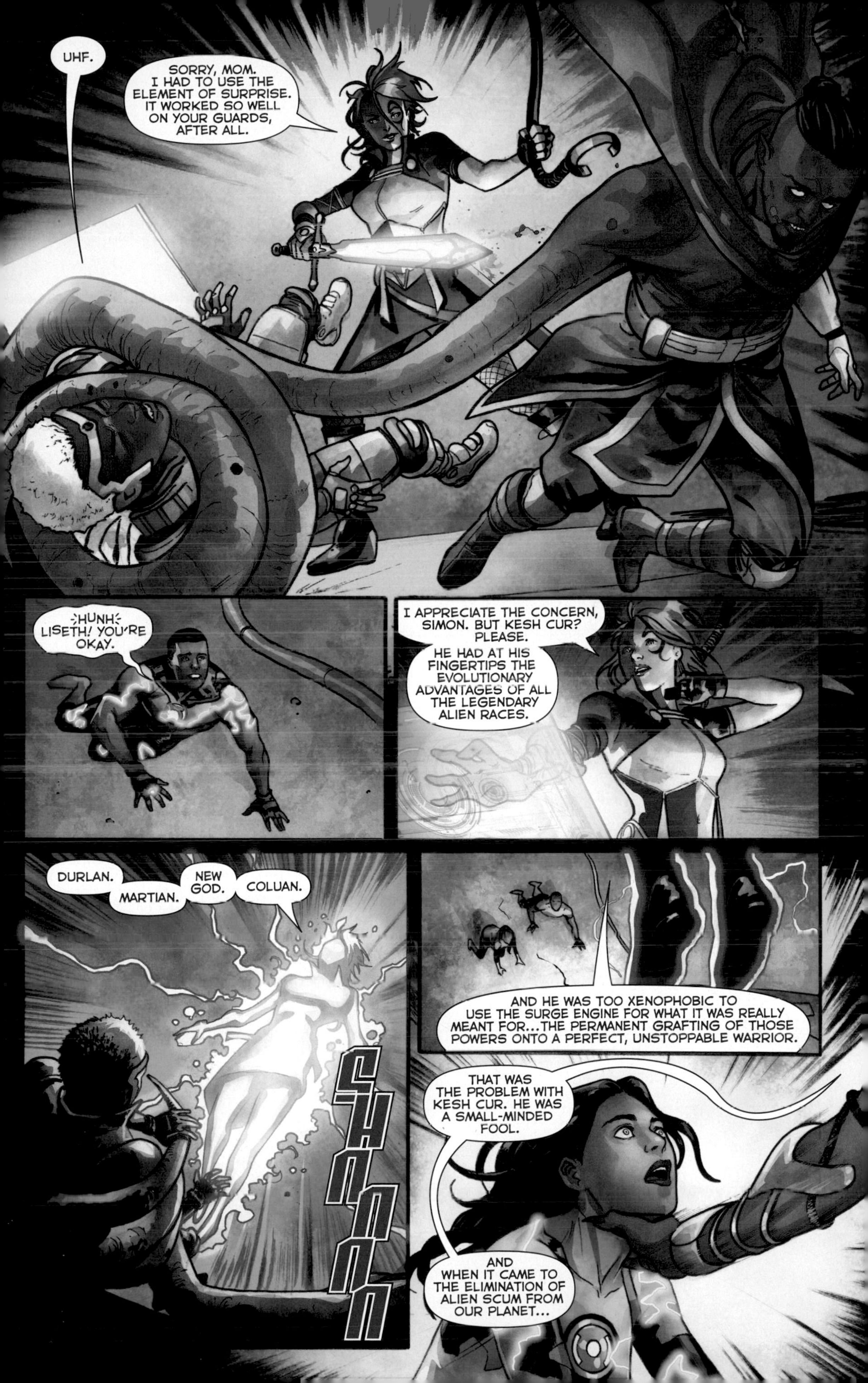
UHF.
SORRY, MOM. I HAD TO USE THE ELEMENT OF SURPRISE. IT WORKED SO WELL ON YOUR GUARDS, AFTER ALL.
HUNH LISETH! YOU'RE OKAY.
I APPRECIATE THE CONCERN, SIMON. BUT KESH CUR? PLEASE.
HE HAD AT HIS FINGERTIPS THE EVOLUTIONARY ADVANTAGES OF ALL THE LEGENDARY ALIEN RACES.
DURLAN.
MARTIAN.
NEW GOD.
COLUAN.
SHHHHH
AND HE WAS TOO XENOPHOBIC TO USE THE SURGE ENGINE FOR WHAT IT WAS REALLY MEANT FOR...THE PERMANENT GRAFTING OF THOSE POWERS ONTO A PERFECT, UNSTOPPABLE WARRIOR.
THAT WAS THE PROBLEM WITH KESH CUR. HE WAS A SMALL-MINDED FOOL.
AND WHEN IT CAME TO THE ELIMINATION OF ALIEN SCUM FROM OUR PLANET...

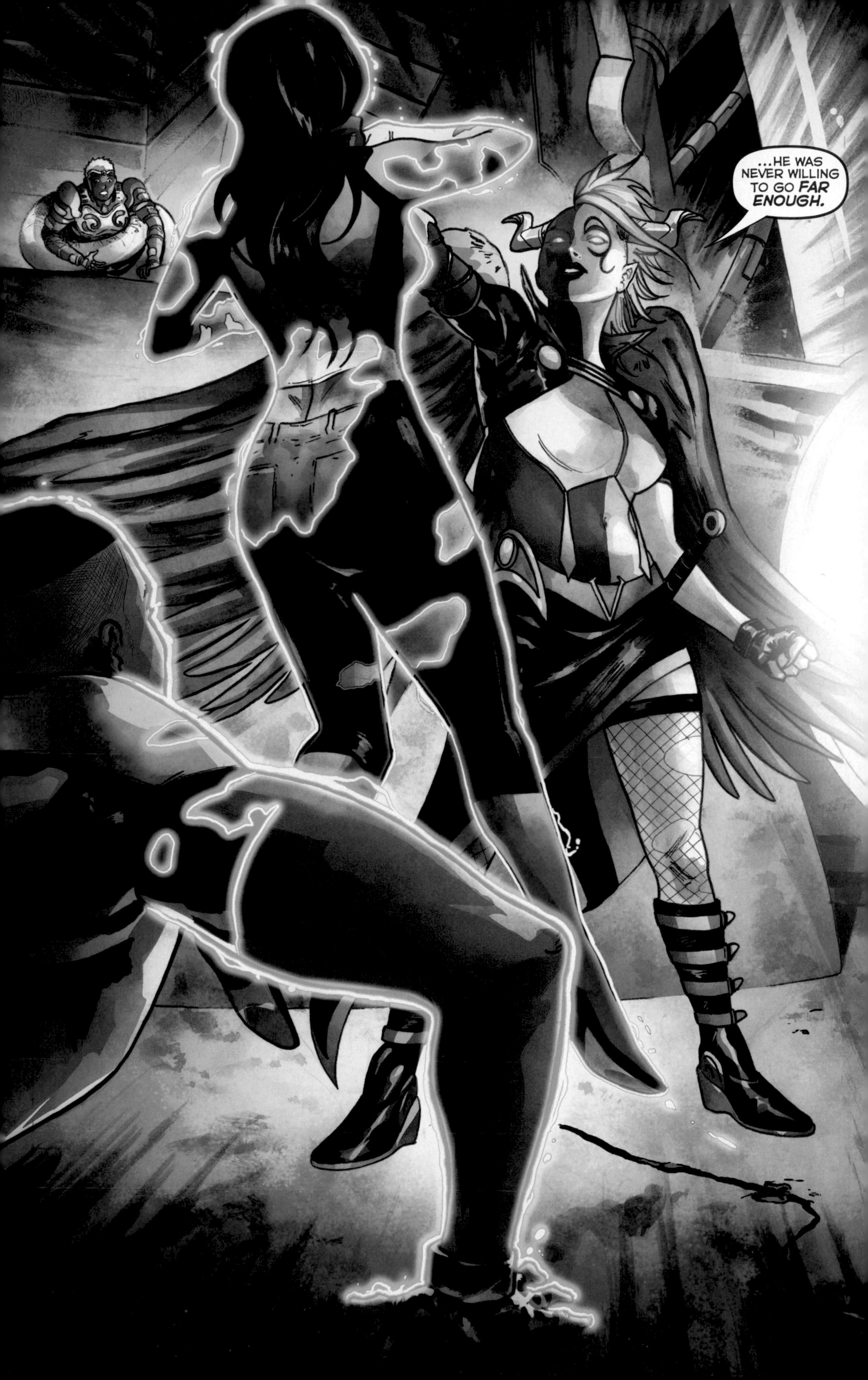
...HE WAS NEVER WILLING TO GO FAR ENOUGH.

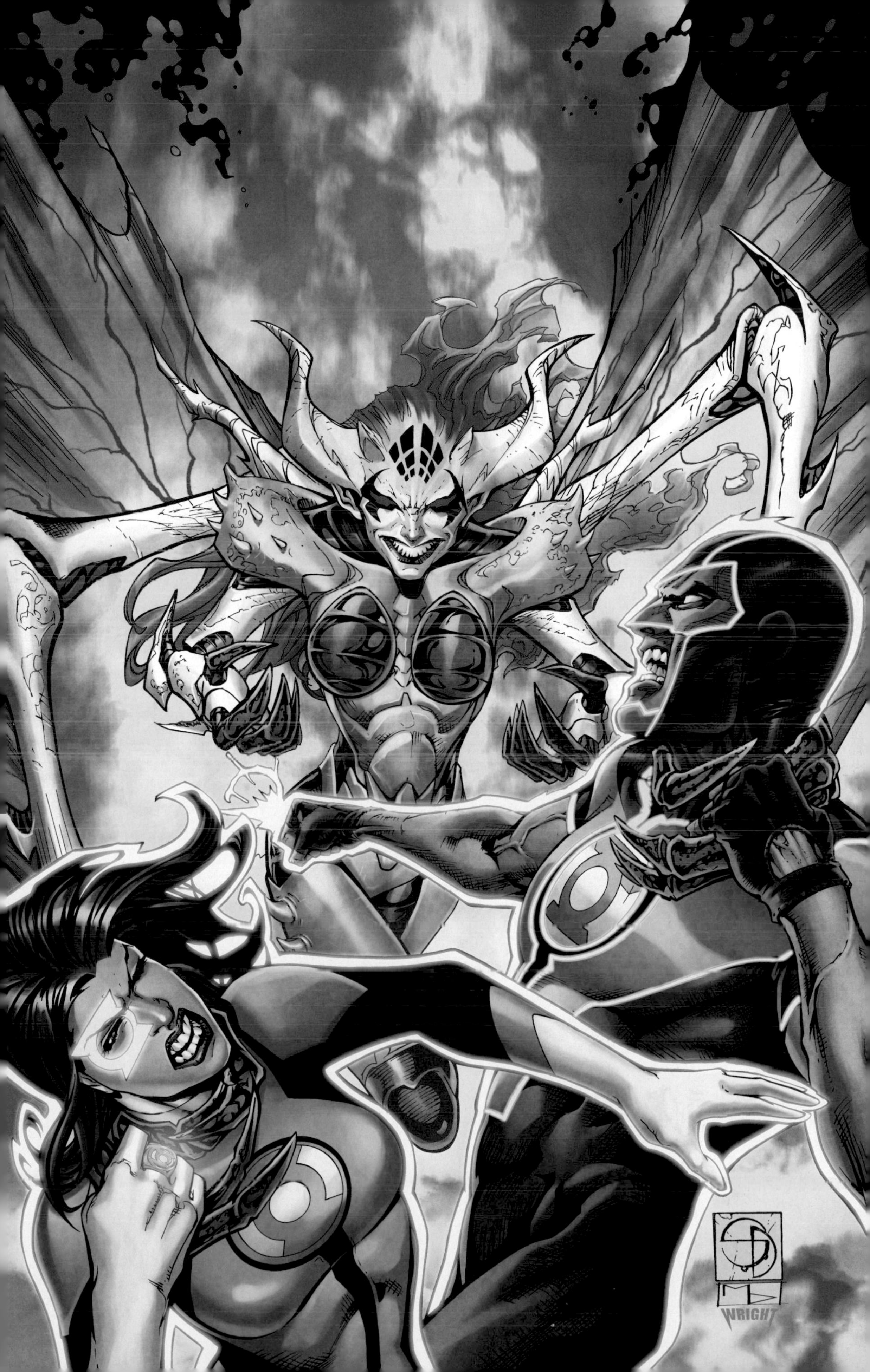
WRIGHT

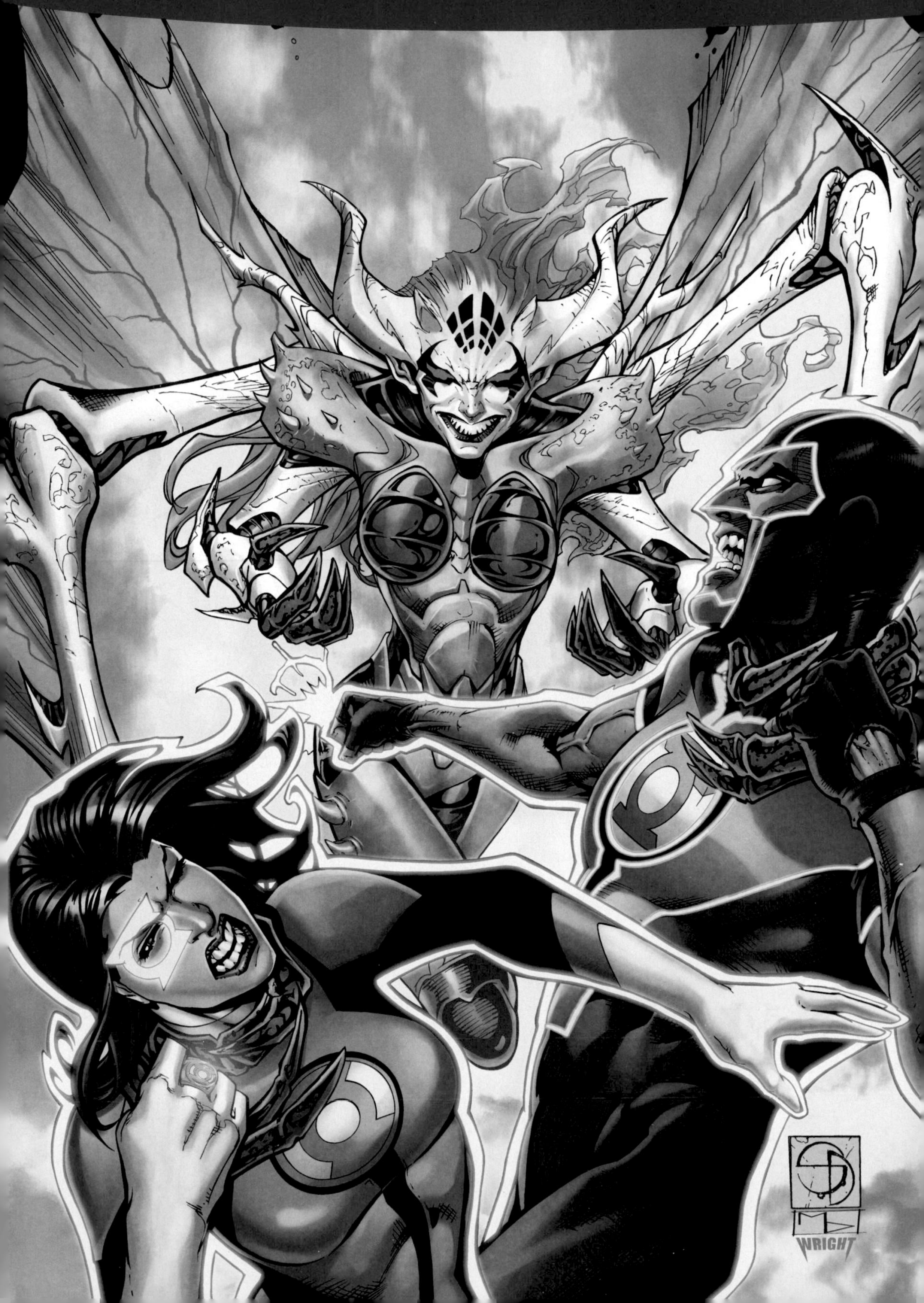
WRIGHT

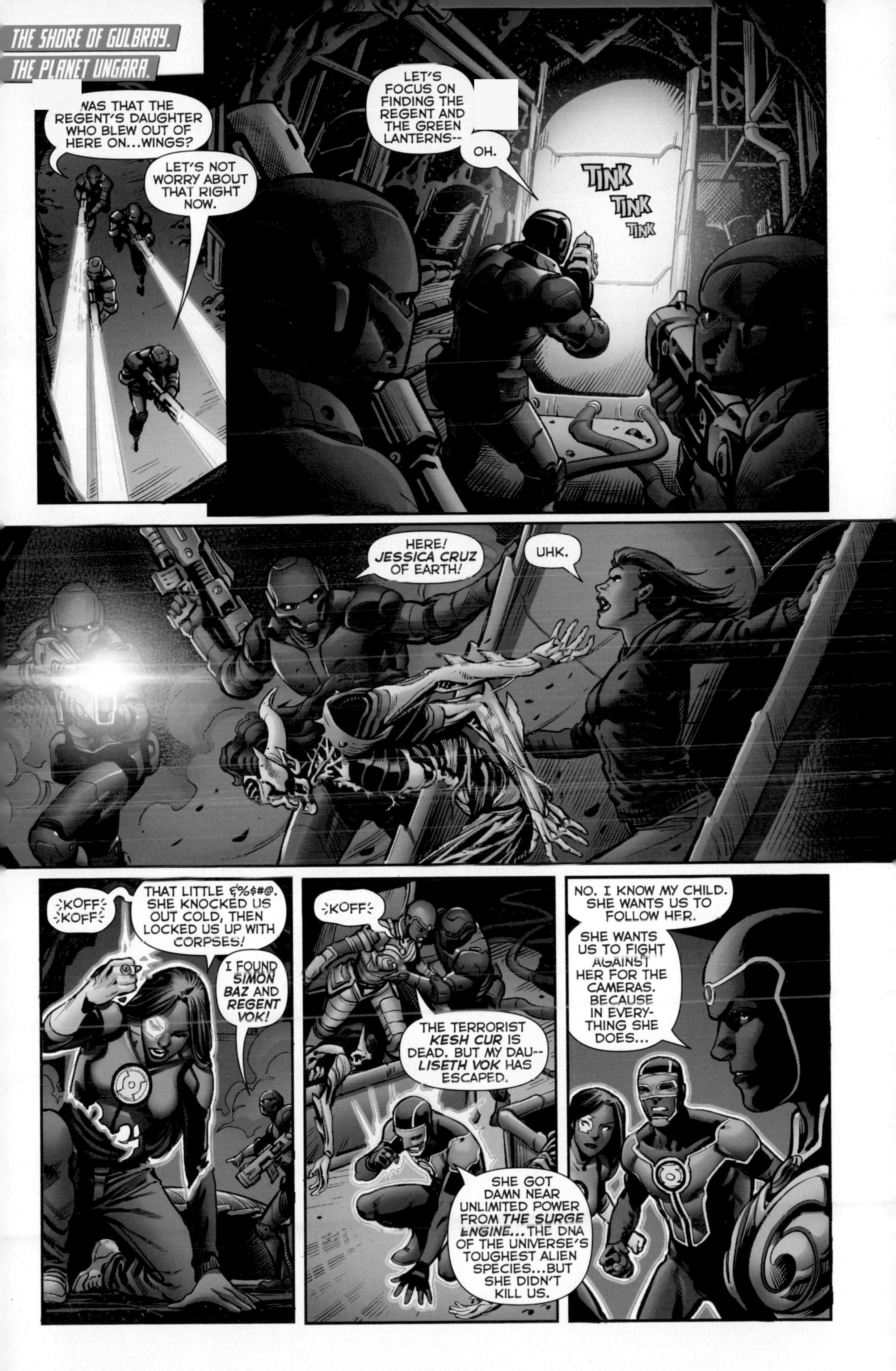
THE SHORE OF GULBRAY.
THE PLANET UNGARA.
WAS THAT THE REGENT'S DAUGHTER WHO BLEW OUT OF HERE ON...WINGS?
LET'S NOT WORRY ABOUT THAT RIGHT NOW.
LET'S FOCUS ON FINDING THE REGENT AND THE GREEN LANTERNS--
OH.
TINK
TINK
TINK
HERE! JESSICA CRUZ OF EARTH!
UHK.
KOFF KOFF
THAT LITTLE &%$#@. SHE KNOCKED US OUT COLD, THEN LOCKED US UP WITH CORPSES!
I FOUND SIMON BAZ AND REGENT VOK!
KOFF
THE TERRORIST KESH CUR IS DEAD. BUT MY DAU-- LISETH VOK HAS ESCAPED.
SHE GOT DAMN NEAR UNLIMITED POWER FROM THE SURGE ENGINE... THE DNA OF THE UNIVERSE'S TOUGHEST ALIEN SPECIES...BUT SHE DIDN'T KILL US.
NO. I KNOW MY CHILD. SHE WANTS US TO FOLLOW HER.
SHE WANTS US TO FIGHT AGAINST HER FOR THE CAMERAS. BECAUSE IN EVERY-THING SHE DOES...

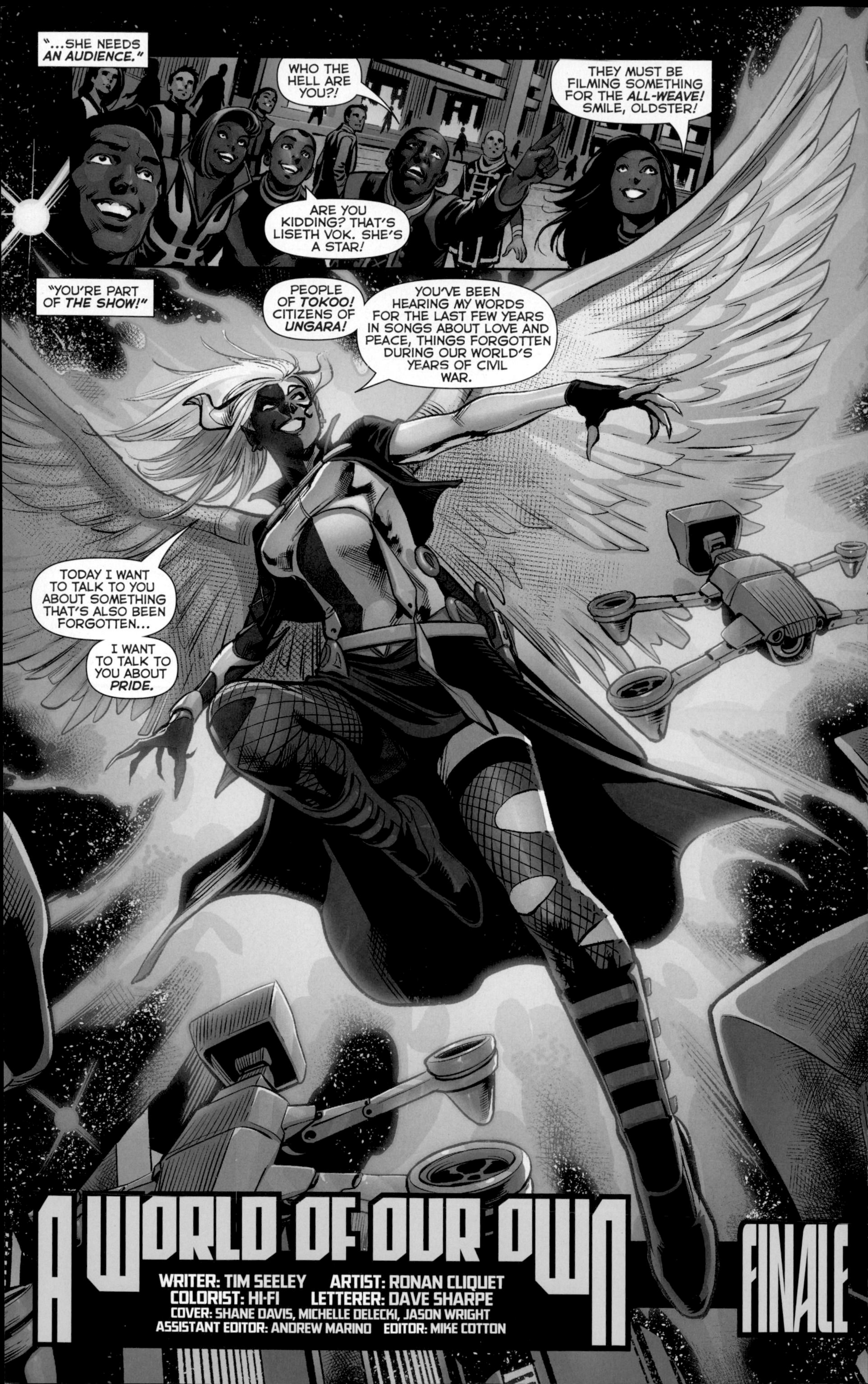
"...SHE NEEDS AN AUDIENCE."
WHO THE HELL ARE YOU?!
THEY MUST BE FILMING SOMETHING FOR THE ALL-WEAVE! SMILE, OLDSTER!
ARE YOU KIDDING? THAT'S LISETH VOK. SHE'S A STAR!
"YOU'RE PART OF THE SHOW!"
PEOPLE OF TOKOO! CITIZENS OF UNGARA!
YOU'VE BEEN HEARING MY WORDS FOR THE LAST FEW YEARS IN SONGS ABOUT LOVE AND PEACE, THINGS FORGOTTEN DURING OUR WORLD'S YEARS OF CIVIL WAR.
TODAY I WANT TO TALK TO YOU ABOUT SOMETHING THAT'S ALSO BEEN FORGOTTEN...
I WANT TO TALK TO YOU ABOUT PRIDE.
A WORLD OF OUR OWN
FINALE
WRITER: TIM SEELEY ARTIST: RONAN CLIQUET
COLORIST: HI-FI LETTERER: DAVE SHARPE
COVER: SHANE DAVIS, MICHELLE DELECKI, JASON WRIGHT
ASSISTANT EDITOR: ANDREW MARINO EDITOR: MIKE COTTON

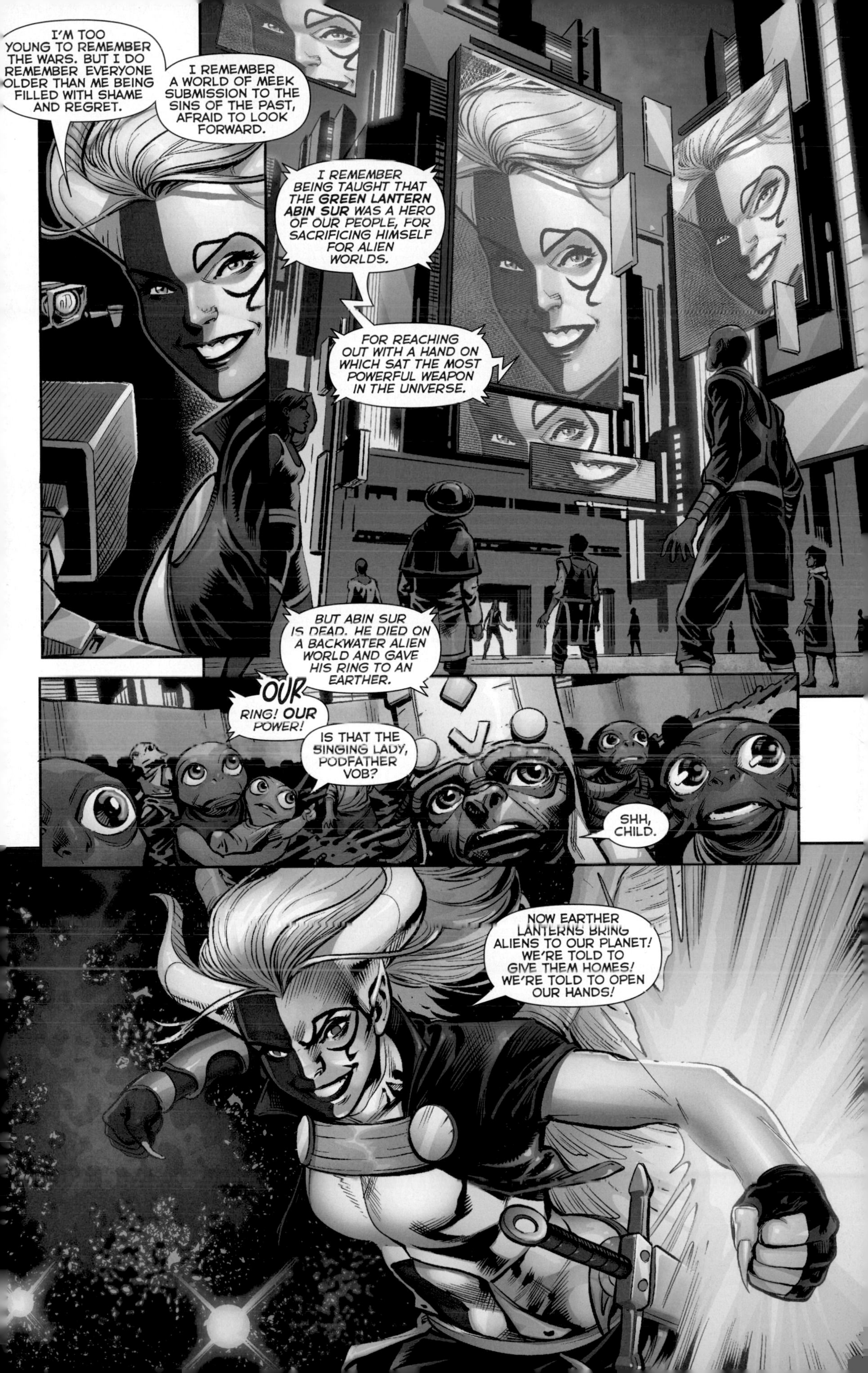

I'M TOO YOUNG TO REMEMBER THE WARS. BUT I DO REMEMBER EVERYONE OLDER THAN ME BEING FILLED WITH SHAME AND REGRET.
I REMEMBER A WORLD OF MEEK SUBMISSION TO THE SINS OF THE PAST, AFRAID TO LOOK FORWARD.
I REMEMBER BEING TAUGHT THAT THE GREEN LANTERN ABIN SUR WAS A HERO OF OUR PEOPLE, FOR SACRIFICING HIMSELF FOR ALIEN WORLDS.
FOR REACHING OUT WITH A HAND ON WHICH SAT THE MOST POWERFUL WEAPON IN THE UNIVERSE.
BUT ABIN SUR IS DEAD. HE DIED ON A BACKWATER ALIEN WORLD AND GAVE HIS RING TO AN EARTHER.
OUR RING! OUR POWER!
IS THAT THE SINGING LADY, PODFATHER VOB?
SHH, CHILD.
NOW EARTHER LANTERNS BRING ALIENS TO OUR PLANET! WE'RE TOLD TO GIVE THEM HOMES! WE'RE TOLD TO OPEN OUR HANDS!

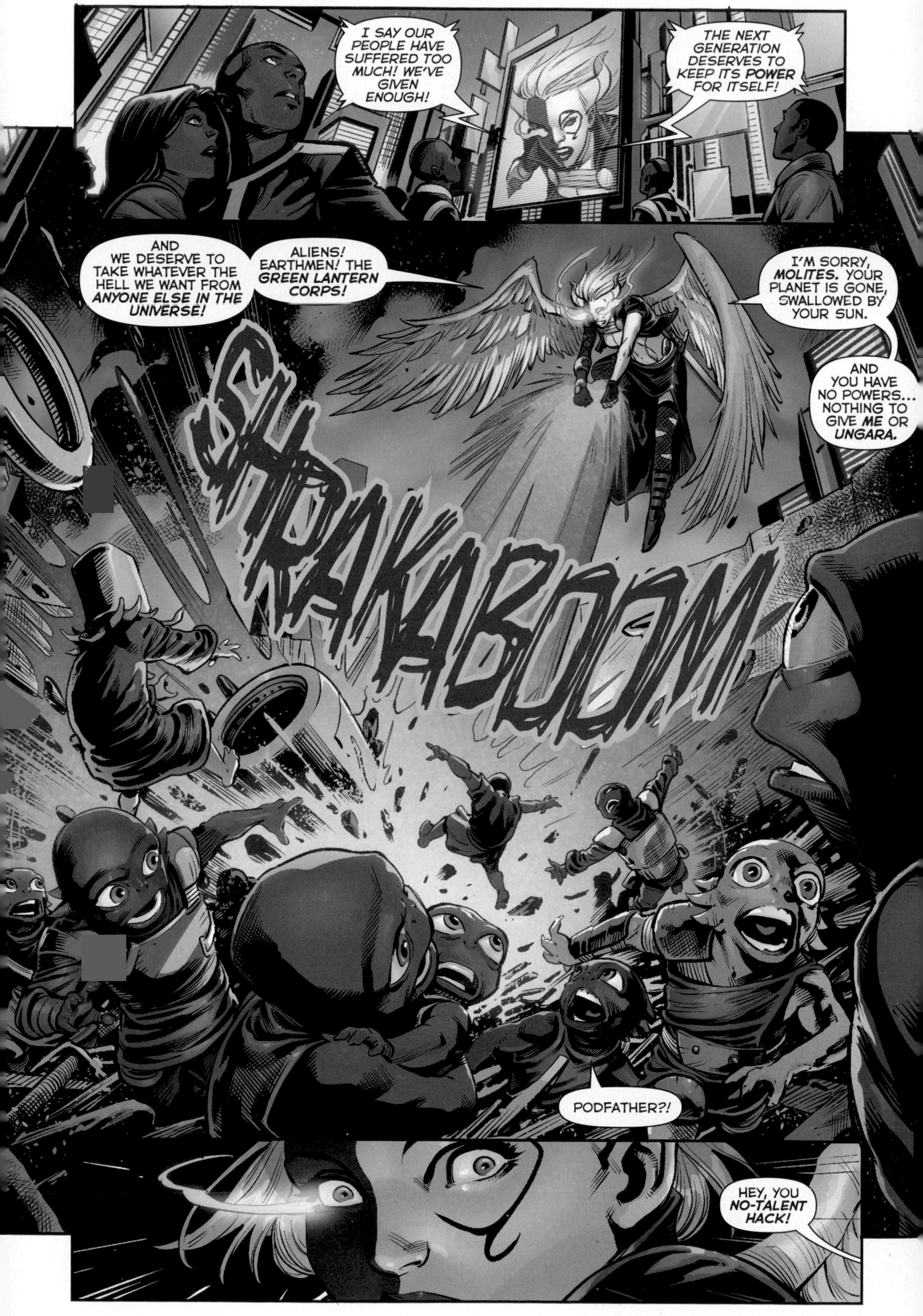
I SAY OUR PEOPLE HAVE SUFFERED TOO MUCH! WE'VE GIVEN ENOUGH!
THE NEXT GENERATION DESERVES TO KEEP ITS POWER FOR ITSELF!
AND WE DESERVE TO TAKE WHATEVER THE HELL WE WANT FROM ANYONE ELSE IN THE UNIVERSE!
ALIENS! EARTHMEN! THE GREEN LANTERN CORPS!
I'M SORRY, MOLITES. YOUR PLANET IS GONE, SWALLOWED BY YOUR SUN.
AND YOU HAVE NO POWERS... NOTHING TO GIVE ME OR UNGARA.
SHRAKABOOM
PODFATHER?!
HEY, YOU NO-TALENT HACK!

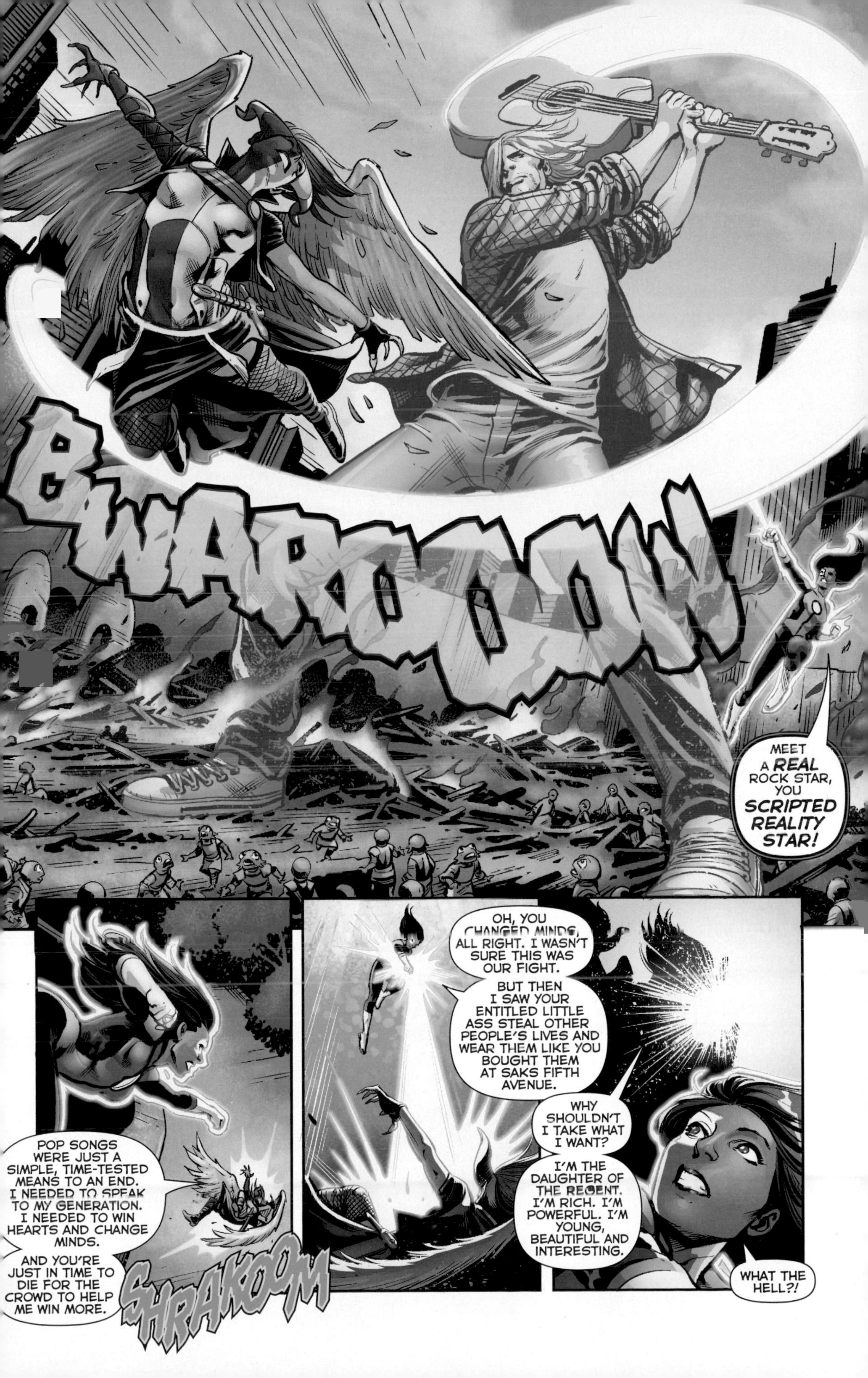

BWAROOOM
MEET A REAL ROCK STAR, YOU SCRIPTED REALITY STAR!
POP SONGS WERE JUST A SIMPLE, TIME-TESTED MEANS TO AN END. I NEEDED TO SPEAK TO MY GENERATION. I NEEDED TO WIN HEARTS AND CHANGE MINDS.
AND YOU'RE JUST IN TIME TO DIE FOR THE CROWD TO HELP ME WIN MORE.
SHRAKOOM
OH, YOU CHANGED MINDS, ALL RIGHT. I WASN'T SURE THIS WAS OUR FIGHT.
BUT THEN I SAW YOUR ENTITLED LITTLE ASS STEAL OTHER PEOPLE'S LIVES AND WEAR THEM LIKE YOU BOUGHT THEM AT SAKS FIFTH AVENUE.
WHY SHOULDN'T I TAKE WHAT I WANT?
I'M THE DAUGHTER OF THE REGENT. I'M RICH. I'M POWERFUL. I'M YOUNG, BEAUTIFUL AND INTERESTING.
WHAT THE HELL?!

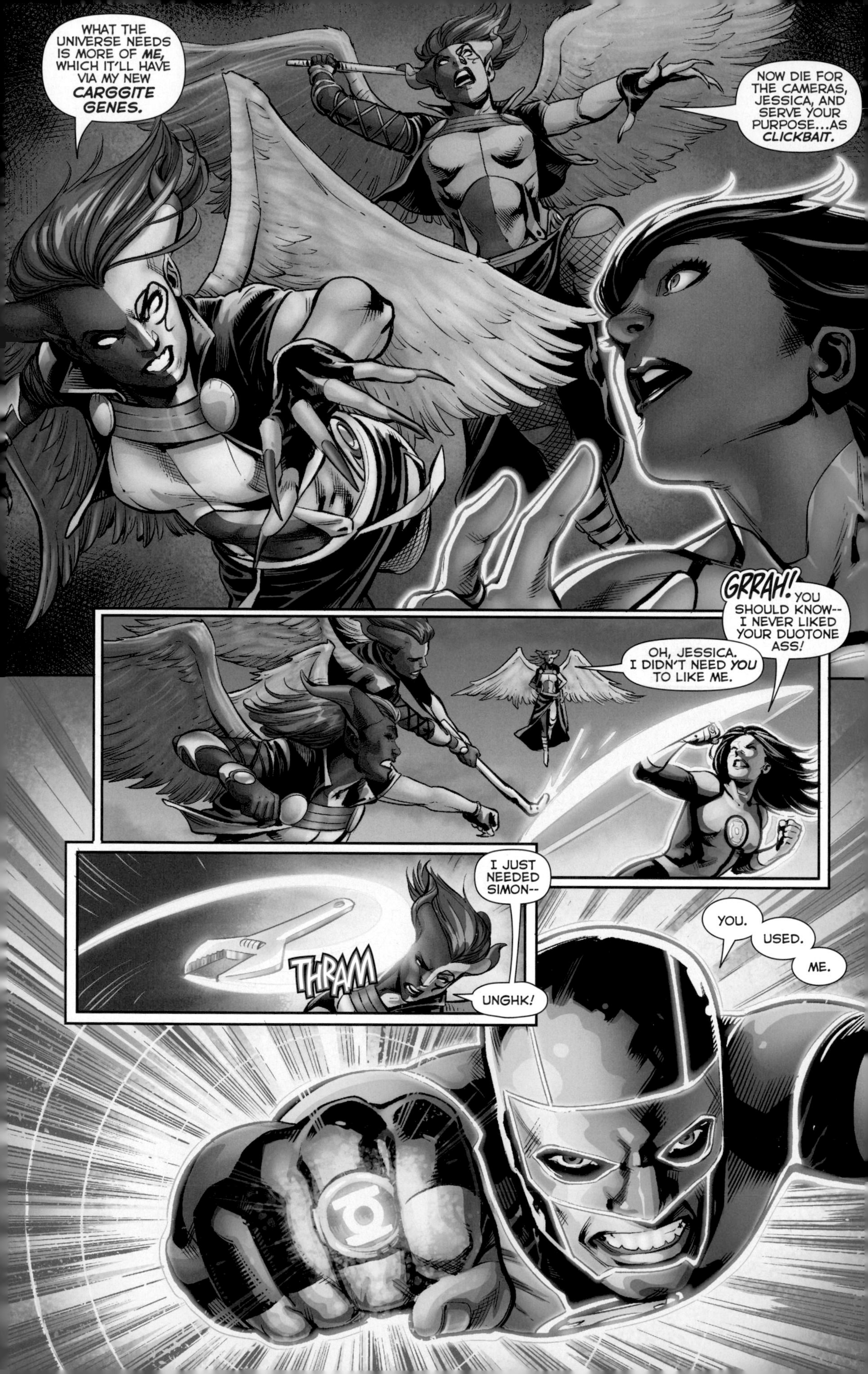
WHAT THE UNIVERSE NEEDS IS MORE OF ME, WHICH IT'LL HAVE VIA MY NEW CARGGITE GENES.
NOW DIE FOR THE CAMERAS, JESSICA, AND SERVE YOUR PURPOSE...AS CLICKBAIT.
GRRAH!
YOU SHOULD KNOW-- I NEVER LIKED YOUR DUOTONE ASS!
OH, JESSICA. I DIDN'T NEED YOU TO LIKE ME.
I JUST NEEDED SIMON--
THRAM
UNGHK!
YOU.
USED.
ME.

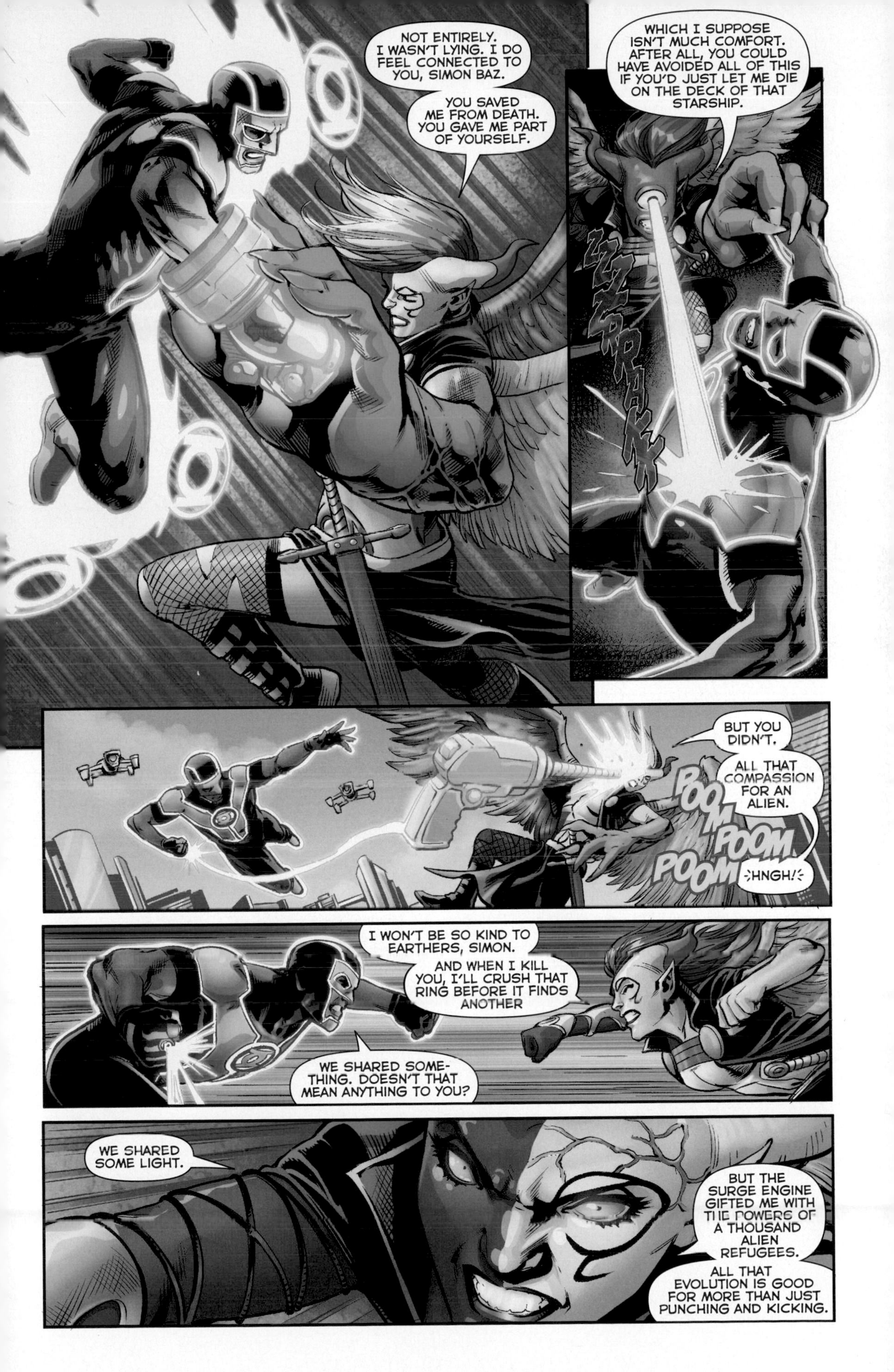
NOT ENTIRELY. I WASN'T LYING. I DO FEEL CONNECTED TO YOU, SIMON BAZ.
YOU SAVED ME FROM DEATH. YOU GAVE ME PART OF YOURSELF.
WHICH I SUPPOSE ISN'T MUCH COMFORT. AFTER ALL, YOU COULD HAVE AVOIDED ALL OF THIS IF YOU'D JUST LET ME DIE ON THE DECK OF THAT STARSHIP.
ZZZZRRAKK
BUT YOU DIDN'T.
ALL THAT COMPASSION FOR AN ALIEN.
POOM POOM POOM
HNGH!
I WON'T BE SO KIND TO EARTHERS, SIMON.
AND WHEN I KILL YOU, I'LL CRUSH THAT RING BEFORE IT FINDS ANOTHER
WE SHARED SOME-THING. DOESN'T THAT MEAN ANYTHING TO YOU?
WE SHARED SOME LIGHT.
BUT THE SURGE ENGINE GIFTED ME WITH THE POWERS OF A THOUSAND ALIEN REFUGEES.
ALL THAT EVOLUTION IS GOOD FOR MORE THAN JUST PUNCHING AND KICKING.

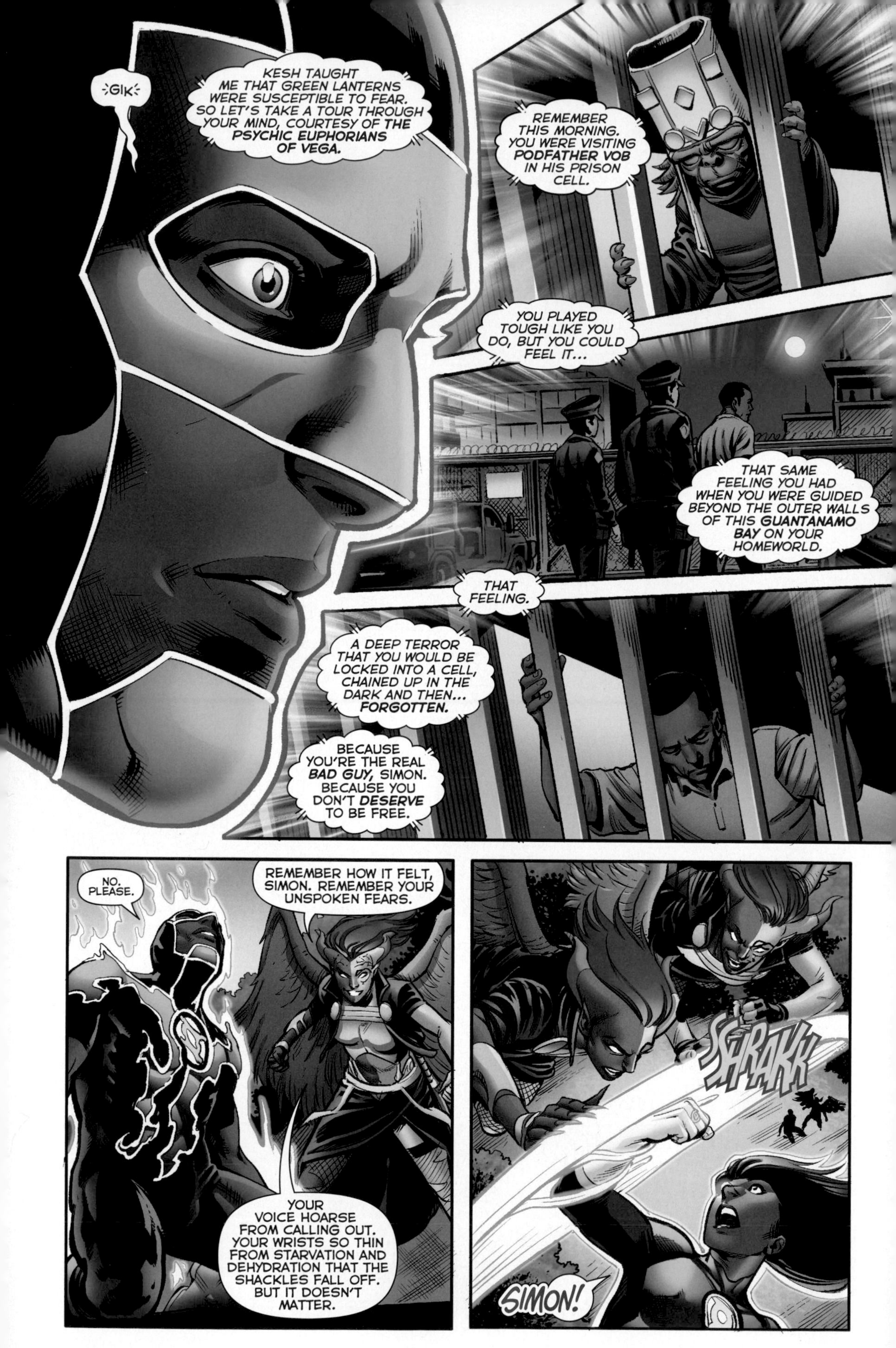
GIK
KESH TAUGHT ME THAT GREEN LANTERNS WERE SUSCEPTIBLE TO FEAR. SO LET'S TAKE A TOUR THROUGH YOUR MIND, COURTESY OF THE PSYCHIC EUPHORIANS OF VEGA.
REMEMBER THIS MORNING. YOU WERE VISITING PODFATHER VOB IN HIS PRISON CELL.
YOU PLAYED TOUGH LIKE YOU DO, BUT YOU COULD FEEL IT...
THAT SAME FEELING YOU HAD WHEN YOU WERE GUIDED BEYOND THE OUTER WALLS OF THIS GUANTANAMO BAY ON YOUR HOMEWORLD.
THAT FEELING.
A DEEP TERROR THAT YOU WOULD BE LOCKED INTO A CELL, CHAINED UP IN THE DARK AND THEN... FORGOTTEN.
BECAUSE YOU'RE THE REAL BAD GUY, SIMON. BECAUSE YOU DON'T DESERVE TO BE FREE.
NO. PLEASE.
REMEMBER HOW IT FELT, SIMON. REMEMBER YOUR UNSPOKEN FEARS.
YOUR VOICE HOARSE FROM CALLING OUT. YOUR WRISTS SO THIN FROM STARVATION AND DEHYDRATION THAT THE SHACKLES FALL OFF. BUT IT DOESN'T MATTER.
SHRAKK
SIMON!

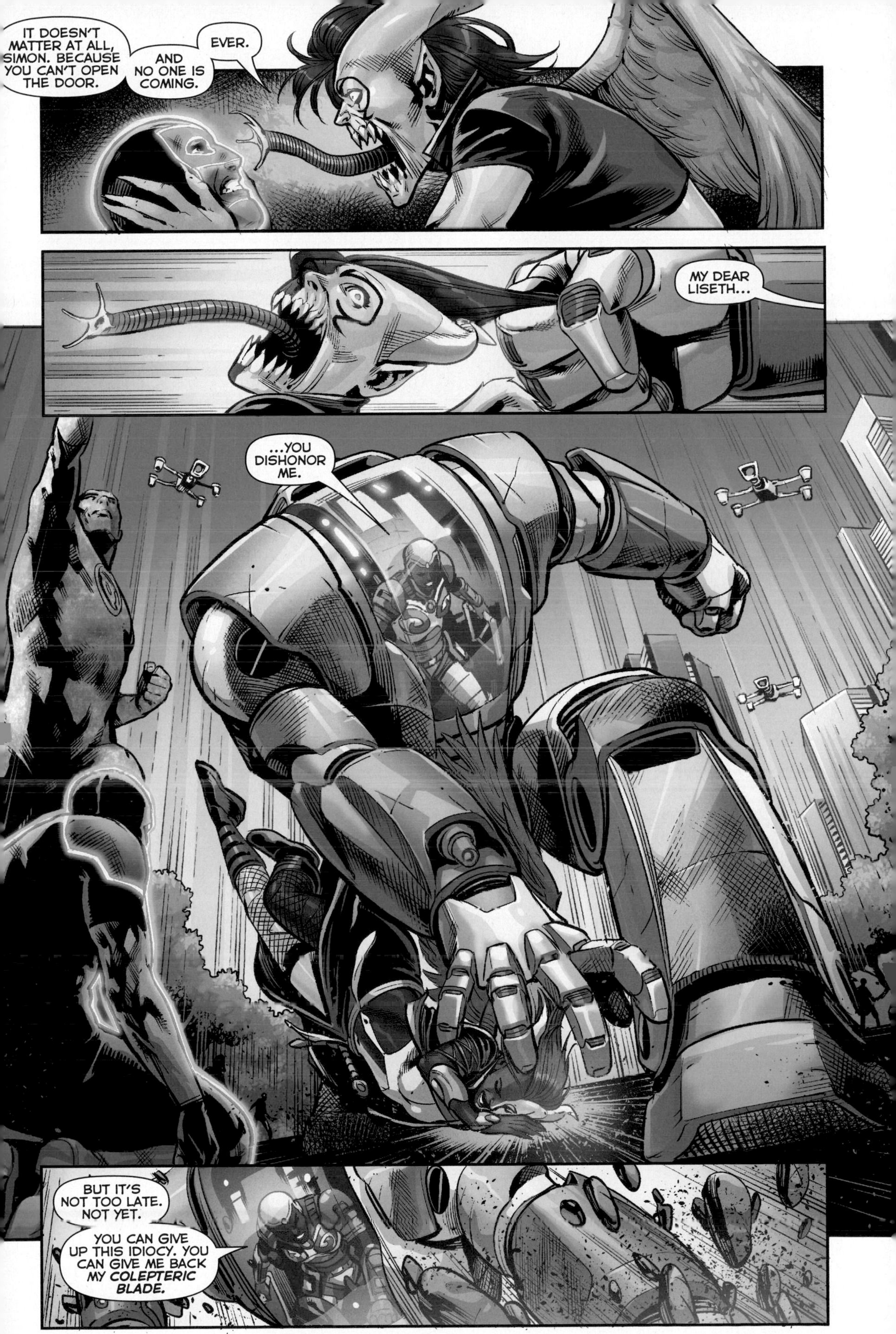
IT DOESN'T MATTER AT ALL, SIMON. BECAUSE YOU CAN'T OPEN THE DOOR.
AND NO ONE IS COMING.
EVER.
MY DEAR LISETH...
...YOU DISHONOR ME.
BUT IT'S NOT TOO LATE. NOT YET.
YOU CAN GIVE UP THIS IDIOCY. YOU CAN GIVE ME BACK MY *COLEPTERIC BLADE.*

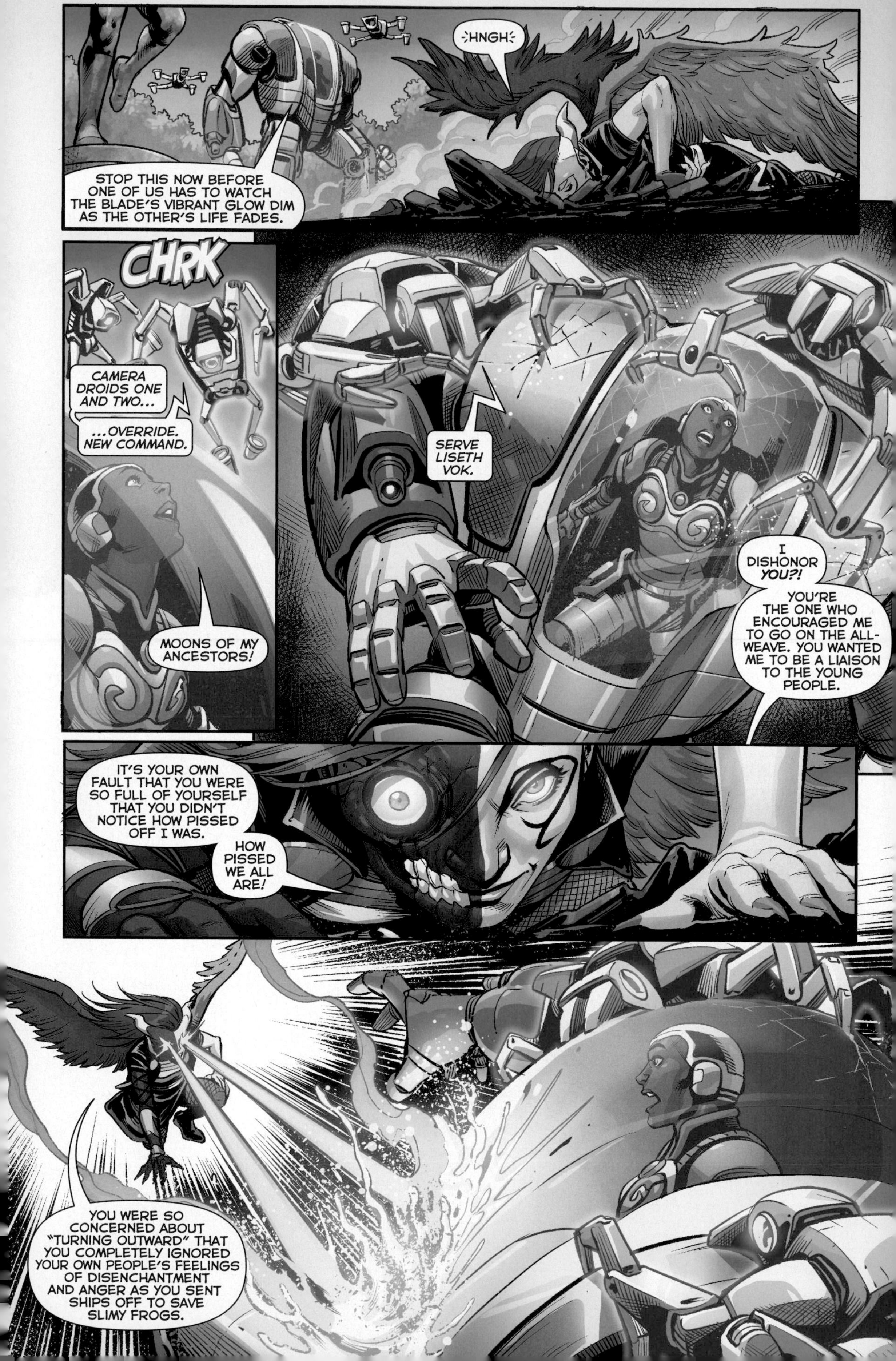

HNGH
STOP THIS NOW BEFORE ONE OF US HAS TO WATCH THE BLADE'S VIBRANT GLOW DIM AS THE OTHER'S LIFE FADES.
CHRK
CAMERA DROIDS ONE AND TWO...
...OVERRIDE. NEW COMMAND.
SERVE LISETH VOK.
MOONS OF MY ANCESTORS!
I DISHONOR YOU?!
YOU'RE THE ONE WHO ENCOURAGED ME TO GO ON THE ALL-WEAVE. YOU WANTED ME TO BE A LIAISON TO THE YOUNG PEOPLE.
IT'S YOUR OWN FAULT THAT YOU WERE SO FULL OF YOURSELF THAT YOU DIDN'T NOTICE HOW PISSED OFF I WAS.
HOW PISSED WE ALL ARE!
YOU WERE SO CONCERNED ABOUT "TURNING OUTWARD" THAT YOU COMPLETELY IGNORED YOUR OWN PEOPLE'S FEELINGS OF DISENCHANTMENT AND ANGER AS YOU SENT SHIPS OFF TO SAVE SLIMY FROGS.

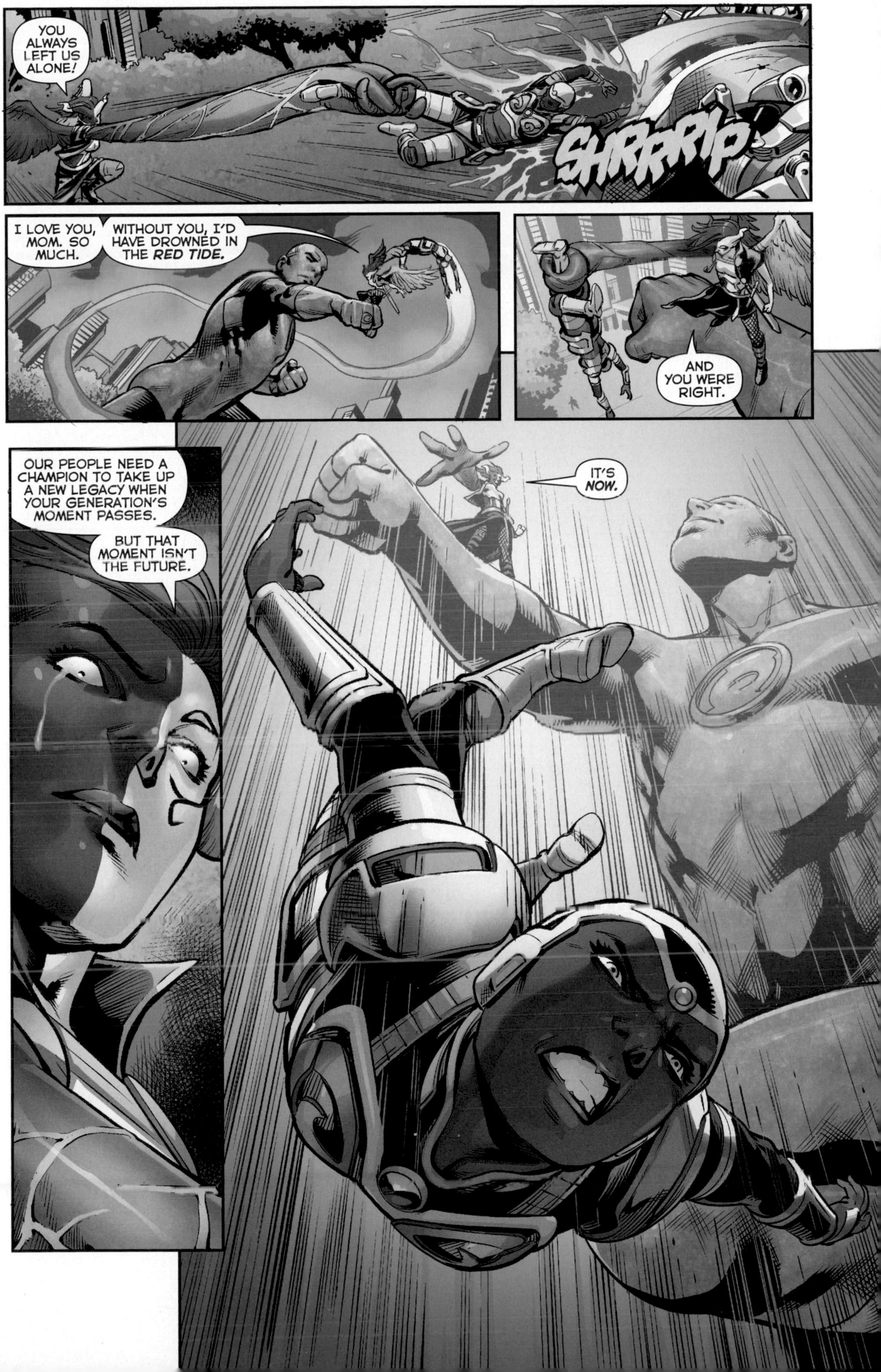
YOU ALWAYS LEFT US ALONE!
SHRRRIP
I LOVE YOU, MOM. SO MUCH.
WITHOUT YOU, I'D HAVE DROWNED IN THE *RED TIDE.*
AND YOU WERE RIGHT.
OUR PEOPLE NEED A CHAMPION TO TAKE UP A NEW LEGACY WHEN YOUR GENERATION'S MOMENT PASSES.
BUT THAT MOMENT ISN'T THE FUTURE.
IT'S *NOW.*

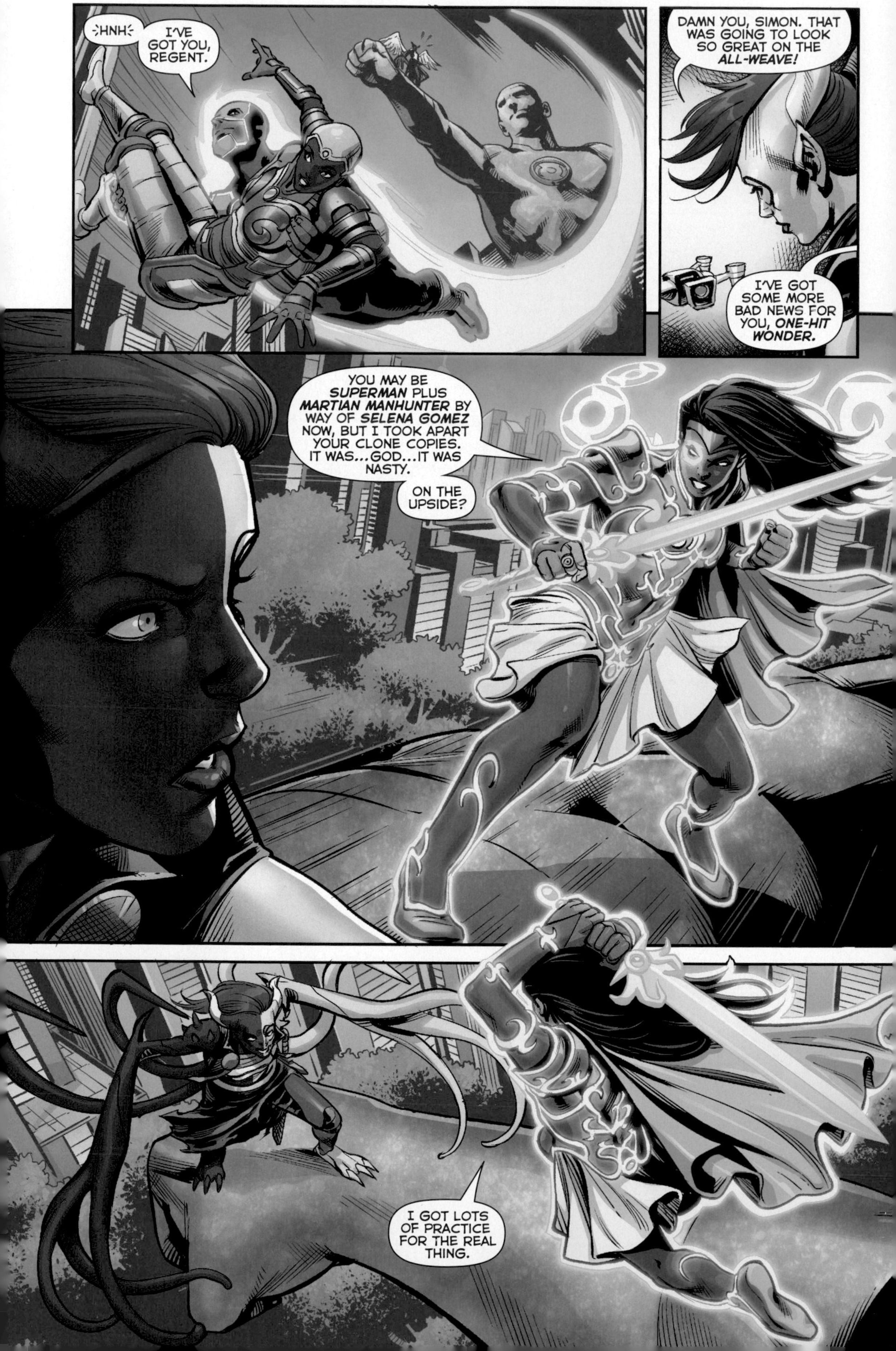

HNH
I'VE GOT YOU, REGENT.
DAMN YOU, SIMON. THAT WAS GOING TO LOOK SO GREAT ON THE ALL-WEAVE!
I'VE GOT SOME MORE BAD NEWS FOR YOU, ONE-HIT WONDER.
YOU MAY BE SUPERMAN PLUS MARTIAN MANHUNTER BY WAY OF SELENA GOMEZ NOW, BUT I TOOK APART YOUR CLONE COPIES. IT WAS...GOD...IT WAS NASTY.
ON THE UPSIDE?
I GOT LOTS OF PRACTICE FOR THE REAL THING.

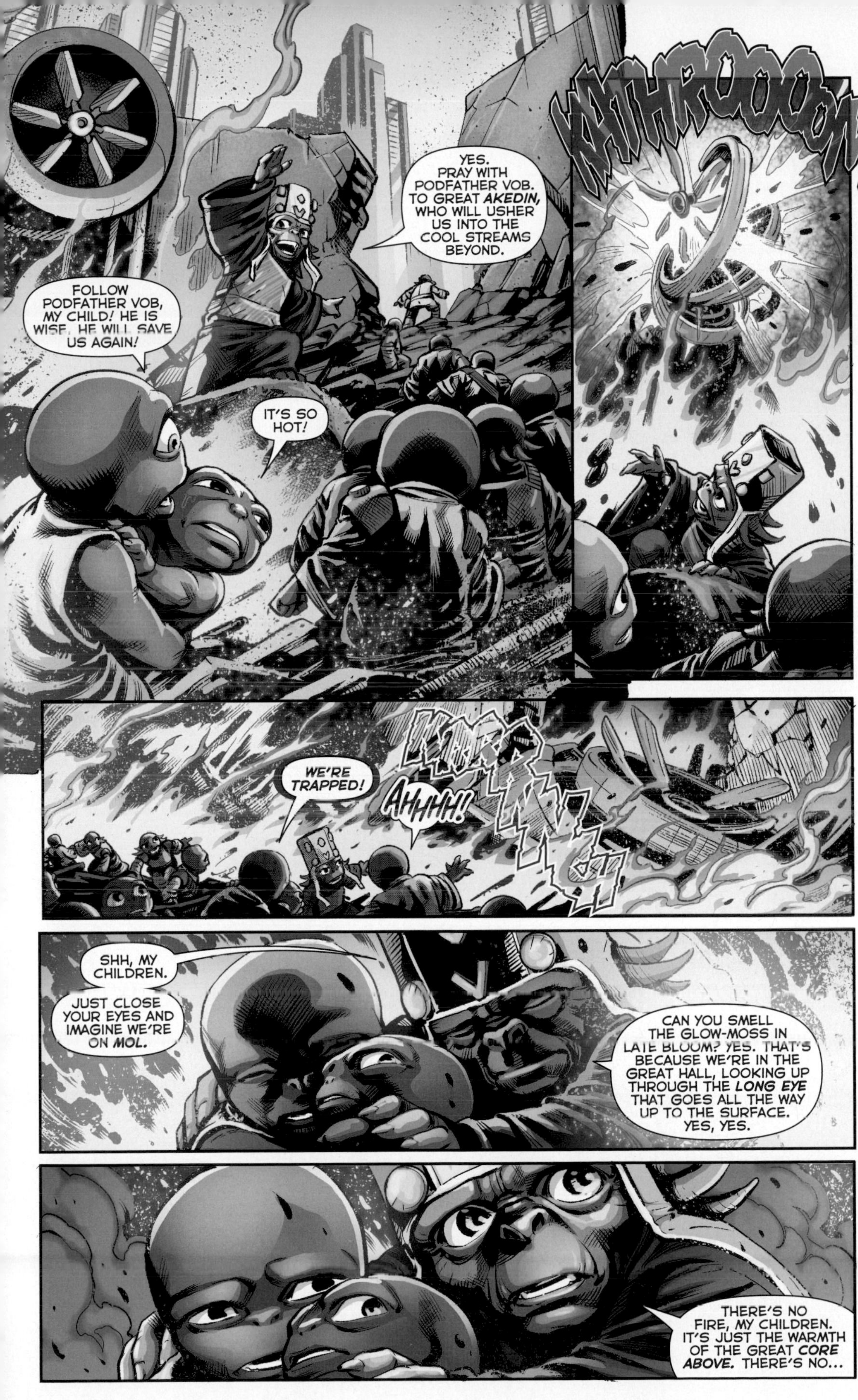
YES. PRAY WITH PODFATHER VOB. TO GREAT AKEDIN, WHO WILL USHER US INTO THE COOL STREAMS BEYOND.
FOLLOW PODFATHER VOB, MY CHILD! HE IS WISE. HE WILL SAVE US AGAIN!
IT'S SO HOT!
WE'RE TRAPPED!
AHHHH!
SHH, MY CHILDREN.
JUST CLOSE YOUR EYES AND IMAGINE WE'RE ON MOL.
CAN YOU SMELL THE GLOW-MOSS IN LATE BLOOM? YES. THAT'S BECAUSE WE'RE IN THE GREAT HALL, LOOKING UP THROUGH THE LONG EYE THAT GOES ALL THE WAY UP TO THE SURFACE. YES, YES.
THERE'S NO FIRE, MY CHILDREN. IT'S JUST THE WARMTH OF THE GREAT CORE ABOVE. THERE'S NO...

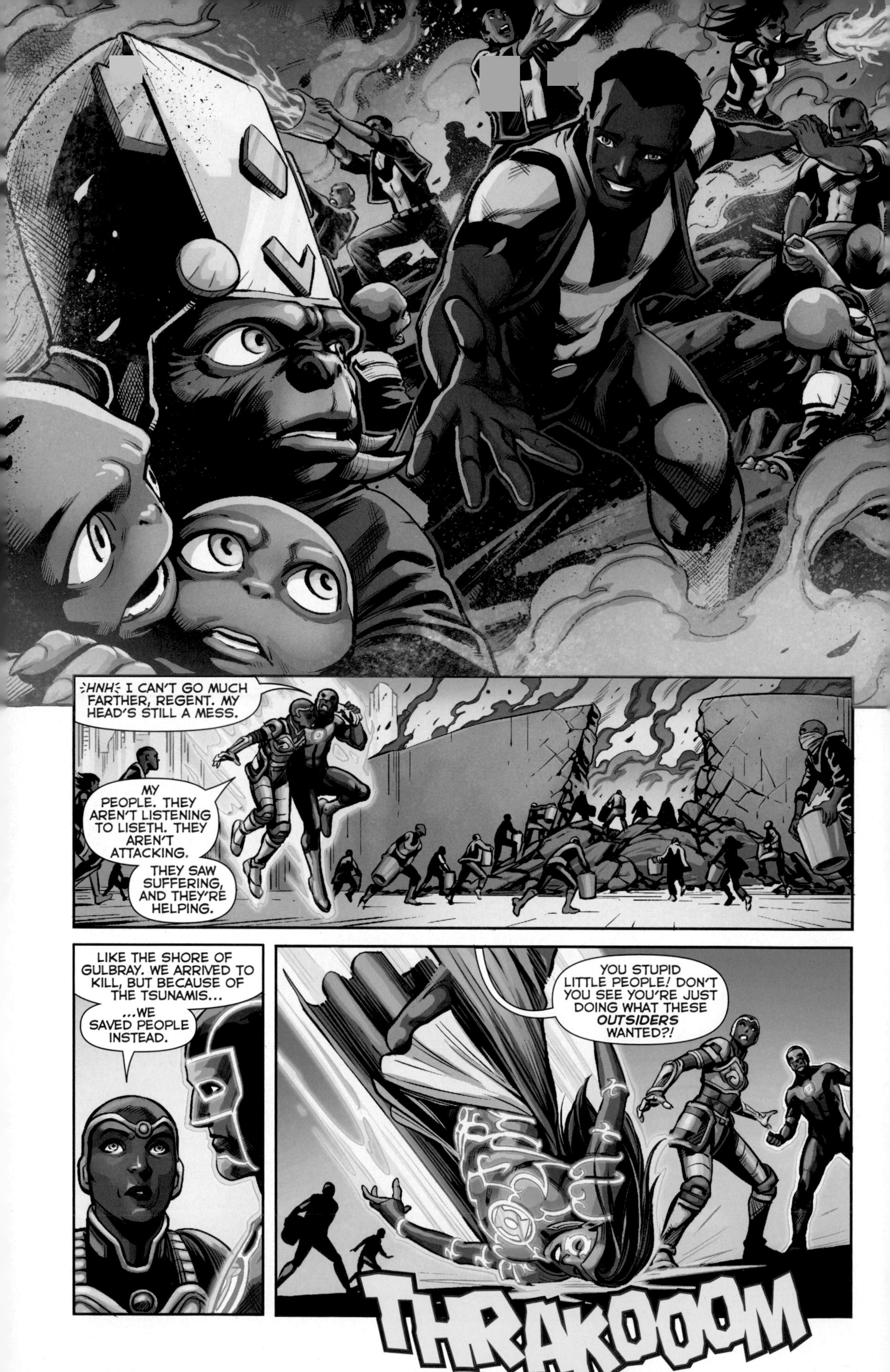
HNH I CAN'T GO MUCH FARTHER, REGENT. MY HEAD'S STILL A MESS.
MY PEOPLE. THEY AREN'T LISTENING TO LISETH. THEY AREN'T ATTACKING.
THEY SAW SUFFERING, AND THEY'RE HELPING.
LIKE THE SHORE OF GULBRAY. WE ARRIVED TO KILL, BUT BECAUSE OF THE TSUNAMIS...
...WE SAVED PEOPLE INSTEAD.
YOU STUPID LITTLE PEOPLE! DON'T YOU SEE YOU'RE JUST DOING WHAT THESE OUTSIDERS WANTED?!
THRAKOOOM

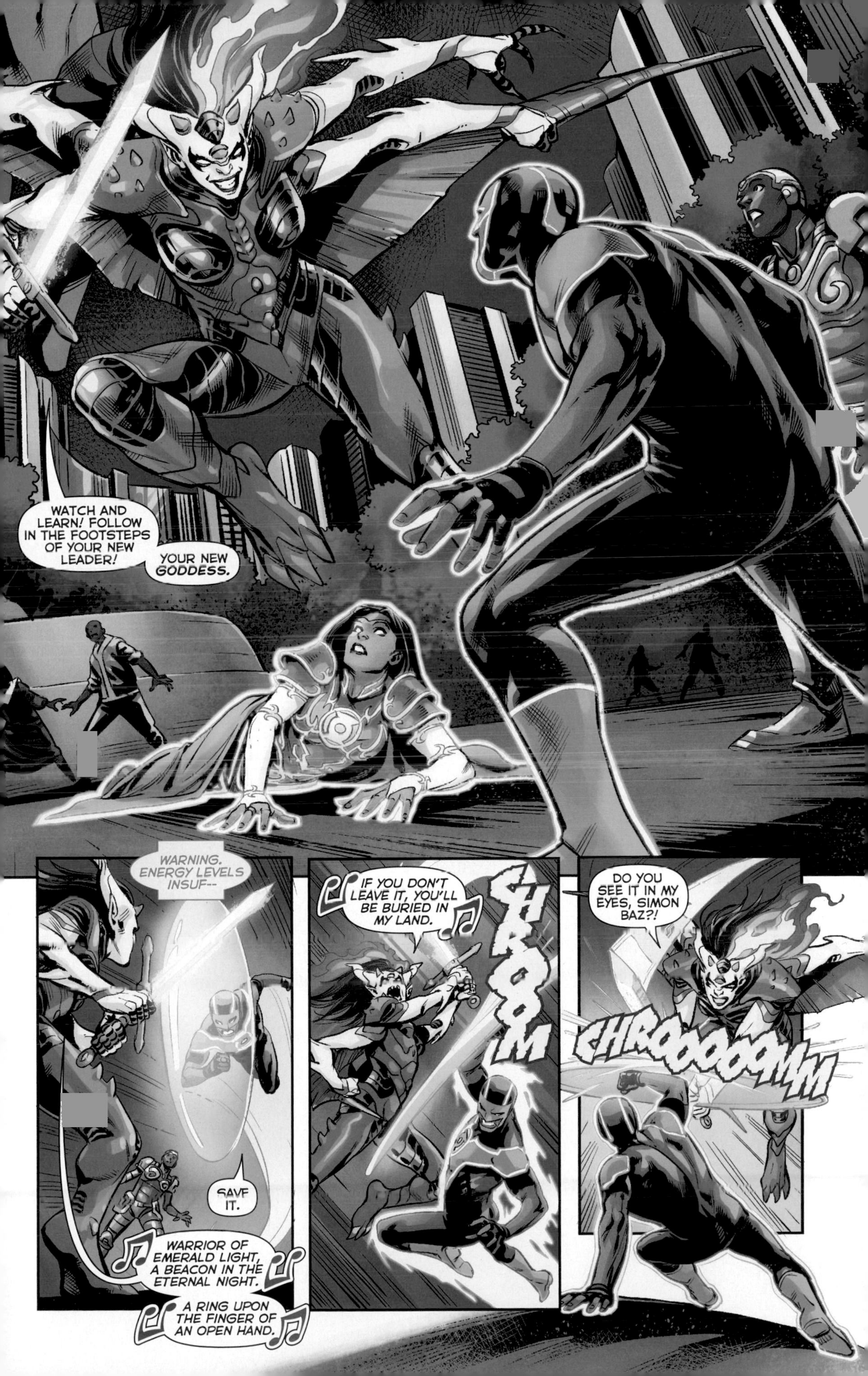
WATCH AND LEARN! FOLLOW IN THE FOOTSTEPS OF YOUR NEW LEADER!
YOUR NEW GODDESS.
WARNING. ENERGY LEVELS INSUF--
SAVE IT.
WARRIOR OF EMERALD LIGHT, A BEACON IN THE ETERNAL NIGHT.
A RING UPON THE FINGER OF AN OPEN HAND.
IF YOU DON'T LEAVE IT, YOU'LL BE BURIED IN MY LAND.
CHROOM
DO YOU SEE IT IN MY EYES, SIMON BAZ?!
CHROOOOOMM

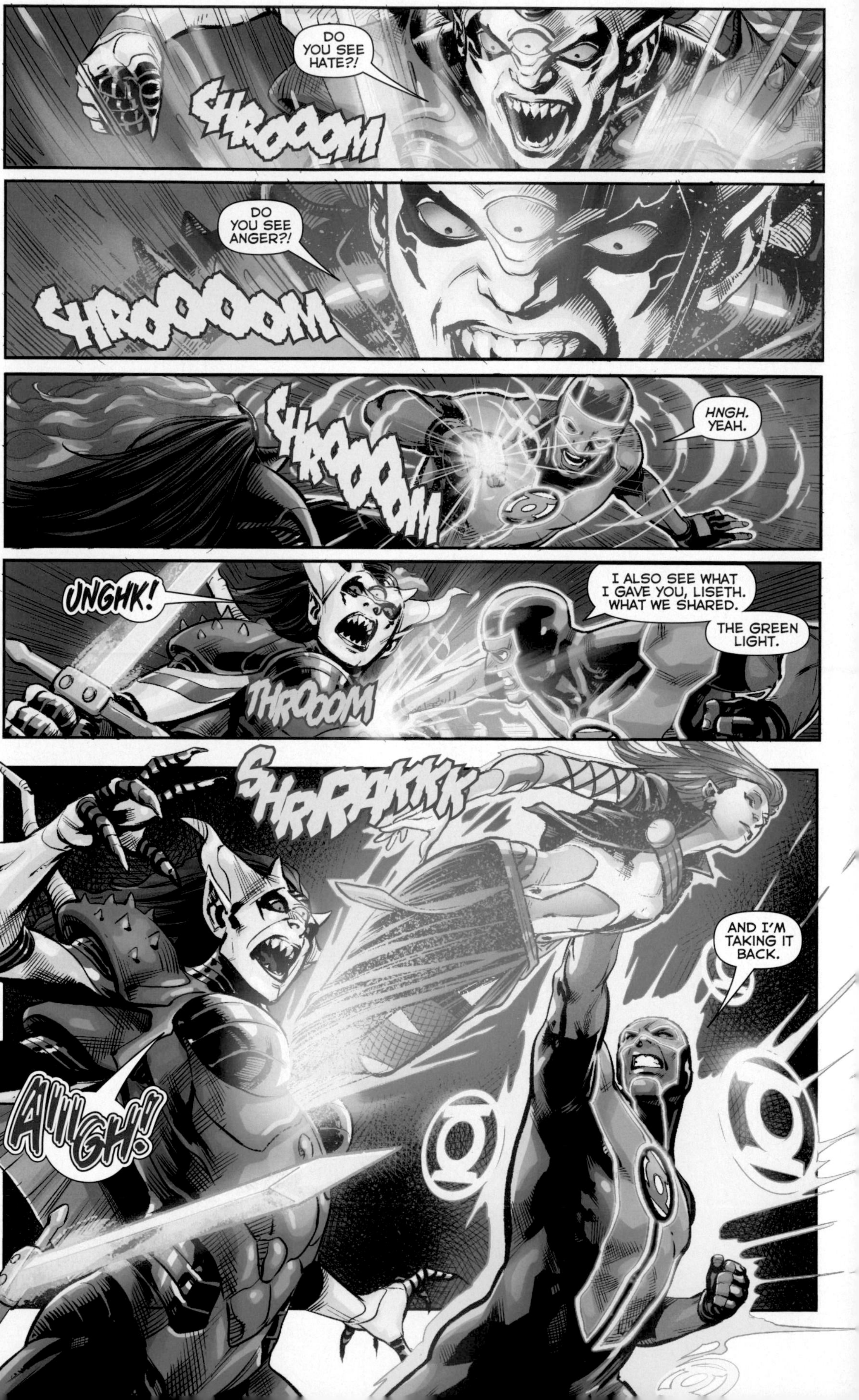
DO YOU SEE HATE?!
SHROOOM
DO YOU SEE ANGER?!
SHROOOOOM
SHROOOOOM
HNGH. YEAH.
UNGHK!
I ALSO SEE WHAT I GAVE YOU, LISETH. WHAT WE SHARED.
THE GREEN LIGHT.
THROOOM
SHRAAKKK
AND I'M TAKING IT BACK.
AAAGH!

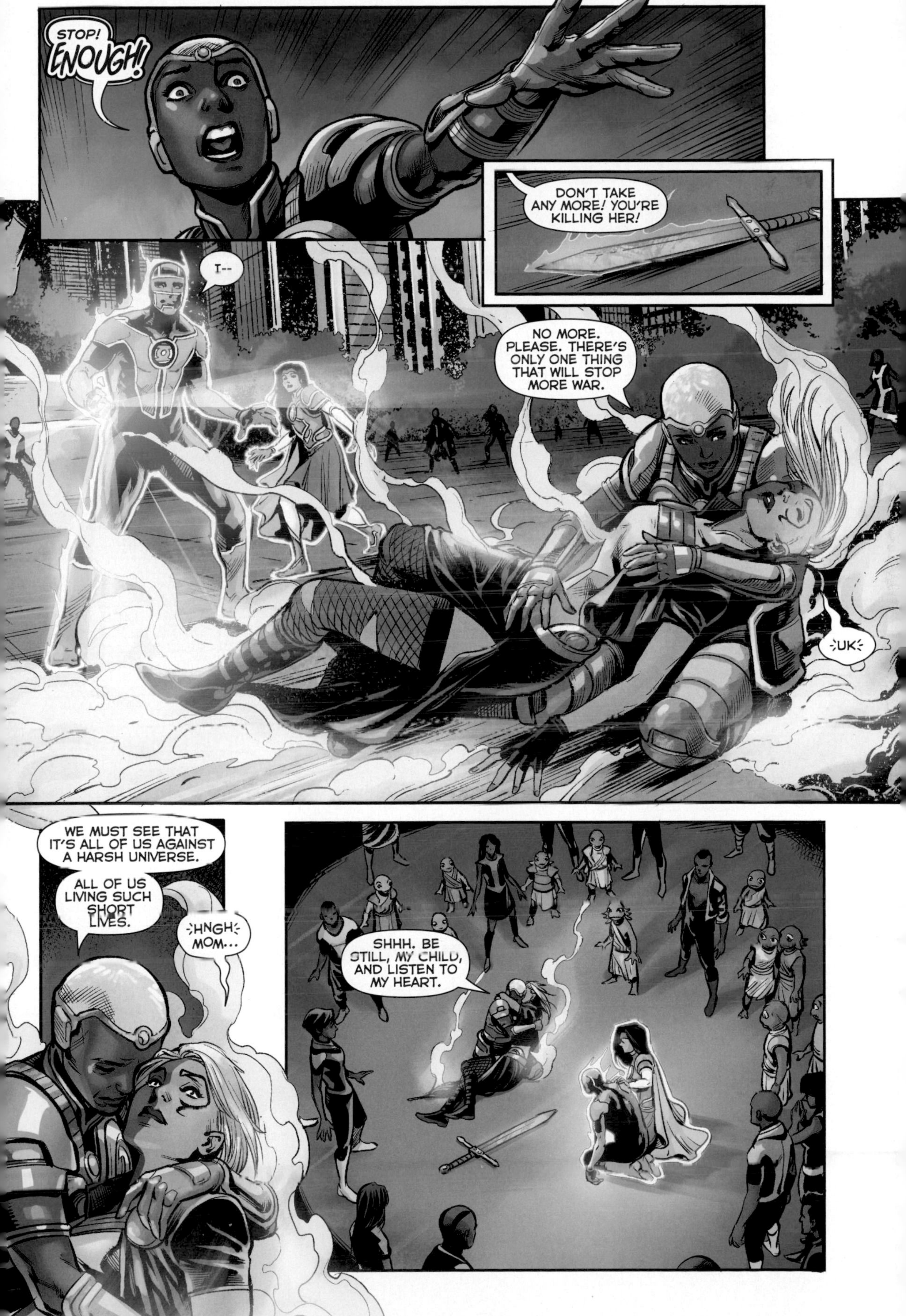
STOP! ENOUGH!
DON'T TAKE ANY MORE! YOU'RE KILLING HER!
I--
NO MORE. PLEASE. THERE'S ONLY ONE THING THAT WILL STOP MORE WAR.
UK
WE MUST SEE THAT IT'S ALL OF US AGAINST A HARSH UNIVERSE.
ALL OF US LIVING SUCH SHORT LIVES.
HNGH MOM...
SHHH. BE STILL, MY CHILD, AND LISTEN TO MY HEART.

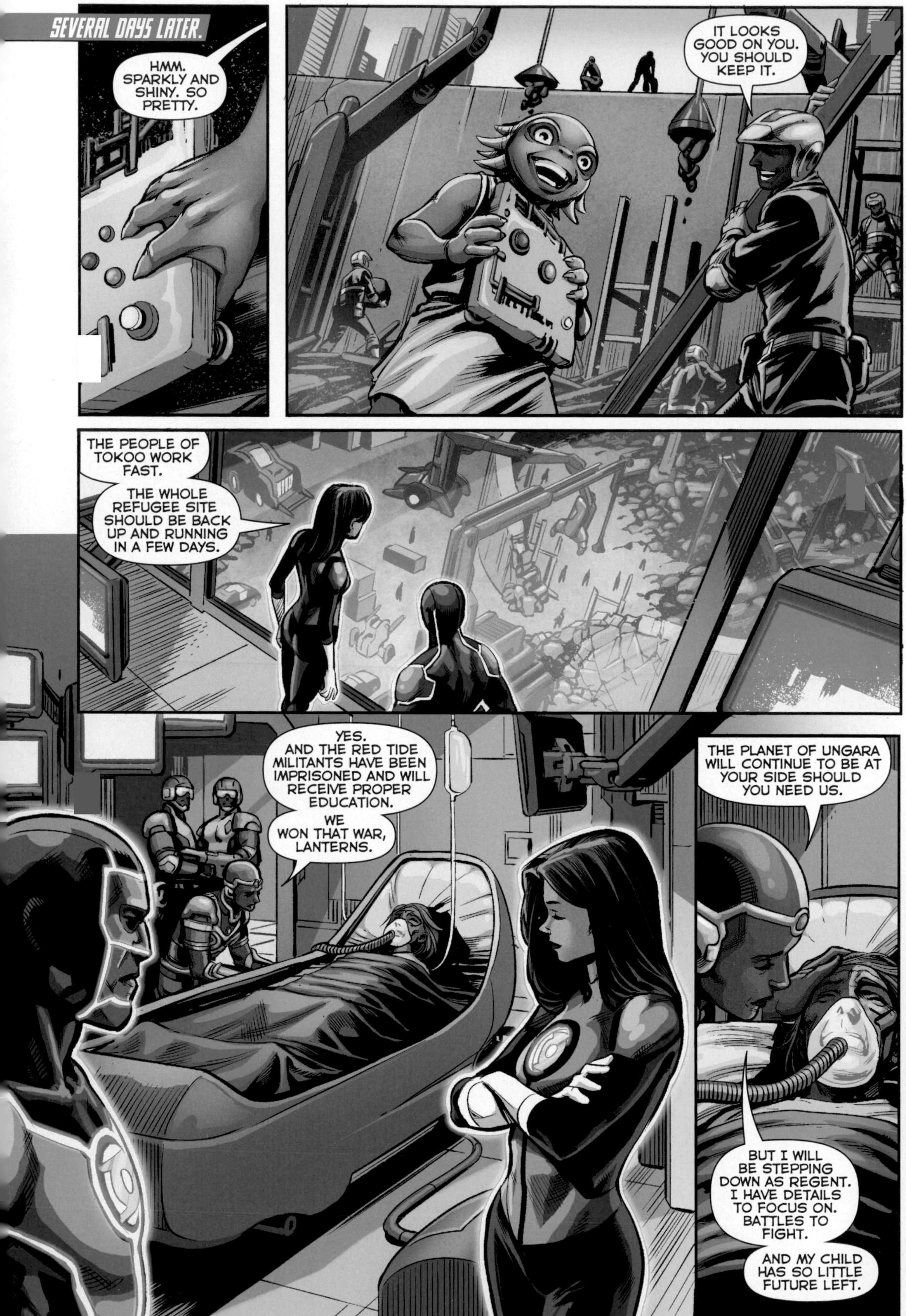
SEVERAL DAYS LATER.
HMM. SPARKLY AND SHINY. SO PRETTY.
IT LOOKS GOOD ON YOU. YOU SHOULD KEEP IT.
THE PEOPLE OF TOKOO WORK FAST.
THE WHOLE REFUGEE SITE SHOULD BE BACK UP AND RUNNING IN A FEW DAYS.
YES. AND THE RED TIDE MILITANTS HAVE BEEN IMPRISONED AND WILL RECEIVE PROPER EDUCATION.
WE WON THAT WAR, LANTERNS.
THE PLANET OF UNGARA WILL CONTINUE TO BE AT YOUR SIDE SHOULD YOU NEED US.
BUT I WILL BE STEPPING DOWN AS REGENT. I HAVE DETAILS TO FOCUS ON. BATTLES TO FIGHT.
AND MY CHILD HAS SO LITTLE FUTURE LEFT.

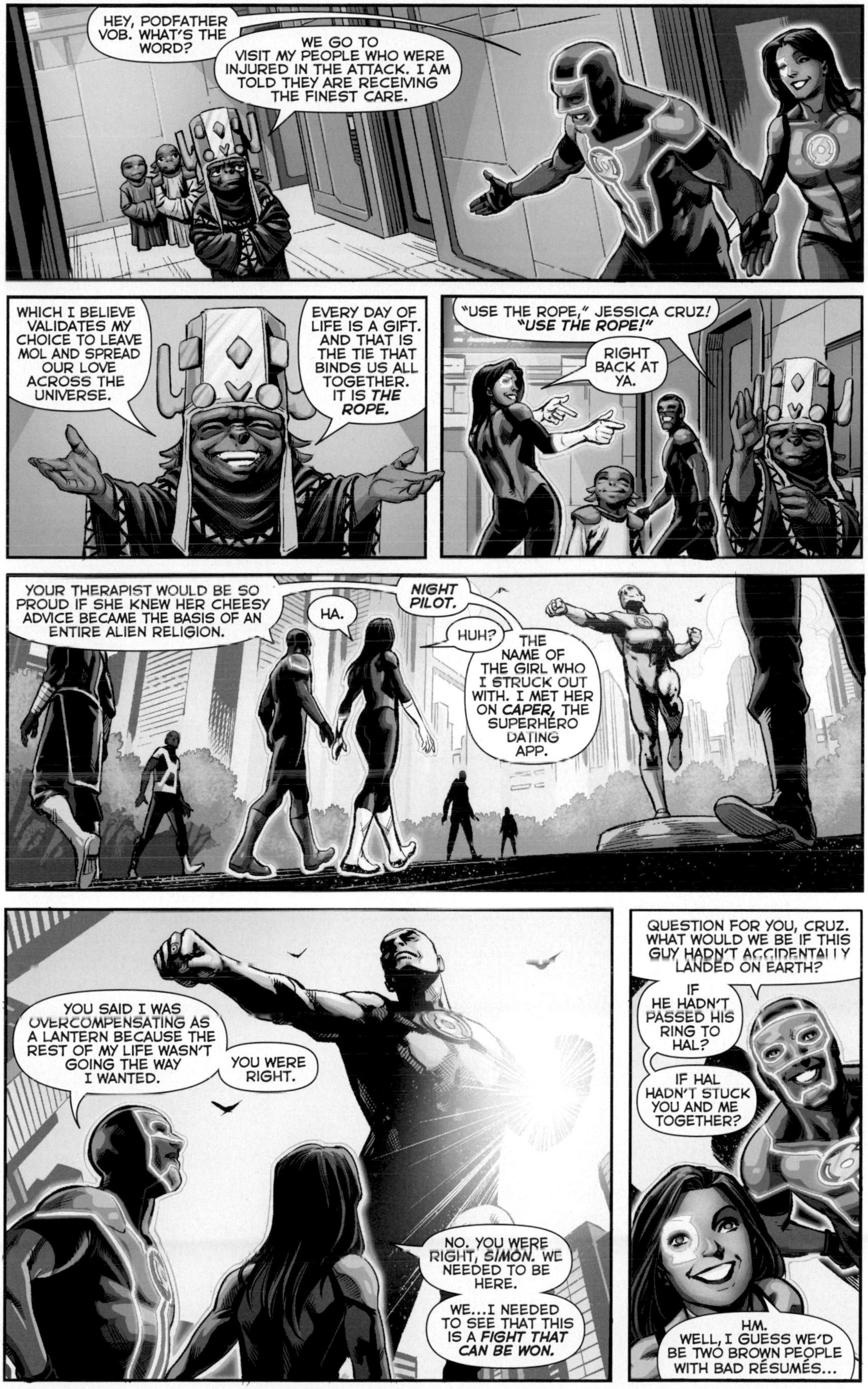
HEY, PODFATHER VOB. WHAT'S THE WORD?
WE GO TO VISIT MY PEOPLE WHO WERE INJURED IN THE ATTACK. I AM TOLD THEY ARE RECEIVING THE FINEST CARE.
WHICH I BELIEVE VALIDATES MY CHOICE TO LEAVE MOL AND SPREAD OUR LOVE ACROSS THE UNIVERSE.
EVERY DAY OF LIFE IS A GIFT. AND THAT IS THE TIE THAT BINDS US ALL TOGETHER. IT IS *THE ROPE.*
"USE THE ROPE," JESSICA CRUZ! *"USE THE ROPE!"*
RIGHT BACK AT YA.
YOUR THERAPIST WOULD BE SO PROUD IF SHE KNEW HER CHEESY ADVICE BECAME THE BASIS OF AN ENTIRE ALIEN RELIGION.
HA.
NIGHT PILOT.
HUH?
THE NAME OF THE GIRL WHO I STRUCK OUT WITH. I MET HER ON *CAPER,* THE SUPERHERO DATING APP.
YOU SAID I WAS OVERCOMPENSATING AS A LANTERN BECAUSE THE REST OF MY LIFE WASN'T GOING THE WAY I WANTED.
YOU WERE RIGHT.
NO. YOU WERE RIGHT, *SIMON.* WE NEEDED TO BE HERE.
WE...I NEEDED TO SEE THAT THIS IS A *FIGHT THAT CAN BE WON.*
QUESTION FOR YOU, CRUZ. WHAT WOULD WE BE IF THIS GUY HADN'T ACCIDENTALLY LANDED ON EARTH?
IF HE HADN'T PASSED HIS RING TO HAL?
IF HAL HADN'T STUCK YOU AND ME TOGETHER?
HM. WELL, I GUESS WE'D BE TWO BROWN PEOPLE WITH BAD RÉSUMÉS...

...BUT WE'D BOTH BE STARING UP AT THE SKY ...WONDERING IF THERE WERE A BETTER WORLD OUT THERE SOMEWHERE.

⟨ᔑᓭᓵᒷ ᔑᓵ ᔑᓵᓭ ᒷᓵᔑᔑ NIGHT PILOT! ⟩

⟨ᔑᓭ ᓵᓵ ᓵᓵ ᔑᓵ ᔑᓵᓭ INTO WORDS YOU'LL UNDERSTAND. ⟩

GET YOUR EARTHER ASS BACK UP TO THOSE FLOATERS AND PUT ANY DUMB IDEAS OUT OF YOUR HEAD! THERE'S ORE TO BE MINED...

...AND YOU AIN'T NEVER GOIN' HOME!

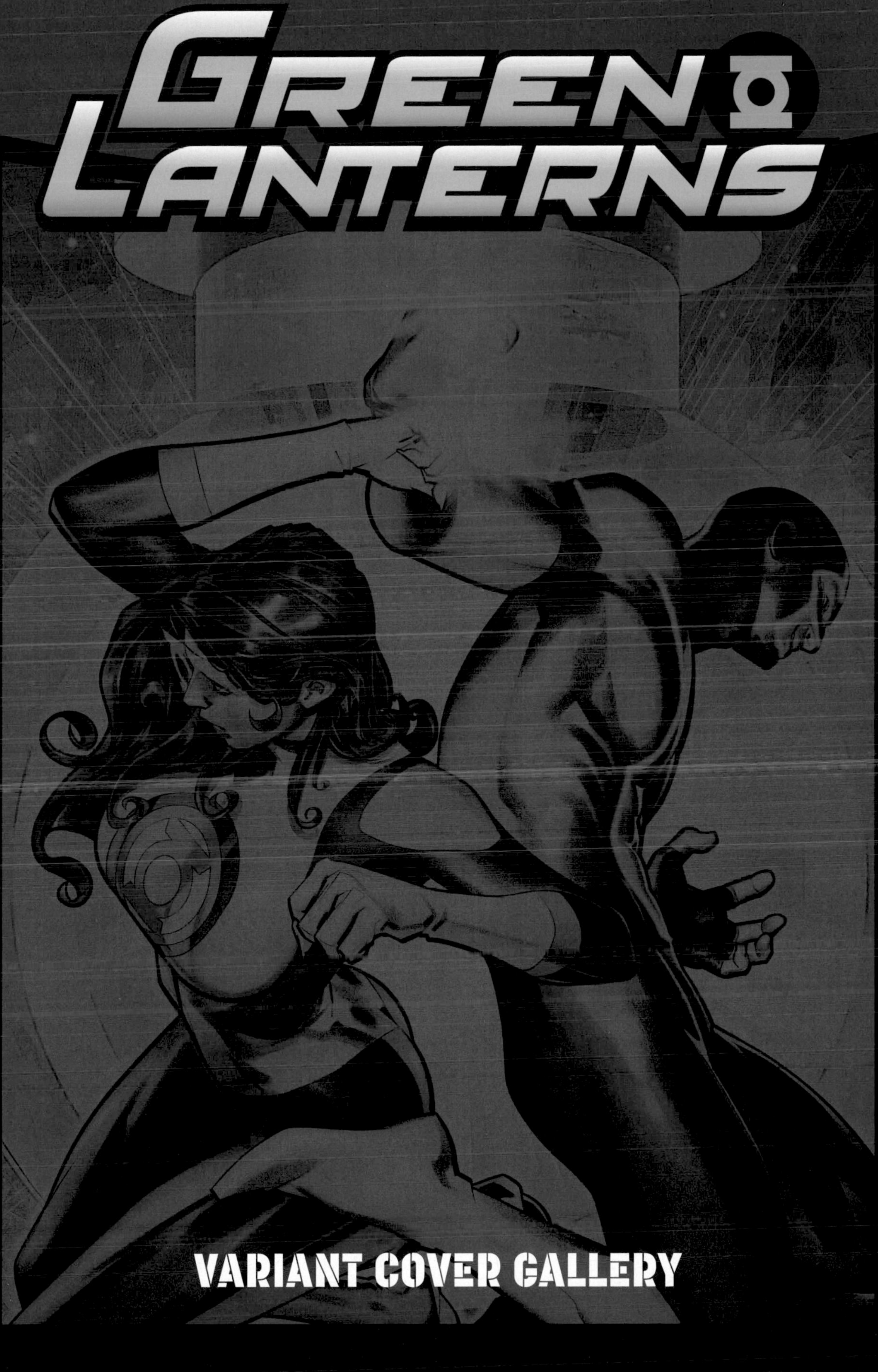
GREEN LANTERNS
VARIANT COVER GALLERY

GREEN LANTERNS #33 variant cover by BRANDON PETERSON

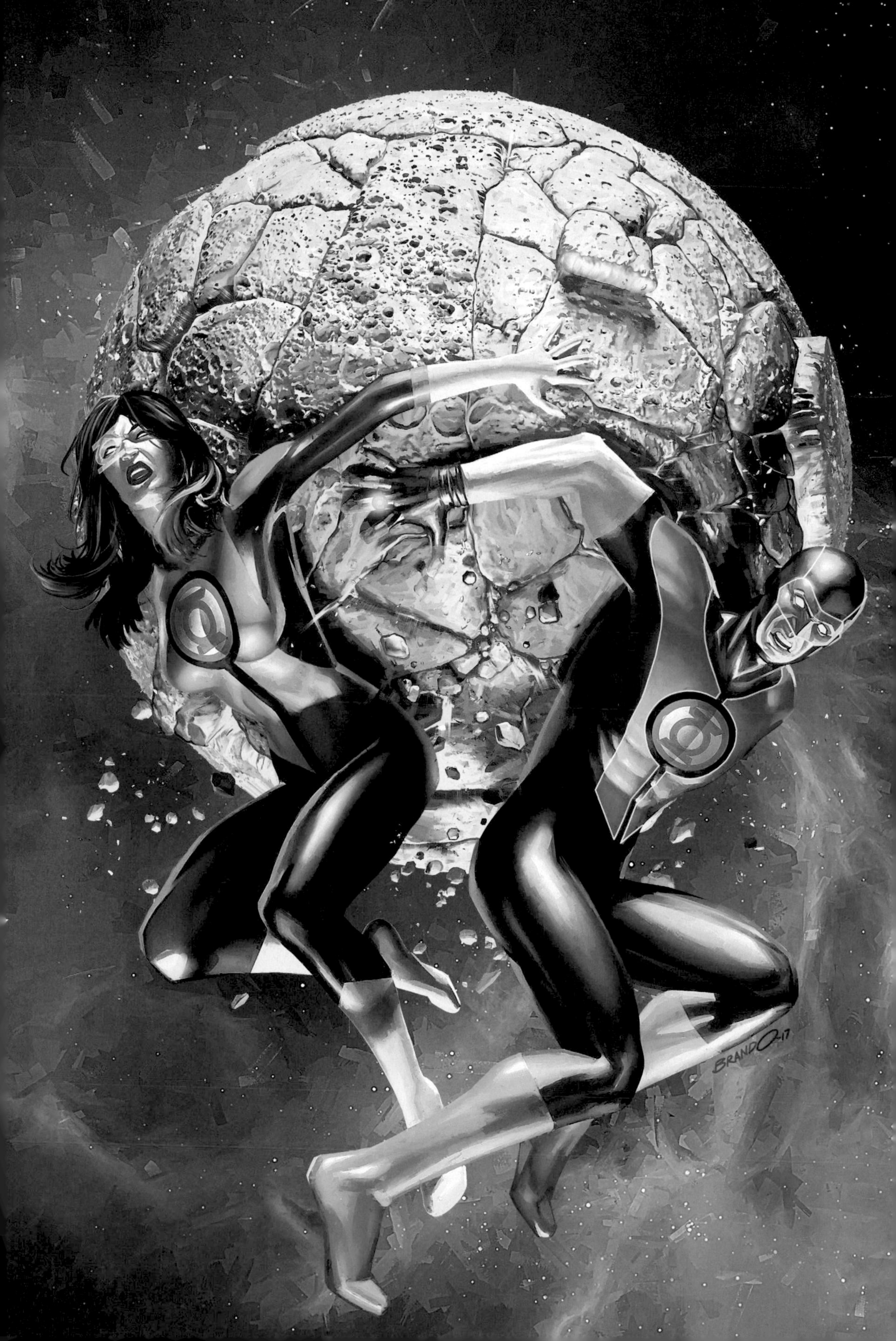
BRANDO '17

GREEN LANTERNS #34 variant cover by BRANDON PETERSON

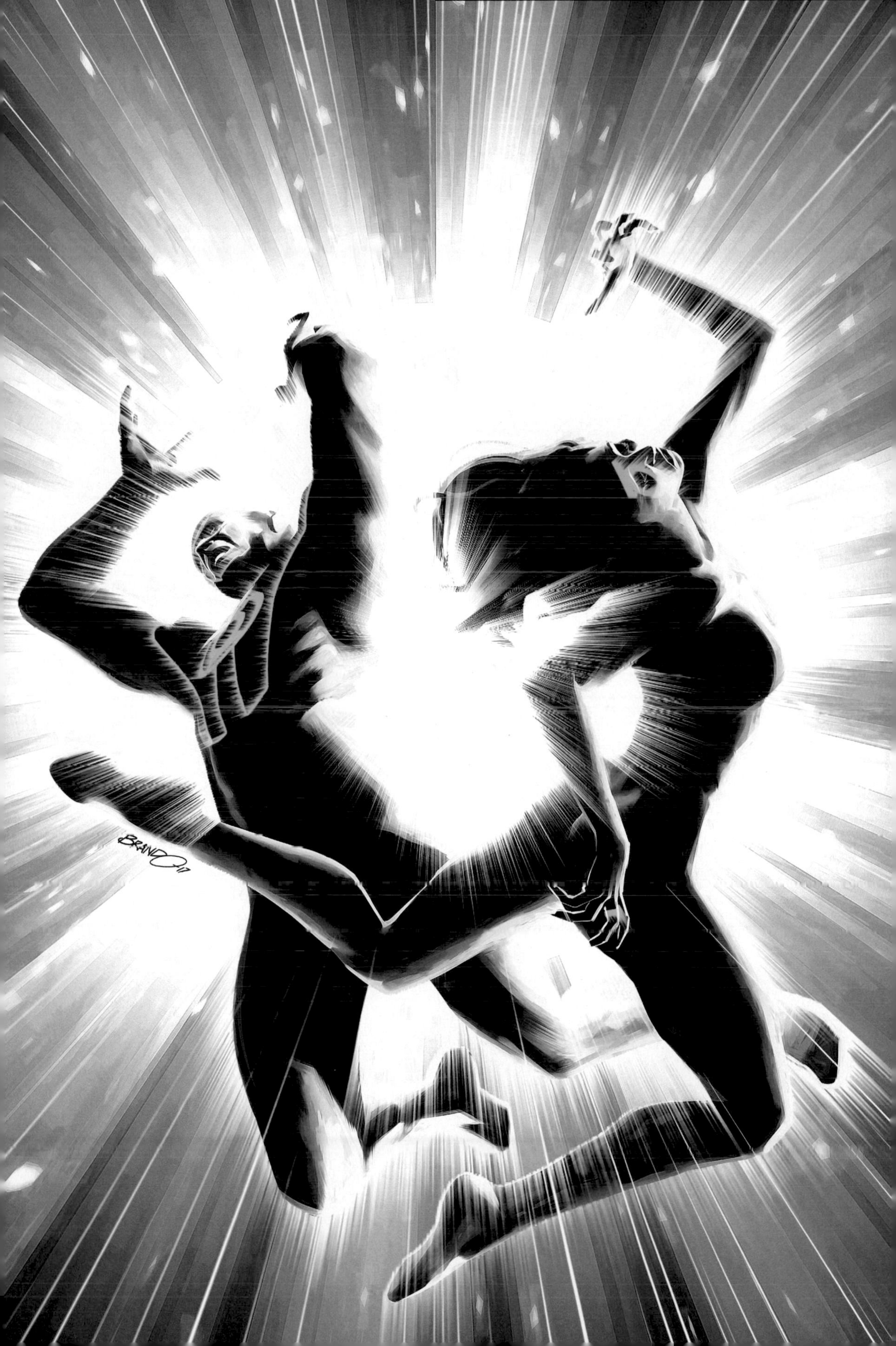
BRANDO '17

GREEN LANTERNS #35 variant cover by BRANDON PETERSON

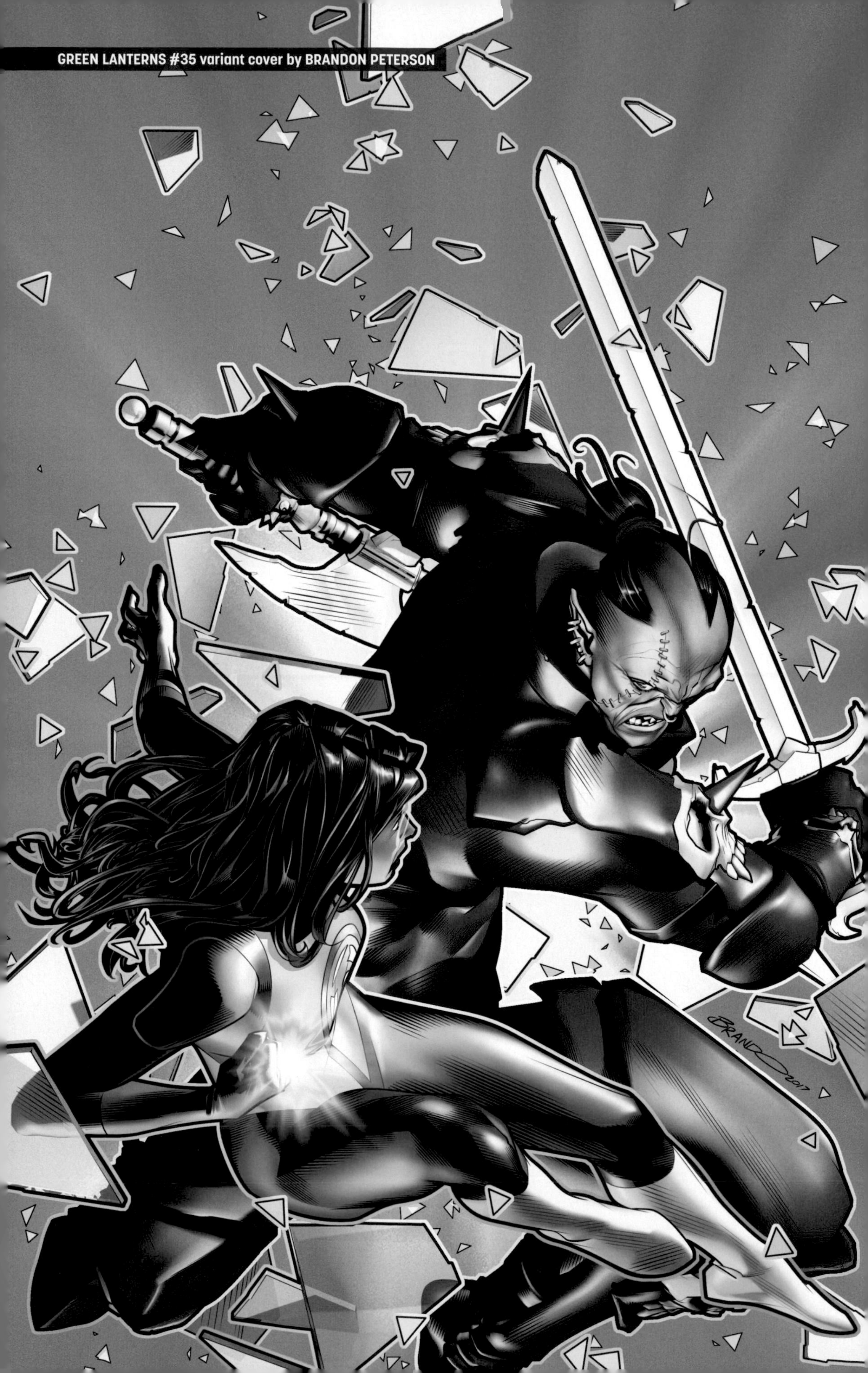
BRANDON 2017

GREEN LANTERNS #36 variant cover by BRANDON PETERSON

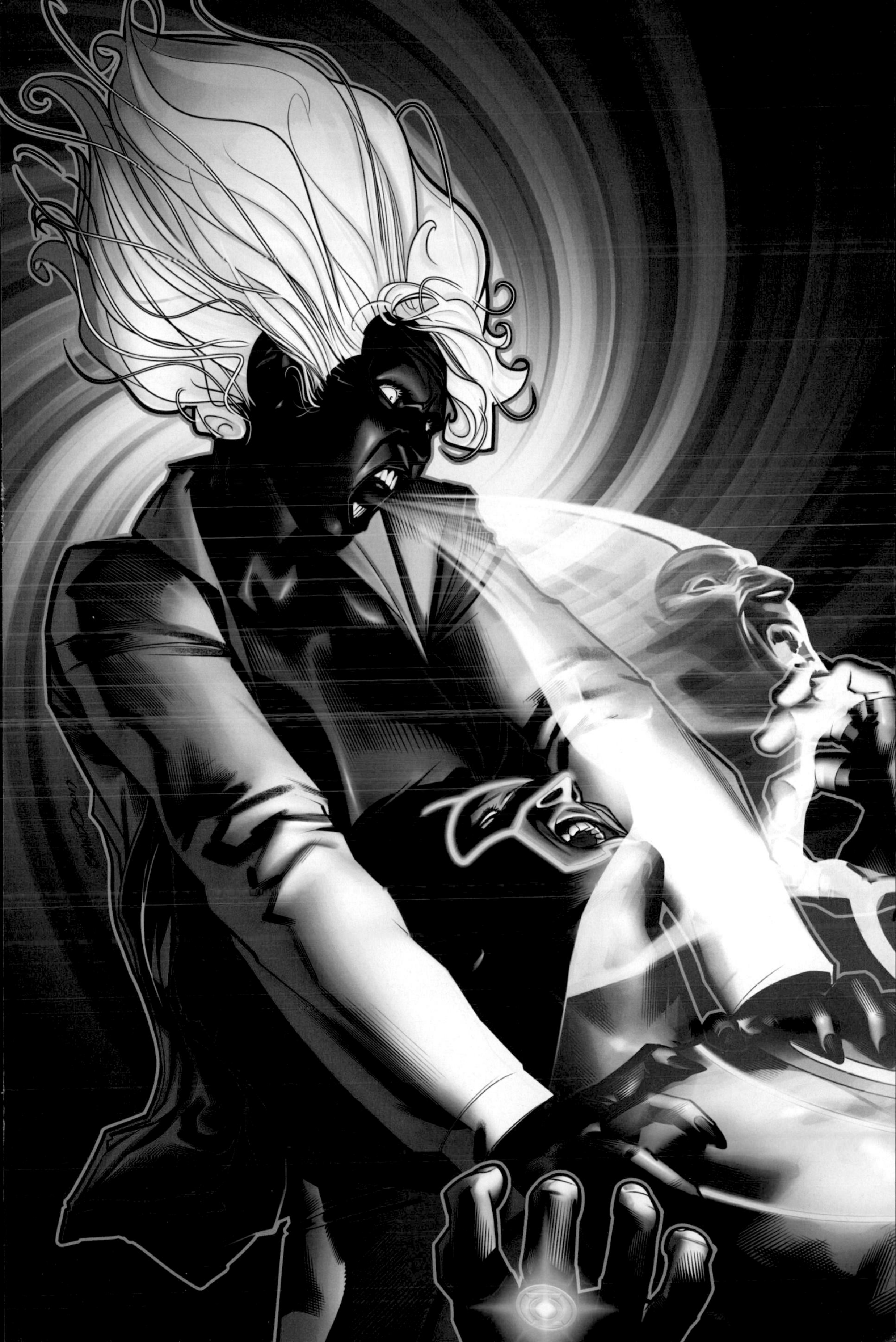

GREEN LANTERNS #37 variant cover by BRANDON PETERSON

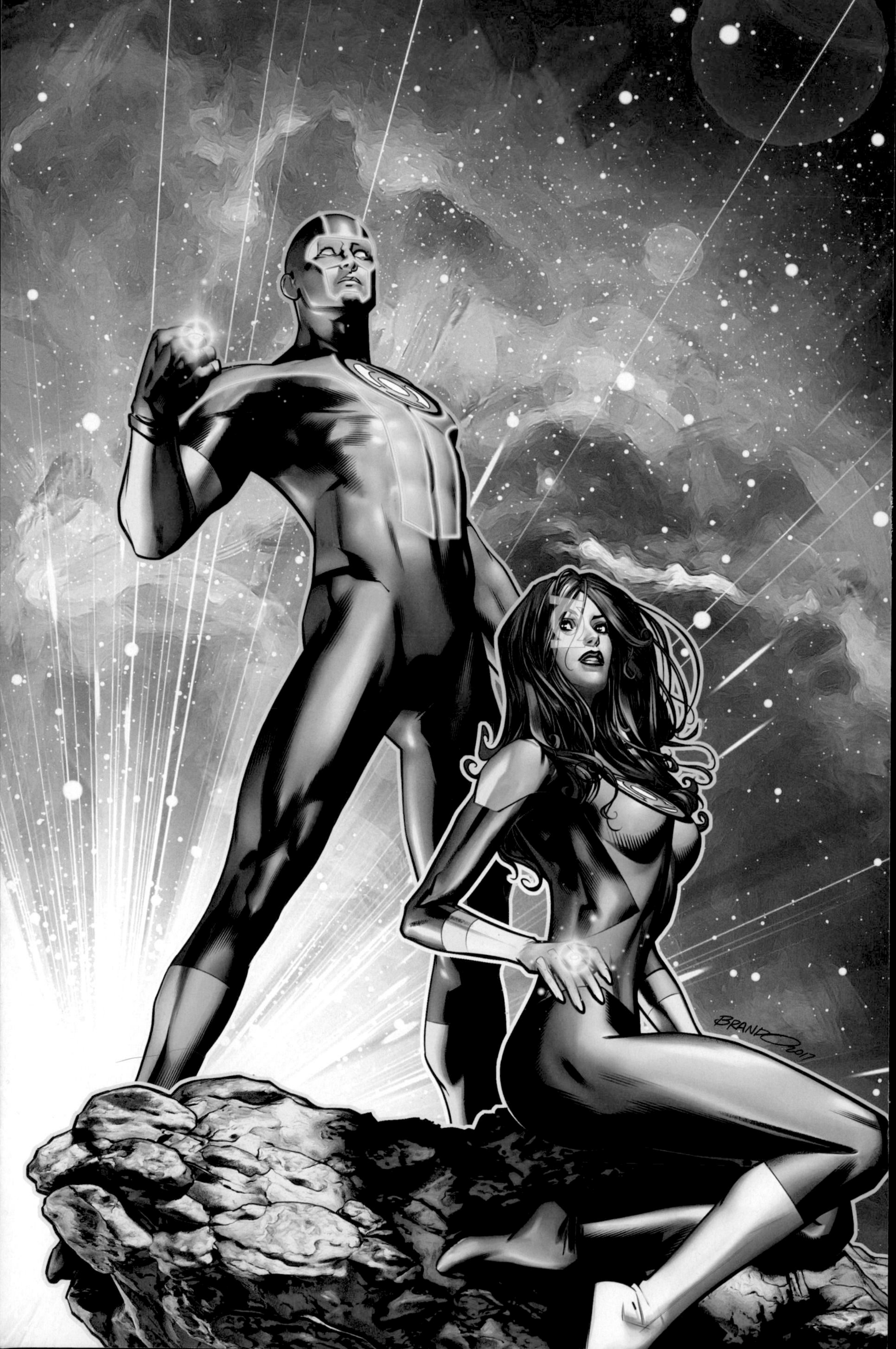
BRANDO 2017

GREEN LANTERNS #38 variant cover by BRANDON PETERSON

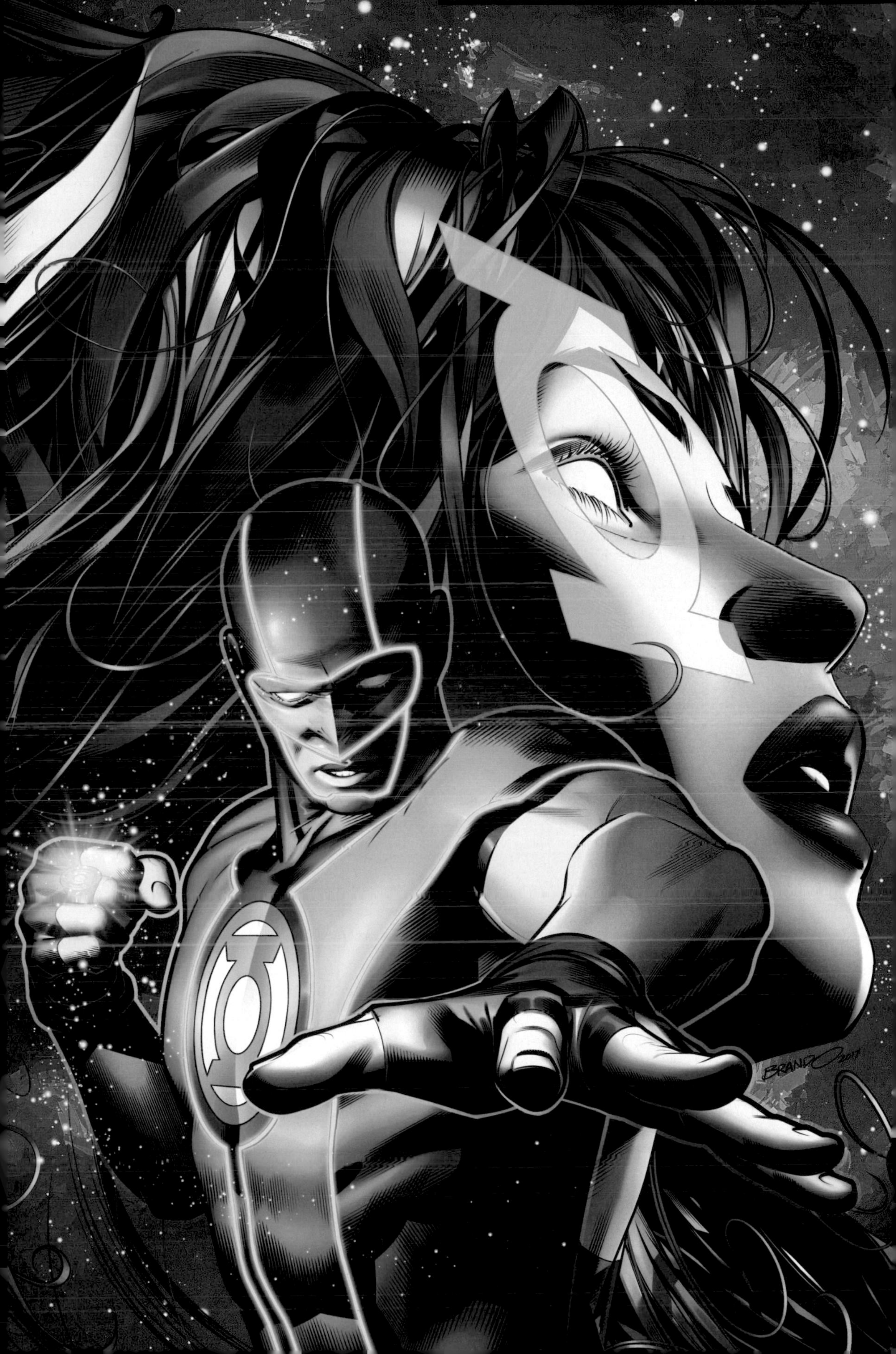
BRANDO 2017

GREEN LANTERNS #39 variant cover by BRANDON PETERSON

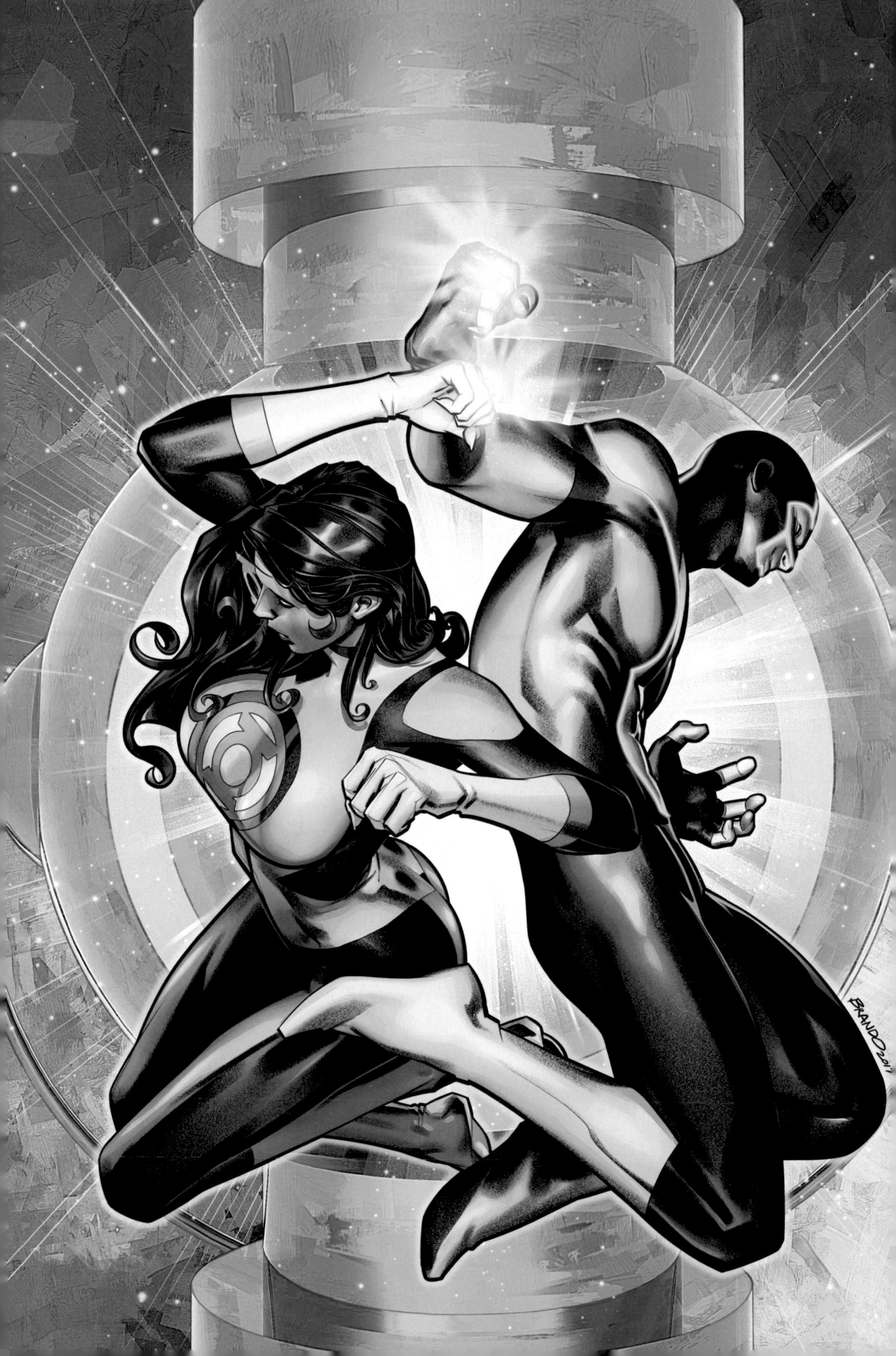
BRANDO 2017

FROM THE WRITER OF
JUSTICE LEAGUE AND *THE FLASH*

GEOFF JOHNS
GREEN LANTERN: REBIRTH

GREEN LANTERN: BRIGHTEST DAY

GREEN LANTERN:
REBIRTH

GREEN LANTERN:
NO FEAR

GREEN LANTERN:
REVENGE OF THE GREEN LANTERNS

GREEN LANTERN: WANTED:
HAL JORDAN

GREEN LANTERN:
SINESTRO CORPS WAR

GREEN LANTERN:
SECRET ORIGIN

GREEN LANTERN: RAGE OF THE RED
LANTERNS

GREEN LANTERN: AGENT ORANGE

GREEN LANTERN: BLACKEST NIGHT

GREEN LANTERN: BRIGHTEST DAY

GREEN LANTERN:
WAR OF THE
GREEN LANTERNS

GREEN LANTERN
VOL. 1: SINESTRO

GREEN LANTERN
VOL. 2: THE REVENGE OF BLACK HAND

GREEN LANTERN VOL. 3: THE END

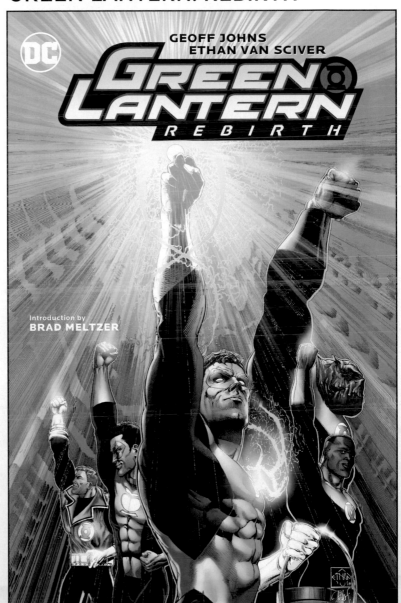

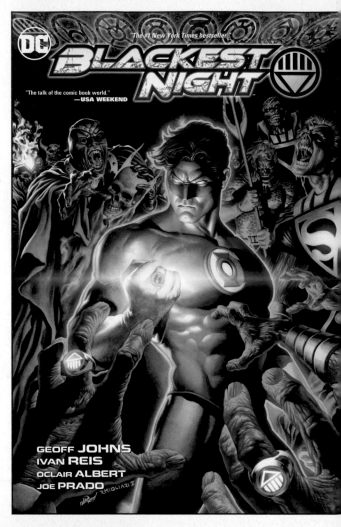
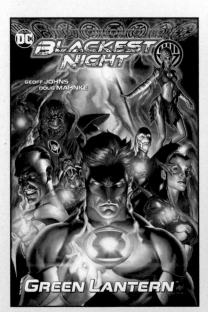